b

**Blackwell
Science**

© David Chappell & Christopher J. Willis 1992,
David Chappell & Andrew Willis 2000

Blackwell Science Ltd
Editorial Offices:
Osney Mead, Oxford OX2 0EL
25 John Street, London WC1N 2BL
23 Ainslie Place, Edinburgh EH3 6AJ
350 Main Street, Malden
    MA 02148 5018, USA
54 University Street, Carlton
    Victoria 3053, Australia
10, rue Casimir Delavigne
    75006 Paris, France

Other Editorial Offices:

Blackwell Wissenschafts-Verlag GmbH
Kurfürstendamm 57
10707 Berlin, Germany

Blackwell Science KK
MG Kodenmacho Building
7–10 Kodenmacho Nihombashi
Chuo-ku, Tokyo 104, Japan

The right of the Author to be identified as the
Author of this Work has been asserted in
accordance with the Copyright, Designs and
Patents Act 1988.

First to fifth editions published by Crosby
Lockwood, 1952–1974
Sixth edition published by
Granada Publishing Ltd 1985
Seventh edition published by
Blackwell Scientific Publications 1992
Eighth edition published by
Blackwell Science Ltd 2000

Set in 10/13pt Palatino
by DP Photosetting, Aylesbury, Bucks
Printed and bound in Great Britain by
The University Press, Cambridge

The Blackwell Science logo is a trade mark of
Blackwell Science Ltd, registered at the United
Kingdom Trade Marks Registry

DISTRIBUTORS

Marston Book Services Ltd
PO Box 269
Abingdon
Oxon OX14 4YN
(*Orders:* Tel: 01235 465500
           Fax: 01235 465555)

USA
Blackwell Science, Inc.
Commerce Place
350 Main Street
Malden, MA 02148 5018
(*Orders:* Tel: 800 759 6102
                781 388 8250
           Fax: 781 388 8255)

Canada
Login Brothers Book Company
324 Saulteaux Crescent
Winnipeg, Manitoba R3J 3T2
(*Orders:* Tel: 204 837-2987
           Fax: 204 837-3116)

Australia
Blackwell Science Pty Ltd
54 University Street
Carlton, Victoria 3053
(*Orders:* Tel: 03 9347 0300
           Fax: 03 9347 5001)

A catalogue record for this title is available from the
British Library

ISBN 0-632-04913-8

Library of Congress
Cataloging-in-Publication Data

Chappell, David.
    The architect in practice/David Chappell,
Andrew Willis. – 8th ed.
        p. cm.
    Includes index.
    ISBN 0-632-04913-8 (pb)
    1. Architectural practice – United States.
    I. Willis, J. Andrew.   II. Title.

NA 1996. C47 2000
720′.68 – dc21   00-029785

For further information on
Blackwell Science, visit our website:
www.blackwell-science.com

The Inspiration

From a pseudonymous letter of a quantity surveyor to
the *Builder*, 9 March 1951

'I have great admiration for an architect who does his job well,
because he has one of the most difficult jobs in the world. He must
be an artist but at the same time in his administration of a building
contract be a business man, and in interpreting it even something
of a lawyer.'

The Dedication

To Arthur Willis, Christopher Willis and Bruce George
and
To the architectural profession

in the hope that the book may encourage that co-operation of
which its joint authorship is a symbol

Contents

Preface to the Eighth Edition

The Architect in Practice was first published nearly fifty years ago in 1952. It was written by two men, one a quantity surveyor and one an architect, both of whom had a flair for writing and who, after working together for some years, came to the conclusion that a textbook on architectural practice was needed. During those fifty years, through seven editions, it has remained a leading textbook used in the education of architects world-wide.

After much heart-searching and after taking soundings in the profession and from the schools of architecture throughout the United Kingdom it was decided to radically change the format for the seventh edition. To the relief of the authors, the revised format was well received and it is continued within this edition. While the format changed, the message and philosophy remain the same: here is a book which tries to present to the reader some of the elementary duties that architects owe to their clients and contractors alike and to endorse the adage that of the many responsibilities that are borne by the architect, the greatest is the duty of care.

Not only has practice changed; in many ways it has become more complicated. For instance there is now a plethora of forms of building contract to choose from, and it is not possible to write in any detail on such a wide subject; it warrants a textbook on its own. The most helpful thing that we can do is to point the reader to relevant sources for this and other allied subjects.

One of the joys of the original book was that it was so readable. Where else could one find such a riveting account of how to organise a foundation-stone-laying ceremony? Sadly this account can no longer be found in this edition and readers faced with organising such a ceremony today must look to past editions. We have, however, retained in many cases the words of wisdom and the spirit of the original authors, which we feel are as relevant and well said today as they ever were.

This edition has been thoroughly revised to take account of the Housing Grants, Construction and Regeneration Act 1996 and the Scheme, changes to the standard forms and adjudication, the Architects Act 1997, the Construction (Design and Management) Regulations 1994 and the Party Wall Act 1996 together with changes in planning and Building Regulations. The new codes of the Royal Institute of British Architects (RIBA) and the Architects Registration Board (ARB) have been described and the new Standard Form for the Appointment of an Architect 1999 (SFA/99). Reference is now made to the Private Finance Initiative (PFI) and partnering and to project management as a distinct role, and a new section has been introduced dealing with techniques for securing employment.

It is a matter worthy of some note that the mantle of quantity surveying author has passed down through three generations of the Willis family.

Finally we hope that our efforts will assist future generations of architects in the way that Arthur Willis and Bruce George assisted our generation.

March 2000   D.M.C.
                                                                  J.A.W.

Acknowledgements

We are grateful to Allan Ashworth MSc, ARICS for his agreement to the use in this book of parts of the text of *Practice and Procedure for the Quantity Surveyor*. We are also grateful to the following for particular assistance:

> Caroline M. Dalziel LLB(Hons), solicitor, for commenting on company law in Chapter 4 and employment law in Chapter 18.
> David Hardwicke DipTP, MRTPI for substantially re-writing planning legislation and practice in Chapter 9.
> Clive A. Marshall FBEng, MCIOB for continued assistance and reworking of the Building Regulations in Chapter 10.

We are also pleased to acknowledge the assistance that we have received from Lawrence Johnston BSc, MSc, ACIArb, RIBA, Head of the School of Architecture, The Queen's University of Belfast; Syd Danks Dip Arch, MSc, RIBA, School of Architecture, University of Central England in Birmingham; Roderick Males MA, RIBA, formerly of School of Architecture, Manchester University; and Jane Oldfield and the staff at the RIBA Information Unit.

The RIBA standard forms are reproduced by permission of the copyright holders; copyright RIBA Publications 1999. The RICS standard forms are reproduced by permission of the Royal Institution of Chartered Surveyors, which owns the copyright.

Abbreviations and Acronyms

AA	Architectural Association
ABE	Association of Building Engineers
AC	Appeal case
ACA	Association of Consultant Architects
ACAS	Advisory, Conciliation and Arbitration Service
ACE	Association of Consulting Engineers
All ER	*All England Law Reports*
ARB	Architects Registration Board
ARCUK	Architects Registration Council of the United Kingdom
ASI	Architects and Surveyors Institute
BBA	British Board of Agrément
BCIS	Building Cost Information Service
BEC	Building Employers Confederation
BLR	*Building Law Reports*
BPF	British Property Federation
BRE	Building Research Establishment
BSI	British Standards Institution
BSRIA	Building Services Research and Information Association
CAD	Computer aided design
CAS	Clients Advisory Service (RIBA)
CAWS	Common Arrangement of Work Sections
CBI	Confederation of British Industries
CC	Construction Confederation
CCPI	Co-ordinating Committee for Project Information
ClArb	Chartered Institute of Arbitrators
CIB	Construction Industry Board
CIC	Construction Industry Council
CIJC	Construction Industry Joint Council
CIOB	Chartered Institute of Building
CI/SfB	Construction Information/Samarbetskommitten for Byggnadsfragor
CILL	*Construction Industry Law Letter*
CIRIA	Construction Industry Research and Information Association
CITB	Construction Industry Training Board
CLD	*Construction Law Digest*
Con LR	*Construction Law Reports*
Const LJ	*Construction Law Journal*

CPA	Construction Products Association
CPD	Continuing professional development
CPI	Co-ordinated project information
CPIC	Construction Project Information Committee
EDC	European Development Council
EPIC	Electronic Product Information Co-operation
EU	European Union
FCEC	Federation of Civil Engineering Contractors
IAAS	Incorporated Association of Architects and Surveyors
ICE	Institution of Civil Engineers
ICW	Institute of Clerks of Works of Great Britain Incorporated
IEE	Institution of Electrical Engineers
IFC	Intermediate Form of Contract
ILA	Institute of Landscape Architects
IMechE	Institution of Mechanical Engineers
IStructE	Institution of Structural Engineers
ISO	International Standards Organisation
JCT	Joint Contracts Tribunal
LI	Landscape Institute
LLP	Limited liability partnership
MW	Minor Works Form of Contract
NBS	National Building Specification
NJCBI	National Joint Committee for the Building Industry
NJCC	National Joint Consultative Committee for Building
NSC/A	Standard Form of Nominated Sub-contract Agreement
NSC/C	Conditions
NSC/N	Nomination
NSC/T	Tender
NSC/W	Warranty
PAYE	Pay as you earn
PDP	Professional development plan
PFI	Private Finance Initiative
PSA	Property Services Agency
QA	Quality assurance
RIAI	Royal Institute of Architects in Ireland
RIAS	Royal Incorporation of Architects in Scotland
RIBA	Royal Institute of British Architects
RICS	Royal Institution of Chartered Surveyors
RSUA	Royal Society of Ulster Architects
RTPI	Royal Town Planning Institute
SMM	Standard Method of Measurement for Building Works
WLR	*Weekly Law Reports*

Introduction

Architecture is undoubtedly one of the professions that can be enjoyed. It offers a wealth of interest in a variety of fields which few other professions can match, and provides an emotional satisfaction which only the other arts can stimulate. It exacts a high price for this enjoyment, however, and in order to derive the fullest pleasure from it architects must devote themselves completely to its study and practice. The more proficient they become and the greater mastery they can acquire the more complete will be their enjoyment. In common with other professions architects owe a duty of care to their clients but they have a greater responsibility than most in that the buildings and environments that they create may well have a profound effect on the population at large.

Ability to design and skill in draughtsmanship or in using computer aided design (CAD) equipment will not alone make an architect. The purpose of this book is to present to architectural students, and perhaps the less experienced practitioners, some indication of the practice and procedure with which they must be acquainted if they are to follow their profession with success. They must find clients to employ them, they must be able to manage an office and be responsible for a good deal of adminstrative work in connection with building contracts, and they must know something of finance, law, the general structure of the building industry and the organisation and requirements of those authorities who exercise so much control over their day-to-day work. Let the readers, therefore, leave their drawing board or move away from their CAD equipment and settle down to their desk or armchair to study an aspect of their work which they may find requires some self-discipline but is nevertheless essential to make them efficient architects.

The architect's work is here looked at mainly from the angle of the private practitioner dealing with the JCT forms of contract, though references are made where appropriate to public service practice and to the government and other forms of contract. Architects in private practice are often commissioned to act for public authorities and they must therefore be able to adapt to the differing conditions which this type of work involves.

The chapters have been arranged in the sequence which the progress of a building contract makes natural. Part I opens with an introduction to the construction industry and is followed by some basic principles of practice, sources of information, legal and administrative matters. Part 2 follows the running of a construction project, the chapters being based on the work stages of the RIBA Plan of Work. Part 3 ends the book with what can best be described as management matters, covering finance, insurance, obtaining work and employing staff. Each chapter includes some illustrations, and ends with notes of law cases together with a selected bibliography.

Part 1
Background to Practice

The Construction Industry

1.1 Introduction

The construction industry is concerned with the planning, regulation, design, manufacture, fabrication, erection and maintenance of buildings and other structures. It includes the separate sectors of activity of building, civil engineering and heavy engineering. However the demarcation between these sectors is blurred. Project values can vary significantly from minor works costing a few hundred pounds to major building schemes costing tens of millions of pounds or major transportation and other infrastructure projects costing several billion pounds. While there are certain similarities in the principles of execution of projects, the scale, complexity and organisation vary enormously.

1.2 Importance of the construction industry

The construction industry is an important part of any economy. In the UK it accounts for approximately 10% of the gross domestic product, although its share of national output has declined over the last 20 years. As such a major industry it is particularly susceptible to trends in both national and international economies, and in particular by such issues as:

■ Uncertainty in business cycles
■ Levels of employment
■ Interest rates
■ Rates of inflation
■ Manufacturing output
■ Market economies

The industry is also a major employer of labour, employing approximately 1.4 million people in the UK, from the unskilled through to the highly skilled technology professional. Therefore, due to its significance, the fortunes of the construction industry provide one of the best indicators of a country's economic performance. An active construction industry generally represents a buoyant economy.

1.3   Characteristics of the construction industry

Particular characteristics that distinguish the construction industry from all others include the following:

- The physical nature of the product
- The product is normally manufactured on the client's premises (i.e. the construction site)
- Most of the products are one-off designs
- The traditional arrangement separates design from manufacture
- It produces investment rather than consumer goods
- Its activities may be affected by the vagaries of the weather
- Its processes include a complex mix of different materials, skills and trades
- Typically, throughout the world it includes a small number of relatively large construction companies and a very large number of small firms

1.4   The people

1.4.1   The employer

The employer is also sometimes known as the *building owner*. The building industry team comprises the designers and the constructors both working at the behest of the employer, perhaps the most important member. It is therefore appropriate that this section should open with an introduction to the person responsible for commissioning the design in the first place and ultimately for the construction.

Employers appear in many guises. They are the clients of the professionals; they are the employers under the building contract and they are the ultimate owners of the building until such time as they dispose of it. It is the building owner who in the long run pays the bill and in that respect calls the tune, which is something that must never be forgotten.

Architects, like most other professionals, must have clients before they can practise. Unlike the painter, the author or the poet, they are not at liberty to choose their own subject. They may of course be their own clients as, for instance, when they design their own houses; but otherwise they are dependent on a commission from somebody else. This applies whether architects are principals or assistants in private practice or are salaried officials in government or local government – in which case their clients will be the council or committee they serve.

Relationships with the client are of prime importance: an architect must not only embark on a process of design (which is a personal thing) but must also attempt to interpret the client's needs and provide a product that is wanted.

An architect acts as the client's agent in spending sums of money, which may be substantial: on the skill and efficiency of the architect may depend the amount of the bill which the client will eventually have to meet. It is essential, therefore, that client and architect should have confidence in each other, particularly as the architect also has certain responsibilities towards the contractor. The old adage that a good building requires a good client as well as a good architect is as true today as it ever was.

How then does a client choose the architect? It may be in one of several ways:

- The client may have approached the client's advisory service of the Royal Institutue of British Architects (RIBA) and have been provided with a short list of suitable architects, from which a choice can be made
- The client may have seen a building or photograph of a building that is liked and finds out the name of the architect
- The architect may be recommended by a mutual acquaintance
- The architect may specialise in designing a particular building type
- It may be through success in an open competition for a particular building or project
- It may be by an entry in a directory or by commissioning external public relations consultants (who themselves must not infringe the code of professional conduct)

1.4.2 The contractor

The building contractor, the second party to the building contract with the employer, is the constructor, whose operations are at the hub of the complex construction industry. Contracting firms vary greatly in their size and capabilities. Many are small firms whose work may vary from one or two houses and some jobbing work to individual contracts of perhaps £250,000 in value. However, the bulk in value of construction work is in the hands of a comparatively small number of larger firms, often with several regional offices, and many carry out work overseas. Most firms are limited companies, some are public companies, but some of the very small contractors still operate as partnerships (see also Chapter 4, section 4.2).

Traditionally the contractor was chosen by competitive tender having priced either a specification and drawings or a bill of quantities. Alternatively work was negotiated with a chosen contractor. Today the procurement processes and the contractual arrangements that are entered into are many and varied. The role of architects when working for a contractor is described in Chapter 3 and their relationship with the contractor regarding procurement procedures, programming and construction is covered in Chapters 7, 8, 12 and 13.

1.4.3 Subcontractors

Subcontractors are, as their name suggests, companies to whom work is sublet. When work is sublet it is delegated; however the contractor is still liable to the employer for any defects in such work. It will be sublet for one of two reasons. It may be the specific wish of the architect that a certain parcel of work be carried out by a particular company, in which case they will be 'nominated' or, depending on the contract, sometimes 'named'. Alternatively it will be the wish of the contractor that work shall be sublet, in which case the subcontractor will be known as a 'domestic' subcontractor. These three types of subcontractor can be defined as follows:

Nominated

A nominated subcontractor is the choice of the architect who, with the employer's agreement, will seek the tenders, evaluate, decide and instruct the main contractor to enter into a subcontract. The JCT forms of contract give both the main and subcontractor rights regarding such matters as extensions of time, loss and expense payments, rights to direct payment in the event of default by the main contractor and renomination if there is default on the part of the subcontractor.

Named

A named subcontractor is the choice of the contractor from a list of not less than three names provided by the architect whose duties and responsibilities do not extend beyond naming (JCT 98 clause 19.3) and the naming procedures contained in IFC 98 (clause 3.3). The subcontractor then becomes 'domestic' (see below) and neither main nor subcontractor enjoys many of the contractual rights of nomination under the main form of contract, albeit the situation becomes complex if the subcontractor's employment is determined or the contract repudiated.

Domestic

A domestic subcontractor is the sole choice of the main contractor who will enter into a direct subcontract unrelated to the main contract. The architect's powers are limited to approving or otherwise the names put forward by the main contractor.

1.4.4 The architect

Architects are the designers of the building project and have the difficult task of translating their client's ideas into an acceptable design and then into working drawings. It should be noted that the profession of architect is, subject to the Architects Act 1997, a registered profession. For business purposes no one can call him or herself an architect in the UK unless they are on the register maintained by the Architects' Registration Board (ARB). Only those qualified in accordance with these regulations can be admitted to the register. However it is only the name 'architect' that is protected; anyone can carry out the role as long as the name is not used.

As the name implies, the architect should be the master-builder – the leader of the building industry team referred to above (the word 'architect' is derived from the Greek root *arch* meaning 'chief' and the word *teckton* meaning 'carpenter or builder'). Architects are qualified to design and administer the erection of buildings, and must possess both theoretical and practical knowledge. Their work is a science as well as an art, for they must produce a structure as well as create form, and must combine aesthetic effect with practical considerations. They must visualise the interior as well as the exterior of the building and must ensure that the accommodation is properly related to the requirements of owners and occupiers, that the form and construction are appropriate to the function of the building and its setting and that the design is developed within the budget set by the client.

Like playwrights, architects are dependent on other people to interpret their designs, and their involvement during the erection of a building is as important to its ultimate success as are the directions given by the producer and stage manager for a play.

The list of duties set out by Hudson in the last edition of *Hudson's Building Contracts* in 1926, is still considered to remain fairly comprehensive today[1]:

(i)   To advise and consult with the employer (not as a lawyer) as to any limitation which may exist as to the use of the land to be built on, either *(inter alia)* by restrictive covenants or by the rights of adjoining owners or the public over the land, or by statutes and by-laws affecting the works to be executed.

(ii) To examine the site, sub-soil and surroundings.

(iii) To consult with and advise the employer as to the proposed work.

(iv) To prepare sketch plans and a specification having regard to all the conditions which exist and to submit them to the employer for approval, with an estimate of the probable cost, if requested.

(v)   To elaborate and, if necessary, modify or amend the sketch plans as he may be instructed and prepare working drawings and a specification or specifications.

(vi) To consult with and advise the employer as to obtaining tenders, whether by invitation or by advertisement, and as to the necessity or otherwise of employing a quantity surveyor. (Engineers do not so often employ a quantity surveyor.)

(vii) To supply the builder with copies of the contract drawings and specification, supply such further drawings and give such instructions as may be necessary, supervise the work, and see that the contractor performs the contract, and advise the employer if he commits any serious breach thereof.

(viii) To perform his duties to his employer as defined by any contract with his employer or by the contract with the builder, and generally to act as the employer's agent in all matters connected with the work and the contract, except where otherwise prescribed by the contract with the builder, as, for instance, in cases where he has under the contract to act as arbitrator or quasi-arbitrator.'

Architects must have a good, practical knowledge of building and allied trades and must have at least a working knowledge of the more specialised aspects of building, such as mechanical and electrical engineering services. Above all they must be creative and dedicated to solving the client's problems as expressed in the brief.

1.4.5 The quantity surveyor/cost manager

The work and services provided by the quantity surveyor today might be described as the financial management of the project, whether it be on behalf of the building owner or the contractor. The term 'quantity surveyor' does not now reflect the services that are provided, since these have been extended during the past 30 years to cover what might be more appropriately termed *project cost management*.

The work of the quantity surveyor can therefore be summarised briefly as:

- Preliminary cost advice
- Cost planning including investment appraisal, life-cycle costing and value analysis
- Procurement and tendering procedures
- Contract documentation
- Evaluation of tenders
- Cash flow forecasting, financial reporting and interim payments
- Final accounting and the settlement of contractual disputes
- Cost advice during use by the client

Traditionally, certainly during the early part of the century, quantity surveyors were employed as preparers of bills of quantities for building projects. Their role was constrained to a limited but important part of the development process. This role was quickly extended to include the preparation of valuations for interim certificates and the agreement of final accounts with the contractor.

During the 1960s the quantity surveyor's role was enlarged to include design cost planning in an attempt to provide the building owner with some form of value for money and cost-effectiveness (see Chapter 9, section 9.3). In more recent times greater emphasis has been placed on the need to examine construction costs in terms of their life cycle rather than solely in terms of initial costs.

It is now advantageous for the quantity surveyor to become fully involved at the outset of a project's development. Although lip service has been paid to this in the past, the designer has often completed this stage of the development process relying only on a very limited input from the quantity surveyor. It is during this stage that the type and size of the project are largely determined and these two factors alone commit a considerable proportion of the total cost. Quantity surveyors can therefore provide a proper and sizeable contribution during the process of strategic planning and by becoming familiar with the special needs of the building owner they can properly evaluate the options that are under consideration.

1.4.6 Other consultants

The other members of the design team who will be involved can include the following:

- Structural engineers
- Building services engineers
- Landscape consultants
- Specialist consultants

Structural engineers

The structural engineers' function is to advise on structural design from foundations to roof including advice on ground conditions on projects where such services are required. The structural stability of the building will be their responsibility, which will include advice, specification, design and supervision of the works in progress. They should be an early appointment as their advice will greatly influence the outcome of the ultimate design, which in many cases cannot be furthered without the basic structural information being available. Some structural engineers will offer drainage and other infrastructure advice, or design input on these issues may be provided by an engineer specialising solely in this type of work.

Building services engineers

Services both mechanical and electrical today form a major part of most projects. Building services engineers provide advice, specification and schematic or detailed drawings and are sometimes responsible for obtaining tenders from specialist firms. Again they should be an early appointment and should be closely involved in ensuring the proper integration of services into the design. Failure to achieve such integration is a frequent cause of delay and disruption on construction sites leading to acrimony, costs and at worst litigation.

Landscape consultants

With the current emphasis on environmental aspects of construction projects it is not unusual for architects specialising in landscape work or specialist consultants to be involved in the design and supervision of what are traditionally known as the external works. Ground formations, planting and arboreal work are the finishing touches which can make or break the external aesthetics of a new or refurbished building.

Specialist consultants

On certain projects there is a need for other specialist consultants. These can include:

- *Acoustic engineers* where concert halls, theatres and the like are involved
- *Theatre consultants* for all types of theatre work
- *Curtain walling engineers* for special cladding work
- *Information technology consultants* for complex data and communications installations
- *Interior or furniture designers* where the employer wishes to use a specialist interior designer

The list of such specialist consultants is not endless but as the years go by more and more such specialists tend to appear as buildings become evermore complex. The specialists all need to be paid and this is something that must always be borne in mind when preparing fee budgets for a building owner, who will need to be convinced of the necessity for their employment.

1.4.7   The clerk of works

The clerk of works is sometimes employed as the employer's inspector on the construction site[2]. Clerks of works are responsible for checking that the materials and workmanship conform to the specification outlined in the contract documents. They may, albeit rarely, be authorised to issue instructions to the contractor but under JCT forms of contract their powers are more limited.

While architects are required to give adequate inspection to check that a building is erected generally in accordance with the provisions of the contract, their terms of appointment rarely require them to make constant inspections. There is, however, often a need for such constant attention, hence the employment of a clerk of works. An architect has to act impartially between the building owner and the contractor, but the clerk of works is only responsible to the building owner. The architect must therefore maintain a delicate balance in dealing with the clerk of works and contractor and, whilst preserving the authority of the clerk of works, must guard against the risk of unfair dictation to the contractor.

The clerk of works' duties and limitations should be clearly understood, and it is the responsibility of the architect to see that they are properly instructed. Good clerks of works can be of the greatest assistance to the architect, who should make a point of getting to know them well and gaining their confidence at the earliest stage. They are usually persons of considerable practical experience who have graduated from a particular trade and the architect should not hesitate to take their advice on practical matters when the occasion demands.

The primary duty of the clerk of works is, as already mentioned, to ensure that the work is carried out in strict accordance with the drawings and specification. The clerk of works' authority is therefore limited to ensuring that the standard required under the terms of the contract is maintained and they can condemn any work or materials that fall short of this standard. The clerk of works must be on site throughout the hours that the contractor's operatives are there (unless only employed on a part-time basis) and, further, must endeavour to be everywhere at once! It is a most difficult job to do well, and requires both tact and knowledge. The architect should recognise this and do everything possible to help.

The clerk of works can also be of considerable assistance by keeping, for instance, a record of any work that is likely to be covered up so that the measuring can be correct. This applies particularly to foundations and other items subject to remeasurement or required for 'as built' record purposes.

Besides these duties there are a variety of other records which the clerk of works should keep. Daywork sheets will be submitted when works may need to be valued on a daywork basis and it will be necessary to certify that the time and materials are correct. Records of operatives on site and what they are doing, visitors, weather records and the like can prove invaluable later on. The clerk of works is altogether a most important person.

1.5   Organisations

1.5.1   Professional organisations

Members of the building team all have their professional organisations that act as learned societies, with library, research facilities and internet web-sites for members and in some cases they provide recognised educational qualifications as well. In the interests of the general public they are responsible for overseeing the conduct of members and practice generally. They also provide a central source for social activities and for the general dissemination of information by way of journals, lectures etc. The major such bodies are:

- *Architects*
  Royal Institute of British Architects (RIBA)
  Royal Incorporation of Architects in Scotland (RIAS)
  Royal Society of Ulster Architects (RSUA)
  Royal Institute of Architects in Ireland (RIAI)
  Association of Consultant Architects (ACA)

- *Clerks of works*
  Institute of Clerks of Works of Great Britain Incorporated (ICW)

- *Engineers*
  Institution of Civil Engineers (ICE)
  Institution of Electrical Engineers (IEE)
  Institution of Mechanical Engineers (IMechE)
  Institution of Structural Engineers (IStructE)
  Association of Building Engineers (ABE)

- *Landscape*
  Landscape Institute (LI)

- *Planners*
  Royal Town Planning Institute (RTPI)

- *Surveyors*
  Royal Institution of Chartered Surveyors (RICS)
  Architects and Surveyors Institute (ASI)

1.5.2   Contractors organisations

In the same way members of the contracting side of the industry have their organisations who look after their members in a similar way and represent their interests in national and regional negotiations on such matters as wages, working rules and contract conditions. The two major bodies in this respect are:

- *Building contractors*
  Construction Confederation
- *Civil engineering contractors*
  Civil Engineering Contractors Association

1.5.3   Manufacturers trade associations

There are a number of associations representing manufacturers from whom useful information and advice can be obtained as to the use of material that their members manufacture or use. Among these are:

- Council for Aluminium in Building
- Brick Development Association
- British Constructional Steelwork Association Ltd
- British Precast Concrete Federation Ltd
- British Woodworking Federation
- British Cement Association
- Clay Pipe Development Association Ltd
- Copper Development Association
- Lead Development Association
- Mastic Asphalt Council Ltd
- Timber Research and Development Association
- Zinc Development Association

In fact, nearly all manufacturers have some sort of publicity organisation for their particular trade[3].

1.5.4   Other organisations

Other organisations exist which further the work of the industry in many ways. Some of the more important of these are described below.

British Board of Agrément (BBA)

This is an official body for the assessment of new building products for which certificates are issued. Since its formation the scope has widened to include traditional construction products which have an export potential. The Board works in conjunction with the European Organisation for Technical Approvals.

British Standards Institution (BSI)

The British Standards Institution has a scope much wider than that of the construction industry alone. It is the recognised authority in the UK for the preparation of national standards covering specifications for dimensions, preferred sizes, quality, performance, methods of testing, terms, definitions and symbols, and codes of practice. All publications are listed in the *British Standards Yearbook*, which is available from the BSI in London. A large number of standards apply to the construction industry. Committees responsible for framing the standards have representatives of contractors, architects, engineers and surveyors as well as experts in the manufacture of the material concerned. British Standards are widely adopted in the Commonwealth countries. The BSI also has an obligation to publish British versions of European Standards, (these are referenced BS EN), and withdraw any conflicting British Standards or parts thereof.

Building Centre

The Building Centre[4] is backed and supported by manufacturers of all types of building product. It maintains a permanent exhibition where samples of a wide variety of materials can be seen. It is an agency from which names and addresses and often leaflets of manufacturers can be obtained, and is particularly useful when only the branded name of a material is known. For those who work some distance from London enquiries can be made by telephone. Similar centres exist in a number of other major cities of the UK.

Building Cost Information Service (BCIS)

Although the BCIS has been largely formulated for quantity surveyors, it is now open to anyone of any discipline who is willing and able to contribute information in accordance with the reciprocal basis of the service. It also distributes up-to-date information on construction economics. The main sections deal with cost analyses, cost indices and trends and market conditions.

Building Research Establishment (BRE)

The BRE's main establishment is at Garston near Watford, Hertfordshire. It undertakes research on building materials and is prepared to advise on difficulties within its sphere of work. A large proportion of its annual budget is spent on research, with the remainder on information activities. It often prepares the results of research in publications, which are available through the Stationery Office. The BRE also includes the Timber Technology Research Station and the Fire Research Station. It is engaged in research across a wide spectrum of activities associated with building.

Construction Industry Board (CIB)

The Construction Industry Board was established to improve the performance of the UK construction industry following the publication of the Latham Report[5]. It brings together suppliers and customers from the private and public construction sectors with central government. It provides both a forum for liaison between the representative bodies of the industry and a channel of communication to institutions and associations, companies and individuals. Its main objectives are to implement the recommendations of the Latham Report and the complementary agenda of the 1998 *Rethinking Construction* Report[6].

Construction Industry Council (CIC)

The Construction Industry Council was established in 1988 with five members. Since then it has grown in size and influence and is now the largest body concerned with all aspects of the built environment. It is the forum for the industry's professional bodies, research organisations and specialist trade associations and speaks as a single body on behalf of the industry.

Construction Industry Research and Information Association (CIRIA)

CIRIA also carries out research activities, but has no laboratories of its own. It acts as a focal point for the approval of projects and provision of funds. For this purpose it obtains government grants, but it also relies on research contracts from industry. Thus it is able to sponsor projects in universities, industrial research centres and government departments themselves.

Construction Industry Training Board (CITB)

The CITB was established under the Industrial Training Act in July 1964. This Act is intended to secure an improvement in the quality and efficiency of industrial training, and to make sure that an adequate supply of people are properly trained for all levels of operation within the industry. The CITB is funded by raising a levy on contracting firms based on the number of employees. In return it is able to offer grants to employers who undertake its courses, and co-operates with Colleges of Technology in providing the courses necessary for such training. A wide range of courses is also offered at its training centres at Birmingham, Erith, Glasgow and Bircham Newton in Norfolk.

Joint Contracts Tribunal Ltd (JCT)

This organisation is composed of representatives of employers, architects, surveyors, contractors and subcontractors. The constituent bodies are as follows:

- Royal Institute of British Architects
- Construction Confederation
- Royal Institution of Chartered Surveyors
- Local Government Association
- National Specialist Contractors Council Ltd

- Association of Consulting Engineers
- Scottish Building Contract Committee
- British Property Federation

It is responsible for drafting the various JCT Forms of Building Contract, for their periodic revision and the issue of practice notes for clarification purposes. Lately, it has undertaken the drafting of co-ordinated professional documents. Its work also includes considering questions raised by and through the representative members on the forms of contract. In the late 1990s the JCT became the Joint Contracts Tribunal Limited with a revised constitution which was in the process of review as this book was completed.

Construction Products Association (CPA)

This association (formally the National Council of Building Material Producers) was originally constituted to represent the collective interests of its members to Government, the Commission of the European Communities, the European Development Councils (EDCs), Confederation of British Industries (CBI), British Standards Institution (BSI) and other trade and professional organisations. It seeks to promote increased collaboration between building material producers. It nominates representatives on government and other committees, and seeks to promote both home and overseas trade. The Council is also able to provide advice on legislation, technical matters, contracts and commercial matters appropriate to its interests. It provides an annual report and weekly information in addition to other technical literature.

Construction Industry Joint Council (CIJC)

The CIJC is the body which determines the wages and conditions for the industry on a national basis. It also arranges negotiations between employers and operatives for the settlement of disputes. It operates a national joint training scheme and works on a regional basis. There are regional joint committees and area joint committees as connecting links between the Council and individual members. The Council has done much to stabilise and improve working conditions in the industry.

1.6 The future of the construction industry

As the construction industry moves into the twenty-first century the demand for improvements in performance are ever increasing, and cannot be ignored. Reviews carried out during the 1990s have highlighted the dissatisfaction among major clients due to the unpredictability of projects in terms of delivery to time and within budgets and to the standards of quality expected. The Latham Report identified that this was due to the fragmentation and confrontation that exists. More recently the *Rethinking Construction* Report again recognised the level of dissatisfaction and put forward proposals for improving performance across the industry as a whole, centred around five key drivers:

- Committed leadership
- A focus on the customer
- Integrated processes and teams
- A quality driven agenda
- Commitment to people

The task force behind the report considered that these drivers together with the application of performance targets provided the focus for considerable improvements within the industry.

This momentum for improvement, together with the evermore sophisticated developments in information technology and communications, will mean that the roles, responsibilities and relationships of all those involved in the industry will change. The industry as a whole and the professionals within it need to respond to the challenge laid down and be ready for such change.

References

(1) May, A. (1995) *Keating on Building Contracts*, 6th edn, Sweet & Maxwell.
(2) *Handbook for Clerk of Works*, 3rd edn (1983), Greater London Council.
(3) *Directory of Official Architecture and Planning* (1992), Longman.
(4) Building Centre, 26 Store Street, London WCIE 7BT. Tel. 020 7637 1022.
(5) Latham, Sir Michael (1994) *Constructing The Team*, Stationery Office.
(6) *Rethinking Construction, the Report of the Construction Task Force*, (1998) Department of the Environment, Transport and the Regions.

2 Basics

2.1 Architectural education and training

The traditional way of becoming an architect was for a young person to be articled to a practising architect for a number of years. It was customary to pay the architect for the privilege and the architect would give the pupil a small allowance each week. The pupil had to pass the external examinations of the Royal Institute of British Architects. That system ended early in the 1960s and full-time education became the norm. The Architects Registration Board (ARB) has a statutory obligation to oversee architectural education. The checking of standards in schools of architecture is undertaken by visiting boards which are composed of members of the RIBA and the ARB.

There are currently 35 schools of architecture in the UK whose examinations are recognised by the RIBA as giving exemption from the RIBA's own examinations[1]. A minimum period of seven years of higher education and training are required. At least one year of practical training must follow the final academic year. The full-time course usually consists of three years at a recognised school, often leading to a first degree in architecture which may be BArch or BA (Hons Arch) depending on the school. This gives exemption from the RIBA Part 1 examination. After that, the student must have a year's practical experience in specific areas of architectural practice, which must be recorded. With the co-operation of practices, the schools operate a system of checks by members of staff to ensure as far as possible that the student is getting appropriate experience.

There follow a further two years of full-time education in a school of architecture, but not necessarily the same school in which the student spent the initial three years. It is always open to a student to apply to another school to complete the course and this can often be beneficial both for the school and for the student. Demand for places at all levels and in all schools is very high. Some students decide after securing their first degrees to look for careers outside the practice of architecture. Interior design, planning and graphics are popular.

At the end of the second period of full-time education successful students will usually be awarded a second degree or a diploma, depending on the establishment. This will give exemption from the RIBA Part 2 examination. A further year in practice is required before the student can present him or herself for the examination in professional practice or the RIBA Part 3 examination, after which the student is entitled to become registered (see section 2.4) on completing some formalities. The Stansfield Smith Review has proposed a number of significant changes, encouraging a more flexible approach.[2] Combining architecture with other courses, specialisation, varied course length and the integration of research are seen as some of the benefits. At the time of writing, the Review is still under discussion.

To enter an architecture course, a student must have at least two A level GCE passes or one A level pass and two AS level passes all in academic subjects, with passes in at least five GCSE subjects including mathematics and English language and a science. Students with the bare minimum qualifications are unlikely to be offered a place unless they have other outstanding qualities. GNVQ and B/TECH Diploma or Certificate passes and merits are also acceptable qualifications for entry although certain schools may view them with suspicion.

It has always been possible to qualify as an architect by part-time study at a small number of schools, but only a small proportion of architects qualify by this method. The minimum period is seven years. Students have to have a post in a firm where they can get appropriate guidance and experience and this normally means living near the schools. There have been moves to change this situation and to open up architectural education to those who cannot attend full-time but would clearly benefit from contact with a school. The system depends on individual part-time students having tutors, usually from the schools, to assist them in achieving the necessary standards to pass the external examinations. The whole system is the subject of much debate at the time this book is being written.

2.2 Continuing professional development (CPD)

An architect would have to be totally cut off from his fellows not to have come across the concept of continuing professional development, commonly known as CPD. It is not, of course, confined solely to architects. The other construction professionals such as engineers, surveyors and planners are required to undertake structured courses of study after qualification. Outside the construction industry, doctors, solicitors and others also have an express obligation in this area. Strictly speaking, it can and is argued that CPD is always implied into the obligations of any professional person – in other words, the obligation to keep up to date. CPD is rather more than that and assumes that the professional will not just keep up to date, but will also develop expertise in specific directions[3].

The RIBA decided that CPD was to be obligatory for its members from 1 January 1993. On 1 April 1999, the RIBA introduced mandatory CPD. The precise difference is not clear. The new rules require every corporate member of the RIBA who is not fully retired to do certain things each year:

- Undertake 35 hours of CPD
- Achieve 100 points of CPD
- Monitor what is done by means of a CPD record sheet
- Plan the activity by means of a professional development plan (PDP)

The RIBA have published an explanatory leaflet which includes a sample professional development plan and CPD record sheet[4]. Valid CPD encompasses any relevant study or any activity which enhances an architect's professional abilities and their development. Whether any particular activity falls into that category is left to the individual architect. Each architect should aim to tailor the CPD to individual needs and, if appropriate, to specialisation. Ideally, architects are encouraged to aim at achieving 50% of CPD activity as formal study – attendance at lectures or courses – with the remainder made up of any other relevant activity. The 1991 leaflet published by the RIBA gave examples of suitable activities:

- Technical and professional conferences, lectures, workshops, seminars and courses
- Teaching/tutoring/mentoring (those not in teaching posts)
- Practice (those in teaching posts)
- Structured home reading; open and distance learning
- Preparing articles for the technical and professional press
- Directed studies during educational and sabbatical leave
- Practice and peer review
- In-house and inter-professional study meetings
- Practitioner research for publication
- Recorded on-the-job research

- Supervised research for further qualification
- Service on BSI or BBA committees and working groups, on RIBA technical and practice- related committees, and service as an RIBA external examiner and on RIBA visiting boards

In addition, the following have been suggested:

- IT and CAD skills
- Financial planning and accounting
- Language skills
- Management development
- Ergonomics
- Working in Europe
- Marketing the practice[5]

The system is to be monitored by a random sample on a yearly basis through registered practices. The sanction for failure to provide evidence that the CPD aims have been achieved may be that the practice is removed from the register.

The biggest spur should be that architects who may be called on to answer in respect of their competence or who are concerned in legal proceedings may be prejudiced if they have neglected their CPD obligations. It is certain to be an important factor in quality assurance (QA).

It will be tempting for architects to concentrate their CPD activities on those areas which they find of most interest, whereas it is likely that they should be concentrating on those areas of practice where interest is lacking. For example, most architects are interested in design; that is why they entered the profession in the first place. They will need little encouragement to attend lectures and carry out research in this area. On the other hand, architects tend to have less interest in the business side of practice or the legal and contractual implications, which is perhaps where effort should be concentrated.

2.3 Distance learning

This is one of those terms which is so simple and self-explanatory that people are often misled. It is used to differentiate from the kind of learning which takes place geographically in the same place as the tutor, for example in college or university. Correspondence courses are examples of distance learning. The concept can obviously serve as part satisfaction of CPD requirements, but there is no substitute for having the tutor alongside the student to explain difficult points as they arise. Thus formal CPD should be a mixture of distance learning (probably the majority of hours), private study and tutor-centred learning. Two examples of types of distance learning are the video packages produced by the CPD in Construction Group[6] and the distance learning library operated by the RIAS in Edinburgh. There are also more elaborate distance learning courses such as those offered by the College of Estate Management.

Learning is a very individual thing. Some persons can only learn if they write or read or discuss with others, some only if they do all those things. Therefore, each person will choose the kind of learning which suits him or her best. After qualification, and for some even before qualification, it is a luxury to attend a seminar or a short course. Distance learning packages are an acceptable short-term substitute provided that the student gets the opportunity to take part in face to face dialogue with a tutor from time to time.

2.4   Registration and practice in the UK

The Architects (Registration) Act 1931 set up the Architects Registration Council of the United Kingdom (ARCUK) as the body controlling the architectural professional in England, Wales, Scotland and Northern Ireland. The Act was followed by the Architects Registration Acts 1939–1969. The principle Act is now the Architect's Act 1997 which consolidates the former Architects (Registration) Acts. ARCUK came to an end and the Architects Registration Board (ARB) came into being on 1 April 1997. Any person wishing to use the title 'architect' for business purposes, must be registered with ARB. The Board prescribes that a person can become registered:

■ By gaining a qualification after passing an examination which is recognised by ARB; *and*
■ By completing at least two years' practical experience supervised by an architect, one of the years being undertaken after completion of a five year course of study and gaining the qualification in 1 above; *and*
■ By passing a written and/or an oral examination in professional practice recognised by ARB

Architects can be removed from the register in the following instances:

- If an architect makes application in writing stating the grounds
- Failure to pay the annual retention fee at the appropriate time after a written request to do so
- If at the time of registration the architect was subject to a disqualifying decision in another European Economic Area (EEA) state, of which ARB was unaware
- Failure to notify ARB of a change of address after being requested to do so
- If an architect is guilty of unacceptable professional conduct or serious professional incompetence or has been convicted of a criminal offence which may have relevance to fitness to practise as an architect

The stated duties of ARB are as follows:

- To maintain a register of architects and to publish it
- To prescribe the admission criteria
- To protect consumers from misconduct or incompetence by architects
- To require appropriate evidence from firms wishing to practise under the title 'Architect'
- To draw up a code of conduct
- To prosecute unregistered persons who practise under the title 'architect'

An unregistered person who practises or carries on business under any name containing the word 'architect' is guilty of a criminal offence. Such a person is liable to a heavy fine. A person who is a member of the RIBA but not registered may not be styled 'chartered architect' and may not even use the affixes FRIBA, ARIBA or RIBA, because they contain the prohibited word[7]. The fact that only the title and not the function is protected has long been a sore point among architects and it has been the source of comment in the courts. The unregistered currently can style themselves 'architectural consultant' or 'architectural designer' if they so wish. Whether such titles will also be put on the proscribed list only time will tell.

The constituent members of ARB are as follows:

- Seven members elected in accordance with an electoral scheme made by the Board with the approval of the Privy Council after consultation with bodies which are representative of architects. All registered persons may take part in such elections.
- Eight members who are appointed by the Privy Council after consultation with the secretary of state and others. These

members represent the interests of the users of architectural services and the general public and no registered person may be appointed.

ARB has set up a European Advisory Group to highlight relevant issues arising from the EU.

2.5   Registration and practice in the EU

Directive 85/384/EEC covers the registration of architects within the European Union (EU). In the UK the Architects Act 1997 takes account of the directive, and in most other member countries appropriate laws have been enacted or amended, the broad effect of which is to make it possible for architect nationals of the member countries to practise in other countries within the community. Registration under the directive is confined to persons, not practices. With some exceptions, it is also confined to nationals of the member countries, so that, for example, an Indian architect may be registered in the UK having satisfied the requirements, but that architect may not seek to practise in the EU on that basis. The Architects Act 1997 makes provision for ARB to maintain a list of visiting EEA architects, but no applications have been received for enrolment onto the list of visiting EEA architects.

Relatively few architects take advantage of the opportunity to practise in other member countries. For example, in the UK the numbers of persons with EU qualifications registering in 1997 was 22, little changed from the previous two years (19 in 1995, 25 in 1996)[8]. The Architects' Directive specifies in very broad terms the areas which must be covered by architects during studies. It also stipulates a minimum of four years full-time study at a university or equivalent institution.

The directive has not had an easy passage and at the time of writing there are still some EU countries which have not fully implemented it. One of the problems is that the education of architects in the various member countries and the role of the persons termed architects are not uniform. Much of this derives from the construction industry practices as a whole in particular countries. In Germany, for example, much construction is carried out on a separate trades basis and architects are expected to carry out the contract site management. In France, by contrast, although a trade by trade contracting system is also common, architects play a less practical role and it is common for production drawings to be prepared by contractors. Clearly, architects in the UK must spend some time in researching such differences before opting to practise elsewhere in the EU. To fully describe the construction industries in European countries is beyond the scope of this book, but useful information is available in a large number of publications[9]. The requirements for registration in EU member countries are complex and advice should be sought from ARB.

2.6 The RIBA Code of Professional Conduct

The RIBA, to which most but not all architects belong, publishes a code of conduct which is binding on its members. ARB also publishes a code which is a completely revised version of the very short code formerly published by ARCUK (see section 2.7). A member of the RIBA may be required to answer inquiries regarding his or her professional conduct. The member is liable to reprimand, suspension or expulsion if the member's conduct is found by the disciplinary committee of the Institute to be in contravention of the code or otherwise inconsistent with status as a member or derogatory to professional character.

The object of the Code of Professional Conduct is to promote the standard of professional conduct, or self-discipline, required of members of the RIBA in the interests of the public. The code regulates the actions of members between themselves, to their clients and to the public at large. The code simply puts into words what most clients would expect of their professional advisors. It is more than just a set of rules for fair dealing; it points out the high standard of behaviour which is expected of a professional person in a position of trust.

A member may engage in any activity, whether as proprietor, director, partner, salaried employee, consultant or in any other capacity, provided that the member's conduct complies with the code. The code is divided into three 'principles', each of which is followed by a set of undertakings which amplify the principles and illustrate their application.

2.6.1 Principle one – RIBA code

'A member shall faithfully carry out his duties applying his knowledge and experience with efficiency and loyalty towards his client or employer, and being mindful of the interests of those who may be expected to use or enjoy the product of his work.'

Where members are acting between parties, they must be impartial. So, for example, they must interpret the building contract fairly between client and contractor. If called upon to decide the line of a boundary between neighbours or any other matter where both sides look to them for expert judgment, they must give an honest opinion. This provision does not, of course, prevent them from representing the client in any such dispute against an opponent. The architect's duty to act fairly will arise only when both sides are relying on his or her judgment.

Before entering into an agreement, members must clearly set out the terms including what services will be provided, responsibilities, any limitation of liability, how fees will be calculated, how the agreement may be terminated and adjudication provision. All such agreements should be in writing and it is sensible to use the RIBA terms of engagement SFA/99, CE/99 or SW/99, as appropriate. Members must state whether they hold professional indemnity insurance.

Members should make sure that they have the resources to carry out commissions and provide a service which meets the RIBA standard of professional performance (see section 2.6.4). Student members should seek guidance from architects if they intend to undertake commissions themselves. Employees are expected to give prior notice to both parties before accepting an engagement elsewhere.

Members must ensure that any offices which are dealing with architecture are under the control of an architect. This rule prevents architects from opening branch offices under the control of unqualified assistants – unqualified in the sense of being unqualified as architects. Architects may well have assistants or even partners who are qualified as surveyors or as architectural technicians. The code precludes these from controlling branch offices.

Members must not sublet work without the client's permission. This merely states the legal position, that if the client engages an architect to do work, the architect must not pass the work to someone else. Naturally, office staff services will be used, but if the work were to be passed on to another architect's practice to carry out, the architect would be in breach not only of the code, but also of the agreement with the client.

Members must not evade their responsibilities by abandoning a commission. This particular undertaking appears to be aimed at architects who may be tempted to desert their clients for an unsatisfactory reason, for example, because the project is becoming more difficult than anticipated. Although SFA/99 and previous editions of RIBA conditions of engagement entitle either architect or employer to bring the commission to an end on reasonable notice, the common law position is more stringent if the RIBA terms are not employed. Architects attempting to bring their commissions to an end may be in repudiatory breach of contract unless they take the greatest care (see Chapter 6, section 6.4). There are many instances, of course, where an architect has little option but to abandon the commission. Such cases arise more frequently than one might wish. Many can be summarised as situations in which the client effectively prevents the architect from carrying out his or her contractual duties. Instances of gross interference with the architect's administration of the contract are not rare.

2.6.2 Principle two – RIBA code

'A member shall, at all times, avoid any action or situation which is inconsistent with his professional obligations or which is likely to raise doubts about his integrity.'

Members' other business interests are covered by this principle. If they are such as might lead the client or employer to question the architect's integrity because they are or appear to be related to the subject of the commission, the architect is obliged to disclose them in writing before being engaged by the client. Obvious examples of such situations are cases where the architect already acts for a contractor in some other matter and the client may wish to employ the contractor to carry out building work, or if the architect owns land adjacent to the client's property and over which it will be necessary to agree an easement. The architect must withdraw unless the client or employer accepts the situation in writing.

If any potential conflict of personal or professional interest arises which is not specifically covered in the code, the architect must do one of three things:

- Withdraw from the situation; *or*
- Remove whatever is causing the conflict of interests; *or*
- Inform the client and anyone else concerned and obtain the agreement of all parties to the architect's continued engagement.

Members must undertake not to make or acquiesce in any statement in which they do not believe or which is misleading or unfair or otherwise discreditable to the profession. This undertaking should be a matter of stating the obvious. It should go without saying that a member of any profession should be a model of the highest integrity.

Members must not hold themselves out to be, or practise as, independent consulting architects if at the same time they:

- Engage in the business of trading in land or buildings; *or*
- Act as a property developer; *or*
- Act as auctioneers or house or estate agents; *or*
- Act as contractors or subcontractors; *or*
- Manufacture or supply goods to or for the building industry, *or*
- Have partners or co-directors who engage in one of the above.

An exception may be made to this rule if members can demonstrate that the firm is clearly identified as and separate from the architectural practice.

Members must not hold themselves out to be independent if they or their employers are contractors. If they practise as both architects and contractors, they cannot pretend to be independent and must inform the client of the right to appoint another architect to act as professional advisor or agent in such matters as quality and financial control. It should be clearly understood that architects who combine architectural and contracting services are offering clients what amounts to package deals (see Chapter 7, section 7.4). Where architects practise in this way, the client has the additional protection that they are bound by the code, but it is for the client to decide whether to engage an architect who is offering this kind of service, to ask for architectural services only, or to engage an architect who has no related interests.

Members must not take any discounts, commissions or gifts as inducements to show favour to anyone. This is corrupt and a criminal offence. Neither must they allow their names to be used in advertising services or products which have any connection with the construction industry. If architects act as contractors, they may take the usual trade discounts customary to the industry. Members must not try to influence improperly the granting of any kind of statutory approval. An example of this might be where an architect sits as a member of an advisory panel to examine planning applications and whose own application comes before the panel. In such a case, the architect would be obliged to declare an interest and, usually, take no part in any discussion of that application.

Members must not have partners or co-directors who are disqualified from registration or expelled from the register or disqualified by reason of expulsion from any other professional body, without the permission of the RIBA.

A member cannot hide behind the provisions of the Companies Acts or any particular form of practice in order to avoid compliance with this principle.

Members who become insolvent or who are disqualified from acting as company directors are obliged to notify the RIBA chief executive.

Members must conform with the rules for client's accounts.

2.6.3 Principle three – RIBA code

'A member shall in every circumstance conduct himself in a manner which respects the legitimate rights and interests of others.'

This portion of the code is designed to regulate the ways in which members can obtain work.

Members must not give discounts or gifts for the introduction of clients or work. If members operate as contractors, of course, they may give all the customary trade discounts.

Members may quote a fee for carrying out commissions. However, they must have enough information to know what a project entails and what services will be required. A member must not offer a quotation unless it has been requested. In effect, therefore, a client can obtain competitive quotations from several architects. Members are not allowed to reduce their fees to take account of quotations which a client may have obtained from other architects. This is to remove the possibility of a 'Dutch auction' taking place. Some architects do not care to participate in quoting competitively. Such an attitude in no way reflects on the quality of their service or the fees they charge. It may be that they do not wish to spend time and effort on such an exercise or they may have had unfortunate experiences in connection with fee tendering in the past.

Provided that the client is not seeking competitive quotations, there is nothing to prevent negotiations with the architect after having received the initial quotation. The architect may be prepared to reduce fees to take account of particular factors which were not clear at the time of the first quotation, or may suggest a reduction in the services. The basic position is that a member must not attempt to supplant another architect. Thus an architect may not approach a client offering services knowing that the client has already entered into discussions with another architect.

The code prevents any member from entering an architectural competition which the RIBA has said is unacceptable. Where a member carries out the duties of a competition assessor, that member may not afterwards carry out any other function in relation to the project.

No member must maliciously or unfairly criticise or discredit another member or that member's work. The fact that it was thought necessary to include this undertaking at all is a sad reflection on architectural practice.

If a client approaches a member to undertake a commission knowing it is being handled, or has been handled, by another architect, the member is obliged to notify the original architect of the enquiry. The member's obligation is to make reasonable enquiries to ascertain whether such a situation exists. The object of the procedure is to enable the original architect to take whatever steps may be appropriate. In the majority of cases, the original architect will do nothing other than acknowledge the notice.

If the client has omitted to pay the fees of the original architect, the client can expect to receive a bill forthwith. In that situation or if the client's reason for changing architects was because of a dispute, the new architect may well ask for further information on the subject and, at the very least, require a payment on account before beginning any work. In some cases, all that will be required is that the client gives the original architect proper notice of termination of appointment in accordance with the agreement. It may be, however, that to give notice to the original architect would be prejudicial to prospective litigation.

Sometimes, an architect may be engaged to give an opinion on the work of another architect. Unless prejudicial to litigation, the engagement should be notified to the first architect. The new architect has no obligation to do anything further.

Significantly, a member must acknowledge the contribution made by others. This is especially relevant to employees, to whom a member has the duty to properly define terms of employment and there is the welcome introduction of an obligation to ensure that professional indemnity insurers waive rights of subrogation in respect of employee architects.

A member now has the duty to report to the RIBA any breach of the code by others. This duty is made subject to restriction imposed by the courts – a provision which is otiose, because it would be a brave, not to say foolish, architect who would attempt to flout the directions of a court, whatever the RIBA may say about it. In apparent conflict with that, undertaking 3.13, which is made subject to the RIBA's disciplinary byelaws, requires members to respect and maintain confidentiality in anything involving breaches or alleged breaches of the code or of the standard of professional competence. Presumably, this should be interpreted to mean that a member must report breaches of the code to the RIBA, but not to others. Members are obliged to report their own indictable criminal offences or disqualification from acting as directors.

2.6.4 Standard of professional performance

'Members are required to maintain in their work and that of their practices a standard of performance which is consistent with membership of the Royal Institute of British Architects and with a proper regard for the interests both of those who commission and those who may be expected to enjoy the product of their work.

Members and their practices will meet the requirements of their engagements with commensurate knowledge and attention so that the quality of the professional services provided does not fall below that which could reasonably be expected of Members of the Royal Institute in good standing in the normal conduct of their business.'

This standard is a new part of the code. The aim is to establish a level of competence. Like the rest of the code, it is fleshed out with a series of undertakings. It is not envisaged that single failure to comply with the standard will result in anything other than an investigation and advice to the member or practice setting out how the standard is to be achieved. However, extreme and irresponsible or repeated failure may result in disciplinary proceedings. If a member is investigated for alleged failure to meet the standard, any failure to comply with the undertakings which amplify the standard may have serious consequences.

The undertakings embrace a wide range of architectural activity.

Members must comply with reasonable instructions from clients and act honestly, competently, diligently and expeditiously to follow agreed timescales and costs. It has to be acknowledged that some instructions given by clients are not reasonable and members must think carefully whether in certain instances the act of compliance itself may be a sign of incompetence; for example, a member who issues a certificate of practical completion because the client so instructs, before a building has reached that condition. It is also unhelpful for the undertaking to set out as one of the ways in which a member can comply with the standard of competence, to '. . . carry out and complete the work . . . competently . . .'. Quite so.

Members must not only fulfil CPD requirements, but must also allow time for employees to do the same.

Every practice must have a complaints procedure for the benefit of clients. This will only really affect medium to large practices where there may be some doubt about the right person to approach.

Members must make appropriate arrangements for cover if they are absent for any reason. This is mainly directed at sole practitioners who are also required to try to establish contacts with other members to avoid the isolation and lack of a balanced view which is the cause of many mistakes.

Members must seek advice if they are faced with a situation which is outside their experience or knowledge. Although architects should have the requisite knowledge to enable them to administer a building contract effectively, there may be a situation where determination is threatened and with which most architects will need external assistance. The same applies to difficult ground conditions or the countless instances where a consultant is indicated. It is perhaps humbling, certainly realistic, but not negligent to admit that help is required. It is negligent as well as a breach of this undertaking to attempt to deal with something for which one is not qualified. In the same connection, a member who is a partner or director of a practice is required to give thought to the capability of staff to whom any matters are delegated. Members must not hold themselves out as having experience or expertise which they do not possess and they must not accept commissions on that basis unless they can arrange for the necessary assistance.

The code concludes with a set of rules which apply where client's accounts are run.

2.7   The ARB Code: Standards of Conduct and Practice

2.7.1   Contents of the code

This code, as may be expected, has many common points of reference with the RIBA code. Failure to comply with the code will not automatically lead to disciplinary proceedings, but it is something which will be taken into account if it becomes necessary to examine the conduct or competence of an architect. Architects who are guilty of 'unacceptable professional conduct' (i.e. conduct which falls short of the standard required of a registered person) or 'serious professional incompetence' (i.e. service which falls short of the standards required of a registered person) may be disciplined in various ways. The standards are set out in the code. They are divided into two sections: conduct and competence, and client service and complaints. What follows is a very brief precis of the twelve standards. There is no substitute for reading the standards themselves.

2.7.2 Conduct and competence

Standard 1: 'Architects should at all times act with integrity and avoid any action or situations which are inconsistent with their professional obligations.'

This is very similar to principle two of the RIBA code. It requires an architect to act with complete honesty at all times and it is to be noted that architects must not make or support statements which are contrary to their professional opinions. This alone would preclude an architect who was instructed by the client to issue (or withhold) a certificate of practical completion, from doing so if the architect had a different view.

This standard also deals with possible conflicts which must be declared and the architect should withdraw if necessary. Architects must not take, as a partner or co-director, anyone who has been struck off the register or disqualified from any professional body. Architects acting as consultants and contractors at the same time must make clear to all that they cannot offer an independent service.

Standard 2: 'Architects should only undertake professional work for which they are able to provide adequate professional, financial and technical competence and resources.'

This duty does not arise until a contract is entered into. Architects doing speculative or competition work are excluded for obvious reasons. Architects are responsible for those under their control and sole practitioners must ensure that procedures are in place to deal with their absences from work.

Standard 3: 'Architects should only promote their professional services in a truthful and responsible manner.'

Architects should promote themselves truthfully and they should not attempt to mislead. It has been said that it is misleading for a sole practitioner architect to be styled 'X and Associates', simply on the strength of occasionally working closely with other disciplines. The point may be debatable, but it would certainly be misleading for a sole practioner to be styled 'X and Partners'. Each architectural office and branch office should be under the control of an architect.

Standard 4: 'Architects should carry out their professional work faithfully and conscientiously and with due regard to relevant technical and professional standards.'

Architects must exercise impartial and professional judgment and carry out work with due skill, care and diligence. This is a change to the generally recognised duty to exercise reasonable skill and care. There is sufficient case law for it to be understood what is meant by reasonable skill and care, but the duty required by the standard is almost certainly more onerous.

Standard 5: 'In carrying out or agreeing to carry out professional work, Architects should pay due regard to the interests of anyone who may reasonably be expected to use or enjoy the products of their own work.'

This is similar to principle one of the RIBA code. The architect has a duty to the wider community to conserve and enhance the environment.

Standard 6: 'Architects should maintain their professional service and competence in areas relevant to their professional work, and discharge the requirements of any engagement with commensurate knowledge and attention.'

This is a clear signal that architects must become involved in CPD. A failure to do so would be significant if ever their competence was called in question.

Standard 7: 'Architects should preserve the security of monies entrusted to their care in the course of their practice or business.'

This standard details the precautions which architects must take with clients' accounts and echos some of the provisions in the RIBA code.

Standard 8: 'Architects should not undertake professional work without adequate and appropriate professional indemnity cover.'

The principal duty is laid on architects who are either sole practitioners or employers. They must ensure adequate cover for themselves and employees. The duty extends to employees to ensure, so far as they can, that their employers have professional indemnity (PI) cover. Many architects carry on professional services outside their main occupation and they should be covered for every kind of work they may perform. Therefore, architects practising as property surveyors, even as a sideline, must have proper insurance. It should be obvious that an architect must have enough insurance cover for every commission. Cover of £500,000 will hardly suffice for a practice called upon to design a £5m development.

Standard 9: 'Architects should ensure that their personal and professional finances are managed prudently.'

Architects who become bankrupt or who are directors of companies which go into liquidation or enter into agreements with creditors may be held to have a wilful disregard of responsibilities or a lack of integrity. Not every architect in this position should be criticised or disciplined, because in practice, this kind of catastrophe may be just bad luck.

Standard 10: 'Architects should promote the standards set out in this Code.'

The standard appears innocuous enough, but the notes make clear that this standard will probably cause most difficulty in practice. Not only must architects comply with the code, they must also report any breaches of which they become aware. There are some exceptions to this rule. If architects are acting as arbitrators, adjudicators, mediators or expert witnesses, their duty may override their obligation to report breaches of the code. Court restrictions or the general law may also prevent such reporting.

Architects must also report their own shortcomings if they are convicted of indictable offences, sentenced to imprisonment, disqualified from acting as a director, made bankrupt or if they are directors of liquidated companies.

Architects who are subject to disciplinary proceedings may be disadvantaged if they have failed to report promptly.

This standard also requires architects to co-operate in investigations. If an architect threatens to bring defamation proceedings in an effort to thwart investigations of a complaint, the threat may be treated as unacceptable professional conduct. This last provision, provided it is properly implemented, provides a welcome protection to innocent parties caught up, perhaps as witnesses, in disciplinary processes.

2.7.3   Client service and complaints

Standard 11: 'Architects should organise and manage their professional work responsibly and with regard to the interests of their clients.'

This standard has similarities to part of principle one of the RIBA code. It sets out very clearly how architects should order their relationships with their clients. A key requirement is that the terms of the engagement must be set out in writing covering scope of work, fees, responsibilities and any limitation, termination provisions and dispute resolution provisions. Any of the RIBA terms of engagement would satisfy these criteria if properly completed. Architects must let clients know that the Architects Registration Board is the disciplinary body in case of unacceptable professional conduct or serious professional incompetence. This seems like tempting fate where some clients are concerned.

At the end of the contract or on reasonable demand, architects must return any documents to which the client is legally entitled. This requirement leaves uncertain the situation where the architect exercises a lien (retains such documents) to force the client to pay fees properly due.

Architects must organise their practices to operate efficiently with sufficient staff to satisfy any time or cost limits agreed with clients and must keep clients informed about progress and of anything affecting quality or cost.

The requirement that confidential information must not be disclosed is implied by law, but it bears repetition.

Standard 12: 'Architects should deal with disputes or complaints concerning their professional work or that of their practice or business promptly and appropriately.'

Every firm must have a complaints procedure with a system of moving the complaint to a more senior person if the designated person fails to resolve the problem. A requirement which will give many architects restless nights is that if they fail to satisfy the complainant, he or she must be advised that the matter can be referred to the Board if there are alleged breaches of the code.

Alternative dispute resolution procedures are encouraged and a strict timetable for dealing with complaints is set out. The Board promises to adhere to the same time limits – where possible.

References

(1) *Schools of Architecture with courses recognised by the RIBA*, RIBA Publications.

(2) *Architecture Education for the 21st Century* by Sir Colin Stansfield Smith (October 1999), RIBA.

(3) Anne Weightman, 'Learning to Survive: CPD in action', *Architects' Journal*, 13 February 1991, pp. 63–4.

(4) *Royal Institute of British Architects Continuing Professional Development Requirements and Guidance Notes*, 1 March 1999, RIBA.

(5) 'CPD New Rules', *Practice*, issue 165, *RIBA Journal*, April 1999, pp. 79–80.

(6) The Continuing Professional Development in Construction Group is part of the CIC. It is based at the Building Centre, 26 Store Street, London, WC1E 7BT and it can be contacted on 020 7637 8692.

(7) *Jones, ex parte the Architects Registration Board* v. *R. Baden Hellard* (1998) 14 Const LJ 299.

(8) ARCUK Annual Report 1994–5, 1995–6, 1996–7.

(9) Spencer Chapman, N.F. and Grandjean, C. (1991) *The Construction Industry and the European Community*, Blackwell Science. *RIBA Architectural Practice in Europe*, a series of guides published by the RIBA. Other series are published by the Construction Industry Research and Information Association, Centre for Construction Market Information, and Building Services Research and Information Association. These publications tend to be fairly expensive. A useful manual covering all the EU countries with much statistical information is *Gateway to Europe*, National Economic Development Council. A useful insight into specifying practice is Atkinson, G.A. (1995) *Construction Quality and Quality Standards*, E. & F.N. Spon.

Employment

3.1   Introduction

Thirty years ago, opportunities for employment were fairly clear cut so far as architects were concerned. They were employed either in private practice or in local government. There was a relatively small number of architects who were employed in other areas, but they were the minority. Moreover, architects in private practice tended to be considered 'real' architects while their fellows in local government were said to lead a sheltered life in which they were not called upon to exercise the full range of architectural responsibilities. Undoubtedly, the kinds of responsibility shouldered by architects in each area of employment is not identical, but if exercised properly, the architects' duties are just as onerous in the local government situation as in the private sector. Indeed, many such public sector offices have effectively been made into self-contained 'private' firms offering their services to a broad spectrum of clients. Moreover, it is generally accepted that a great many opportunities exist for architects outside the usual fields of employment.

In general, it must be said that other areas of employment have always existed, but architects have tended to ignore the variety in favour of the traditional. The uncertain economic situation forced many architects to seek work totally outside the construction industry where their hard won skills were sometimes of little value. In other cases, architects have looked more seriously at occupations within the industry which were not popular. In some of these occupations the architect is employed largely in a traditional way, in other cases just one facet of the architectural 'package' is used; for example, design, project management, drawing ability and so on. One of the great advantages of an architectural education is that because it is so broadly based, the architect has the chance to examine in some detail a great many possibilities.

The following brief summary cannot be comprehensive because the range of possible opportunities is as long as individual ingenuity makes it.

3.2   Private practice

Private practice is still considered by most lay people as the area wherein architects are employed. An architect will opt for private practice for many reasons:

Because the type of work is likely to be varied

This is the kind of statement which in practice scarcely bears examination. There are certainly practices both large and small which handle an amazing variety of work, but most practices tend to have certain project types in which they profess particular expertise and they tend to get commissions for work for which they have a reputation. Even in a large office handling different project types, the individual architect will often find that he or she is always given a particular kind of work to do.

Because of the particular type of work

There are some private firms which tackle projects that an architect would not encounter elsewhere: very large and prestigious buildings or buildings under the direction of a famous and much sought after master architect or highly specialised building types. Although many organisations such as banks, radio and television, railways and hospitals have their own architects' departments, the design of a new radio station, hospital and so on is rarely left to the 'in house' architects. Therefore, an architect seeking to gain experience in such specialised buildings must join those private firms which specialise in them.

This is not really the place to enter into a long discussion about whether a client is better to engage a private firm which specialises in hotels to design a new hotel or whether a firm which has no previous hotel experience would actually produce a refreshingly different solution to an old problem. In theory, every architect can design any building after going through the appropriate processes of briefing, analysis and synthesis, but in practice, time is money and the architect with previous experience of a particular building type will most likely be put to design the next such building commission to come into that office.

The opportunity to become involved

This is very closely related to the next reason.

The opportunity to take responsibility

Certainly, in the small to medium sized office an architect will be encouraged to take responsibility, provided the architect can demonstrate the appropriate ability. In larger offices, there may be more bureaucracy at work, but even there, an architect prepared to work hard and gifted with ordinary competence can enjoy a fulfilling life. With greater than ordinary competence or a real flair in some field, there is no reason why the architect should not rise to the top of the firm in due course. Although the authors have not seen statistics, many years of observation suggest that it is much more likely that a competent hardworking architect will gain promotion by staying a number of years in a private office than if the same architect stayed for the same number of years in a public sector office.

The opportunity to advance to principal status

This is closely linked to the last reason. An architect who feels involved in the firm's fortunes, who takes on responsibility above that which is indicated in the job description (if any) and who demonstrates ability is almost certain to rise to the top of any private firm. This is because such a firm owes its existence to satisfied clients who return with new commissions. A private firm cannot afford to carry passengers, because they must be paid for out of the income generated by the rest of the staff. A really first class architect, generating more than his or her fair share of fee income for the firm and attracting and keeping clients, eventually becomes the firm in that if such an architect left, the firm would be hard pressed to survive long afterwards. That scenario is more common among small practices, but the principle holds good in any practice. It is possible for an architect employed in a private practice to become the firm or a very sizeable portion of it.

There are many one-person practices in the country and a few large multidisciplinary practices employing over 50 staff. Most of the practices, however, fall into the category of medium to small employing 3–30 persons. Indeed, 65% of all practices have fewer than 10 staff[1]. Some architects prefer the small office because of its friendly atmosphere. It by no means follows that a small office is friendly and a large office unfriendly. Indeed, a clash of personalities which can be absorbed within a firm employing 50 people would be disastrous in an office of five people. The larger office may offer certain advantages in the form of backup and benefits which may not be available in a small office. There may be greater freedom in a small office, but there is less flexibility to meet sudden surges in workload. The most notable point about a private office is that there is always the pressure to earn the income to pay the bills. For the architect at the bottom of the hierarchy, the pressure is more noticeable in the smaller firm where the key policy decisions can be readily seen in a fairly crude way. Such pressure gives many people a sense of excitement. We suspect that it is an important, if perhaps unrecognised, factor in the decision to work in private practice.

3.3 Local authority

Many architects are employed in local government or in government departments. After the 1974 reorganisation of local government, most county councils and district councils appointed an architect as one of the chief officers at the head of a department. The size of department and the precise responsibilities varied with the authority. For some years now, certain local authorities have adopted a policy of making the architects' department a separate entity from the other council departments, economically more accountable than before and often able to take on commissions from other organisations. In some instances, a department has been made completely independent. In such an instance, it becomes a private practice rather like any other except that its birth took place under unusual circumstances. In other instances, the architects' department has ceased to exist altogether, certainly as an identifiable unit.

The character of local government offices varies greatly and so does the scope of the work. Some operate, as noted above, as large departments under the leadership of a chief officer responsible to the council. In other cases, the department may be part of the surveyor's or engineer's department, or it may be part of the council's building department.

The work of an architect in local government is basically the same as that of the architect in private practice. The council will in effect be the client although the relationship between council and architect will be that of master and servant. The architect will be governed by the council's standing orders. However, in carrying out duties, the architect must always remember the obligation to behave in a thoroughly professional manner particularly when called upon to carry out duties under the contract such as certifying or giving extensions of time. Not only should the council not prevent the architect from acting in this way, the council has a positive duty to ensure that the architect carries out his or her duties properly[2].

Architects in local government have certain advantages. If the authority is of reasonable size, they have the authority's other departments, legal, public health, building control, planning and so on, available for advice. In the larger authorities, the architects' departments will doubtless contain many specialist sections such as quantity surveyors, mechanical and electrical engineers, structural engineers, landscape architects and interior designers. Architects operating in that kind of office will in effect be in a multidisciplinary environment able to call upon any assistance necessary.

It is sometimes said that local government offices do not offer as much scope as do private practices. The truth, of course, is not quite so simple. Many offices have a high reputation and such offices will tackle all the authority's prestige works. Smaller offices may confine themselves to fairly routine tasks or smallish projects, handing out the occasional large project to a private firm on a consultancy basis. Any architect contemplating working in local government must make appropriate enquiries first. It must never be forgotten that not all architects want to design very large and prestigious projects. Very many feel more at home working on smaller jobs. A particular feature of working in local government is that architects who put in a number of years' service with the same authority will build up an understanding of the philosophies of the departments who regularly require building work. There is the opportunity to make considerable progress through the development of briefs for particular purposes. Such architects have a unique opportunity to evaluate the performance of existing buildings and to feed back the information into current design.

There are also many opportunities for architects in the planning departments of local authorities, influencing design and planning on a larger scale, perhaps through structure plans or local plans or through involvement in town design, listed buildings, conservation areas and the like. Very often, such architects are also members of the Royal Town Planning Institute.

The opportunities for advancement may be slower and along more rigidly defined lines than is the case in private practice, but the staff will be divided into recognised grades. Each has a maximum and minimum and regular annual incremental increases. Promotion tends to be based on seniority as well as technical and administrative ability. There are well defined conditions of service which include such matters as holidays, sick leave, superannuation (which is generous) and hours of service.

3.4   Other public organisations

Other public organisations such as health authorities and trusts tend to offer rather specialised experience. Regional architects' departments are often a feature and they are closer in organisational structure to a local government office than a private practice. They offer a unique opportunity to develop a profound expertise in a particular building type. This can be a very satisfying experience. For example, many architects gain enormous satisfaction from a professional lifetime spent in the rapidly developing world of health care. The principal disadvantage of such industries stems from the same root: the difficulty in moving to an office carrying out different kinds of projects unless the particular expertise is required.

In this category, it is also possible to group universities and large chains of shops and hotels which very often employ their own architects to deal with minor building works, investigation of defects and maintenance and to liaise with independent consultants. It is possible to gain considerable experience in dealing with a wide variety of building structures in such offices. The buildings can vary from the very old and historic to the brand new.

Ecclesiastical authorities generally entrust new building to private architects. There are limited openings for the post of diocesan surveyor to carry out church inspections and maintenance work. The Church of England has a well-organised system. The Roman Catholic, Methodist and other non-conformist churches have few official posts, most work being undertaken on an ad hoc basis as required.

Some housing associations have their own architects' departments, but most work is carried out by independent consultants and increasingly on a design and build basis by contractors.

3.5   Large companies

Some large companies have their own architects' departments. The work tends to be highly specialised, but it very much depends on the company. The atmosphere is more commercial than in local government, but there are similarities, particularly in the way in which the architect works for the employer rather than in an independent capacity for a client. The career structure and conditions of service are also likely to be better defined than in many private offices. Work within one company can vary, i.e. laboratories, warehouses, offices and housing for employees. Many companies have overseas branches and the chance to travel is attractive to some architects.

3.6   Contractors

Some large contractors employ their own architects. The quantity surveyor has always had a place in building contracting and it seems natural that the architect should be involved also. Architects, however, have a poor reputation among building contractors and they are more likely to be employed in a design capacity than in a practical quality control role. The majority of medium sized contractors carrying out design and build work will engage private firms of architects on a project basis, because it is more cost effective than maintaining an architects' department. Some of the larger contractors, however, do maintain departments of their own and very often having the facility to inject major capital sums into CAD and other expensive equipment, they can create a stimulating and exciting environment in which to work.

Although architectural designs emanating from contractors have aroused adverse comment from time to time, there are many good examples. In addition, there is often a good opportunity for quality control and detailed administration. This is particularly the case because changes to the design are very significant to contractors when it is they who pick up the cost not, as is usual, the building owner. There are opportunities for architects who are sufficiently flexible. Indeed, there is no reason why an architect should not rise to director level.

Many architects dislike the idea of working for a contractor because they feel a split duty between the contractor, as their employer, and the ultimate purchaser of the building. In practice, this need not be a problem. The contractor's objective is to construct a building which satisfies the requirements as laid down in the contract and to make a reasonable profit. In addition, the contractor wants the purchaser to be happy with the building. Very few contractors are rogues. Some may be hard business men, but many are just the opposite – hence the large number of bankruptcies in the industry. There are just one or two things to remember:

- A contractor who has an architect as an employee will not ask him to act contrary to his professional judgment. That is probably why the architect was appointed in the first place.
- An architect employed by a contractor cannot give the contractor's client independent advice[3]. An architect must always make the position clear to the client. It is especially important when it appears that the architect is acting in the capacity of an independent consultant. This can happen, for example, when the contractor undertakes a design and build project and the architect is involved in settling the client's brief.

Every architect should spend some time, if possible, working for a contractor. There is much practical experience to be gained together with an indefinable empathy with the contractor's difficulties.

3.7 Manufacturers

Product design and development has traditionally had a valuable input from architects. Furniture design is a good example where many architects try their hands. Some classic pieces of furniture are named after the architect who designed them. A less common area of employment is in the field of building components. There is a multitude of products which would and in some cases do benefit enormously from architectural input. Electrical fittings, ironmongery, floor wall and ceiling tiles and panels, glazing units, doors, windows, etc. In many instances, a relatively common building component might be improved by an experienced architect. The number of architects who work in this field is small and it is usually an interest which develops.

3.8 Teaching

There are good opportunities for architects in schools of architecture if they have an interest in teaching. That is the most important thing. Most schools advertising for staff lay stress on skill in design, but they also expect a prospective lecturer to offer one or two other subjects about which they feel confident to lecture. A lecturing post, therefore, will usually involve a number of hours lecturing every week together with studio, workshop and some administrative responsibilities. There are some who regret the emphasis on design skills and argue that while design is the distinguishing architectural skill, every school should have some lecturers whose principal skills lie elsewhere, for example in construction, building procurement, professional practice and building sciences. It is probably important that these people are also qualified architects.

There are also openings for lecturers in other construction disciplines such as surveying or building, and besides universities, there are many colleges of building where architects can make a valuable contribution.

Starting salaries are often considered to be low compared with salaries for architects of equivalent experience in other fields, but salaries in the new universities may be higher than in older establishments. It actually varies with the economic climate. As a result, lecturing tends to attract younger members of the profession, because as an architect gains experience outside teaching, he or she cannot afford to take a drop in salary in order to make the move from, say, private practice to teaching. Experience in practice is the great difference between the requirements for a lecturer in architecture and a lecturer in, say, mathematics or history. The budding lecturer should, therefore, gain as much experience as possible before becoming a full-time teacher. Most posts have opportunities for research and consultancy work.

Architects who do not wish to take up lecturing as a full-time career, but who are interested nonetheless, can often contribute useful practical input by doing part-time lecturing. The financial rewards tend to be modest, but there is a great deal of satisfaction to be gained.

3.9   Other specialisation

All professionals tend to specialise in one way or another as they gain experience. This is for the perfectly natural reason that they realise that their own profession is not just doing one activity, but is a collection of activities which are performed to different degrees. There are many opportunities for architects to specialise within the profession. For example, architects may specialise in a particular building type. Many architects specialise in housing or schools or hospitals, industrial buildings and so on. They may also specialise in the tasks they do. For example, they may do only design, or production drawings, or survey work, or contract administration, or model making, or perspectives, or information technology. These are to some extent fairly obvious ways in which architects can specialise. There are other less obvious specialisms, such as investigating defects, expert witnessing, contractual advice, adjudication and arbitration.

Few architects can help some degree of specialisation as they gain experience, because the range of skills traditionally required of the architect is just too great now that each skill is becoming so complex. To many architects, however, the most satisfying element in their work is the chance to be involved in so many different ways in the production of a building. These architects will always fight to retain a degree of broad architectural activity against which to practise their specialisms.

3.10   Adjudicator, arbitrator or expert witness

None of the activities in this section can really be pursued as a full-time occupation. Architects sometimes combine all three roles and manage to make a reasonable living, because they are good and in demand. For most architects, however, these particular activities will be followed alongside practice in the more traditional architectural role.

Following the coming into force of the Housing Grants, Construction and Regeneration Act 1996 and Construction Contracts (Northern Ireland) Order 1997, adjudication has really started to take off and it is set fair to replace arbitration as the dispute resolution procedure of choice for contractors. As the number of adjudications increases, the requirements for adjudicators will increase accordingly. Although in theory any architect can be an adjudicator, in practice adjudicators must have certain qualities. They must have experience in the construction industry sufficient to make them wise in the ways of the people they are likely to encounter. In addition, they must have technical expertise and legal expertise. They need not be qualified lawyers, but they must understand rather more than the basic principles of contract law. Ajudicators need to be skilled in assimilating facts quickly and applying logical analysis in order to reach a decision.

There are courses for architects wishing to become adjudicators, but care must be taken in choosing the right course. Some are little more than a brief survey of the relevant legislation and a few watchpoints. Even the best and most comprehensive courses cannot produce an adjudicator from an architect overnight. In practice, although adjudicators can be named in the contract or agreed between the parties when a dispute arises, most are appointed by a nominating body to which one of the parties has made application. Therefore, an architect wishing to practise as an adjudicator must apply to and be accepted onto its register by such a body.

Many architects practise as arbitrators. This role requires rather different skills to those exercised by adjudicators. Arbitrators have the luxury of more time in which to consider the issues in dispute, but they are more likely to have to decide complicated procedural questions. Unlike the decision of an adjudicator, the award of an arbitrator is final and binding unless, rarely, appealed to the court. The Chartered Institute of Arbitrators runs training courses for prospective arbitrators. Most arbitrators belong to panels of arbitrators held by the construction professions.

The role of the expert witness is undergoing change since the implementation of the Woolf Report and the revision of the Civil Procedure Rules. Essentially, anyone can be an expert if they have the required expertise in the appropriate area. In practice, most architects who practise in this field tend to be expert, not only in their chosen subject but also in the job of being an expert. There are particular skills involved and experience is important. Although an expert is usually chosen by one side of the dispute or the other (although this may change), the function of an expert is to assist the court or the tribunal to find the truth. Experts must never be partisan – a difficult and delicate problem when receiving a fee from just one of the parties. Although there are courses available for budding expert witnesses, nothing can really compare with the experience of being cross-examined in court by counsel. Good experts are difficult to find and most construction lawyers are constantly looking for architects willing and able to produce good reports and give convincing testimony.

References

(1)   *Architect's Employment and Earnings* (1998), RIBA.
(2)   *Perini Corporation* v. *Commonwealth of Australia* (1969) 12 BLR 82.
(3)   Principle 2, undertaking 2.5, RIBA Code of Professional Practice.

4

Types of Practice

4.1 Sole principal

Many architects carry on practice as sole principals. The latest figures at the time of writing suggest that 50% of all practices are organised in this way. Precise figures are not available. Because a practice is run by a sole principal, of course, does not mean that it is a one person practice. The sole principal may indeed work entirely alone or may employ a dozen staff of various kinds. The following are factors:

- In times of recession an architect might set up in practice alone as the only way of getting employment. If successful, the architect continues, but if not, he or she will look for opportunities in employment again when the recession is over.
- Many young architects look upon sole practice as an ambition.
- A successful sole practitioner cannot remain alone for very long. The workload will become too big and some form of partnership becomes necessary.
- Some architects become sole practitioners by purchasing a practice from a retiring architect.
- Sometimes an architect moves from being a member of staff into partnership as a temporary measure for two or three years, and when the old sole practitioner retires, becomes a sole practitioner.
- An architect will sometimes build up a private practice as a spare time occupation before taking the plunge and becoming a sole practitioner.

It is probably the most difficult form of practice, but it is potentially very rewarding personally and financially. An architect contemplating this form of practice must have considerable reserves of self-reliance and an iron nerve to face alone all the problems of architectural practice. Most of these problems will have little to do with architecture. They will concern the business. Even though an architect in this situation may have no shortage of friends with whom to talk over important decisions, such as whether expansion should take place, they have nothing riding on the correctness of the decision.

4.2 Partnership

The latest, admittedly over ten years old, statistics[1] suggest that nearly 40% of architectural practices are carried on in the form of partnerships. Anecdotal evidence, however, suggests that the figure has been reduced somewhat by companies opting for limited liability (see section 4.4). Partnership is defined by the Partnership Act 1890 as 'the relationship which subsists between two or more persons carrying on business in common with a view to profit'. It is important to remember that simply sharing accommodation or staff with another on financial terms is not 'carrying on business in common'. If the courts have to decide whether in any particular case a partnership exists, a crucial factor is whether or not the parties share the profits or losses. In general, if they do, it is a partnership.

Partners are jointly and severally liable for the acts of the partnership. Thus, they are liable both as a group and individually and one partner is liable for the act of his or her partner provided only that it was carried out in the course of the partnership business. Normally, in the case of partnership contract debts such as the purchase of IT equipment, they are only jointly liable.

Actions against architects seem to be on the increase. A party seeking damages can pursue all the partners or individual partners in turn or any combination of partners until the damages are recovered in full. This can be disastrous to both the partnership and to the individual partner, because the sums of money involved can be quite beyond the means of a private person and bankruptcy may be the outcome. In the case of a simple contract debt, the party requiring payment is only entitled to choose one of the options. Invariably, a party seeking recovery of a debt or of damages against a partnership will take action against all the partners together.

A partner is responsible to the full extent of his or her personal wealth for the acts of the partnership. That is irrespective of a partner's particular partnership share. To take an example: if partner A has a one third share and partner B has a two thirds holding, and partner B is not available to pay the appropriate share of a debt, partner A will be obliged to pay the whole amount. If the firm is worth less than the amount of the debt, partner A will have to make up the difference. If partner B subsequently becomes available, of course, partner A can sue for the appropriate amount to cover partner B's share. If all partners are available to pay, they will normally contribute according to the proportion of their share holding (see also Chapter 17, section 17.5).

A partnership usually has a written partnership agreement. Although it is not strictly necessary, it can save disputes about trivial things getting out of hand. Written evidence of the agreement is not necessary in order to indicate the existence of a partnership to third parties (who would not know, in any case, that a written agreement existed). It can be seen from the firm's notepaper, bearing the name of the firm and probably the names of the individual partners. As far as third parties are concerned, it is usually sufficient if the architect either states that he or she is a partner (whether or not this is true) or acts as though that was the case.

The advantages of a partnership are as follows:

- When the business expands beyond a certain point (which will vary depending on the architect concerned), the principal will not have full knowledge of every project or the ability to give proper supervision. A choice must be made: either to have a very experienced architect at high salary to help with the administration or to have a partner to share the burden, not necessarily on equal terms, but on terms satisfactory to both parties. A partner will have a real interest in the success of the business and an incentive to contribute to the utmost.

- Economy in expenditure can be effected by the pooling of accommodation, equipment, or staff by partners. Whereas one principal might not have enough work to employ three assistants, two jointly might be able to do so. The two partners and staff of three might be accommodated in two rooms, whereas as separate businesses they would need four. Of course, both staff and accommodation can be shared without any partnership existing. Each principal would have his own work, the time of staff being recorded and their salaries allocated accordingly.

- Two or more partners should be able to generate more ideas and attract more work together than the sum of such ideas and work separately.

- There may be more capital available for expansion.

- A partner establishes a goodwill value to a business (more about goodwill later). If an architect is in practice alone, there may be virtually no goodwill value, because if such an architect dies or retires, existing clients are little more likely to continue with a totally new architect who may take over the business than they are to go elsewhere. In both cases they are venturing into new territory. A new and younger partner, however, will be able to maintain a continuity of personnel and establish a relationship, even if not primary, with all the firm's clients.

Goodwill is difficult to define. It is the benefit which a practice acquires by virtue of its prestige and the fact that clients return for further commissions. A partnership should not be thought of as stationary. At any time there may be partners leaving or joining and the workload will vary according to the economic climate. All this has a bearing on the goodwill. It used to be the custom for a new partner to have to buy a share in the partnership by bringing in a large capital sum. It was known as 'buying a share of the goodwill'. Figure 4.1 shows one method of calculation.

If a new partner could not afford to put up the initial capital sum, it was sometimes agreed that payment could be made on an instalment basis – a certain fixed sum every year for a given period.

Profits	Year 1	£55,000
	Year 2	£85,000
	Year 3	£100,000
Total		£240,000
Average: $\frac{240,000}{3}$	=	£80,000
Value of goodwill: £80,000 × 2*	=	£160,000
Existing partners' share: A at 60%	=	£96,000
B at 40%	=	£64,000
New partner buys, say, 20% share at cost of $\frac{20 \times 160,000}{100}$	=	£32,000

A and B might sell 10% each, thus receiving £16,000 each.
If the following year's profits were £100,000, the partners would share as follows:

A at 50% = £50,000
B at 30% = £30,000
C at 20% = £20,000 (new partner)

* The multiplying factor is somewhat arbitrary, but it is not less than 1 and seldom more than 2.

Fig. 4.1   Buying a share of the goodwill.

As a result, many partners lived in near poverty for years until they paid off the capital sum required and they only attained a comfortable income late in life. It is now becoming common for goodwill to be given a nil value. More emphasis is placed on attracting a person with the right professional attributes into a partnership. The chances of doing this are obviously increased if the incoming partner is not required to contribute a substantial amount to the partnership coffers. The new partner is given an appropriate share in the partnership and the actual income which the share will generate will clearly bear a relationship to the total fee income over the year.

The new partner, in return, will be expected to leave a proportion of earnings in the practice to act as working capital. It has to be said that existing partners who may have been obliged to purchase shares in the partnership are not always receptive to this approach, because it denies them the chance to sell their own shares to a new partner. Against this must be weighed the consideration that new partners are the lifeblood of any practice and without them income can decrease and existing partners' shares may decrease in value. In essence, the modern approach is a change from looking at capital gains to increases in annual income.

It is obviously advantageous if partners have similar views regarding the general philosophy of a partnership, but there is merit in healthy differences regarding the methods of attaining desired ends. Partners should have the utmost trust and confidence in one another. This suggests that they should know one another quite well before the final step of partnership is taken. It is, therefore, most common for a firm to take its new partners from its own staff, whose capabilities and suitabilities are known and have been judged over a lengthy period.

If a new partner is introduced to facilitate a continuance of the business, age is a factor which must be taken into consideration. 'A' (aged 50) might take a partner aged, say, 35. In 10 or 15 years' time, 'A' retires and the new partner continues the business, looking for a successor and so on. Life, and partnerships, never work out quite so neatly, but that is the theory.

It is usual that the rights and duties of each partner are set out in the form of a legal agreement drafted by a solicitor experienced in that kind of work. Although the agreement (which will be in the form of a deed) can be as long or as short as the partners wish, it is advisable to include any matter which it might be anticipated can cause problems. Typical heads of terms include the following:

- Name of the firm
- Place of business
- Date of commencement
- Value of goodwill
- Amount of capital provided by each partner
- Treatment of work in progress
- Duties of partners
- Proportions of profits or losses between each partner
- Amount of cash drawings per partner per month
- Banking arrangements
- Termination provisions
- Outgoing partners
- Power of attorney
- Partner insurance
- Professional indemnity insurance and any other professional requirements
- Partnership perks
- Arbitration of disputes

In fixing the amount of drawings, it must be remembered that the firm is assessed income tax on the basis of its profits. The cash drawings must allow for this and it is good practice for the partners to set aside an appropriate amount to tax every month as they make drawings. The advice of the firm's accountants should be sought on this and other aspects of the agreement. Unless the agreement specifies a period of notice, a partnership agreement may be terminated by any partner simply by giving notice to that effect. All partnerships are terminated by death and by the taking of a new partner or the retirement of an old partner. This is one of the essential differences between a partnership and forms of corporate body which continue although the persons constituting the membership may change.

Termination of a partnership does not remove liability from any of the partners and it is usual for partnerships to maintain professional indemnity insurance in respect of retired members. Problems can arise if all the partners split up and there is no continuing partnership to carry on insurance premium payments. In these circumstances, some insurers offer special deals (see Chapter 17, section 17.5).

Many practices use the designation *associate* to signify that the particular member of staff has attained a status which is higher than other members of staff, but short of partnership. Often, it is an indication that the person concerned will eventually become a partner. Although it is usual to list the names of associates on the letterhead, it is good practice to separate the associates from the partners by putting the associates at the bottom of the page. This signals to the public that an associate is not a partner. It is an important safeguard as far as the associate is concerned who otherwise could be liable as a partner if a court decided that the associate had held him or herself out as such.

Associates are normally appointed by letter, but some firms like to give the arrangement some additional solemnity by having a deed prepared. Associates do not have any share in the partnership profits except that they may have a share in a bonus scheme like other members of staff and they often have extra benefits such as payment of private telephone charges, a better than average car, health care package and so on.

In the early 1990s, the practice of appointing *salaried partners* appeared to be dying out. Unfortunately, it seems to have taken on a new lease of life. Salaried partners suffer the worst of both worlds. They are often considered to be full partners if there is a question of liability and certainly in the eyes of the public it is likely that such would be the case. On the other hand, they normally receive a very small share in the profits on top of their salary. It is a position to be avoided because they are often undifferentiated from other partners on the letterhead and, therefore, they are just as likely to be sued. Although the partnership agreement may contain an indemnity for all salaried partners from the full partners, the indemnity will be of no avail if there is a large claim which claims the assets of the firm and the individual partners and the professional indemnity insurance does not cover it.

Although it is common for a person to be designated *consultant* on the letterhead, the reality is often that the architect is a retired partner of long standing who is kept on the letterhead to reassure clients that there is a continuity in the partnership. The consultant, more often than not, will be paid a small retainer. A consultant, in these terms, may be called in by the remaining partners occasionally in order to contribute a recollection of an old project or perhaps to deal with some particular small matter which can be kept within precise boundaries.

4.3 Unlimited liability

An unlimited liability company finds little favour with architects' practices; only about 2% of firms are set up in this form.

The principal advantages are that a director of such a company is free from liability after a period of 12 months has expired from leaving the company and there is no requirement for filing reports with the companies registrar. There are, however, some formalities. An unlimited company is one stage removed from a partnership. The members of such a company are liable to contribute in the proportion of their share holdings if the company's assets are not sufficient to pay debts. There may be a maximum of 50 members.

4.4   Limited liability

Limited liability is a company where the liability of the members is limited to the nominal value of the share holding, hence the name. If the company is faced with a debt which is greater than the company's assets, the company can be wound up and the shareholders have no further liability. The situation may sound attractive to architects as a protection from liability and indeed that is probably the chief reason for the growth in limited liability companies in architectural practice. In 1989, limited liability companies formed about 7.5% of all practices. It is likely that this figure is now somewhat greater. Although there was no legal reason why architects should not form limited liability companies, the idea was frowned upon by both ARCUK and RIBA until 1981. Trading with limited liability is not without its problems, of course, and the Insolvency Act 1986 provides severe penalties for directors who continue to trade whilst insolvent. The court has power to order them to contribute to the company's debts out of personal assets. There are other measures the court may order against culpable directors, for example that after insolvency liquidation, a former director may not be involved in the formation of a company with a similar name for a period of five years.

The principal difference between a limited company and a partnership is that when the shareholders (members) form a company, they are creating a separate legal entity. If the shareholders are also directors, they are employees of the company. Directors are paid a salary by the company and if the year end shows a profit, a dividend may be declared and shareholders share in the dividend according to the amount of their share holding. In the case of architectural practices formed as limited companies, it is likely that the directors will also be the shareholders holding a similar percentage of the shares as they would have done in the case of a partnership. It is quite possible, however, that some shares may be held by persons not employed by the company or for some directors not to hold shares at all.

The advantages of a limited liability company are:

- Except in exceptional circumstances, the directors are not personally liable for the debts of the company[2].
- It is more flexible than the partnership, because trusted members of staff can be promoted to director status on a salary without giving them a part of the company.
- Directors can be removed with far less difficulty than is the case with a partner.
- The company does not dissolve when a director leaves or when shares change hands. Therefore, there are no complex legalities involved. The company simply continues as normal.
- Companies attract capital more easily than do partnerships. This is important if expansion is planned. This is because other firms are used to doing business with companies.
- Companies, but not partnerships, are internationally recognised and, therefore, in a better position than partnerships to develop business overseas.

There are disadvantages:

- A company is governed by the Companies Acts 1985 and 1989. It comes into existence only after registration by the Registrar of Companies. From that time, it can act only in accordance with the Acts. If the company carries out transactions before registration, they may be treated as the transactions of a partnership.
- Every company must file accounts with the Registrar where they are open to public inspection. Partnership accounts are private to the partners.
- A very important restriction is that a company may only act in accordance with the 'objects clause' which is to be found in the Memorandum of Association. This clause sets out the purpose of the company and what its powers are. A company which attempts to do something which is not included in the clause is said to be acting *ultra vires* (i.e. beyond its powers). Such actions can lead to many problems, for the company itself and for those who trade with it. For this reason, the objects clause should always be drafted with great care by an experienced company lawyer.
- There are certain formalities associated with the running of a

company. The Companies Acts require that at least one general meeting of shareholders must be held every year.

■ The dissolution of a partnership can be a fairly simple, though traumatic, process, but a company must be wound up. This can take a long time.

■ No discretion can be exercised over the apportionment of dividends. They must be divided strictly in accordance with the shareholding.

■ In general, a director's tax position is not as good as that of a partner's, because a director pays tax on the PAYE system and there is no opportunity to take advantage of some advantageous 'self-employed' tax concessions. This situation, however, is subject to change depending on government policy.

■ A client may dislike doing business with architects practising as a limited company (even though the client may also be a limited liability company) because it is considered by some to be unprofessional.

Although the shareholders together wield power over the way a company is run and they have the power to dismiss a director, they must act within the Companies Acts and the company's objects clause and a single shareholder has no power to bind the others by any of his or her actions. A company can be tailor-made by a solicitor quite inexpensively. It is even cheaper to buy a company 'off the shelf'. Such companies are ready formed. All the paper work is complete and they generally have a code name. The objects clauses are drafted for various purposes in fairly broad terms and after purchase it is a relatively simple matter to change the name. Some key points in relation to private limited companies are:

■ They must have one director (public companies must have two)

■ There must be a company secretary who cannot be the same person as a sole director

■ A private company cannot offer shares to the public

■ There is no limit on the number of members, but if the number falls below two for six months, personal liability can be incurred

■ There must be a Memorandum subscribed to by at least two people taking at least one share each

■ The Memorandum must include the following clauses:
  □ Name
  □ Office where registered (e.g. England and Wales, Northern Ireland or Scotland)

☐ Objects
☐ Liability (whether limited)
☐ Capital

- The name must have 'Limited' as the last word
- The name must appear in full on business correspondence
- The name cannot be registered if there is another company of the same name on the index, if the name is offensive or if it would be a criminal offence
- Business correspondence must also include the registered number
- There must be printed Articles of Association
- The Articles must be signed by the subscribers
- The company can use another name provided that the company name also appears on correspondence
- A register of directors must be kept and the registrar must be notified of changes
- There must be a qualified independent auditor
- There must be at least one AGM and unless otherwise unanimously agreed by those entitled to attend, 21 clear days' notice must be given

4.5 Public company

A more recent development has been for some architectural practices to carry on their business as public companies and, indeed, a few large practices have already taken this route. It is important, of course, that control of the company remains in the hands of architects. That is something which is much more difficult to ensure in the case of a public rather than a private company. The essential difference between private and public companies is that members of the public can buy and sell the shares of the latter. In theory, it is possible for a publicly quoted company to be completely controlled by people who are not architects. Since, however, that would fall foul of the Architects Registration Board (ARB) which insists that an architectural practice should be controlled by architects, such a move would be self-defeating. It is clearly a valuable asset for a company to be able to describe itself as 'architects'. Any kind of agreement to restrict the number of shares on sale to the public (e.g. keeping 51% for architect directors) would be frowned on by the Council of the Stock Exchange.

Members of the public who buy shares receive a share of the profits each year depending on the dividend announced. Therefore, trading as a public company is a useful way of generating finance for expansion. The regulations with regard to public companies are more stringent than is the case with private companies. For example, the nominal value of its allotted share capital must be not less than £50,000. In addition, a public company must put the status or the letters 'PLC' after its name. A public company is normally formed after a period as a private limited company. Floating a company is a specialised operation. It is not essential in order to be a public company, but it is a means of attracting more investors. In order to achieve a successful flotation, the prospective shareholders must be convinced that the company has a good chance of giving a worthwhile return on money invested. Some kind of track record is essential.

4.6 Limited partnership

In a limited partnership, at least one partner must be responsible for all the liabilities of the partnership. In an architectural practice, this partner must be an architect. There can be one or more additional partners who contribute capital to the partnership and whose liability is limited to the amount of capital they contribute provided that they have no part in the management of the partnership. Such partnerships must be registered under the Limited Partnership Act 1907.

This is a comparatively little used form of partnership whose chief advantage appears to be the possibility of using funds injected by the limited partners for which they receive appropriate shares in the profit.

4.7 Limited liability partnerships

A recent development has been the promotion by the UK Government of the concept of a limited liability partnership (LLP). A consultation paper was published in 1997, identifying the key features of LLPs:

- They will be separate legal entities distinct from the owners (members)
- Members of LLPs will not be jointly and severally liable in the normal course of business
- They will be treated as partnerships for the purposes of UK income tax and capital gains tax

- A partnership which evolves into an LLP will not undergo a 'deemed cessation' for income tax purposes
- They will have to file audited public accounts similar to a limited company
- They will require two or more designated members who will carry out tasks similar to those of a company secretary, for example, signing the annual return

Therefore, the new LLPs combine certain crucial structural features of both companies and partnerships, the general intention being that the LLP will have the internal flexibility of a partnership but external obligations equivalent to those of a limited company. In common with partnerships, the members of an LLP may adopt whatever form of internal organisation they choose. However, they are similar to limited companies in that the members' liability for the debts of the business will be limited to their stakes in it and, therefore, they will be required regularly to publish information about the business and its finances (including the disclosure of the amount of profit attributable to the member with the largest share of the profits). Also, they will be subject to insolvency requirements broadly equivalent in effect to those that apply to companies.

In February 1999, the Report of the House of Commons Select Committee on Trade and Industry was published for public comment and it is anticipated that a bill will be placed before parliament to enable firms to convert to LLP status during 2000.

4.8 Co-operative

Although some practices operate as co-operatives, the members must have particular views in common. To operate in this way could be said to be making a social statement as much as acting as a business. Control is on the basis of one member equals one vote. Responsibility and rewards are shared. If it is intended to register under the Industrial and Provident Societies Acts a co-operative must have a minimum of seven members. If there are fewer than seven members, they must practise as a partnership or a limited or unlimited company. If the co-operative faces large debts to the extent that liquidation is necessary, the liability of individual members is confined to the amount of their shareholdings. Generally, the members have shares of only nominal value.

4.9   Group practice

Group practice is a comparatively recent development. The idea is that independent firms of architects associate themselves to mutual benefit, but they do not share profits neither do they have joint responsibility to their clients. They may share staff and offices, telephones and other overheads, dividing the expenses on an agreed basis. The firms may well be situated in different localities; indeed this is often an advantage in easing the pressure by sharing the load. If one practice is badly affected by recession, another in the group may be able to share out tasks. It is a very worthwhile form of practice provided that all parties are committed to the same ends. There are seven common types of group practice:

■ *Group association*: a loose association of firms for the purpose of sharing experience and knowledge. Each firm has a clearly separate identity as far as clients are concerned.
■ *Shared facilities*: No real association other than sharing accommodation, equipment and, occasionally, staff.
■ *Single project group practice*: Usually formed for the purpose of carrying out a specific commission, because it is too large for any of the firms to tackle it individually. When the purpose of the association has been accomplished, it automatically comes to an end.
■ *Group co-ordinating firm*: Another way of carrying out a large project is for one of the firms involved to act as co-ordinator and the other firms to take responsibility for specific parts of the scheme. Obviously, this kind of arrangement can only work for large projects where the parts can easily be identified. The co-ordinating firm normally takes overall responsibility so far as the client is concerned.
■ *Group partnership*: a partnership composed of individual firms which continue to practise separately, but which combine on certain large or complex projects on a regular basis.

The distribution of liabilities can be extremely complex in any kind of group practice. It needs little imagination to see that some forms are more risky than others. Whenever group practice is contemplated, it is essential to take proper legal advice, not from the family solicitor but from someone experienced and knowledgeable in the pitfalls to be avoided.

4.10   Developer/architect/contractor

Subject to the provisions of the codes of conduct (Standards of Conduct and Practice and, if the architect is a member of the RIBA, Code of Professional Conduct: see Chapter 2, section 2.6) an architect can practise in any combination of the above. An architect may even act as an estate agent. It is to be welcomed as giving the architect greater flexibility, but an architect choosing to practise simultaneously in two or more of these activities must take great care that his or her professional integrity is preserved. It is important that a client properly understands that, for example, such an architect cannot act as a builder for a development and at the same time give truly independent advice on that same development as an architect.

References

(1)   *Census of Private Architectural Practices 1988* (1989) RIBA Market Research Unit.
(2)   *Williams & Anor* v. *Natural Life Health Foods Ltd* [1998] 2 All ER 577.

5 Sources of Information

5.1 Basic library

Every practice needs a basic library. The extent to which an architect must refer to and rely on technical information cannot be overemphasised. The size and complexity of the library will depend on the size and needs of the practice.

Various kinds of information need to be on hand. First there will be technical books on such matters as design, building construction, and contract law. Some of these will be retained from student days; others will be acquired as the practice develops – sometimes new, sometimes secondhand. Textbooks, particularly those dealing with the law, have a habit of becoming out of date very quickly and, despite the inevitably high costs, have to be replaced as it is essential that all references are kept up to date. Such books should be kept on a library shelf and if the practice cannot run to the luxury of a specialist librarian then a system should be devised whereby a record is kept of who has taken a book for reference and when, as it is very easy for books to be mislaid causing unnecessary frustration to a prospective user who cannot find what is wanted when it is wanted.

The second type of information that needs to be held is technical information on products. Some will be in the form of well-prepared and fully illustrated catalogues, preferably in strong, clearly marked loose-leaf binders. This permits revised sheets to be inserted and the superseded sheets removed and, if not wanted as a record for an old job, destroyed. Other information will be in pamphlet form which can be stored in folders kept in open-ended boxes for ease of retrieval. Again, it is essential that all information is up to date; some practices go so far as to acquire new information every time it is wanted. There is a great temptation to take information which is two or three months old and assume, often quite wrongly, that it is still current; some material will almost certainly have been withdrawn and new introduced with concomitant numbering alterations.

A third category of information that needs to be available is government and statutory publications. Examples of this type of information include technical circulars from government ministries on such matters as health and education, design criteria and technical requirements. A particular requirement in an architect's office is an up-to-date set of the current Building Regulations and a summary of all British Standards and in many cases the full standard as well[1].

5.2   Classification and proprietary systems

5.2.1   Classification

The great increase in technical and trade information in recent years has swamped ad hoc systems of classification devised by individuals for their own use. There are three systems in use in the UK.

CI/SfB

This is currently the most common system of classification. It originated in Sweden; the letters SfB stand for *Samarbetskommitten for Byggnadsfragor* (the name of the Swedish committee concerned). Using this system it is possible to give any book, catalogue, official bulletin or pamphlet used by architects a classification according to its contents. The classifying symbols are easily remembered, and frequent use will enable the architect quickly to find the material wanted.

The SfB system classifies information into four main tables:

- Table 0   Built environment
- Table 1   Elements
- Table 2/3   Construction form and materials
- Table 4   Activities and requirements

Tables 1 and 2/3 include most technical and trade literature while tables 0 and 4 include most technical references, text books, official publications and regulations. Much technical and trade literature has an SfB classification already printed on it, and this greatly facilitates the incorporation of such material into the library.

EPIC

Electronic Product Information Co-operation (EPIC) is a relatively new internationally recognised classification for construction projects. It originates from a European committee of organisations which provide product information. Although EPIC is probably mainly used in the UK to classify information intended for other countries, information originating in other countries may also be classified according to this system.

Uniclass

This system was developed by the Construction Project Information Committee (CPIC) representing all construction professionals based on principles set out in the International Standards Organisation (ISO) standard which deals with classification of construction information. It is closely related to EPIC, from which it draws some bases. Support was given by the DOE Construction Sponsorship Directorate and the project was led by NBS Services after industry wide consultation. It is particularly useful where it is desired to arrange files in computer databases.

5.2.2 Proprietary systems

The need to keep a library up to date is all important and great care has to be taken with incoming information, including allocating an SfB, EPIC or Uniclass reference if one is not provided. It is also necessary to keep the office index up to date, as it is of little use having information stored on a shelf or elsewhere without having the facility to find out firstly whether what is sought is available and second, if it is, where it can be found.

All this can be very time-consuming and there are a number of commercial undertakings which provide an information service for architects' offices. They obtain the trade and other information, provide files and shelving to keep it in, give a regular up-dating service to the library and, in some cases, an information advisory service by telephone or post. However, remember that these firms have to operate at a profit. Some charge a fee to the firms whose trade literature they circulate, while others charge a fee to the offices receiving the service as well. In each case the trade literature supplied will not be all-embracing, as there will be firms who will rely on advertising their products directly to the profession and the industry.

5.3 Information technology

Vast amounts of information are now available through the Internet and the World Wide Web. The RIBA has its own web site (www.riba.net) with links to other useful information centres. Government departments are also well represented and it is possible to download a variety of publications. A disadvantage of the web, which is either a major or minor irritant depending on temperament, is the relatively long period required to move from site to site. 'Surfing the web' is rather less exciting in practice than it sounds.

A major breakthrough in recent years has been the availability of information in readily accessible form on CD-rom. It is now possible to have whole libraries on a few discs.

5.4 Selected project records and feedback

It will be found very useful to keep a record of all notes and data about a project in a separate file, with a simple history sheet in front to summarise what stage has been reached. The various stages of the work (e.g. sketch plans, applications, approvals) should be listed and the dates on which action was taken inserted against them; references and file numbers should be added as appropriate. This will not only save a considerable amount of hunting through files, but it will also make it that much easier if it becomes necessary to hand the project over to someone else. A specimen project history sheet is shown in Fig. 5.1.

When the project is complete, all the office information (files, drawings, bills of quantities, etc.) becomes history, but for some years at least, important history. Careful decisions will need to be made as to what is destroyed and what is kept (see Chapter 15, section 15.6 for more information on filing material).

Much time and effort is put into every project and as much use as possible should be made of the information which arises, hopefully to save similar efforts next time. For instance, the possibility of standard detailing for another occasion may arise, or specification information may be able to be reused, never forgetting the need to check and amend if necessary. The quantity surveyor will usually have made a cost analysis of the tender and will have provided the architect with a copy so that cost information arising from the project can be utilised (after suitable

PROJECT HISTORY SHEET

Project . . . .   Project no . . . .

Address . . . .

Client . . . .

Address . . . .

Tel. no . . . .   Fax no: . . . .   E-mail: . . . .

Local authority . . . .

Adjoining owner(s) . . . .

. . . .

Party wall surveyors . . . .

Date of instructions . . . .

Final design approved . . . .   Estimated cost . . . .

Production drawings commenced . . . .   Completed . . . .

Application for planning consent . . . .

      Approval received . . . .   Reference . . . .

Application for Building Regs approval . . . .

      Approval received . . . .   Reference . . . .

Application for approval of means of escape . . . .

      Approval received . . . .   Reference . . . .

Quantity surveyors . . . .   Tel. no . . . .

Consultants . . . .   Tel. no . . . .

. . . .   Tel. no . . . .

. . . .   Tel. no . . . .

Bills of quantities commenced . . . .   Completed . . . .

Tenders invited . . . .   Tenders received . . . . .

Successful contractor . . . .   Tel. no . . . .

Address . . . .

Contract amount . . . .   Date of contract . . . .

Nominated subcontractors and suppliers

. . . .

. . . .

. . . .

. . . .

Agent/foreman . . . .   Tel. no . . . .

Clerk of works . . . .   Tel. no . . . .

Starting date . . . .   Completion date . . . .

Defects liability period commences . . . .   Expires . . . .

Final account certified . . . .   Amount . . . .

Fig. 5.1 A specimen project history sheet.

updating) if a similar project is being considered. Finally, the needs of the lawyers should not be overlooked. If an architect is unfortunate enough to be involved in a project which has ended in arbitration or the courts, the information he or she holds may be vital to their client's case. It is an established truism that the side which presents the best records is the side most likely to win – all other things being equal of course.

5.5 Legal/administrative

5.5.1 Textbooks

Every practice should have a comprehensive set of textbooks dealing with the law and also with what might be described as the business side of architectural practice. Architects are expected to be neither lawyers nor tycoons, but they are expected to have a fairly detailed understanding of the law as it affects them and to be able to understand and apply basic business techniques. An architect must be able to advise the client on choosing the correct form of contract and must understand the principles behind such matters as extensions of time, liquidated damages, variations, determination and the like. It is also conceivable that the client may need some initial advice on easements, boundaries, party walls, rights of light and basic obligations during the progress of the building contract. In some of these areas all that is required of the architect is to know enough to appreciate when it is appropriate to consult, or advise the client to consult, specialised legal, management or other practitioners.

The criticism most often levied at architects is in this area of business and law. It should be obvious that the person administering the contract should be at least competent in these necessary skills. It should not be something merely left to be picked up as the architect does the job. Although everyone needs practical experience, it is only useful as a way of tempering theoretical knowledge. Without the theory first, there is nothing to temper and the architect simply amasses a motley collection of information, often inaccurate and incomplete. The groundwork should have been laid in the schools of architecture. Schools vary in the time they devote to these topics, but in any event and at best they can only provide a framework which the student or young architect must flesh out by private reading.

There are two kinds of textbook: the simple and the complex.

Serious legal textbooks will not only state the law, but also give copious references together with a discussion of difficult points. This kind of book is fine for the lawyer. It is also useful to have on the shelf as a reference for the architect who takes a keen interest in such things. For most architects, however, an altogether simpler approach is welcomed and, generally, it is all that is necessary. The same thing can be said about management textbooks. Every office should have a standard text, but also numerous easy-to-read guides.

Standard forms of building contract loom large in the average architect's working life and architects should be expert in this particular field; after all, they are the professionals whom most forms assume will administer the contract. Guidance and explanatory texts dealing with all the standard forms should be on every practice shelf. It must never be forgotten that architects who cause their clients to suffer loss through ignorance in administering a contract may be liable for professional negligence. Thus architects who made several errors when certifying, including deducting liquidated damages in the certificate and deducting them before the contract completion date had been reached, narrowly escaped suffering the consequences of these errors. In passing, the court considered that the architects in question were 'doing their incompetent best'[2].

Specific topics which should be covered by appropriate textbooks:

- *Law*
  A simple general exposition[3]
  A construction law book[4]
  A good book on contract law[5]
  Some books on specific topics such as planning law[6], design liability[7] or warranties[8]

- *Standard forms of building contract*
  One or two general texts[9]
  Texts dealing with specific contracts, such as JCT 98, IFC 98[10], MW 98[11].

- *Management*
  One or two standard management texts[12]
  Some texts with special relevance to managing a practice, managing contracts, etc.[13]

- *Professional Liability*
  One or two texts[14]

5.5.2 Acts of Parliament

Acts of Parliament do not normally make easy, or even engrossing, reading. Indeed, it sometimes taxes the courts to decide on the true meaning of the words used. Nevertheless, there are some Acts which a practice must have on its shelves[15]. Care must be taken to keep the Acts regularly updated. Statutory Instruments and Regulations are regularly issued under powers conferred by Acts of Parliament and it may be the Regulations which are most important so far as the busy architect is concerned[16]. It is essential that, in the absence of a librarian, someone in the practice is given the responsibility of making sure that the Acts, Instruments and Regulations are up to date.

5.5.3 Selected law reports

The English legal system depends in large measure on the doctrine of judicial precedent. That means broadly that, in general, a court must follow the decision of previous courts in similar circumstances. To be precise, a court must follow the ratio decidendi (the reason for the decision). There may be many other things which a judge will say in the course of giving judgment, but it is only the ratio which is binding. The other statements may have persuasive force on another court, perhaps depending on the judge uttering them. The idea behind the doctrine is to impart some degree of certainty into the law. However, there is considerable scope for a court to depart from a previous decision if it is considered that aspects of the earlier case are significantly different from the case being tried. When a court decides not to follow a previous decision, it is said to 'distinguish' the earlier case. The courts may do this to avoid injustice in a particular case.

The general rule is that every court binds a lower court by its decisions. The hierarchy of the courts is shown in simplified fashion in Fig. 5.2. A decision of the House of Lords is binding on all other courts, but it has the right to depart from its own decisions in future cases for very good reasons. It occasionally does so. The Court of Appeal binds itself and all courts below. Most construction cases are dealt with and disposed of, if not appealed, by specialist judges who deal with cases which have a high technical content. Their work is not confined to construction cases, but the construction industry is the major user of their services. This used

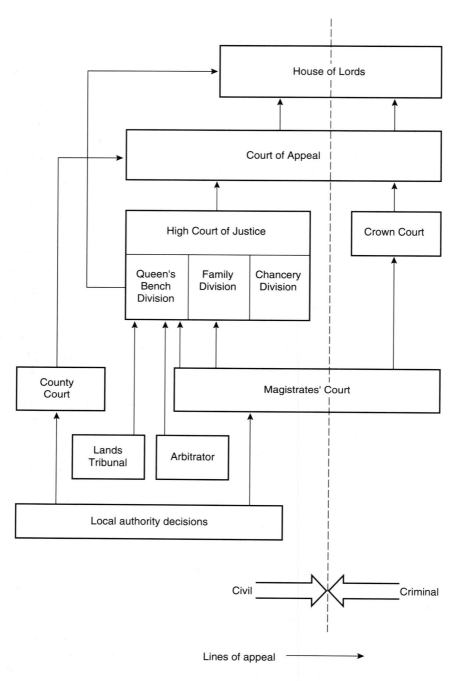

Fig. 5.2   Court hierarchy.

to be called 'Official Referee's Business' but is now referred to as the Technology and Construction Court.

In order for this system to work, it is essential that reports of the judgments in decided cases are easily available. Law reports have been available for about 700 years in various forms. It is perhaps a peculiarly English trait that, in spite of the importance, there is no official system of law reporting. Reporting depends on private enterprise. The nearest thing to an official set of reports is the Weekly Law Reports published by the Incorporated Council of Law Reporting since 1965. The are many other series, such the 'All England Law Reports', 'Lloyds' Law Reports', 'Times Law Reports', etc. Not all decisions are reported and until comparatively recently, many decisions of importance to the construction industry went unreported.

It is unrealistic to expect architects to read every law report or even to read all the reports relating to construction. However, architects should be aware of legal decisions which might affect them and they should know where to lay their hands on the full report of the judgment. Architects should, of course, be wary of attempting to identify the ratio in each case. Courts often appear to have grave difficulty in this regard when examining the judgment of higher courts which they are expected to follow. Nevertheless, the reports can provide valuable insights in certain circumstances.

There are now a number of series of reports which are concerned only with construction cases. No one series covers all the cases:

- *Building Law Reports* (BLR): Fully indexed series, usually giving full judgments and each case is prefaced by a brief resume of the key facts and decisions together with a useful commentary on some of the features of the case in question. Published by LLP Limited (paperback with annual hardback volume).
- *Construction Law Reports* (Con LR): Fully indexed series, usually giving full judgments and each case is prefaced by a brief resume of the key facts and decisions. Concentrates, although not exclusively, on the judgments of the Technology and Construction (formerly Official Referee's) Courts. Published by Butterworths (hardback).
- *Construction Law Journal* (Const LJ): Fully indexed series, generally giving full judgments and each case is prefaced by a brief resume of the key facts and decisions. Each issue also contains articles on some aspect of construction law and contracts, and book reviews. Published by Sweet & Maxwell (paperback).
- *Construction Law Digest* (CLD): Fully indexed series, dealing

with specific aspects of construction cases of interest, together with details of standard contract amendments, Acts of Parliament, etc. Each issue has a penetrating insight into key issues of construction law. Published by Blackwell Science (paperback with hardback yearly binder).

■ *Construction Industry Law Letter* (CILL): Fully indexed series, giving brief reports on cases of interest together with short commentary. Also contains occasional articles on construction law topics, details of Acts of Parliament, standard contract amendments, etc. Published by Monitor Press Ltd (paperback with hardback binder).

CLD or CILL are probably the most useful for a busy architect, but the practice should back up these 'immediate' quick reports with one or more of the other series in order to be able to refer to the full judgment of a particular case.

References to law reports (there are some references given in the notes to chapters of this book) are given by means of a standardised abbreviation system. The abbreviations referring to the reports noted above are given immediately after the titles in each case, but in addition it is necessary to include further information to enable location of the precise report. Usually that is achieved by giving the volume number and the page number. Therefore, '32 BLR 51' refers to volume 32 of Building Law Reports, page 51. (CLD and CILL have slightly different systems).

5.5.4   Professional publications

Professional journals offer a quick way of keeping up to date with construction law and standard contract amendments. Many of them offer a regular series of updates on these matters. *Building*, the 'Practice' part of the *RIBA Journal*, and in Northern Ireland the *RSUA Practice Bulletin* are all valuable in this respect. Specialist construction law journals *Construction Law* and *Building Law Monthly* are filled with useful articles.

5.6   RIBA information line

An information line was instituted by the RIBA on 1 May 1995. It is operated by expert staff of the information unit of the British Architectural Library. It is accessed via a premium rate telephone line which helps to pay the running costs. The service is available only to RIBA members. A broad range of architecture and architectural practice matters are covered and details of books, articles and seminars can be sent by fax or post. The unit can call upon the services of a panel of specialist advisors who are prepared to give brief preliminary advice free to members who may then commission them on a consultancy basis if the query warrants it.

References

(1) Details of all published construction standards are available on CD-rom produced by Technical Indexes Ltd entitled *Concise Construction Standards*. Complete Picture (UK) Ltd also produce a CD-rom, *Complete Regulations*, which contains much useful information.

(2) *Lubenham Fidelities & Investment Co* v. *South Pembrokeshire District Council* (1986) 6 Con LR 85.

(3) Barker, D.L.A. & Padfield, C.F. (1998) *Law Made Simple*, 10th edn, Butterworth-Heinemann.

(4) May, A, *Keating on Building Contracts* (1995) 6th edn, Sweet & Maxwell; Speaight, A. & Stone, G. *Architects's Legal Handbook* (1998), 6th edn, Architectural Press.

(5) Furmston, M.P. (1996) *Cheshire, Fifoot and Furmston's Law of Contract*, 13th edn, Butterworth.

(6) Heap, D. (1991) *An Outline of Planning Law*, 10th edn, Sweet & Maxwell.

(7) Cornes, D. L. (1994) *Design Liability in the Construction Industry*, 4th edn, Blackwell Science.

(8) Winward Fearon & Co (2000) *Collateral Warranties*, 2nd edn, Blackwell Science.

(9) Chappell, D. (2000) *Understanding JCT Standard Building Contracts*, 6th edn, E. & F. N. Spon; Powell-Smith, V. & Furmston, M.P. (2000) *A Building Contract Casebook*, 3rd edn, Blackwell Science.

(10) Jones, N.F. & Bayles, S. (1999) *Jones & Bergman's JCT Intermediate Form of Contract*, 3rd edn, Blackwell Science.

(11) Chappell, D. & Powell-Smith, V. (1999) *JCT Minor Works Form of Contract*, 2nd edn, Blackwell Science.

(12) Drucker, P.E. (1968) *The Practice of Management*, Pan; Drucker, P.F. (1968) *The Effective Executive*, Pan; Peter, L. (1971) *The Peter Principle*, Pan; Townsend, R. (1985) *Up the Organisation*, Penguin.

(13) Cox, S. & Hamilton, A. (1998) *Architect's Handbook of Practice Management*, 6th edn, RIBA Publications; Beaven, L. Cox, S., Dry, D. & Males, R. (1995) *Architect's Job Book*, 6th edn, RIBA Publications; Chappell, D. (1996) *Contractual Correspondence for Architects and Project Managers*, 3rd edn, Blackwell Science; Barrett, P. & Males, R. (1991) *Practice Management*, E. & F. N. Spon.

(14) Lavers, A. & Chappell, D. (2000) *A Legal Guide to the Professional Liability of Architects*, 3rd edn, Lavers; Cecil, R. (1991) *Professional Liability*, 3rd edn, Legal Studies & Services.

(15) Late Payment of Commercial Debts (Interest) Act 1998; Architects Act 1997; Housing Grants, Construction and Regeneration Act 1996; Party Wall Act 1996; Arbitration Act 1996; Building Act 1984; Companies Act 1985, 1989; Consumer Protection Act 1987; Copyright, Designs and Patents Act 1988; Defective Premises Act 1972; Health and Safety at Work Act 1974; Insolvency Act 1986; Latent Damage Act 1986; Misrepresentation Act 1967; Occupiers Liability Act 1957 and 1984; Partnership Act 1890; Sale of Goods Act 1994; Sale of Goods and Services Act 1982; Unfair Contracts Terms Act 1977.

(16) A good example is the Construction (Design and Management) Regulations 1994.

Part 2
Running a Project

6

Stage A: Architect's Services

6.1 Enquiries

Marketing is dealt with in Chapter 19. The results of marketing should be enquiries from prospective clients. Enquiries can take many forms. Ideally, they come in the form of a letter, stating requirements and courteously requesting details of fees and conditions of engagement. The reality is almost never like that. Established architects will usually have clients with whom they do business on a continuing basis. In such cases, the enquiry is likely to be quite informal, during a meeting about some other matter or by telephone. Many new clients make their first approach by telephone; very few call personally at the architect's office in the first instance.

The way in which a client makes an enquiry can often tell the architect a great deal about the kind of client he or she is. It is always wise to respond to any kind of approach from a new client by arranging a meeting. At the meeting, the client can assess the architect and the architect can decide whether he or she wishes to work with that client. As in every other field, personalities have a major part to play in the equation. Clients are dealt with in Chapter 1, section 1.4.1. A client may sometimes be a friend or relative, but more generally, a complete stranger. Some may have built before, others will be building for the first time. By its nature, the production of a building may take a very long time from inception to completion. It is important to start the relationship on a firm foundation or it will not survive.

6.2 Extent of services

There is some confusion regarding the services provided by the architect. On the one hand, it is often firmly believed that the architect's fee for a commission will include anything and everything the client may require, provided only that it has some relationship to the project. On the other hand, and equally erroneously, it is believed that the architect will prepare a set of plans, but anything else the client may need will cost extra. There is a grain of truth in each belief, which is why it is often difficult to explain the architect's services satisfactorily.

The question of fees is dealt with below, but it is worth remembering at this point that architects sell their services just like anyone else. If, for example, an architect is asked to prepare a sketch scheme to satisfy the client's requirements, that is what will be done. It is totally unreasonable to expect preparation of working drawings, invitation of tenders and inspection of work in progress at no additional cost. Moreover, the client may not like the sketch scheme produced by the architect, but provided that it satisfies the requirements given by the client, the architect is entitled to the fee.

In practice, most architects are prepared to carry out considerable reworking of their schemes until the client is entirely happy. This is very worthy and in the best traditions of professional service, but it is not strictly necessary and in an era of fee competition it is not always practical to achieve. To overcome this problem, the early stages of the architect's work are often carried out on a time charge basis.

It is unfortunately true that many clients are astonished, if they have never built before, that at the end of the initial stages of the architect's work there is often nothing visible except a set of two or three presentation drawings for which they are expected to pay what may appear to be an exorbitant fee. To take this attitude, of course, is to ignore the vast amount of work which has gone before the preparation of drawings. The prudent architect will usually avoid that situation by involving the client as fully as possible in every stage of the work. Although this approach is in line with best practice, the architect should assess each client, because some want nothing better than that the architect goes away and returns in a few weeks with his or her proposals. The architect, therefore, is expected to be something of a psychologist alongside all the other skills required.

The relationship between architect and client is that of agent and principal. The agent exercises contractual powers on behalf of the principal and in doing so the principal is bound by the agent's properly authorised acts. The agency relationship may be created in one of four ways:

- ■ *Expressly*, when the client specifically appoints the architect either in writing or orally. This is the most satisfactory, particularly when done in writing, because there is little scope for misunderstandings or mistakes.

■ *By implication*, when it is clear to others that the architect must be acting as agent. Such an instance may occur because the client behaves as if the architect was acting in an agency capacity or simply because the architect is doing the kind of things normally done by an agent.

■ *By necessity*, when the architect acts for the client in an emergency and otherwise there would be no agency. There will be very few instances when an agency comes into being in this way so far as architects are concerned. One might just visualise a situation where the architect must give an instruction on the client's behalf in order to save the destruction of property even though the architect may not be empowered to give that particular instruction.

■ *By ratification*, when the architect performs some act which the client subsequently ratifies. Two conditions must be satisfied: (1) The architect must carry out the action on behalf of the principal. (2) The principal must have been capable of carrying out the act at the time it was performed.

The agent's authority is important. It may be actual or apparent (ostensible). An architect's actual authority is defined by the terms of the conditions of engagement. Apparent or ostensible authority is the authority the architect appears to possess so far as parties other than the architect and client are concerned. An architect is liable to the client for acting beyond authority, but provided the architect is behaving in the way in which others expect him or her to act, the client will usually be responsible for such actions to third parties. For example, an architect carrying out functions under a building contract may issue instructions to the contractor. Provided the contract expressly empowers the architect to issue such instructions, the contractor is entitled to carry out the work and be paid. It matters not that the architect may be obliged, under his or her conditions of engagement, to obtain the client's authorisation for such instructions. Of course, in that situation, the architect may expect to be required to reimburse the client for any loss sustained.

The duties of an agent are:

■ To act. Failure to act if action is called for is actionable.
■ To obey instructions. The instructions must be lawful and reasonable.

■ To exercise skill and care. The kind of skill and care normally to be expected from a member of that particular profession.
■ Not to take any secret bribe or profit. The principal may recover damages including the amount of such bribe.
■ To declare any conflict of interest.
■ Not to delegate without authority.
■ To keep proper accounts.

One of the greatest dangers for an architect is that of exceeding the authority actually given by the client. The possible consequences have already been touched upon. When in doubt, the client's written authority should be obtained. Next best is to confirm instructions to the client. Another danger may arise if the architect fails to disclose that he or she is acting for a client. The architect may become personally liable to the third party in such cases.

Agency may be terminated by the death of the agent or principal, by the performance of the agent's contract, by mutual consent, by breach on the part of either agent or principal and by bankruptcy of the principal, but not necessarily of the agent.

At one time it used to be thought that the architect was in the position of a quasi-arbitrator or acting in a judicial capacity when carrying out some functions under the building contract. Such things as giving extensions of time or certifying monies due were thought to be in this category. Such notions were dispelled with the case of *Sutcliffe* v. *Thackrah* (1974)[1]. The architect has a duty to act fairly in these circumstances, but the duty is owed to the client, not to the contractor: *London Borough of Merton* v. *Stanley Hugh Leach* (1985)[2]. If an architect is negligent in the performance of any duty under the contract, the client may issue a claim against the architect direct, or arbitrate under the conditions of engagement as appropriate, in respect of any loss suffered, but the contractor must take action against the client, probably in arbitration, under the building contract[3]. Recent developments in the law, however, have suggested that there may be circumstances where an architect could be said to assume responsibility to a contractor who can be shown to have relied on his decisions. The position is complex and not yet clear[4].

The architect's services fall into two parts:

(1) Services which an architect will undertake as part of the overall design and administration of an entire project from beginning to end.

(2)   Services which are available from an architect, but not as part of 'normal' entire project services.

A detailed description of these services is included in the RIBA Standard Form of Agreement for the Appointment of an Architect 1999 (SFA/99) (see section 6.4.3) available from the RIBA.

All architects will be prepared to offer the 'normal' services to their clients, but some of the additional services may call for a degree of expertise in fields which not every architect will be prepared to offer. In addition, although the architect is still usually the lead consultant and contract administrator, it is no longer a foregone conclusion and some clients are appointing a project manager to act as team leader and contract administrator (an explanation of the two very different roles which can be played by the project manager is given in Chapter 7, section 7.3). In such instances the architect's management services will not be required.

For charging and other purposes, the work is divided into stages. Figure 6.1 shows them in diagrammatic form. It should be noted that the RIBA Plan of Work has recently been amended. It is the amended plan of work outlined here. This part of the book is divided into the same stages for convenience and what follows is a brief description of each stage, which will receive more detailed treatment in succeeding chapters. It is not always easy to pinpoint activities within a particular stage, because the whole process is continuous and some activities can be accommodated in several stages. For example, application for full planning permission and selection of specialist subcontractors will take place at a time to suit the circumstances.

Stages	
A	Appraisal
B	Strategic brief
C	Outline proposals
D	Detailed proposals
E	Final proposals
F	Production information
G	Tender documentation
H	Tender action
J	Mobilisation
K	Construction to practical completion
L	After practical completion

Fig. 6.1 The RIBA Plan of Work (title of stages only).

6.2.1 Normal services[5]

A Appraisal

During this initial stage, an important function of the architect is to obtain the client's brief. It can be a laborious process if clients are not, and sometimes if they are, sure of what they want. It is the architect's task to separate what the client wants from what he or she really needs. The architect will need to ask many questions regarding finance available, time schedule and the function required of the building. It is likely that several meetings will be required before the architect is satisfied. If there is any advice the client requires or the architect thinks it proper to give at this point, it will be given. For example, the architect may say at the first meeting that the project is not feasible because of cost, siting or some other reason.

Generally, assuming the scheme is not aborted, the architect will visit the site to get some idea of what is involved. It is at this stage that the architect will be able to provide a rough idea of the cost, time and fees likely to be involved in proceeding with the scheme. If the work the client has in mind is very small, for example an extension to a house, the whole process may take no more than a day or so. In the case of larger projects, a correspondingly longer time will be required. Where extremely large and complex projects are concerned, this stage may be very protracted. On anything other than small projects it represents a considerable body of work at the end of which the architect might prepare a report, depending on the size and complexity of the project, for examination by the client. Instead of a report, the architect's conclusions might be presented orally.

This is the stage during which the architect will check thoroughly that the project is feasible, that it can be built for the money the client wishes to spend, that there are no obstacles in the form of planning objections from the local authority or the site conditions and so on. There will be involvement in discussions with statutory authorities and any consultants appointed and every matter which might affect the client's intention to proceed must be investigated. For example, if the client is proposing a speculative housing development, it might well be prudent to include for the client's information, details of local schools, shops and bus services near the site. If the site is in a designated conservation or urban redevelopment area, the architect will explain how that will affect the scheme[6].

At this stage, alternative ways of tackling the design will be suggested and will conclude by a request to the client to make certain decisions. The decision may be simply whether to proceed, or it may involve matters thrown up by the investigations. This is not too early for the architect to consider with the client the procurement alternatives.

B Strategic briefing

The strategic brief will be prepared, possibly by the client, but normally by the architect. This brief takes into account all the preparatory work and the client's decisions on any points thrown up by the appraisal. The key procedures must be identified, together with the way in which the architect intends to organise the design team to deal with the project. The client can then be given some preliminary thoughts on the need for consultants and specialist subcontractors.

C Outline proposals

This stage is probably better known as 'sketch design'. Taking into account all previous discussions including the client's decisions at the end of stage A, the architect will develop the brief into a full briefing document for the project, intended to indicate the client's requirements in every particular. The architect will then commence to prepare drawings to illustrate the proposed solution to the client's problem. The drawings will not be detailed, but they will be sufficient to show what the architect has in mind in a general way. It should be possible to see the general massing and external appearance of the building, its disposition on site and the arrangement of the interior.

To produce these sketches, the architect will have to have analysed and considered all the information gleaned during the previous stages. The client should be asked to approve an approximate estimate of cost at this stage. In giving such an approximate estimate of cost, an architect is wise to ensure that it makes proper allowance for the outline nature of the design at this stage, by building in an estimating tolerance. This is particularly important, because this is the figure that the client will always remember! Where the project is other than small, the cost estimation should be carried out by a quantity surveyor who should be involved at an early stage.

D   Detailed proposals

On small projects, this stage is combined with the previous stage. The architect must take into account any comments the client makes about the outline proposals, complete the full briefing document and work with any consultants who may be appointed to produce a more detailed design for the client's approval. At this stage, the client should have a very clear idea about the appearance of the building, the materials proposed and the layout of the interior. A fresh estimate of cost will be prepared and the dates proposed for commencement and completion. The architect will require the client's final approval to the scheme, time-scale and cost at this point.

Assuming that the client does approve with little or no amendment, the architect should apply for planning permission. Although an application for outline permission will almost certainly have been made at feasibility stage and thereafter the planning authorities will have been closely consulted, there is unfortunately no guarantee that planning permission will be granted. In the majority of cases, the procedures adopted by the architect avoid a refusal at this stage, but it is not uncommon for the planning authority to require some changes before they will grant permission. Both architect and client will find it frustrating if this happens; in addition it will cause the architect much extra work.

At the end of this stage, the architect should advise the client that any subsequent changes of mind will be costly in terms of time and money. The scheme now should be regarded as fixed.

E   Final proposals

As soon as the architect obtains the client's approval to the scheme design, every part of the scheme must be developed in great detail. This is the first part of what is commonly called 'working drawings'. If consultants are appointed, they will be involved in similar detailed design work. The client will be asked to approve many of the details, particularly as regards standards and quality. The cost of building the project must be kept constantly under review by the quantity surveyor as each detail is finalised. The drawings produced during this stage will be highly technical, dimensioned, noted and coded. On the basis of these drawings, all further negotiations and approvals with statutory bodies will be finalised.

The architect should advise the client that if any subsequent changes are required which are other than trivial, the building programme will be disrupted and the client will incur considerable extra cost. The client's idea of 'trivia' may well not accord with the architect's views.

Clients often fail to understand why a change of mind which, on the face of it, appears to reduce the overall cost of the building should result in additional costs. The architect should, therefore, clearly explain that if the client changes something, the architect has to begin again the process of consultation with statutory bodies (including, on occasions, re-applying for planning and other permissions), consultants and any specialist subcontractors. Drawings have to be redone, fresh calculations made and new costings carried out. The architect's careful programming of office resources will be upset and there is the very real danger that mistakes will be made. It is the architect's duty to give clear advice in this regard if the client wants any changes. It would be wrong to simply carry out the client's instructions and present a large bill for additional services at the end.

F   Production information

During this, usually fairly lengthy, stage, the architect and any consultants should be busy producing all the information which will be required for tendering and, additionally, the information that a contractor will require to proceed subsequently to erect the building. In addition to the drawings prepared during the last stage, details and schedules will be produced together with a specification of all the materials and items of work required. Applications in connection with the Building Regulations and any other necessary statutory approvals should be finalised during this stage.

G   Tender documentation

If the system of procurement warrants it (see Chapter 7, section 7.4), bills of quantities should be prepared by the quantity surveyor from information supplied by the architect and other consultants. The architect must be ready to supply any additional information which the quantity surveyor requires. Unless the project is such that the contrary is suggested, the architect should know the building in detail at this stage. The documents must be assembled in a suitable form to allow the prospective contractors to tender. All relevant information should be included so that the contractors can include for every aspect of the work.

It is usual for the architect or quantity surveyor at this stage to prepare a final cost estimate to ensure so far as possible that the client will not receive an unpleasant surprise when tenders are returned.

The planning supervisor will be producing the pre-tender health and safety plan and the architect must pass on copies of the final production information.

H   Tender action

Prior to this stage, the architect should have advised the client on the most appropriate way of obtaining a price for the work. It may be by means of negotiation or tendering. During this stage, everything needing to be done before prices are obtained should be organised and, if tendering is decided on, tendering information should be sent out to all the contractors on a list which the client has previously approved. A prudent architect will have requested references from every contractor on the list and at the same time ascertained by discreet enquiry some idea of their financial stability. This is essential[7]. In some cases, a formal pre-qualification process will be carried out in order to produce a shortlist of the most appropriate contractors. In the case of public sector tendering, the relevant EU procurement legislation must be satisfied.

The architect will in due course, together with the quantity surveyor, assess all tenders received and advise the client accordingly. If the lowest tender is too high to suit the client's pocket, the architect may be involved in revising the project. Unless it is the architect's fault that the project is too expensive, an additional fee is appropriate for this work.

J   Mobilisation

During this stage, the architect should give advice to the client with regard to contractual matters, insurances and the like and should be ready to answer any questions. Discussions will have taken place concerning the appropriate form of contract, including any necessary amendments, before tender stage, and the contract documents prepared for signature. All the information to enable construction to commence on the appointed date must be assembled and it is usual for a number of meetings to be held with consultants, specialist subcontractors, the contractor and possibly representatives from statutory authorities.

K   Construction to practical completion

During the course of work on site, the architect will carry out his or her duties under the contract and make regular visits to site to inspect the general progress and quality of workmanship and materials. It may be necessary to supply further production information from time to time or as set out in an information release schedule. The client should be kept up to date on the progress of the work and supplied with financial reports from time to time depending on the client's requirements and the size and complexity of the project. The client should be given any additional advice required concerning the project.

L   After practical completion

When work is completed, the architect must ensure that all defects are made good and that loose ends are tied up, and must generally make sure that the financial aspects are settled accurately with the help of other consultants as appropriate. The client should be supplied with some general notes on maintenance together with a set of drawings showing the building and the main lines of drainage and the services installations which will be required for the health and safety file.

6.2.2   Other services

Sites

The architect can advise on site suitability and negotiate on the client's behalf. He or she can prepare survey drawings and undertake site investigations, in collaboration with the appropriate consultant.

Buildings

The architect can produce survey drawings of buildings and pre-pare schedules of conditions. Depending on the skills within the office, it may be possible to carry out structural surveys and investigate defects and failures. The preparation of specifications in connection with repairs can be undertaken, and the inspection of work in progress. Advice may also be offered on many other building problems, such as energy conservation, fire protection, change of use and economic costs in use. For completed buildings, architects can provide as-built drawings and maintenance and operational manuals.

Development

The architect should be an expert in the production of special plans for many purposes in connection with building development. Elaborate models and perspectives are available from some offices; other specialist services which may be available include montages, detailed plans and specifications for roads and sewers, demolition and environmental studies and conveyancing plans.

Design

The architect should be able to offer a wide variety of services under this general head. Among them are interior design, the design and selection of furnishings and decoration, exhibition design, shop-fitting and advice on the commissioning or selection of works of art. He or she may be able to offer specialist services in acoustical investigations, development and testing of systems of building including testing of prototypes or models.

Financial

Depending on the disciplines within the architect's office, it may be possible to offer complete cost planning of building projects, advice on cash flow requirements, life cycle cost analyses, value management and engineering, valuation of buildings, preparation of schedules of rates or quantities, estimates and negotiations in connection with fire damage and grant negotiations. Otherwise these matters are best left to a quantity surveyor.

Negotiations

It is common for architects to offer services in connection with planning appeals and special negotiations, building regulation relaxations, submissions to bodies such as English Heritage and submissions to landlords, etc.

Legal

The architect should be able to offer a substantial knowledge of the law as it relates to construction and provides services in connection with easements, party wall negotiations and rights. With appropriate experience and training, it should be possible to give expert evidence in proceedings and advise during conferences with solicitors and counsel. Although in theory all architects can act as adjudicators or arbitrators in appropriate cases, in practice only those architects who have had proper training and experience should do so (see Chapter 3, section 3.10).

Management

Management services include entire project management of building works, provision of constant site inspection, co-ordination of separate trade contracts, co-ordination and supervision of direct labour contracts and services to either party in connection with design and build contracts. 'As built' drawings can be prepared together with detailed maintenance manuals and maintenance programmes.

Historic buildings

Some architects can offer services in connection with historic buildings and conservation areas, embracing research, inspections, detailed reports and applications for planning approvals in connection with listed buildings and conservation areas.

Consultants

If architects have appropriately qualified personnel within their practices, they will be able to offer services normally provided by the appropriate consultant. They will be able to offer these services either on projects for which they are the project architects or project managers or on projects for which another architect has been engaged (with the agreement of that architect). An architect may also be engaged as an independent consultant on a regular basis if required.

Planning supervisor

Many, although not all, architects have undertaken training to enable them to offer services as planning supervisor in connection with buildings under the Construction (Design and Management) Regulations 1994. The RIBA have produced special terms of engagement for the purpose. It is not uncommon for an architect to combine both architectural and planning supervisor services on the same project.

Summary

The services which the architect may offer as part of the normal or additional services cover every facet of construction work and the care and maintenance of buildings in use. It should be noted that, although all architects will be willing to offer some of the services outlined above, architects, like other professionals, tend to develop their own specialisms. There will be serious legal implications for architects who hold themselves out as qualified to offer a competent service in something which they are not equipped to do. In addition, of course, it must not be forgotten that architects should not offer services for which they do not have appropriate professional indemnity cover (see Chapter 17, section 17.5).

6.3   Fee negotiation or tendering

At one time, architects used to have a mandatory fee scale. The RIBA then published recommended fee scales. That has also vanished, although the RIBA does publish indicative percentage fee scales for architects' services in the form of percentage fee graphs for new works and works to existing buildings, and a classification of building types based on the ones which used to form part of the RIBA Architect's Appointment (the 'Blue Book')[8]. Because the scales are merely indicative, it means that architects are free to charge whatever they consider to be the proper rate for the work to be done – whether they will persuade clients to pay is another matter. Negotiations can take place with a prospective client to arrive at a mutually agreeable figure. There is a point, however, below which the architect cannot give a satisfactory standard of service. To negotiate a fee below that point is commercial suicide to say nothing of being unprofessional. In practice, it seems that architects commonly do work for less than the scale fee and sometimes for nothing at all if a reasonable commission may result.

The numbers of architects prepared to do so-called 'speculative work' in this way shows no signs of decreasing and some unscrupulous clients use, as an excuse for not paying, that they thought the architect was working speculatively. Although everyone in business must face commercial reality, architects do the profession no favours by working for very low fees or for nothing at all.

The fees negotiated will depend on many factors of which the following are the most significant:

- The amount of work the architect has in progress
- The size of the office related to turnover and hence the overhead costs
- Whether the project is 'one off' or simply the first of many similar jobs which the architect can expect to receive from the same client
- Whether the project is particularly interesting to a particular architect

Most architects use the published fee scales or at least they use them as a basis. A small, one man, office may charge less, but offer fewer resources than a larger firm which may charge more to cover its larger overheads. The smaller firm may argue that it is giving a more personalised service. It is now possible for a client to obtain competitive quotations from a number of architects for the same project. It is necessary to ensure that the terms are absolutely clear and on the same basis for each of the architects involved in giving a quotation.

The basis of fees is usually either:

- A percentage of the construction cost of building; *or*
- A time charge; *or*
- A lump sum.

6.3.1 Percentage charges

Architects will normally charge a percentage of the actual construction cost if they are providing the normal full service. The RIBA published indicative percentage fee scales divide buildings into classes and provide graphs showing indicative percentages for each class over a range of construction costs. Class 1 buildings are the simplest, class 5 are the most complex. The recommendations are detailed and, if the architect does propose using them, he should study the implications carefully. Among points worthy of note are the following[9]:

- Consultants' work is included in the total cost even if carried out under a separate contract
- Specialist subcontractors' design fees are excluded
- If the architect carries out work on parts of the building which are eventually omitted, the total construction cost will be estimated for fee purposes
- Built-in furniture and equipment is included in the total cost
- If clients carry out any work direct or supply materials at their own cost, the architect should estimate the value and include it in the total construction cost for fee purposes
- Where there is a substantial element of repetition, the fees may be reduced

It is normal for fees to be paid in instalments based on the estimated final cost. The final fee account will be adjusted to take account of the actual final cost of the building. Payment should be agreed as being made at the end of each stage, or better, monthly. It is essential that the charge is settled before the architect undertakes any work.

6.3.2 Time charges

Time charges are based on an hourly rate. The RIBA Standard Form of Agreement for the Appointment of an Architect 1999 (SFA/99) sets out no recommendations, but it has been suggested elsewhere that indicative hourly rates should be as shown in Fig. 6.2.

| | | Type of work | |
	General	Complex	Specialist
Partner/director or equivalent	£90	£130	£170
Senior architect	£70	£100	£130
Architect	£50	£70	£90

Effective from 1 January 1998 and reviewable annually.

Fig. 6.2   Indicative hourly rates.

This matrix originally appeared in *Practice*, issue 152, *RIBA Journal*, March 1998, page 83. Publication was approved by the RIBA Council to complement the existing so-called 'indicative fee scales'. The figures were said to include office costs, but not travel and other expenses. Most architects would be delighted to be able to charge these kinds of fees. Sadly, anecdotal evidence suggests that the general level of hourly rates is substantially below these indicative figures. However, principals offering special expertise or experience normally charge a relatively high rate. The rate will also vary with the complexity of the work to be carried out.

The actual amount charged per hour varies from practice to practice and from one part of the country to another. Charges are usually higher in the London area than in the regions and larger practices usually charge more than small practices. In the latter case, the large practice will probably argue that the increased cost arises from higher overheads needed to maintain a better standard of service.

It is very difficult to arrive at a figure for an hourly rate, because the rates from practice to practice are not generally known. Thus, an architect fixing an hourly rate for his technical staff may wonder where to start. A commonly used guide used to be the $1 \times 1 \times 1$ formula where the rate was made up of equal parts of salary, overheads and profit. In practice, the architect worked out the amount he paid a staff member per hour, then multiplied by three to find the hourly rate to be charged to the client. It was a very rough guide and current evidence suggests that the profit element is now very much below a third of the total. Architects should go through the exercise, perhaps using 0.3 for the profit (i.e. $1 \times 1 \times 0.3$) to see if they are charging anything like this figure. It is our experience that most architects and surveyors, particularly outside London, charge very low hourly rates when compared with other professions.

Work for which an hourly rate would be appropriate could include:

- Constant site inspection
- Partial services
- Additional services
- Any instance where the client has agreed with the architect that a time charge should be made
- Additional work beyond the architect's control such as:
  - □ Revisions to documents due to changes in the law
  - □ Changes in client's instructions
  - □ Delay or disruption in building operations caused by others

Many clients are wary of paying on an hourly basis. They tend to liken it to a blank cheque. It is, however, perfectly possible for an architect to state an hourly rate and to give a rough estimate of the length of time needed. Another variant is the hourly rate plus ceiling figure beyond which the architect must not go without further authorisation. Rendering monthly accounts in such instances assists both architect and client to keep control of the situation. In certain instances, there is no option but to state an hourly rate. It need not be more expensive than a lump sum (see below) because the architect is certain to make a reasonable profit from an hourly rate, whereas he must add something for contingencies when arriving at a lump sum.

6.3.3   Lump sum charges

There is nothing to prevent the architect from quoting a lump sum fee to cover all the work expected to be carried out. Indeed, clients may require that approach. However, this should only be done if:

- The extent of the work required is absolutely clear
- The time-scale of the service is known

It would be unusual, for example, if an architect was to quote a lump sum fee for carrying out negotiations with a local authority in regard to development work. On the other hand, a small project requiring full services over a comparatively short time-scale is the sort of job architects can cost in their offices and for which they can give a firm quotation.

There is a danger for the client if he or she requires a lump sum quotation, and the architect has a duty to explain the implications fully. Clients must know precisely what they want; they must not cause delay or change their minds. If architects are involved in additional work clearly not included in the original sum, the client can be required to pay additional fees. Where architects are requested to quote on a lump sum basis, they must take care to specify precisely the services which are included, particularly whether or not they are inclusive of VAT, expenses, etc.

An architect may not take part in a Dutch auction so as to effectively undercut another architect's fee quotation. The RIBA Code of Professional Conduct is clear about that (see Chapter 2, section 2.6).

The practice of project team fee negotiations is very popular among many clients. These clients commission buildings which, of their nature, require a considerable input from consultants in several disciplines. Traditionally, such clients would be left to negotiate terms and fees with each consultant individually as recommended by the architect, and clients fear that this is an expensive process. Moreover, experience has shown that different consultants do not always fit together harmoniously. Indeed, many disputes arise out of conflicts between the approaches of differing disciplines. The idea of project team fee negotiations is that an integrated approach is presented to the client consisting of all the consultants under the co-ordination of a lead consultant (who may not be an architect). Fees and the individual responsibilities are expressly set out, including specific professional indemnity responsibilities.

6.3.4   Work to existing buildings

If the work the client requires to be done involves an existing building, a larger fee is chargeable. This is because the architect will be involved in much more work due to the constraints of the original structure, planning, services, etc. If, in addition, the building is of architectural or historic interest, if it is a 'listed building' or in a conservation area, the client may also be paying for the architect's special skills in dealing with buildings of that type. Even if the building is a new construction to be joined onto an existing building, the client will be charged a higher fee for that portion of the work where new and old connect. It is impossible to give other than such rather general indications, because each old building has its own special identity which requires individual consideration. For example, a very ancient town wall of considerable length might attract a lower percentage fee than a complicated Victorian building. It is very risky, from the architect's point of view, to agree to take on this kind of work for a lump sum.

6.3.5   Determination

Just whether and how much the architect can recover in respect of fees in the event of determination will depend on whether formal conditions of engagement have been entered into and the circumstances of the determination. SFA/99 provides that either architect or client can determine on 14 days' notice. It also provides that the architect is then entitled to fees for all work he has completed up to the time of determination. The exact method of calculating the fees will depend on the basis originally agreed. The architect is entitled to charge all expenses arising from determination if due to the client's determination or breach of contract. An architect in the middle of producing working drawings, specifications and schedules for the contractor cannot be expected to move staff onto other work immediately.

If there is no formal agreement between the architect and the client, there will be no provision for determination and no provision for subsequent recovery of fees. In this situation the parties will find themselves locked into litigation unless they suddenly display a streak of reasonableness which, had it been present in the first place, may have resulted in an agreement on clear terms (see section 6.4). Anecdotal evidence suggests that many architects do find themselves in awkward situations as a result of a failure to enter into a proper formal agreement with clients. Architects are not only the authors of their own misfortunes in this situation, they are also in breach of principle one of the RIBA Code of Professional Conduct.

Ignoring what may be in the terms of engagement, it is worth remembering that an architect's engagement is a contract and that it may be brought to an end in the same way as any other contract (see Chapter 13, section 13.1).

6.3.6   Expenses

There is no automatic right to expenses. A client is entitled to assume that they are included in any fee quoted unless they are specifically stated to be extra. It is also advisable to state precisely what the architect considers to be reimbursable expenses. A distinction must be made between expenses and disbursements. Disbursements are sums which are expended on behalf of a client and they are usually recovered as a net amount. Statutory fees and direct payments to consultants fall into this category. Common expense items are:

- Postage, telephone, fax, e-mail and other means of communication or delivery
- Hotel and travelling expenses (mileage rates should be stated in the agreement)
- Charges for travelling time if the time spent on travelling is exceptional (this should also be agreed in advance)
- Printing, reproduction and purchase of all drawings, documents, photographs and models, etc. which the architect must or the client requests him to produce in order to carry out the work
- Payment for specialist advice which the client has authorised, for example, legal advice
- Special hire charges for equipment if authorised

6.4   Terms of appointment

6.4.1   The basic contract

The relationship between an architect and his or her client is contractual. There may also, depending on circumstances, be a tortious liability. Principally, however, the relationship will depend on the terms of the agreement made between the parties.

There are two types of contract:

- A simple contract (under hand)
- A specialty contract (a deed)

There are important differences. In the case of a simple contract, there must be consideration present (each party must contribute something to the bargain) or the contract will not be valid. In addition, an action for breach of that contract can be defended by reference to the Limitation Act 1980 if brought by one party against the other more than 6 years after the date of the breach. A specialty contract does not require consideration to make it valid and the limitation period is 12 years from the date of the breach. There are other differences, but the two noted above are the most important so far as architects are concerned. Effectively, the result is that an architect who enters into an agreement as a deed with the client doubles the length of exposure to actions under the contract or for breach of its terms.

A contract is a binding agreement between two or more persons which creates mutual rights and duties and which is enforceable at law. There must be an intention to create legal relations. In the case of agreements between business people, such an intention is implied. In the case of friends or relatives, the intention normally has to be demonstrated. For a valid contract there must be:

- An offer by one party
- Unqualified acceptance by the other party
- Consideration (except in the case of a specialty contract)
- Capacity to contract. Certain persons, e.g. drunkards, the insane and minors, have very limited capacity to contract
- Intention to create a legal relationship
- Genuine consent, i.e. there must be no duress
- A legal objective
- An objective which is possible

A simple contract can be entered into in writing or orally. The problem with an oral contract, of course, is uncertainty about its terms. Even if there are witnesses, they may later disagree regarding what they heard. Many architects are engaged purely on the basis of an oral agreement and, indeed, some clients may appear offended if asked to put the commission in writing, as though it was some reflection on their honour. In truth, the purpose of recording the terms in writing is to protect both parties, not only against sharp practice, but more commonly against imperfect memory or plain misunderstanding. At the very least, the architect should confirm in writing the terms of the appointment at the earliest opportunity.

It used to be the case that a specialty contract had to be made under seal[10]. This was usually a round piece of red paper on which a seal was embossed or it could be a rubber stamp or, indeed, anything so long as the parties clearly intended the document to be sealed[11]. However, the Law of Property (Miscellaneous Provisions) Act 1989, in the case of individuals, and the Companies Act 1989, in the case of companies, removed the necessity to use a seal. Indeed, the use of a seal alone will not create a deed.

In the case of a company all that is required is for the document to state on its face that it is a deed and for it to be signed by two directors or one director and the company secretary. In the case of an individual, the document must state on its face that it is a deed and it should be signed by the person making the deed in the presence of a witness who must attest the signature. Alternatively but rarely, an individual may authorise another to sign on his behalf in which case there must be two witnesses who must attest the signature. The stamping of such documents is not generally required unless part of a conveyance.

An important principle is privity of contract. That is the rule that only parties to a contract can bind or be bound by that contract. In recent years, however, it has been thought that such a rule can result in unfairness in certain circumstances and, at the time of writing, the Contracts (Rights of Third Parties) Act 1999 is due to come into force to allow persons who are not parties to a contract to enforce rights under the contract.

6.4.2   The effect of the Construction Act

All terms of engagement entered into by architects after 1 May 1998 are subject to the Housing Grants, Construction and Regeneration Act 1996 (commonly referred to as the 'Construction Act'. In Northern Ireland legislation to the same effect is the Construction Contracts (Northern Ireland) Order 1997). Part II of the Act deals with construction contracts and every architect should have a copy. Part II is only a few pages long. Included in the definition of such contracts is an agreement 'to do architectural, design, or surveying work, or . . . to provide advice on building, engineering, interior or exterior decoration or on the laying out of landscape in relation to construction operations'.

'Construction operations' are defined in some detail. Broadly they are the construction, alteration, repair, etc. of buildings, structures, roadworks, docks and harbours, power lines, sewers and the like. They also include installation of fittings such as heating, electrical or air conditioning, external or internal cleaning carried out as part of construction and site clearance, tunnelling, foundations and other preparatory work and painting or decorating. Excluded are such things as drilling for natural gas, mineral extraction, manufacture of certain components, construction or demolition of plant where the primary activity is nuclear processing, effluent treatment or chemicals, construction of artistic works, sign writing and other peripheral installations. More importantly, it does not bite where one of the parties intends to take residence in the subject of the construction operations.

The provisions of the Act apply only to 'agreements in writing' and there are detailed provisions as to what that entails. Apart from the obvious, it also covers situations where there is no signature, where the parties agree orally by reference to terms which are in writing and where agreement is alleged in arbitration by one party and not denied by the other.

The Act requires that all construction contracts must include certain provisions. They are:

■ *Adjudication*
  Either party must have the right to refer disputes to adjudication with the object of obtaining a decision within 28 days of referral. A party may give notice of intention to refer at any time and the referral must take place within 7 days. The 28 day deadline may be extended by up to 14 days if the referring party wishes or indefinitely if both parties agree. The adjudicator may take the initiative in ascertaining the facts and the law. In other words, the adjudicator does not have to wait until one party raises a point, but can ask for evidence. The adjudicator's decision is binding until the dispute is decided by litigation, arbitration or by agreement. The parties may agree to accept the adjudicator's decision as final. The adjudicator is not to be liable for acts or omissions unless there has been bad faith.

■ *Stage payments*
  A party is entitled to stage payments unless the duration of the project is less than 45 days. The parties are free to agree the intervals between payments and the amounts of such payments.

■ *Date for payment*
  Every contract must contain the means of working out the amount due and the date on which it is due and must provide a final date for payment.

■ *Set-off*
  Payment may not be withheld, or money set off, unless notice has been given particularising the amount to be withheld and the grounds. The notice must be given no later than the agreed period before final payment.

■ *Suspension of performance of obligations*
  If the amount properly due has not been paid by the final date for payment and no effective notice withholding payment has been given, a party has the right, after giving a 7 day written

notice, to suspend performance of obligations under the contract until payment has been made.

- *Pay when paid*
  Except in cases of insolvency, a clause making payment dependent on receipt of money from a third party is void. This is intended to outlaw the so-called 'pay-when-paid clause', but it may not be sufficient to do so. It does not take effect if the third party is insolvent.

To the extent that a construction contract does not include these provisions, the Scheme for Construction Contracts (England and Wales) 1998 comes into effect just as if the clauses contained in the Scheme were written into the contract. Most standard form construction contracts and all the RIBA terms of engagement comply with the Act and, therefore, the Scheme is not relevant where such terms are used. Where architects contract on the basis of an exchange of correspondence or on terms drawn up by the client's legal advisors, it is likely that some, if not all, of the Scheme will be effective.

6.4.3 The RIBA Standard Form of Agreement

Some bodies insist that the architect contracts on the basis of their own particular terms and conditions. In such cases, the architect should take the greatest possible care, including if necessary obtaining expert advice. Wherever possible, the architect is well advised to contract on the basis of standard terms of which the best known is the RIBA Standard Form of Agreement for the Appointment of an Architect (SFA/99). Although it is possible to incorporate these terms by stating in a letter to a client that they are so incorporated, such a practice can lead to confusion because the terms are intended to be applied on the basis of a Memorandum of Agreement which provides for the inclusion of certain matters as appropriate. Simply to incorporate the document as a whole without qualification could lead to ambiguity. Another difficulty which can arise is that the document is drafted with a traditional contractual arrangement in mind. If some other arrangement, such as employment by a contractor or in connection with a management contract, is intended, some amendment of the terms will be necessary.

The Architect's Appointment[12] was introduced by the Royal Institute of British Architects in 1982. It was the successor to the

Conditions of Engagement and followed the report of the Mono-
polies and Mergers Commission on architects' and surveyors'
services and remuneration. There was also a small works edition.
In 1992, the RIBA introduced SFA/92. Significantly, it allowed for
changes to the services when something other than the traditional
architect's role was required. Therefore, it had supplements for use
with historic buildings and for community architecture work.
There was also a special edition for use with design and build
where the architect was employed by the employer or by the
contractor. A version designed for use with projects for which IFC
84 might be used was issued in 1995 (CE/95) and then a version for
use for small works (SW/96). These documents had a mixed
reception, many architects continuing to use the Architects
Appointment. The impetus for a new set of terms of engagement
was a general dissatisfaction with the existing forms, the Latham
Report[13], calling for a suite of interlocking contracts and the
Construction Act which necessitated certain revisions to the
existing forms in any event. The new forms are:

SFA/99	For general use for the appointment of an archi-tect.
CE/99	For use in 'straightforward situations where it is considered preferable to the more formal agree-ment (SFA/99) or the small works form (SW/99).
Amendment DB1/99	For use with SFA/99 or CE/99 if the architect is acting for the employer under a design and build contract.
Amendment DB2/99	For use with SFA/99 or CE/99 if the architect is acting for the contractor under a design and build contract.
SW/99	For use where the professional services are rela-tively straightforward, construction works are of no more than about £150,000, where MW 98 is used on the basis of a simple contract (i.e. not a deed) and the applicable law is England and Wales.
SC/99	For use where an architect appoints a sub-consultant to perform part of the architect's services.
PS/99	For use where a planning supervisor is appointed.

SFA/99 is the standard terms of engagement and it will be
considered in more detail. It is in the following parts:

- *Articles of agreement*
  Although the parties have the right to adjudication, they are also given the option of choosing either arbitration or litigation. Previously arbitration was the designated method of dispute resolution. Arbitration offers distinct advantages over litigation. The arbitrator can be an architect agreed on by the parties, the proceedings are private and they are usually considerably faster than legal proceedings. Arbitration also has an element of finality which is absent from litigation. The recent reforms in legal procedure (the Woolf reforms) are aimed at streamlining the legal process. Whether this will be successful only time will tell.

- *Schedule 1*
  This is for the insertion of a description of the project. It is really the client's brief and any change may result in varied services and fees.

- *Schedule 2*
  This is for the architect to set out the services to be provided.

- *Other activities*
  A ready printed list of activities which the architect may be willing to carry out, but which will attract additional fees.

- *Schedule 3*
  Here the fees and expenses payable by the client are to be set out.

- *Schedule 4*
  Space to set down the names and addresses of other persons appointed by the client in connection with the Works and parts of the project to be designed by others.

- *Services supplement*
  This sets out the architect's possible design and management services. The individual services are to be deleted if not required and it is possible to substitute another set of services (e.g. DB1/99) instead.

- *Conditions of engagement*
  These consist of a set of defined terms and the clauses themselves.

It is worth looking at the conditions of engagement in greater detail.

The definitions speak for themselves and we will refer to them as necessary in what follows. The meat of the contract begins at *clauses 1.4 and 1.5* which set out the requirements for notice and state that when calculating periods of time within which actions must be performed, public holidays are excluded. That means, of course, that ordinary weekends are included. All notices must be in writing.

Clause 1.6 places a duty on both the architect and the client to advise each other if they become aware that there is a need to vary the services, timetable, fees or, indeed, any part of the agreement or if there is incompatibility in or between the client's requirements, instructions, cost, timetable or approved design. Anything else likely to affect progress, quality or cost and any information or decisions from the client must be notified as soon as they become apparent.

By *clause 2.1* the architect is to exercise reasonable skill and care in conformity with the normal standards of the architect's profession. This term simply states what is the general law. In *Bolam* v. *Friern Hospital Management Committee* (1957)[14] the judge defined the standard required of a professional person:

> 'But where you get a situation which involves the use of some special skill or competence, then the test whether there has been negligence or not is not the test of the man on top of the Clapham omnibus, because he has not got this special skill. A man need not possess the highest expert skill at the risk of being found negligent. It is well established law that it is sufficient if he exercised the ordinary skill of an ordinary competent man exercising that particular art.'

Clause 2.2 is very important. It sets out the architect's authority to act on behalf of the client. It gives the architect power of agency in respect of the matters set out or implied in the architect's appointment, but it must be read with *clause 2.3* which stipulates that the architect must obtain the client's authority before beginning any service or work stage. The architect as agent has been discussed in section 6.2.

Clause 2.7 serves to qualify the architect's actual authority in that substantial changes from the approved design must not be made without the client's agreement unless it is a matter of urgency in which case the architect must notify the client without delay. The architect must also inform the client if the overall authorised cost or contract period is likely to be varied. It is good practice to send progress reports to the client at such intervals as seems appropriate to the type and size of project. Unless the client is familiar with the construction industry, the reports should be couched in straight-forward terms so that the implications can be grasped immediately.

It should be noted that the contractor is only concerned with whether the architect acts within the powers given by the building contract. If the contract empowers the architect to instruct the contractor to carry out extra work, it matters not that the architect has not obtained the client's permission. The contractor is entitled to do the work and be paid by the employer. In such a situation, however, the employer might well have a valid claim against the architect for exceeding his or her actual authority as set out in these conditions.

Clauses 2.4 and 3.8 to 3.11 and 3.13 deal with consultants. The case of *Moresk Cleaners Ltd* v. *Thomas Henwood Hicks* (1966)[15] decided that architects have no implied authority to delegate design responsibility and unless they obtain the client's agreement they will be held liable to the client if a delegated design proves to be defective. The architect is to advise the client about the appointment of consultants (other than those already named in schedule 4) to design, carry out parts of the Works or to give specialist advice. It is for the client to appoint and pay each consultant and confirm to the architect the services which they are to perform. However, either architect or client may propose the appointment of consultants at any time for the other's agreement.

A very important provision states that the client will hold each consultant, and not the architect, responsible for the competence, inspection and performance of the work carried out by them. That is a very good reason, quite apart from the question of professional indemnity cover (see Chapter 17, section 17.5), why the architect should not undertake to carry out what would normally be consultants' work by direct engagement of consultants. The efficacy of this clause which in effect limits the architect's liability has been accepted by the court in *Investors in Industry Commercial Properties Ltd* v. *South Bedfordshire District Council* (1986)[16] where a similar clause in the previous RIBA Conditions of Engagement was considered. The client must ensure, that is virtually guarantee, that consultants co-operate with the architect both by providing drawings and other information in good time and by their willingness to consider and comment on the architect's work to enable any necessary changes to be made. If this term was not expressly included, it would have to be implied to enable the carrying out of the architect's duties.

Many problems have been caused by the architect's obligation to inspect the Works. Nowhere does it state that the architect must 'supervise' the Works although the courts, and architects themselves, regularly refer to the architect's duty to design and supervise. Supervision implies constant inspection and direction. In building contracts, this duty lies with the contractor.

Clauses 2.5, 2.8 and 3.10 refer to site inspection. The architect is required to make such visits to site as are reasonably expected to be necessary at the date of the appointment. Clearly, it is not expected that the architect should make frequent or constant inspections. If such a degree of inspection by the architect is agreed to be necessary, a part-time or full-time resident architect may be appointed or otherwise a clerk of works will be employed and the architect should advise the client about this.

The clerk of works should be employed by the client, but under the direction and control of the lead consultant. This may or may not be the architect. In the case of *Kensington & Chelsea & Westminster Area Health Authority* v. *Wettern Composites* (1984)[17], it was held that the damages awarded against the architect should be reduced by 20% to take account of the negligence of the clerk of works. As the clerk of works was employed by the client, it was held that the client was vicariously liable for the clerk of works' actions. It is clearly in the architect's interest that the clerk of works is employed directly by the client.

Clause 3.12 is especially useful to bring home to a client the true situation in respect of the building contract, although it only states what is the general law. In practice, a client will always blame the architect if anything goes wrong with a project. This clause makes clear that where the client has entered into a building contract, the contractor, not the architect, must be held responsible for the contractor's methods and for the proper execution of the Works.

Clause 2.6 requires the architect to co-operate with any of the persons listed in schedule 4. Such co-operation will take the form of supplying drawings and information as necessary and commenting on their work. In addition and significantly, the architect is made responsible for integrating into the architectural design any relevant information provided by the consultants.

Clauses 3.1 to 3.7 are procedural in character and provide that the client will provide necessary information, decisions and approvals when requested and will set down the relative priorities of brief, cost and timetable. Such a provision must be implied or the architect will be unable to function properly. The client must nominate a responsible representative for the giving of instructions. This is a sensible procedure which would probably be adopted in any event. The representative may well be a project manager acting in this capacity rather than actually managing the project. Obviously the client must have authority to issue instructions to the architect. The client is to issue such instructions only through the lead consultant, whoever that might be. Perhaps surprisingly, the client is required to instruct when applications for statutory and other consents are to be made. The way in which the clause is structured is unfortunate. In practice, the architect would advise when such applications were required and the client would make a decision about the advice. That might well be an instruction, but the client is reacting rather than taking the lead. The client must also comply with the CDM Regulations and appoint a planning supervisor and a principal contractor. The clause uses the word 'competent' before each such person, but it must be redundant because the alternative is for the client to appoint incompetent persons which can never be intended.

Clause 3.13 states that the client must obtain legal advice and provide 'such information and evidence as required for the resolution of any dispute between the Client and any other parties providing services in connection with the Project'. It is not clear what this clause means. It is tempting to assume that it merely refers to a situation where the client has a dispute with the contractor, but it probably has wider implications in regard to consultants and clerks of works. The architect is also a party providing services.

Clause 4.1 prohibits either party from assigning the whole or any part of the agreement without the other's written consent. This is simply stating the position under the general law whereby a party may usually assign a right, but not a duty without consent. Applied to architectural practice, it simply means that the architect must perform his or her part of the contract, say to make application for planning permission, and the client must do his or her part, i.e. to pay the architect's fees. *Clause 4.2* forbids subletting by the architect without consent, but the consent is not to be unreasonably withheld.

It is important to understand the difference between assignment and delegation. If an architect delegates (which as is noted above may not be done without permission) any duties, he or she still retains responsibility for the proper carrying out of such duties. If, however, some of those duties are allowed to be assigned, the architect is no longer responsible for them. The responsibility passes to the person to whom they have been assigned. To properly carry out an assignment a three-way contract must be drawn up, called 'novation', between the assignor (the person assigning), the assignee (the person to whom the duty is assigned) and the third party (the person to whom the duty is owed).

Clauses 5.1 to 5.17 deal with payment of fees and expenses. Fees are to be either:

- A percentage of the construction cost; *or*
- A lump sum; *or*
- A time charge; *or*
- Another agreed method.

The principle of percentage fees is well understood, but less so is the way in which such fees are to be calculated at various stages in the project. What constitutes the construction cost is set out in the definitions. But it will not be properly ascertained until the end of the contract when the final certificate is able to be issued. Before tenders are obtained the calculation will be based on the approved estimate of the construction cost. Between that time and when the contract is let, the lowest acceptable tender is used. After letting, it is either the certified value or the anticipated final account. After letting, therefore, there appears to be a choice of widely differing amounts. The certified value will be a very low figure at the beginning of the contract, gradually increasing at each certificate. The anticipated final account, on the other hand, will certainly vary as work progresses, but only to the extent that it takes into account variations and claims. It will always be a substantial sum greatly in excess of the certified value in the early stages of the contract.

Where a lump sum is to be the basis of fees, there are options, two of which, to varying degrees, alleviate the risk for the architect. It can be either:

- Calculated by using the percentage in the schedule of fees applied to the approved construction cost at the end of stage D; *or*
- Calculated, stage by stage, by using the same percentage, but applying it to the approved construction cost at the end of each stage and arriving at a lump sum for the next stage; *or*
- A fixed lump sum as generally understood.

Time charges need little explanation. Travelling time to and from the architect's offices is chargeable. Lump sum and time charges are reviewable every 12 months in accordance with the retail price index.

There is extensive provision for additional fees in *clause 5.6*. This is a difficult topic. The main reason is probably because architects vary tremendously in what they are prepared to do for the fee. In most cases, architects are prepared to do rather more than should be expected of them. The important criterion is that the extra work or expense caused to the architect must be for reasons beyond his or her control. The second consideration is that remuneration for the extra work must not be covered in some other way. If those criteria are satisfied, payment is to be on a time basis unless the architect and the client agree some other method. That is a perfectly adequate clause, but it was clearly considered to be necessary to give some examples and although the reasons are stated not to be limited to the examples, the danger is that clients will not be prepared to look beyond them. Some of the examples are that the client varies the scope of the services, or the architect must develop a new design, or there is delay and disruption by others.

If the architect does not complete the services, payment is to be in accordance with schedule 3 for complete services or stages, otherwise the fee is to be proportioned based on the architect's estimate of the percentage complete.

The architect is only entitled to recover expenses which are specified in schedule 3 unless the client has given prior authority for the expenditure. Expenses can amount to a substantial sum and architects can easily be caught out by this provision. Disbursements are to be reimbursed in the usual way. The architect must keep records of all expenses and disbursements and also of time spent, if that is to be the basis of charging. The client has the right to see the records.

An important clause deals with payment and makes clear that payment is due on the issue of accounts. The final day for payment of each account, to conform to the requirements of the Construction Act, is 30 days after the due date. Each fee account is to include all additional fees and expenses and the basis, if appropriate, is the architect's estimate of percentage completion. The client may not set off against payments to the architect unless the set-off has been agreed by the architect or awarded in adjudication, arbitration or litigation. The client is to give notices within 5 days of the due date, stating the amount to be paid and how it is calculated, and not later than 5 days before the final date for payment if it is intended to withhold money from any payment. Interest is payable on overdue amounts.

Where the client determines or suspends the architect's performance, the architect is entitled to all fees due at that date. If the architect suspends or determines due to the client's breach, the architect is to be paid all expenses and other costs necessarily incurred. This could be substantial and should roughly equate to what the architect could claim for repudiation at common law.

The copyright position is regulated by the Copyright, Designs and Patents Act 1988. There is also case law which has a bearing on the situation. There is no copyright in ideas or concepts, but only in the way in which they are expressed. Section 1 of the Act states that copyright is a property right in, among other things, original literary, dramatic, musical or artistic works. Section 4 makes clear that 'artistic work' includes 'a work of architecture being a building or a model for a building' and that 'building' includes any fixed structure and part of a building or fixed structure; 'artistic work' also means 'a graphic work, photograph, sculpture or collage, irrespective of artistic quality'.

In general, copyright remains with the originator or creator for his or her lifetime and for 50 years thereafter. Work produced by an employee is the copyright of the employer. Section 2 of the Act makes clear that no one may reproduce or copy any work without the consent of the originator. Assignment of copyright from the creator of the work to another may only be accomplished in writing. Such assignment can never be inferred (section 90). It is not usual to transfer copyright, but rather to grant a licence to use the copyright material for a particular purpose or for a particular period of time. It is not necessary to register ownership of copyright in any way, but in published works it is usual to indicate a claim to copyright thus: © John Smith (1991).

The Act introduces the concept of 'moral rights' (sections 77(4) to (5)). An architect has the right to be identified as the originator of the building where: 'in the case of a work of architecture in the form of a building or a model for a building, a sculpture or a work of artistic craftsmanship, copies of a graphic work representing it, or of a photograph of it, are issued to the public'. Section 77(5) states that: 'The author of a work of architecture in the form of a building also has the right to be identified on the building as constructed or, where more than one building is constructed to the design on the first to be constructed.' The creator must assert the right to be identified in this way before an infringement can take place.

Architects have copyright in their designs and a client usually has a licence, which may be express or implied, to reproduce the design as a building. In the absence of any agreement, the client must have paid a sufficient fee before a licence will be implied:

Stovin-Bradford v. *Volpoint Properties Ltd* (1971)[18]. In any event, even if sufficient has not been paid for a licence to reproduce in the form of a building to be implied, the client will be entitled to possess the drawings: *Gibbon* v. *Pease* (1905)[19].

The architect's normal remedy for infringement of copyright is to take out an injunction to prevent the carrying out of the work. This will not normally be granted if building work has already commenced on site: *Hunter* v. *Fitzroy Robinson and Partners* (1978)[20]. The alternative remedy is for the architect to sue for damages. Large amounts of damages will not usually be recovered unless it can be shown that the infringement of copyright was flagrant or a substantial benefit accrued to the infringer. Section 107 of the Copyright, Designs and Patents Act 1988 makes certain instances of infringement a criminal offence with penalties of fines and imprisonment. That particular provision is unlikely to have much application to the architect.

Clauses 6.1 and 6.2 do not attempt to amend the position under the general law. They simply clarify the architect's position. Copyright in all the architect's drawings and documents and in any building produced from such documents is the property of the architect and the architect asserts the right to be identified as the author of the project. The client, however, is to have a licence to copy the architect's drawings and other documents or software and to allow the other consultants to do the same, but only for the purpose of constructing the building on the site to which the design relates and related maintenance, operation, promotion, leasing or sale.

There are three important provisos:

- The architect is not to be liable if his designs are used for any purpose other than the purpose for which they were intended. It is probably useful to spell out this point although that would be the legal position in any event.
- If the client wishes to use the designs after the architect has completed the last service, but before the building has reached practical completion, there are two situations: the client must seek the architect's consent if RIBA stage D has not been completed or, if the architect has completed stage D, the client must pay the architect a reasonable licence fee (unless set out in schedule 3). This is probably somewhat stricter than the position under the general law.
- A valuable right is given to the architect to refuse to allow the client to use the documents, etc. if the client has not paid any monies properly due. The architect must first give 7 days'

notice. The client may resume the use once the outstanding sums are paid.

Clauses 7.1 to 7.3 contain valuable protection for the architect. The architect quite specifically does not warrant that the services will be completed in accordance with the timetable, that planning or other permissions will be granted, that the performance, work or products of others will be satisfactory or that any other body will be solvent even if the architect recommended the body. Given the propensity of architects to recommend products and contractors to their clients, this last is a very useful safeguard. The client may not start any action against the architect in contract or in tort after a period which is to be stated in the appendix has expired. The period is to be calculated from the date of completion of the last service or from the date of practical completion of the project, whichever is earlier. This is the opportunity for the architect to reduce the period of time for which he or she will be liable.

Clause 7.3 is an attempt to limit the architect's liability, but the clause is so complex (the first sentence is over 12 lines long) that there must be some doubt whether it will achieve that end. The pity is that it replaces two of the clauses in the Memorandum of Agreement of the former SFA/92 but, at least in the view of these authors, it does not do so with anything like the same clarity. The SFA/92 clause restricting liability to no more than a specified sum was upheld in a case in 1998[21]. In essence, the new clause appears to say that a sum to be inserted in the appendix will be the limit of the architect's liability, but that if the architect's responsibility for loss or damage is less, that is what must be paid. The way in which any lesser liability is to be assessed is the extent to which it is 'just and equitable' having regard to the architect's liability for the damage in question compared to the responsibilities for the damage of others concerned and assuming that the others have provided contractual undertakings to the client which are as stringent as the architect's undertakings.

Clause 7.4 obliges the architect to maintain PI insurance for the amount and during the period stated in the appendix. There is the usual proviso that the insurance is available at commercially reasonable rates. The architect must produce insurance documents on request and inform the client if such insurance ceases to be available.

Clause 7.5 makes clear that if the client has informed the architect that a warranty will be required, the terms of the warranty must be attached to the agreement (see section 6.5).

Clauses 8.1 to 8.8 deal with the position if the contract is suspended or terminated. Without such a provision, neither party would be entitled to terminate or suspend unless they could establish grounds at common law, e.g. repudiation. It is worth noting that usually there is no right to terminate at common law because the client fails to pay. That is simply a breach of contract for which the remedy is damages. The client is entitled to suspend any or all the architect's services by giving 7 days' notice. To comply with the Construction Act, the architect may also suspend performance on 7 days' notice if the client fails to pay. The notice must state the grounds for suspension and, strangely, the obligations affected. The Act does not require the specifying of the obligations affected and under the Act, a party may suspend all obligations. The architect must resume performance when the money is paid in full. Insofar as the contractual provision falls short or is more onerous than the Act, the Act applies. The Act also provides that a suspending party is entitled to have the period of suspension ignored when the total period for performance of obligations is calculated. In effect, the architect will be entitled to an extension of time. SFA/99 extends that principle to cover suspension by the client. Any suspension by either architect or client which lasts longer than six months entitles the architect to request instructions. If no instructions are given within the next 30 days, the architect can treat his obligations as determined.

Either party may determine any or all performance of the architect's obligations by the giving of 14 days' written notice to the other. The notice must state the grounds for determination and the services affected. This provision is a welcome improvement on the equivalent SFA/92 clause which referred to 'reasonable notice' – always a difficult concept. It is not immediately obvious why the notice should state the grounds for determination, because no particular required grounds are set out in the agreement. Neither, it seems, must the grounds be such as would entitle a party to treat the agreement as repudiated under the general law. Presumably the requirement will be satisfied by the flimsiest of reasons. An alternative provision for determination allows the deed to be done immediately on notice by either party if either become insolvent or the architect cannot continue with the commission due to death or incapacity. After determination for any reason and if the client requests, the architect must give the client copies of the drawings and other documents, etc. which the client has a licence to use, but subject to the copyright restrictions in clause 6.2 and payment of the architect's reasonable charges for copying. Were it not for that last provision, the architect would be obliged to provide the documents without being reimbursed for copying.

There is a provision preserving the parties 'accrued rights and remedies'.

Dispute resolution is dealt with under *clauses 9.1 to 9.6*. Clause 9 is complex. There are four possible methods of resolving disputes. It is essential that the parties do not make a mistake in deciding on the appropriate method or there may be financial consequences. The methods are:

■ *Negotiation or conciliation*
This is optional and the parties may attempt to settle their differences by means of the RIBA Conciliation Procedure 1998. The only purpose in including this method in the conditions is simply to draw the parties' attention to an alternative to confrontation.

■ *Adjudication*
Where the Housing Grants, Construction and Regeneration Act 1996 applies, either party may opt to have any dispute or differences arising under the agreement settled by an adjudicator. The procedure is to be as set out in the Model Adjudication Procedures published by the Construction Industry Council. The remainder of this provision is designed to comply with the Act.

■ *Arbitration*
Where the parties have opted for arbitration as the principal method of dispute resolution, they may agree a person or, failing agreement, a person may be appointed at the application of either party by the appointor named in the appendix. If no one is named, the default provision is for the President of the Royal Institute of British Architects to appoint. This is an agreement to arbitrate which falls under the Arbitration Act 1996. There is a proviso that, if the law of the agreement is stated to be the law of England and Wales, either party may choose to pursue a remedy through the courts if they are seeking to recover a sum of money not exceeding £3,000 or whatever other sum is set out by legislation in accordance with section 91 of the Arbitration Act 1996. In addition, if the claimant in an arbitration is an architect under an unamended SFA/99, the arbitrator does not have the power to award security for costs[22].

- *Litigation*

    If, in the articles of agreement, the parties have opted for litigation instead of arbitration, any dispute can be dealt with in the courts. The parties must give careful thought to the possibility of litigation although most architects would welcome an architect arbitrator appointed by the President of the RIBA rather than a judge to deal with disputes about the appointment.

Very importantly, the client must indemnify the architect for all the architect's costs in any proceedings together with a reasonable sum for the architect's time if the architect gets a judgment or award for fees and expenses or if the client fails in any claim against the architect. This has the effect of reimbursing an architect who is successful in arbitration or litigation for virtually the whole amount of costs. Without such a provision, a successful litigant can usually expect to recover anything between 60% to 90% of costs, depending on circumstances.

6.5 Duty of care agreements (collateral warranties)

Strictly speaking a collateral warranty[23] is a contract which runs alongside another contract and is subsidiary to it. Such documents have proliferated in recent years and it is common for contractors, nominated and domestic subcontractors and suppliers and all the consultants to be required to execute a collateral warranty in favour of the building owner, the fund providing the money for the project and/or any number of prospective tenants. It used to be the view that such an agreement was not very important because it merely stated in contractual terms the duties which everyone knew the architect owed to a third party in tort. That view is no longer tenable.

Before looking at some of the provisions commonly encountered in forms of warranty, or duty of care agreements (as they are often called when used in relation to consultants), it should be understood why they are so important to the building owner. There is a fundamental contract principle that only the parties to a contract have any rights or duties under that contract. The principle is called 'privity of contract'. For example, in a contract between a client A and an architect B, each has rights and duties to the other. B has a duty to design a building for A, but he has no duty to any third party C to design that building. That would be the case even if the contract stated that he had such a duty.

To put it at its most basic, if A and B include a term in their contract that they will each pay £100 to C, the term will be ineffective in that if they fail to honour it, C will be unable to enforce it, because C is not a party to the contract. In a similar way, if A and B include a term that C will pay each of them £100, they will be unable to enforce it. At the time of writing, a bill is passing through Parliament dealing with third party rights in contract. The bill threatens to overturn some of these cherished concepts in favour of giving third parties mentioned in contracts some entitlement to enforce provisions in their favour. However, it appears that parties to a contract will be able to exclude third party rights by inserting a provision to that effect in the contract. If that is correct, the position is likely to be largely unchanged in practice.

Applying this principle to the architect's conditions of engagement, if something goes wrong with the building which is clearly a design fault, only the client can take action against the architect for breach of the conditions of engagement. For example, if an architect designs a house for the client, the house is sold on to a third party and a design defect then becomes apparent, the third party cannot take action against the architect under the conditions of engagement between the architect and client. At one time, the third party would have been able to overcome this kind of problem by suing in the tort of negligence if there was no contractual relationship. A plaintiff suing in negligence must show that:

- The defendant had a duty of care to the plaintiff; *and*
- The defendant was in breach of that duty; *and*
- As a result of the breach the plaintiff suffered damage of the kind which is recoverable.

So, in the first place, the plaintiff would try to show that the defendant architect owed a duty of care. The courts appeared willing to find such a duty in many instances. But the House of Lords case of *Murphy* v. *Brentwood District Council* (1990)[24] made it very difficult for a third party to successfully sue in tort for a defective building.

In broad terms, the decision in *Murphy* means that if an architect negligently designs a building, recovery in the tort of negligence will only be possible if the defective design causes injury or death to a person or if it causes damage to property other than the building which is the subject of the defective design. Even then, the recovery will be limited to compensating for the injury or damage to other persons or property and will not cover rectification of the original design defect. The concept is much the same as product liability and the Lords saw no reason for making any distinction.

The result is that a third party can no longer rely on suing an architect in negligence except in very circumscribed situations such as if the action can be brought under the reliance principle set out in *Hedley Byrne* v. *Heller* (1964)[25]. Contracts are concerned with achieving specific results and contain many terms relating to quality. Tort is concerned with remedying wrongs. The courts now emphasise the difference. To take a simple example: if an architect specifies the wrong external cladding which soon deteriorates, that is a breach of contract for which the law lays down remedies as between the architect and the client. If the cladding is so inadequate that it falls off the building and injures a passer-by, that may be negligence for which the passer-by has a remedy against the architect in tort. The situation has been muddied in recent years by a number of legal cases which have enabled the original party to a contract to bring an action against the other party for breach of contract even though the original party has since sold on the building to a purchaser and received full value for it[26]. However, the situations where that can occur are likely to be limited, because it appears that if the original party (but no longer the owner of the property) is to be able to take action, among other things the other party must be shown to have known at the time of entering into the contract that the building was to be sold on or tenanted.

The purpose of a duty of care agreement is to create a contractual relationship between the architect and third parties who otherwise would be unlikely to have any remedy if design defects became apparent after completion. At the time of writing, there is a standard form of warranty (CoWa/F) in favour of funders and (CoWa/P&T)[27] in favour of purchasers or tenants. There are also a great many other forms of warranty in circulation, some of which have been especially drafted by solicitors with a greater or lesser experience of the architectural profession and the construction industry generally. The following are points which architects should bear in mind when called upon to sign a duty of care agreement.

6.5.1 General

The basic problem is that, by virtue of the agreement, the architect acquires liabilities towards a party who has paid no fee for the privilege. If the architect does not take care, greater duties may be undertaken towards the third party than those which the architect already owes to the client under the conditions of appointment. If it can possibly be avoided an architect should not enter into a duty of care agreement. Some architects take the view that they should not resist requests to execute duty of care agreements because, as professionals, they should be prepared to take responsibility for their actions. This is a most laudable sentiment, but architects should consider whether they wish to accept a greater burden of liability than the general law would impose. That is the situation where a duty of care agreement is executed as in any other freely negotiated contractual situation. If architects do execute such agreements, there seems to be no good reason why they should not charge an appropriate, rather than a nominal, fee for the warranty. The opportunity afforded to a third party to take legal action should be worth a substantial sum. However, in this as in most other matters, commercial pressures may force the architect into executing such agreements without charge.

6.5.2 Execution

The essential differences between a deed and a simple contract have been explained in section 6.4.1. Architects will usually be asked to enter into a duty of care agreement in the form of a deed, because it extends the potential liability period to 12 years and no consideration is necessary. If the original conditions of engagement are under hand, an architect could be in the position of having a longer period of liability to the third party than to the original client. In duty of care agreements executed as simple contracts there will always be a term stipulating that the architect receives a small sum, usually about £10, in order to make a valid contract. This is because the agreement is always very one-sided and, without the nominal sum, it is very unlikely that any other consideration on the part of the third party would be present.

6.5.3 Skill and care

There is usually a term by which the architect warrants reasonable skill and care in the performance of his or her duties. This is the normal professional standard of care and as such it is not inherently objectionable. Some warranties, however, take the position further and ask the architect to warrant 'due' or 'all proper' skill, care and 'diligence'. Because it is not at all certain what greater liability such terms may impose, architects should be wary about entering into agreements on that basis and should stick to tried and tested definitions of their professional obligations. There should also be a proviso that the architect will under no circumstances have a greater liability to the third party than the architect already owes to the client. An architect should never warrant fitness for purpose. That is clearly a very much higher standard of care.

6.5.4 Materials

Architects are often asked to warrant that they will ensure that certain materials will not be used in the construction of the building. An architect cannot warrant any such thing. The best that can be done is to warrant that the architect will not specify certain precisely defined materials. References such as 'any materials known to be deleterious' are to be avoided. The use of blacklists is gradually deceasing in favour of reliance on the architect's specifying skills. At least one manufacturer has mounted a successful legal challenge against the blacklisting of its products and there is scope for further challenges in the future[28].

6.5.5 Copyright

There is no sensible reason why a professional should surrender his or her copyright. It is enough to grant a licence for certain specific uses such as repair and maintenance. If an architect does agree to assign copyright in the designs, it seems that the architect would not be precluded from reproducing particular details in another design provided a major part of the original design was not reproduced. Architects should beware the granting of an *irrevocable* licence to use their designs, because it means exactly what it says and the licence could not be withdrawn in the future even if the client fails to pay.

6.5.6 Assignment

Assignment is a provision which allows the party to whom the architect gives the warranty to assign the benefits of the warranty to other parties. It is this clause which gives the agreement much of its value. The biggest problem with the right to assign is that the architect has no control over the identity of the future warrantee. The worst clauses allow assignment, without consent, to unlimited numbers of people for an indefinite period. If the architect agrees to an assignment clause, it should allow assignment once only within a limited period of time, say two or three years subject to the architect's consent.

6.5.7 Professional indemnity

The party taking the benefit of the warranty will principally be interested in the architect's professional indemnity insurance. Many architects enter into duty of care agreements with terms so onerous that the insurance would be repudiated by the insurers if ever a claim was made. Every agreement must be put to the insurers before it is signed, or the indemnity insurance will be at risk. A term by which the architect agrees to maintain indemnity insurance cover at a particular level for a specific number of years is very common, but virtually useless for practical purposes. The most an architect can do is to agree to use best endeavours to keep such a policy in force provided cover remains available at commercially viable rates.

An interesting question concerns the damages which a client could recover from the architect for breach of such a condition. If the breach was not discovered, as seems likely, until the occurrence of an event which warranted calling upon the architect's indemnity insurance, there would be no such insurance to meet the claim and, therefore, presumably no money to pay damages caused by the breach. Those damages would, in any event, be what the client would have lost. The client would have lost the chance to call upon the architect's insurance.

6.5.8 Funders

Where the third party is providing financial backing for the development, they will require some kind of control over the situation if things go wrong between architect and client. It is usual for a term to be inserted which provides that if the architect wishes to terminate the appointment, the architect must give a specified number of days' notice to the funder. If the funder then gives notice to the architect, the architect loses the right to terminate or accept repudiation and must, thereafter, accept the funder's instructions in respect of the development. This type of clause poses two basic difficulties: first, the original client may object if he or she is not a party to the warranty; secondly, the architect loses the right to terminate. If architects agree to the inclusion of this type of term, they should ensure that the funder can only take over the appointment by novation subject to payment of all outstanding fees.

References

(1)   (1974) 1 All ER 319.

(2)   (1985) 32 BLR 51.

(3)   *Pacific Associates* v. *Baxter* (1988) 6 Con LR 90.

(4)   See *Calil* v. *Sallis* (1987) 4 Const LJ 125; *Pacific Associates* v. *Baxter* (1988) 6 Con LR 90; *Henderson* v. *Merritt Syndicates* (1994) 69 BLR 26; *Conway* v. *Crow Kelsey* (1994) 39 Con LR 1.

(5)   See Green, R. (1995) *Architect's Guide to Running a Job*, 5th edn, Architectural Press Ltd.

(6)   Chappell, D. (1996) *Report Writing for Architects and Project Managers*, 3rd edn, Blackwell Science.

(7)   See *Partridge* v. *Morris* (1995) CILL 1095 and *Valerie Pratt* v. *George Hill* (1987) 38 BLR 25.

(8)   The current indicative scales are taken from the RIBA's *Engaging an Architect: Guidance for Clients on Fees* (1994, revised 1996).

(9)   It should be noted that the RIBA 1999 forms of agreement do not reflect this position.

(10)   At the time of writing that is still the position in Northern Ireland.

(11)   See *Whittal Builder* v. *Chester-Le-Street District Council* (the 1985 case) (1996) 12 Const LJ 356.

(12)   Described in the last edition.

(13)   Latham, Michael, (1994) *Constructing the Team*, Stationery Office.

(14)   (1957) 2 All ER 118.

(15)   (1966) 4 BLR 50.

(16)   (1986) 5 Con LR 1.

(17)   (1984) 1 Con LR 114.

(18)   (1971) 3 All ER 570.

(19)   (1905) 1 KB 810.

(20)   (1978) 10 BLR 84.

(21)   *Moores* v. *Yakeley Associates Ltd* (1998) CILL 1446.

(22)   Section 38(3) of the Arbitration Act 1996 and clause 9.5.1 of the SFA/99 Conditions.

(23)   Winward Fearon (2000) *Collateral Warranties*, 2nd edn, Blackwell Science.

(24) (1990) 50 BLR 1.

(25) [1964] AC 465, and see section 6.2, page 84.

(26) *St Martins Property Corporation Ltd and St Martins Property Investments Ltd* v. *Sir Robert McAlpine & Sons Ltd and Linden Gardens Trust Ltd* v. *Lenesta Sludge Disposals Ltd, McLaughlin & Harvey plc and Ashwell Construction Company Ltd* (1992) 57 BLR 57; *Darlington* v. *Wiltshire* (1994) 69 BLR 1.

(27) Published by the British Property Federation.

(28) *Kirkforthar Bricks* v. *West Lothian Council* (1995) unreported. See also 'Blacklists', *Practice*, issue 150, *RIBA Journal*, January 1998, pp. 83–4.

Chapter 7

Stage A: Appraisal

7.1 Feasibility studies

Once the architect has found out what the client wishes to build, where and when, the next stage is to decide whether it is feasible to build. If not, the project will abort at that stage. Feasibility, however, may depend on any one of a number of factors or a combination of several factors. The decision to proceed or to stop lies with the client of course, but it is the architect's function to present the appropriate information to the client in a structured way so that it is made as easy as possible for the client to come to a decision. Clearly, the client's decision may be influenced by matters which are not known to the architect; therefore, it is always wise for the architect to investigate more rather than less widely. Because it is difficult at this stage to decide just what data might be relevant, the architect should always include rather than exclude information.

There are some very small projects for which a formal feasibility study may be inappropriate. It should be remembered, however, that it is not the size of the project which determines whether a feasibility study should be done, but associated factors such as complexity, situation, type of development, and so on. It is a sensible procedure for the architect always to approach a feasibility study as though the client requires a formal report to be prepared. In some cases, particularly in the case of a large company or any organisation whose officers have to satisfy others besides themselves, a feasibility report will be mandatory.

Whether the architect is to produce a report or simply to investigate and report orally to the client, it is vital to have a check-list in order to prevent the inadvertent omission of an important item. The following check-list and brief notes are not intended to be exhaustive, and some of the items will apply only to certain developments, but it is a suggested starting point which architects can mould to suit individual requirements.

Terms of reference

It is always sensible to bear in mind the terms of reference, or put another way, what it is that the architect is being asked to do. It is prudent to make a list of the assumptions being made so that the client knows what is known for certain, what is estimated and what is merely assumed for the moment. Typical areas for assumption are that a proper measured survey has not been carried out, in the case of an existing building a structural analysis may not have been done and the structural stability of the building may be assumed. If there is any reason to doubt the structural stability, short of a detailed structural survey and calculation, no assumption should be made and the architect should obtain authority to have the structure properly investigated. Other assumptions which may have to be made concern boundaries and the ground condition.

Consultants

Consultants who might be involved in the study include:

■ Quantity surveyor/cost manager
■ Structural engineer
■ Geotechnical engineer
■ Mechanical and electrical services engineer
■ Acoustics engineer
■ Landscape architect

Authorities

Statutory and other authorities and suppliers who may be involved are:

■ Planning
■ Highways
■ Drainage
■ Housing
■ Education
■ Police
■ Transport
■ Fire
■ British Coal

- Electricity
- Water
- Gas
- British Telecom
- The Commission for Architecture and the Built Environment
- Forestry Commission
- English Heritage
- National Trust

Site location

Site location should be considered in relation to the distance from the nearest centre of population and the general topography. Neighbouring watercourses, use of adjoining land and any possible nuisance should be examined.

Access

Means of getting to the site is always important; in some cases it can be crucial to the success or otherwise of the project. Bus, train and air services can be vital to a building which hopes to prosper as a conference centre. Road routes are also important.

Shops

The type of project will determine the importance of nearby shops on its viability. Housing must be reasonably near to shops, and elderly person accommodation is more attractive if it has a few small shops nearby such as newsagents, chemists and general stores. Mobile shops should not be forgotten and the distance of the project from, and ease of access to, the nearest large shopping centre should be recorded.

Health

The following are important:

- Doctors' surgeries
- Dental surgeries
- Opticians

- Chiropodists
- Clinic
- Health centre
- General hospital facilities
- Proposed future provision

Social and recreational

It is worthwhile making a complete list of this type of provision in the area for certain kinds of proposed development. The only accurate way to compile such a list is for the architect to walk over every part of the surrounding area.

Education

A wide range of educational provision is possible and in the case of residential development it is essential that appropriate provision is available. Any projected educational developments in the area must also be noted.

Employment

The names and locations of principal employers in an area may be a crucial factor in the viability of housing developments.

Rights

The following rights should be recorded if existing or if thought to exist:

- Light
- Way
- Support
- Party walls
- Easements
- Covenants (restrictive or otherwise)

Planning points

- Whether there is any agreement in principle
- Whether there is any earlier permission concerning the same site
- The usual standard conditions inserted in planning permissions in that area
- Specific requirements in regard to storey heights and number, densities, access provision, permitted materials, parking provision
- Any other planning permissions for nearby sites
- Building lines
- Improvement lines
- Road proposals

Licensing

If required.

Drainage

General provision and problems.

Architectural/historical

Matters such as whether the building, if an existing building is being examined, or whether the site is in a conservation area should be considered. Even if there is no statutory protection for the building, the architect will want to record whether there are any interesting and attractive features. The reaction of local amenity societies should also be considered. Although not decisive, opposition from such a quarter can cause serious delays to the process of obtaining appropriate statutory approvals.

Geological factors

Fault lines, unusual ground conditions and mining subsidence are all problem areas.

Statutory undertakings and services

What services, if any, are readily available to the site or can be connected without undue problems. Any easements or diversions required. Other points regarding street lighting, high voltage cables overhead or underground, sub-stations.

Policy

Whether there is any local or central government policy which affects the scheme.

Grants

If any are available.

Structural analysis

Comments on existing structures, if any, in relation to the proposals.

Access

Number of entries to site and width, if metalled surface or special difficulties.

Design possibilities

Options available in broad terms with regard to disposition of various elements set against the site factors, structural options, aesthetics, historical and urban factors.

Estimate of cost

In broad terms, stating the basis of the estimate (i.e. 'current prices'), whether VAT is included and so on. Some clients insist on a fairly sophisticated life cycle analysis which the architect would usually request the quantity surveyor to carry out. In fact, there is little to be gained from such an exercise at this stage, when very little is known about the building.

Programme

Possible design team programme and future building programme in the form of key start and finish dates.

Conclusions

Advice to the client, with short reasons.

Approvals/decisions

A list of the approvals and decisions required from the client and a time schedule for receipt if the programme indicated earlier is to be implemented. This is a valuable method of getting the client to respond.

Additional material

Whatever is useful to assist the client in understanding the issues and reaching a decision, such as charts, graphs, maps, drawings and photographs.

7.2 Consultants

A consultant is someone who gives expert advice or assistance. Common types of consultants in connection with construction work are:

- Quantity surveyor/cost manager
- Structural engineer
- Electrical engineer
- Mechanical services engineer
- Planner
- Interior designer
- Landscape architect

A consultant, of course, can be anyone the architect considers necessary to assist in the development of the project. The architect may be a consultant on the same basis as the others in those instances when another construction professional has been chosen to be the lead consultant or where a project manager has been engaged to administer the contract. In many cases, however, the architect is the lead consultant because of the particular breadth and scope of training he or she has undergone and we will assume that this is the case in this instance (see section 7.3 for a discussion of project managers).

If the project is small, the architect may feel capable of carrying out the whole of the design work. The professional indemnity insurance, however, must always include all the kinds of work the architect undertakes to carry out. On larger projects, the architect should nominate such consultants as are required to deal with those areas of work which are outside the architect's competence. Consultants are employed either directly by the client or by the architect. It is better for the architect if the consultant is employed directly by the client, because there is a direct contractual link established between consultant and client which is clearly useful in the case of problems with liability and fees (see Chapter 6, section 6.4). Where the architect appoints the consultant, any action in respect of the consultant's negligence will be taken by the client against the architect. In order to recover the whole or a contribution to any damages, the architect will join the consultant as third party. Therefore, care must be taken that the consultant has appropriate professional indemnity insurance and provides the architect with an indemnity in respect of the work carried out.

It is good practice, indeed almost essential, to employ consultants as soon as their need is identified. In practice, this will be shortly after the architect has clarified the brief with the client. It is sometimes difficult to convince a client that consultants are necessary. The client is conscious of the additional fees. It is part of the architect's duty to advise the client when consultants are required. To delay the appointment of consultants may result in the redesign of large parts of the project at a late stage.

However consultants are appointed, they must be made aware of the extent of the services required from them. Ideally, this information should be imparted during the first design team meeting (when all consultants and the client are present), carefully recorded and made the basis of the contract of engagement. All consultants must report to the architect unless another construction professional has the co-ordinating role.

The standard forms of contract do not generally make any reference to consultants other than the quantity surveyor. The exception is the JCT Management Contract 1998, but there the reference is confined to the Articles and they are not mentioned in the conditions. All consultants should report to the architect. Obviously, it is essential that they inspect their own work on site, but no contract gives them power to give instructions. A consultant who wishes to issue an instruction should first submit it to the architect who may incorporate it into an architect's instruction. Indeed strictly they can only enter the site if the architect makes them authorised representatives for the sole purpose of inspecting their own portions of the works. The architect should obtain an appropriate certificate from each consultant in respect of the practical completion of each specialist section of work.

7.3   Project managers

Although at one time architects were considered to be the obvious choices as the professionals most suited to lead the building team, that is no longer necessarily the case. Over the last few years the concept of project management has steadily gained ground. A project manager, however, may not be the same person as the lead consultant or the contract administrator. All these terms contain a mixture of the woolly and the legally specific. A definition of a project manager which was approved by the RIBA was:

> 'The Project Manager is a construction professional who can be given *executive authority and responsibility* to assist the client to identify the project objectives and subsequently supply the technical expertise to assess, procure, monitor and control the external resources required to achieve those objectives, defined in terms of time, cost, quality and function.'

That definition is worth careful study. Clearly the kind of person capable of carrying out that role will be formidable. The reference to 'control the external resources' opens up a whole new dimension and one wonders how feasible it is to have one person in this position. It could never be said of architects in traditional scenarios that they controlled external resources. To control is to dominate and to regulate. It could never be said that architects controlled contractors.

Project management considered in the vacuum, unfortunately all too common, is the subject of many books and articles. The concept of project management is not particularly linked to construction; there is no good reason why it should be so linked. It is well expressed by the following definition:

> 'Project management is a collection of loosely connected techniques, some of which are useful in bringing projects to a successful conclusion. Clearly, the project manager manages. He must think about motivation, team building, career growth, financial control, and all the other things that concern managers. In addition he has to head off into the unknown. His path is not clear, his path has not been trod before, but his objective will be clear.
>
> Something that is special about project management, something that separates project management from plain old management, is the need and the emphasis on planning. Simply because the project management team is following no known path, they must think ahead all the time. They are continually faced with decisions about the route ahead and must plan for events that are long distant in the future. Hence here is a formula that neatly paints a picture:
>
> $$\frac{management + planning}{project\ management}\text{'}^{[1]}$$

Project managers may be divided broadly into two categories:

- Project managers type 1 who act as the technical arm of the employer
- Project managers type 2 who carry out the contract administration role in regard to building contracts

The contractual relationships are quite different. If this difference is not appreciated, very serious consequences may result.

Project managers type 1

Project managers type 1 act as the employer's representative. Generally they act as agent for the employer with the power to do, in relation to the project, everything the employer could do. They will interview and appoint consultants and carry out the briefing exercise, having first been briefed by the employer. The advantage to the employer is that he has a skilled professional looking after his interests and being paid to watch the other professionals. The project manager has no powers under the building contract. Indeed, most building contracts do not even acknowledge his existence. There is now provision under JCT 98 for an employer's representative to be appointed to carry out the employer's functions. Unless the standard form contracts are amended, the project manager has no right to enter site, or to attend site meetings. Most project managers in this position tend to be notable for strong views forcibly expressed. A contractor taking instructions from a project manager in this position does so at his peril. A project manager has no status on site during the progress of the Works. This is probably the usual position occupied by the person termed project manager. It should be noted that it does not replace the traditional architect's role. There is still a need for a lead consultant, whoever that might be.

Project managers type 2

A project manager type 2 performs all the functions of a contract administrator in regard to the building contract. Only he may issue instructions and certificates. Where this kind of project manager is employed, it is essential that the appointment documents of the other construction professionals reflect the situation. For example, the project manager is responsible for co-ordinating their roles and must have the authority to do so. The project manager in this situation wields a great deal of power. If the project manager's function is to manage the project, this type of project manager is closest to that role. However, it is comparatively rare to find a project manager in this position. Because this is the role traditionally taken by architects, an architect trained in project management techniques makes a good type 2 project manager.

Whatever the role, and it is possible to find a project manager working solely for a contractor, the project manager is supposed to have certain skills. Depending on the role of the project manager, the required skills may vary. Shorn of excessive jargon, they are:

- Management
- Construction law
- Contract law
- Value management
- Value engineering
- Procurement and contract options
- Project planning
- Briefing
- Cost control

- Risk management
- Contract administration
- Dispute resolution

There are various courses on which a budding project manager may enrol. Before choosing a course, the prospective project manager may care to reflect on the fact that project management is not a universal skill. Project management of a building project with its many disparate elements is quite different from, say, project management of a new product through a factory.

7.4 Procurement paths and implications for the professional

The procurement system should be the most appropriate in the light of the criteria signalled to the architect by the client during and after the briefing stage. In choosing a procurement path, the key criteria are the client's priorities in respect of:

- Time: economy and certainty
- Cost: economy and certainty
- Control: apportionment of risk
- Quality: in design and construction
- Size/value: small/medium/large
- Complexity: complex/simple

There are as many different procurement systems as there are pebbles on the beach, but some of them are different only in detail. The principle systems may be expressed as follows:

- Traditional
- Project management
- Design and manage
- Management contracting
- Construction management

7.4.1 Traditional

Very broadly, the traditional system is where the client commissions an architect to take a brief, produce designs and construction information, invite tenders and administer the project during the construction period and settle the final account. If the building is other than small and straightforward, the architect will advise the client to appoint other consultants to deal with particular items, such as quantities and cost estimating services generally, structural calculations and heating design. The contractor, who has no design responsibility, will normally be selected by competitive tender or there may be good grounds for negotiating a tender.

The essentials are that the architect is the independent advisor to the client carrying out the design. The contractor is only responsible for executing the work in accordance with the drawings and specifications produced by the architect and other professionals. Figure 7.1 shows the relationships of the parties in diagrammatic terms.

7.4.2   Project management

Although project management is a somewhat imprecise term, it has much in common with the traditional system (see section 7.3 for a description of the role). However, the architect is not the leader of the team; the project manager is the leader. The project manager, of course, can be an architect and most architects would say that an architect is the obvious choice for the post in view of his or her particular training. Essentially, the project management system places most emphasis on planning and management. Therefore, a person, whether architect, engineer or surveyor, with the relevant project management skills is required. The project manager is likely to appear in one of two principal roles: either simply as the technical agent of the employer for the purposes of the project or as the professional with the authority to manage the project, including organising and co-ordinating all consultants. In either case, the project manager acts as a link between the client and the design team. Depending on the particular kind of project management chosen, the contract administrator may be the project manager or the architect. Figures 7.2 and 7.3 show the relationship of the parties in diagrammatic terms.

7.4.3   Design and build

Design and build is a system which has grown in popularity and which appears in various guises. It places responsibility for both design and construction in the hands of the contractor. There are variations in the name and there are subtle differences in meaning. *Design and build*, for example, refers to the basic system where a contractor carries out the two functions. *Design and construct*

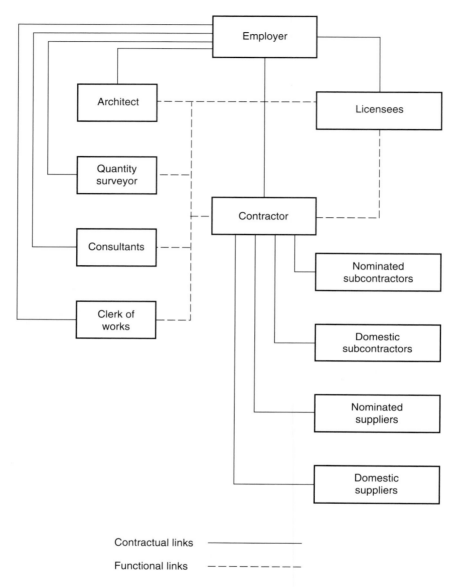

Fig. 7.1 Traditional contract.

includes design and build and other types of construction such as purely engineering works. *Develop and construct* often describes a situation where a contractor takes a partially completed design and develops it into a fully detailed design. *Package deal* can be used to refer to either of these. In theory, the term suggests that the con-

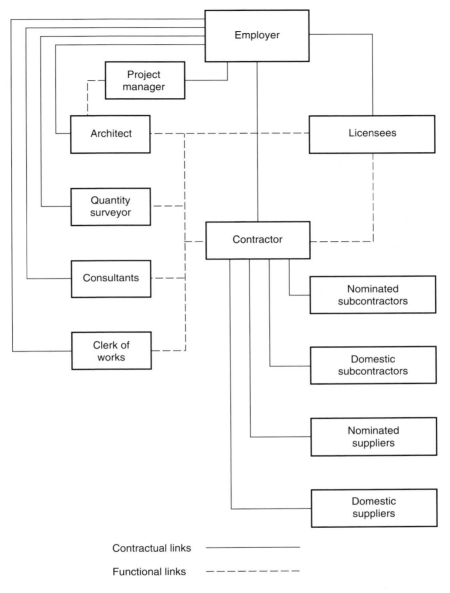

Contractual links ────────────

Functional links ─ ─ ─ ─ ─ ─ ─

Fig. 7.2 Project management type 1.

tractor is responsible for providing everything in one package and it is particularly apt when referring to an industrialised building. *Turnkey* contracting is a system in which the contractor really is responsible for everything, including furniture and pictures on the

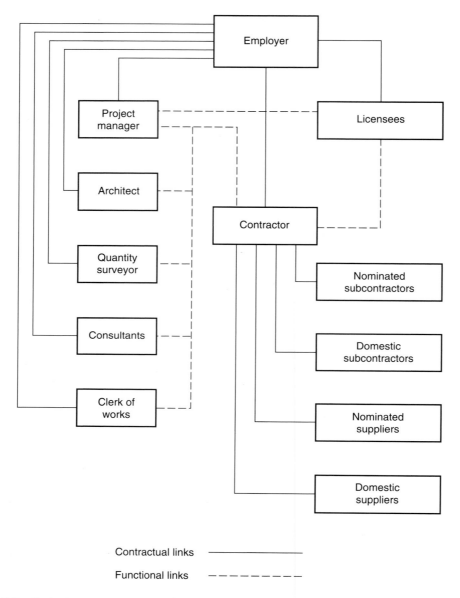

Fig. 7.3   Project management type 2.

walls if required. The idea is that the employer simply turns the
key and begins using the building – hence the name.

Many architects are unduly concerned about design and build as
though every such contract is one less for an architect to design.
Nothing could be further from the truth. Unless the building is

very simple, the contractor will seek an architect to carry out the design including all the preliminary briefing and feasibility work where necessary and also the preparation of constructional drawings. From the client's point of view, an independent advisor is required to look after the client's interests before, during and after construction. There is no doubt that the architect's role is different from the traditional image, but that should not be a problem. It does not necessarily mean, because an architect has a contractor for a client, that he or she will be unable to produce good architecture. It is very much in the contractor's interest that the client is happy with the finished building.

The employer may approach a design and build contractor as soon as the intention to build starts to form. The contractor then takes charge of the project until completion. The architectural function will either be carried out in the contractor's own architects' department or, more commonly, by subletting the work to a firm of architects in private practice. An architect in such an instance will owe a duty to the contractor which will depend on the conditions of engagement agreed for the work. Generally, the duty will probably be to carry out the architectural functions in obtaining and satisfying the brief and perhaps to carry out quality control duties on behalf of the contractor during the construction period. An architect in those circumstances will have no duty to the employer other than the common law duty to ensure that the design will not result in injury or death to the employer or those who will use the building and damage to property other than the building itself[2].

Alternatively, the employer may engage a full design team to complete the design of the building and a great many production drawings in some detail before seeking tenders from contractors to complete the design and construct the building. Most commonly, the employer will engage an architect to prepare an outline scheme together with a performance specification on which contractors will be invited to tender. The contractor will engage an architect to do the detailed design development work and to produce the production information to satisfy the performance specification.

A system which is increasing in popularity involves what is known as a 'consultant switch'. In this system, an architect or even a full design team is engaged by the employer to prepare all the initial material, and tenders are invited on the basis that the successful contractor will take the design team on board as the contractor's consultants to complete the work. The architect must remember who the client is at any particular moment, because the contractor will require somewhat different service from that which was given to the employer. After the switch, the employer must either do without independent advice, or engage another architect for that purpose. The very worst thing that an architect could do would be to try and act for both employer and contractor. There is a clear conflict of interest. This system is often wrongly referred to as 'novation'. Novation is similar in general effect, but with some important differences. It is a legal procedure by which a contract between the architect and the employer is replaced by another contract on identical terms between architect and contractor. Because, as noted above, the contract between architect and employer and between architect and contractor will require different terms, novation agreements commonly incorporate a schedule of changes. The agreement must be made between all three parties. It is sometimes seen as a means of assembling all the design responsibility in one place more effectively than can be achieved by other means. Whether that is so is open to question.

A particular point which architects should watch if they are asked to carry out work for contractors in a design and build scenario is the extent of the design obligation. An architect's normal obligation, like that of any other professional, is to use reasonable skill and care. In contrast, the normal design and build liability, unless expressly amended, is to produce an end result which is fit for its purpose if that purpose is made known. The contractor may well attempt to engage an architect on 'fit for purpose' terms. Quite apart from the fact that such liability is very onerous and admits of no 'state of the art' defence, the architect's insurers are almost certain to refuse cover (see Chapter 17, section 17.5).

Figure 7.4 shows the relationship of the parties in diagrammatic terms.

7.4.4 Design and manage

Design and manage is not as yet very common in the UK. Single point responsibility rests with a professional who may be an architect, engineer or surveyor. Besides being responsible for the design of the project the professional also manages the project in the sense of managing the other professionals and also the construction process in the form of, probably, a number of sub-contractors and suppliers. Figure 7.5 shows the relationship of the parties in diagrammatic terms.

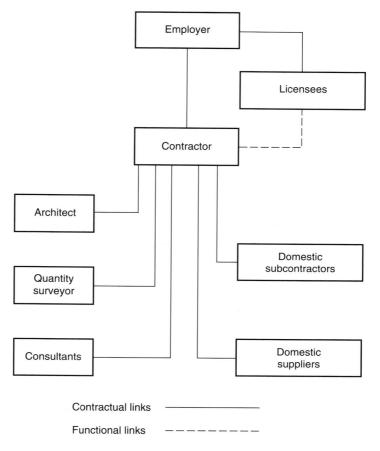

Contractual links —————————

Functional links – – – – – – – –

Fig. 7.4 Design and build.

7.4.5 Management contracting

Management contracting seems to be waning in popularity as design and build increases its stake in the construction market – or perhaps design and build is gaining in popularity as management contracting is decreasing.

The contractor is selected at an early stage. Although not normally responsible for carrying out any of the construction work, the contractor simply has a management function for which a fee is paid. The construction work is divided into a number of packages with the contractor's advice and tenders for these individual packages are invited as appropriate to suit the programme.

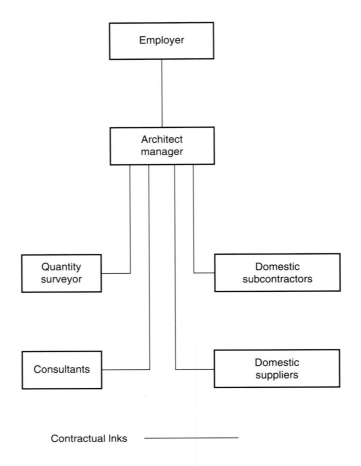

Contractual lnks ————————

Fig. 7.5   Design and manage.

The works contractors are in contract with the management contractor.

This type of contract has much in common with a traditional contract in which all the work is sublet to nominated sub-contractors. The system is commonly said to allow the employer considerable freedom for change of mind while preserving price and end date. Such a contention is clearly contradictory and management contracts in practice appear notable for escalating costs and shifting end dates. The employer takes more risk under a management contract than would be the case under a traditional procurement system, but this is the price paid for greater control over the work.

This is the system most often referred to as 'fast track', the idea being that work begins on site as soon as sufficient information has been produced to enable the first works contractors to start. The architect and other consultants are then involved in a constant race against time to produce the remainder of the drawings in time for the succeeding works packages. The architect must also be sufficiently organised to ensure that subsequent drawings do not necessitate the reconstruction of work already executed.

A few years ago, architects who worked in this way were heavily criticised by quantity surveyors, contractors and clients alike. From that point of view management contracting could be said to have made a virtue out of necessity. Architects should not be misled, however, by the apparent glamour of fast track. The architect's liability is exactly the same. The system imposes a tough discipline on all sides. The employer must be precise in requirements and prepared to hold fast to decisions. The preparation of information must be scheduled and on target, and the management of the contract must be tight. Any disputes which may arise can usually be traced to a failure to adhere to these principles.

It is, of course, quite difficult to perform under conditions of stress such as occur during fast building. It can be compared to driving a car: the faster the car is driven, the better the road and the mechanics have to be, and the further the driver has to see ahead. The driver is called upon to exercise more, not less, skill. The fast driver who has an accident is told that he or she should not have been driving so fast. The architect who makes a mistake purely as a result of fast building techniques must be told to get out of the fast lane.

Figure 7.6 shows the relationship of the parties in diagrammatic form.

7.4.6 Construction management

Once again, this system calls upon the contractor to act simply in a management capacity for which a fee is paid. The design team is often appointed directly by the employer, but in some instances the contractor may appoint. In such cases, the system has some of the flavour of project management. The key difference between this system and management contracting is that the individual works contractors (they are usually termed 'trade contractors' under this system) are in contract with the employer.

This overcomes a number of problems encountered under the management contracting system, notably that the contractor, as

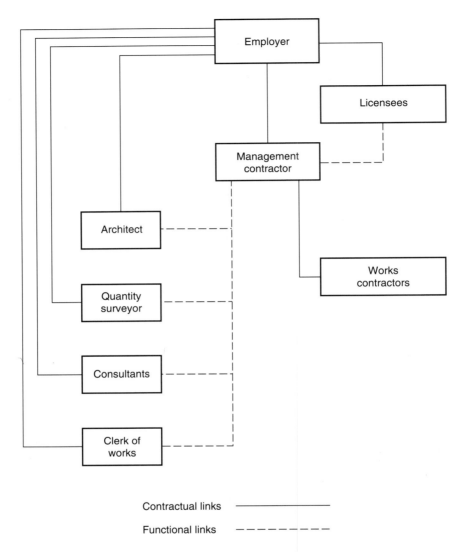

Contractual links ———————————

Functional links — — — — — — — —

Fig. 7.6   Management contracting.

construction manager, can become one of the team alongside architects, engineers, quantity surveyors, etc., and the trade contractors are liable for their breaches directly to the employer without the problems of an intervening contractor in the contractual chain. Although details vary, the construction manager is usually responsible for managing not only the trade contractors, but also the other consultants. Some very large projects have been carried out using this system which calls upon the same kind of skills from the design team as required under the management contract. Figure 7.7 shows the relationship of the parties in diagrammatic form.

There are other ways of separating systems, such as by method of price determination, i.e. measurement or cost reimbursement contracts which must in any event be taken into account, and by reference to the method of contractor selection, i.e. competitive tender or negotiation.

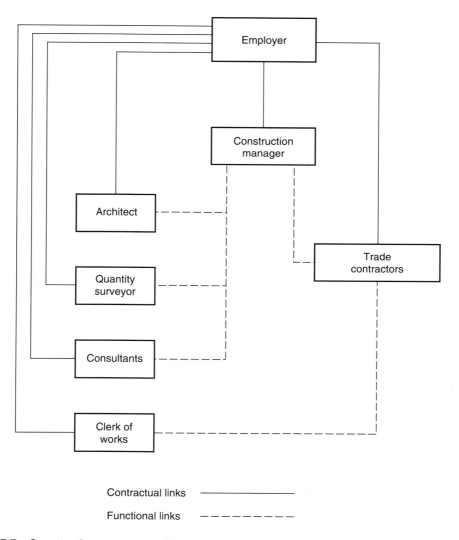

Fig. 7.7 Construction management.

7.5   PFI contracts

The Private Finance Initiative (PFI) was introduced in 1992. It is not a procurement system, because any of the systems set out in section 7.4 can be used with PFI. It is becoming clear, however, that procurement routes based on some form of design and build, certainly contractor led, are becoming the standard. The idea was that the private sector should be involved in providing and operating various assets which might otherwise never have been started. The system envisaged the eventual return of the project to the public sector. The return to the private sector was to be achieved during the intervening period. The idea had much to commend it and many PFI projects have been commenced. Private finance invested in the public sector introduces a high level of technical, managerial and financial skills and experience. By this means, a construction company might actually be in the position of creating its own workload.

It is usual for a special purpose vehicle (SPV) to be set up for the express purpose of obtaining finance and carrying out the project. More often than not it is a joint venture company between the finance providers and the building contractor. In order to ensure that the SPV secures a satisfactory return on investment, the agreements with central or local government are normally for periods of as much as 25 years. While apparently ensuring the time to make a substantial profit, the long time period places a high level of risk on the SPV which will have entered into several undertakings about the services to be provided. The system is not yet proven and there are misgivings among some construction companies who have indicated that they have had to bear most of the losses.

Some types of development which the government has said would be suitable for PFI schemes include hospitals, prisons, public sector offices, types of housing, roads and railways. There are many complications and, of course, a whole new set of jargon is being created. Nevertheless, this is part of the future and architects must have a thorough grasp of the implications[3].

7.6   Partnering

Partnering has been defined as:

'A management approach used by two or more organisations to achieve specific business objectives by maximising the effectiveness of each participant's resources. The approach is based on mutual objectives, an agreed method of problem resolution and an active search for continuous measurable improvements.'[4]

It is important to know the difference between 'partnering' and 'partnership'. Partnership has been described in Chapter 4, section 4.2. When parties enter into partnership, they intend to, and do, enter into a very specific legal relationship. This is not what is intended by parties who enter into a partnering arrangement. Very often the parties will prepare a 'charter' which will set out their joint aspirations. It is rare for the charter to define a legal relationship although it may sometimes overlap into that territory. There is still a necessity for a legally binding contract.

Partnering was one of the recommendations in the Latham Report[5]. Ideally, it should be a means to enable employers and contractors, or contractors and subcontractors, or professionals and clients, to work together with the object of reducing costs for mutual benefit. It should also have the effect of reducing conflict between the parties. It is not a procurement system, rather it is a commercial system. If all the people interested in getting a finished building on site are working in the same direction instead of constantly fighting, there should be benefits all around. Some basic principles have been established. Not all of them are common to all partnering arrangements:

- Interests of all the participating parties must be identified.
- Potential conflict areas must be identified and eliminated if possible, or if not possible they should be reduced.
- A system of incentives and rewards must be established which enables all parties to share in the rewards.
- Quality and production targets must be set for each project and improved upon in succeeding projects. Systems of measurement against those targets must be devised.
- Systems must be put in place to encourage the parties to work ever more closely together.
- Each party must be open with the other – the so-called 'open book policy'. The employer must have access to the contractor's costs.

Any kind of building contract can be used to procure the project, but very often some kind of cost plus or target cost arrangement is used. The idea is that the contractor is always sure of getting the costs of the project, even if there is no profit. Theoretically, the contractor cannot actually make a loss, although the employer certainly can.

One of the problems is that partnering can suffer from the same affliction that bedevilled such concepts as 'fast track' and 'management contracting'. Many people are unsure what constitutes partnering. They have heard that it is 'a good thing', but they are not sure why that is. Just as every self-respecting large contractor billed themselves as 'managing', so no project seems to be worth considering unless 'partnering' is in there somewhere. Partnering is more about setting in place a particular ethos than anything else. Concepts of good faith and fair play are important. No two partnering arrangements need be, and probably are not, the same.

The chances of successful partnering are very much increased when there is a prospect of a continuous string of projects, because the carrot of further work and turnover is always there in the future even if the current project is a bit of a disappointment. The chances are lowest if just one project is involved or when tackling the last of a series of projects. Cynics may point out that partnering is merely serial contracting with attractive packaging. There is nothing wrong with that of course.

'Serial contracting' works like this. On the basis of the successful tender for the first contract, further contracts are negotiated. To operate properly, the projects should be similar in construction and type so that negotiation for future contracts on the basis of original contracts is feasible. It is usual for the employer to make some sort of limited commitment to the contractor for the whole series. However, it is not something which can be legally enforced since it is always subject to the successful outcome of negotiations. The advantage is that one set of tendering takes place and the contractor can use the experience gained on the first contract to improve efficiency on the second and so on. The maximum benefit is gained for the employer if the basic terms for the whole series can be established when calling for the initial tender. An intended programme for all the contracts in the series should be set down at the outset if the contractor is to be able to calculate the potential benefits to the full. The system should produce savings for both parties.

The results of the first partnering arrangements are making themselves known. Anecdotal evidence suggests problems arising from either employers or contractors using the cover of partnering to disguise business as usual. There are also success stories. The procedures will not be capable of serious analysis until they have been in place for a number of years or over a number of projects.

References

(1) Reiss, Geoff (1995) *Project Management Demystified*, 2nd edn, E. & F.N. Spon. This is an excellent book, particularly for the uninitiated.

(2) *Murphy* v. *Brentwood District Council* (1990) 50 BLR 1.

(3) *The Private Initiative: the Essential Guide* (1996) RICS Business Services.

(4) *Trusting the Team* (1995) Centre for Strategic Studies in Construction, University of Reading and the Reading Construction Forum.

(5) Latham, Sir Michael (1994) *Constructing the Team*, Stationery Office.

Stage B: Strategic Briefing

8.1 Sequential framework and plan of work

For every activity there is a need for a sequential framework so that the correct operations can be carried out at the right time and, probably most important, in the right order. The things which an architect has to do throughout the process of design and construction of a building are so numerous, complex and interactive that, without such a framework, chaos would soon result. Architects have long produced such frameworks for themselves. Sometimes they were not much more than lists. In 1964, the RIBA Plan of Work was first published in the *RIBA Handbook of Practice Management*[(1)]. The intention was to provide a model procedure for the design team. It was never the intention that the Plan of Work would be slavishly followed under all circumstances. Indeed, certain assumptions were made:

- A building cost of about £300,000 and a full team of designers. It is now considered relevant to most building projects.
- The architect is responsible for leading the building team. That is not now necessarily the case.
- The earliest possible appointment. What the architect does may vary according to the time of his appointment.
- The degree of complexity was such as to involve the stages set out in Fig 6.1, the objective of each stage being to commence the next.
- In each stage the cycle of work is:
  - ☐ stating objective and assimilation of relevant facts
  - ☐ assessment of required resources and setting up of appropriate organisation
  - ☐ planning the work and setting timetables
  - ☐ carrying out work
  - ☐ making proposals and recommendations
  - ☐ obtaining client decisions
  - ☐ setting out objectives for the next stage.

The Plan of Work was revised in 1999 as part of the revision of the appointment documents SFA/99 etc. Although the revisions are largely cosmetic, they take account of some perceived changes in architectural practice, other professions, the JCT development of multidisciplinary documents and BS 7000 part 4: the Guide to Managing Design in Construction. The Plan is an ideal tool provided it is remembered that it is only the basic outline. There are many instances when two or more stages may be combined. The stages may often interweave and it is rare, certainly up to stage H, that there is any definite point at which it can be said that the project is moving from one stage to another.

The Plan, in its complete form, indicates the principal tasks for the major participants at the stage when the tasks are usually carried out and shows the architect's tasks in two sections: design function and management function. The architect should not slavishly follow this time schedule, but must carefully assess each project in the light of the Plan and adjust the Plan to suit. A very full fleshing out of the Plan of Work was represented by the RIBA Architect's Job Book[2]. The use of the Plan of Work will not eliminate mistakes, but it will very much reduce their incidence by ensuring that crucial steps are taken in logical order and by paving the way for the architect to co-ordinate the members of the design team (see also Chapter 6, section 6.2.1 for a description of each stage).

8.2   Site and building acquisition

In most instances clients already have a site when they approach an architect for the first time. Giving advice on site or building acquisition is one of the additional services which the architect can offer. Clearly, the choice of site should follow the architect's assessment of the client's brief (see section 8.4). If a new building is being considered, the shape of the site, the contours and the location can have a marked influence on the finished building. There are some buildings, such as factories, which require virtually flat sites, others which need sites in sunny locations, by a railway or central road network, in an urban centre and so on. A key factor is the size of the site and whether it is acceptable to erect a high rise building. There are several factors which can influence this kind of decision. Among them are the attitude of the Planning Authority, market value of floor area at different storey heights above ground level and, particularly in the case of dwellings, social considerations.

It is even less likely that an architect will be asked to advise on the acquisition of a suitable building although it does sometimes happen if the client is seeking a suitable building to convert to a specific purpose. In such a case, the architect has to start from the brief and assess the ease with which any particular building can be converted to its new purpose and the degree to which it is capable of fulfilling the client's brief when so converted. It can be a difficult and complicated task. The key factors to be considered are:

- *Structure* In most instances a structural survey will be required[3]. In addition it will be necessary to consider the constructional implications of:
  Columns
  Internal heights
  Changes in floor level
  Unusual roof shapes
  Towers, spires, etc.
  Basements
  Windows and doors
  Special architectural features, e.g. finials, drip moulds, etc.
  Decay

- *Heating and insulation*
  Need to change
  Compatibility of electricity, gas, solid fuel, solar heating, organic heating, etc.
  Compatibility of systems such as radiators, warm air, pressured air, underfloor heating, ceiling panel, etc.
  Insulating qualities (heat and sound) of existing fabric
  Ease of upgrading the insulation
  Any obvious restrictions on materials

- *Materials*
  Durability
  Appearance
  Appropriateness
  Consider floor, walls and ceiling and roof
  Heat retaining qualities
  Susceptibility to condensation

- *Ventilation*
  Natural
  Artificial

- *Lighting*
  Natural
  Artificial

■ *Acoustics*
Materials
Room shape and volume

■ *Design considerations*
Possibility of division vertically and/or horizontally
Possibility of creating large unobstructed spaces
Means of escape in the event of fire
Pedestrian and vehicular access
Disabled access
General shape as existing compared to the required or ideal
shape

■ *Environmental requirements*
Internally: problems in heating, lighting, humidity, ventilation,
damp penetration
Externally: effect of alterations on external appearance and the
relationship to other buildings and spaces

■ *Possible adaptation techniques*
Complete gutting
Partial gutting
Virtually complete retention of existing structure

■ *Likely costs*

In practice, the architect will not separate the above into separate
categories. Indeed, it can be seen that some factors fall into or have
relevance in several categories. Part of the architect's skill in
assessing whether an existing building is appropriate for a particular use is to keep all these factors in mind and weigh one against
another in arriving at a considered view. There are certain other
legal considerations which are considered later in this chapter.

8.3 Surveys

Whether the architect advises on the acquisition of land or buildings or whether the client presents a fait accompli, a survey will be
required before the architect can proceed with design work. 'Survey' is an imprecise term referring to an activity which may range
from taking a detailed set of measurements, including levels, and
translating them into careful drawings, to an inspection of varying
degrees of thoroughness resulting in a written report. It is, therefore, very important for the architect to establish from the outset
the kind of survey which will be required.

For example, if the client is simply considering purchase and development of existing property, an inspection and written report is indicated together with a rough sketch containing a few key dimensions. If the architect is presented with a site and instructed to produce a feasibility study, a very general idea of the dimensions, levels and other features is required sufficient to determine whether the project can be fitted onto the site. A wholly different set of information must be considered (see Chapter 7, section 7.1). In practice, however, the most common kind of survey in which the architect will be interested is the measured survey.

The next thing the architect must decide is whether to advise the client to engage a surveyor (land surveyor or building surveyor as appropriate) to carry out the work. If the site is relatively small and uncomplicated or the existing building and its proposed alterations are simple in character, the architect can probably do the survey work without difficulty[4]. For anything other than the simplest sites or buildings, a survey produced by an independent surveying firm is indicated. The main reason is that surveying is becoming very sophisticated and the equipment tends to be highly expensive. It makes no economic sense for the architect to have that kind of equipment unless he can use it on a regular basis. Moreover, in the case of complex surveys, the architect cannot hope to compete with the surveyor who is doing the job full time.

8.3.1   Preliminary enquiries

Before tackling the survey or instructing the surveyor to do the work, the architect should make certain enquiries. Some of these enquiries will produce information which is vital to the survey or which assists the architect at feasibility stage. It is suggested that the following should always be consulted:

- *Local Planning Authority:* They have a wealth of information and they will advise on such things as the structure plan, local plans, unitary development plans, conservation areas, listed buildings and trees with preservation orders. In addition, of course, they will have a view on the acceptability of the proposed development.
- *The Building Control Office:* Old deposited drawings may be very revealing, but often the building control officer may be the best source of information
- *Local History Department of the Public Library:* The curator will

normally have a great deal of information in the form of old maps and plans of the area or of the building. Such things as ancient quarries, river courses and even tunnels may be discovered in this way.

- *Local inhabitants:* They can give helpful information, but it should always be supported in some other way if possible. Pointers to the possibilities of easements may be obtained (see Chapter 9, section 9.6.6), but watch out for petty rivalries which may fog the memory. It has been known for an elderly person to positively remember that the site in question used to harbour an old mineshaft only for it to be discovered much further down the road.
- *The mineral valuer:* Useful in respect of the nature of the subsoil and the possibility of faults, filled ground, etc.
- *British Coal:* For a fee they will provide a short report about the past and projected mine workings which may affect the site. For a larger fee, they will supply more detailed information which may require an expert to interpret.
- *Deeds Registry or County Office:* They tend to be the repository of legal information and deed plans, but it is amazing what can be discovered in the conveyancing history of a piece of land.
- *The client's solicitor:* With the client's permission, of course, for advice on any matters affecting the land, such as covenants or easements.

8.3.2 Site investigation

Site investigation has come to mean the investigation of the ground under the site. Some of the information discovered when conducting the preliminary enquiries will give valuable hints regarding the kind of site investigation which should be carried out. If the building is other than relatively small and light, a specialist consultant engineer should be engaged by the client to advise on and oversee the investigation. Such a consultant should be nominated by the architect. There are firms which specialise in ground investigations, but it is essential that they are given a proper brief so that they can form conclusions regarding the scope of the investigation. Even where the proposed building is very light and the ground has no known problems, the architect will have some trial pits dug in order to confirm that all is well. It is usual to set out the positions of the pits with regard to the actual siting of the building. If a specialist firm is employed, the type of investigation proposed will depend on the proposed building and the kind of ground conditions expected. The usual method is to sink boreholes and measure the samples, taking various tests for acidity, sulphate content, strengths under varying conditions and so on. If the height of the building suggests that piles will be required, the boreholes may well be sunk to great depths. The firm will prepare a report which will repay careful study. If in doubt, the architect should never hesitate to request the firm or specialist to produce a further report to explain the first.

8.3.3   General considerations

Other considerations which should be carefully studied are the aspect, orientation, shelter, overshadowing from adjacent buildings, existence of services such as sewers, water, electricity and gas, means of access to the public highway and communications. In rural districts the suitability of the site for sewage disposal plant or the sinking of a well may also have to be considered. Topographical and other features of the site must be recorded – such things as levels, dimensions, bench-marks, positions and types of trees, existing buildings on and near the site and their character, overhead cables and poles, rivers, lakes, springs, rocky outcrops, fissures and the type of vegetation.

The architect must never make the mistake of thinking that a first class survey is a substitute for visiting the site. Not even a superb set of photographs taken from every angle or a video of the site will suffice. It should not be discounted how often an architect will get a feeling for the kind of building required during the first site visit. It may be because of a particular view or a grouping of existing buildings or something as intangible as the atmosphere. Site visits are certainly essential.

Even if a surveyor has been engaged to carry out the survey, the architect should make a point of walking all over the site or, in the case of a building, throughout the building and actually enter every room. Only by doing this will the architect thoroughly know the site or building and satisfy the duty of care owed to the client.

8.3.4   Surveys of existing buildings

Unless it is absolutely out of the question, the architect should always carry out an existing building survey[5]. Not only will the architect know precisely what is required in the form of illustrative drawing so far as difficult details are concerned, he or she will learn about the way the building is constructed by the very process of carrying out the survey and plotting the results.

If a simple extension is to be made to an existing building as opposed to the alteration of the building itself, it will be sufficient to survey only the part of the building immediately adjoining the proposed extension. Some suitable point on the existing building will probably be chosen as a temporary benchmark which may or may not be related to ordnance levels. The exact positions of all plinths, string courses, openings and other features on the elevations which have to be taken into consideration should be noted. The precise level of every floor should be established, carefully checking that the floors are themselves level and, if not, taking several levels along the edge of each floor at the point of extension. The thickness and construction of any walls to be cut through should be determined also. In old buildings, it is not unusual to find dummy columns, pilasters and even the wall thickness itself may consist of battened out voids covered in thick plaster or stucco. The levels of the external ground must be established.

The first thing the architect will do after arriving at the building is to take a general walk around and observe the surroundings, the condition of boundary walls and fences and any outbuildings. After looking at the outer elevations and looking into each room internally, the architect will be able to form an opinion regarding the overall condition and place it in one of the following categories:

- In good repair
- Neglected, but basically sound structurally
- In poor condition structurally, perhaps in a dangerous state

In some instances, the architect will find a very serious problem during the initial walkabout. In such circumstances, there is no alternative but to telephone the client immediately for further instructions. Clearly, there is little point in continuing to survey a building which is only fit for demolition. Whatever the client's instructions may be, the architect should always confirm them in writing.

During the survey, it may be necessary to obtain the client's authority to employ a builder to assist the investigations by taking up floorboards or exposing part of the foundations. This kind of investigation cannot be carried out if the client does not own the property unless the actual owner has given express permission.

The architect is always wise to get such permission in writing through his client.

Investigations should encompass the various services – whether they exist and if they do, what is their condition? Gas, water, electricity, drainage, hot water, cable TV, etc. may all require substantial overhaul or renewal. The condition of the roof, eaves, flashings, rainwater pipes and gutters, damp-proof course and any other features which prevent moisture from penetrating into the building deserve particular attention, as all the money spent on improving or redecorating the property may be wasted if some fault in these areas is overlooked. It would not be overstating the point to say that damp is at the root of most building defects.

Although it may be that the eventual scheme for the building will only affect certain parts, it is usually best to make an accurate measured survey of the whole, including all internal heights, so that sections can be drawn through any part without much difficulty. The only exception to this general rule is if the architect knows clearly in advance just which parts of the building are to be affected. Some architects advocate the making of a rough survey in the first instance, to be followed by a thorough survey only when the new design has been approved by the client. Down that road lies disaster. The architect will often find that he or she is faced with trying to make a scheme work which the later detailed survey shows cannot work, possibly because of an impossible change in levels or of headroom.

The golden rule is never to make assumptions. Inevitably, the architect will discover, when plotting, that certain dimensions have been forgotten. There is no alternative but to return to the building and check them. This can be difficult if the building is some distance from the office. In those circumstances, the prudent architect will take equipment along to enable the building to be roughly plotted out as a check.

Each room or space on the survey drawing must be given a number so that they can be identified easily by giving them the same number on the alteration drawings. It is good practice to provide the contractor with a set of drawings of the building as existing so that comparison of existing and proposed can be made readily. The following is a brief check-list covering the major areas to be considered when carrying out a survey:

Building site

Development
Permitted development and restrictions under the structure and
    local plans
Zoning, density, floor space index, etc. as applicable
Improvement lines
Proposed adjacent development

History of the site
Rights of public and adjoining owners
Boundaries or party walls or fences

Nature of ground and subsoil
Trial holes or other evidence of nature of subsoil
Precautions against subsidence, seasonal variations in subsoil and
    water table
Safe bearing capacity of subsoil
Report from mineral valuer and geologist
Liability to flooding

Condition of site
Levels and gradients
Bench marks
Shelter or exposure from surrounding ground
Direction of prevailing wind
Aspect and orientation
Dimensions and area of site
Existing trees and features
Existing buildings on the site and on adjoining land
Overhead cables and poles

Services
Position, size and depth of public sewers
If no sewer, suitability and possible siting of septic tank and
    overflow outlet
Utility services available, such as gas, water, electricity, etc. with
    names and addresses of supply undertakings
Position and pressure of water main
Electricity supply, voltage, capacity of any existing cables
Position and size of gas main
Telephone service
Possibility of sinking well

Communications
Means of access
Nature and proximity of public highway
Rights of way across site

Existing buildings
(in addition to the foregoing, so far as applicable)

Drawings
Plans, elevations, sections, details as necessary, drawn to scale

Construction
Type and method of construction of foundations, walls, floors and
    roof
Wall and floor thicknesses
Hidden construction features
Special finishes

Condition of structure
Signs of rot, beetle or other infestation etc., in timber
Decay or spalling in concrete
Excessive rusting or distress in steel members
Looseness of plaster surfaces
Damp penetration through roofs, flashings and gutters
Condensation
Damp-proof course to walls
Settlement cracks
Windows and doors, etc.

Condition of services
Gas, water, electricity, drains, central heating, hot water, TV cable
    or aerial, vacuum, computer, specialised gases or other links
Possibility of extending the services

History of the building
Age
Purposes of previous occupation
Quality of previous maintenance work

8.4   The brief

One of the architect's most important functions is the taking of an
accurate brief from the client. Yet many architects are very careless

in this respect. The brief is the client's instructions to the architect. It may be intensely detailed and complex and, since the architect's task is to satisfy the brief, it is essential that it is as clear as possible. Of course, it may not be possible to produce a very clear brief. Indeed the very essence of some briefs is the vagueness and the freedom of the architect to produce a solution within very broad parameters. This is probably because in those instances, the client does not know what he or she wants.

That raises another important point. The architect's function is really to produce not what the client wants, but what the client needs. That is the function of every professional person. The process of setting down what the client needs may take a long time. Once it is accomplished, the design process may be swift. In some cases, such as the brief for a new hospital, the pace of development may be so quick that there is never any hope of the architect producing anything more than a loose brief designed, hopefully, to accommodate as many changes as possible so that the design will never be finally fixed until the contractor has left site.

The traditional method of taking a brief would result in a schedule of accommodation required. That system should long since be defunct in favour of a user requirement study or some development of that principle. The idea is that the architect analyses the client's needs in terms of activities and identifies, in respect of each activity, a number of key criteria including areas, volumes, requirements for finishes, orientation and aspect, interaction with other activities and to what extent, numbers of persons involved, special requirements ancillary to the activity, social and psychological needs.

A great deal of work may be necessary to produce a brief of this nature in terms of research or operational study or both. In many cases, it will not be justified if the proposed building is a common building type. Even if that is the case, the architect should always be wary that the brief which the client has come to know and love over the years may be flawed or may have become flawed with the passing of time and the introduction of new processes, etc.

The result of any briefing exercise will be something in writing or, in some instances, in graphical form. Wherever possible, the architect should try to schedule information in logical form and to confine other written material to note form. There will be much information in the form of hard facts, but there will also be much in less tangible form. It is often useful to separate the two. The brief should always be confirmed to the client before the next stage is commenced.

8.5 Reporting

Architects are expected to report to their clients at various stages throughout the design and construction period. Stage B is probably the earliest stage at which a client can expect a formal report and, of course, such a report will not always be in writing. Indeed, for a very small project and an unsophisticated client, a written report is probably quite inappropriate.

It is often difficult to decide when to report and when a report is unnecessary, but it is usual to make a report of some kind whenever an architect wants some kind of decision from the client. The purpose of the report in such an instance is to acquaint the client with the appropriate information on which to base a decision. There will be other instances when the architect requires no decision, but it is simply good client relations to report on progress. A client, like anyone else, always likes to know that he or she is not forgotten.

The following list indicates typical reports the architect may produce while running a project, not all of which will be applicable on every project:

- Feasibility
- Outline proposals
- Scheme design
- Progress reports
- Extension of time
- Loss and/or expense
- Special reports, i.e. before determination, after insurance risk damage, etc.

The architect will also be responsible for passing on and, if appropriate, commenting on reports received from other consultants. For instance, cost reports from the quantity surveyor, reports on structural condition from the structural engineer, etc. Sometimes such reports are submitted direct by the consultant concerned and the client may particularly require cost reports to be submitted directly. However, from an organisational point of view, it is better that they pass through the hands of the architect so that the employer deals with one person and a possible clash of professional interests is avoided. Some brief comments on report writing are given in Chapter 15, section 15.5.

References

(1) The latest edition is Cox, S. and Hamilton, A. (1986) *RIBA Handbook of Practice Management*, 6th edn, RIBA Publications.

(2) Beaven, L., Cox, S., Dry, D., & Males, R. (1988) *Architect's Job Book*, 5th edn, RIBA Publications Ltd.

(3) Milka S.L.J. (1988) *Structural Surveying*, 2nd edn, Macmillan.

(4) J. Clancy (1991) *Site Surveying & Levelling*, 2nd edn, Edward Arnold.

(5) Hollis M. & Gibson C. (1990) *Surveying Buildings*, RICS Books.

Chapter 9

Stages C and D: Outline and Detailed Proposals

9.1 Design data

The RIBA Plan of Work describes stage C as:

> 'To determine general approach to layout, design and construction in order to obtain the authoritative approval of the client on the outline proposals and the accompanying report.'

During this stage the architect will be involved in developing the brief, carrying out user requirement studies, gathering appropriate information, trying out solutions in consultation with other members of the team and preparing an outline proposal. It has already been seen (Chapter 8, section 8.4) that the architect must prepare a brief on the basis of client needs rather than client wants if there is a conflict. If the brief is considered as a problem, the architect can only start to find the answer when all the data necessary has been assembled.

Much of the data will be collected as part of the feasibility study (see Chapter 7, section 7.1). Other factual material will concern relevant Acts of Parliament, Statutory Instruments and Regulations and the recommendations of appropriate bodies (e.g. Sports Council). In addition to this material, the architect will be concerned with user requirement studies. Some of this work may have been carried out while preparing the brief, but it is usual for more detailed studies to take place after the feasibility stage has been completed.

User requirement studies, put simply, attempt to encapsulate in easy reference form all the criteria which the user requires of the building. All buildings have more than one user, and there is the problem. Each user may have slightly, or even widely, differing requirements. Sometimes, different classes of person use the same building but they have almost opposing requirements. An example of a building where this is the case is a courthouse, where not only are the requirements of judges, prisoners and public quite different, the circulation routes must not cross. When one takes into account the needs of police, court officials, solicitors and others involved in the cases for trial, not to mention the complex administration requirements, a courthouse of any size becomes a very complex building. There are other buildings with equally complex user requirements.

Some part of the user requirement study will be factual, other parts will be more subjective and need to take into consideration such things as suitable environmental, social and psychological factors. During this stage, the architect will try to visit some good examples of the building type under consideration. Much other design data will be standard for most projects (see Chapter 5, section 5.4).

The point to appreciate is that all relevant design data must be available before the architect can seriously attempt to formulate even outline proposals. There is a need to emphasise this point because the temptation to launch into the design stage of an interesting project before all information is to hand can be hard to resist.

9.2   Outline proposals and development

This is not the place to discuss architectural design. It is beyond the scope of this book. Most clients are not at all interested in design theory; they are only interested in results. If the results are bad, the theory is irrelevant.

As a basic principle, the architect should always keep the client informed of the progress of the design work. This is especially the case if the architect wants to attempt something rather different from the norm. In such a case, the client's agreement should be obtained first. In most cases, a client is interested only in such fundamentals as whether the building will successfully keep out the rain and the cold, how well it works and how much it will cost to build and to run. An architect who can keep a client happy on those points will have little to worry about.

As a general rule, the architect should only present one proposal to the client. There are exceptions to this as to every other rule, but they will be rare. The client looks to the architect and other members of the design team to produce a solution to the problems contained in the brief. Above all, a client expects advice. The team may well come to the conclusion that any one of a dozen different schemes could be developed into an acceptable project, but it is their function to recommend the one they consider to be the best. Unless the client has expressly asked for alternative proposals, one proposal shows that the architect is carrying out the job of eliminating options. Most options should be eliminated by a consideration of the brief, and the rest at feasibility stage. To present proposals which show major differences at this stage suggests that the architect has not carried out earlier tasks adequately.

During this stage the architect will perform certain management functions. Co-ordination of the design team is an ongoing process throughout the design and construction stages of any medium to large project. As part of this process, during this stage the architect will be concerned with putting in place the procedures which will ensure that the team works as a team and not as a group of individuals, although it must be admitted that the ideal is easier to envisage than to achieve. A key factor will be the lines of, and frequency of, communication. As a general rule, all communications should be to the architect whose job it is to see that the appropriate information is properly distributed. Although it is vital that the structural engineer has all the information needed to enable a proper contribution to be made to the project, the architect must take care that individual team members are not swamped with information 'just in case' it might prove useful. This is where the managerial qualities of the architect should come to the fore.

It is useful to have a meeting for the team at the beginning of this stage to establish the following (adapted from the RIBA Plan of Work):

- The objectives (often overlooked, see Chapter 14, section 14.1).
- Available information regarding the brief, basic design data (see section 9.1), cost limits, timetable set by client or other restraints.
- Matters to be dealt with as priorities.
- Design team procedures, including roles and communications.
- The very important topics of procurement systems and contractual arrangements, tendering, type of bills, specification, schedules, and work methods.
- Any particular drawing techniques or systems (such as computer aided design). It may indeed be a little late in the day to decide this point and it is something which the architect should consider at briefing stage. The reason is that some consultants may not be willing to work within any given system of drawing. They may in fact have a fully operational computer drawing system which is incompatible with the architect's own system.
- System of carrying out cost checks during design.
- List of actions to be taken.

■ Programming and progress techniques for the design team and for the project in construction.

Either at the end of Stage C or in the early part of Stage D, the architect will apply for outline planning approval. At the end of Stage D or during the early part of Stage E, full planning permission should be sought (see section 9.4).

The RIBA Plan of Work describes Stage D as:

'To complete the brief and decide on particular proposals, including planning arrangement, appearance, constructional method, outline specification and cost and to obtain all approvals.'

The team should have a very clear idea of the brief during this part of the work. Indeed, there should be no question of changing the brief once this stage is complete and the client should be so informed, otherwise much time and money will be wasted. What was thought of in terms of concepts during the last stage now has to be developed, with the advice of appropriate consultants, into a design which is quite detailed, i.e. the staircase must be capable of being made to work without altering its dimensions, and space allocations for columns, beams and services ducts must be adequate. It is during this stage of work that every member of the team has to make a determined effort to work together. It really is no use the architect saying that all the other members must fit their designs into his or her master design, neither should any other consultants stick out for their own particular choice. Unless the final design is a true combination of all the team working single-mindedly to solve the client's problems, the end result will be lacking in validity. A modern building is so complex that single-handed design is not feasible.

At the end of this stage, the architect should be able to present the client with design drawings which show how the building will work and look and, if up to date computer techniques are employed, how the users will experience living and working in and around the building as part of the overall environment.

The management function is much the same as in Stage C, except that the procedures set up then should be fully operational and the architect is simply in the position of setting fresh objectives and timescales and ensuring that every member co-operates properly and at the right time. In addition, the architect will be ironing out any problems with relevant authorities, the most important of which will be:

- Water
- Electricity
- Gas
- Highway
- Fire
- Telephone
- Environmental health
- Cleansing

Many of these authorities require layout plans before they can comment sensibly and it is essential that the architect has agreements before this stage is completed or the whole scheme can be put at risk. Even something like refuse collection may pose severe problems if not tackled early with the support rather than the opposition of the local cleansing department.

It is useful for the architect to submit a written report with the presentation drawings in which the major strengths can be emphasised and any weaknesses made clear. The architect should ask the client for agreement to proceed to tender stage through the more detailed design, production information and bills of quantity stages.

9.3   Cost estimates and planning

The quantity surveyor is the expert on costs. There is a world of difference between producing an estimate of the probable cost of a building from a set of drawings and producing a similar estimate from a brief and as the design develops putting together a cost plan which enables the architect to work within known costs limits in respect of each element. An experienced architect may make a reasonable attempt at the former, but only a skilled and experienced quantity surveyor will be able to carry out the latter with sufficient accuracy to be useful.

The client will have stated what can be afforded, but the architect may have to use some strategy in getting the true figure. On the basis that all building work costs more than expected or planned, the client will often present the design team with a reduced figure. When this happens, the team set their sights accordingly and when construction is nearing its end the client sometimes indulges in an orgy of expenditure and uses up his hidden balance in pointless extras when it would have been put to better use in perhaps increasing the overall floor area, or heights, or other fundamental provision. Be that as it may, the team can do no other than work to the figure given by the client. To do other would amount to negligence and, at the very least, the professionals would lose their fees.

Although the client may say that the maximum expenditure is, say, £5,000,000, that information is of little help to the architect except in very general terms. It can be translated into rough areas or volumes on the basis of different constructional systems and finishes, e.g. expensive or basic. What the quantity surveyor can do is to produce a cost plan for the designers which allocates a sum of money to each element. For example, the cost of walls may be expressed as x per square metre, similarly for floors, roofs and so on. Allocations for furniture can be made on a room by room basis. More importantly, the quantity surveyor can give the architect an idea of what those sums of money represent in terms of construction and finishes by giving a range of examples in each case. In order to be able to do this, the quantity surveyor has to be able to call on a file or database of cost information and trends built up over a considerable period.

The cost plan can be presented in different ways, so that for example, if a housing estate is being considered, a price per dwelling may be expressed together with a figure for district heating, another for roads and footpaths, landscaping and so on. Over the years, several professional journals have featured buildings whose costs have been presented in this way.

Irrespective of the level of detail within the cost plan, the overall accuracy of the costs is ultimately dependent on the design detail available and the extent of outstanding risks with potential cost implications at the time of estimating.

9.4 Town Planning applications and approvals

9.4.1 Administration of planning control

By and large, planning organisation has two main tiers: a central government tier under the mantle of the Secretary of State and a local government tier in the shape of local planning authorities.

At government level, Town and Country Planning comes within the remit of the Department of the Environment, Transport and the Regions (DETR) which was set up in 1997 to succeed the Department of the Environment (DOE). Ultimate responsibility for the DETR rests with the Secretary of State for the Environment who is supported by a number of ministers.

At local level, administration of the planning system on a day-to-day basis rests largely with local planning authorities. In the shire counties, there is a two tier system with the planning function split between the county councils and the district councils. In metropolitan areas, the planning system is administered by a single tier of metropolitan districts which are unitary authorities. Local planning authorities are responsible for preparing development plans and processing planning applications for development. Decisions are normally made by planning committees made up of elected members or by planning officers under delegated powers.

In recent years the Secretary of State has also made provisions for other agencies, such as development corporations and joint planning boards, to have the same powers as local planning authorities.

9.4.2   Legislation

Town planning legislation is consolidated into four Acts:

■ The Town and Country Planning Act 1990
■ The Planning (Listed Buildings and Conservation Areas) Act 1990
■ The Planning (Hazardous Substances) Act 1990
■ The Planning (Consequential Provisions) Act 1990

The Planning and Compensation Act 1991 made many new provisions for what was controlled in those four Acts and made some important new changes to planning law, including changes in relation to development plans, the definition of development, appeals, enforcement and other matters.

These five Acts together, along with a number of rules, regulations and orders, comprise the Town and Country Planning Code which controls development and use of all land and buildings in England and Wales. Some of the more significant statutory instruments made by the Secretary of State in recent years are:

■ The Town and Country Planning (Use Classes) Order 1987 which provides that certain changes of use are not material (i.e. important) and, therefore, are not development.
■ The Town and Country Planning (General Permitted Development) Order 1995 which provides that certain minor developments will be deemed to be permitted, often subject to extensive qualifications and restrictions. Development speci-

fied in the Order is commonly referred to as 'permitted development'.

■ The Town and Country Planning (General Development Procedure) Order 1995 which specifies the procedures to be adopted in the making and processing of applications.

The government also lays down policies for the guidance of the local planning authorities in the exercise of their day-to-day control duties. These policies are normally contained within government circulars and planning policy guidance notes (PPGs) which cover a wide range of topics including General Policy and Principles (PPG1 1992), Green Belts (PPG2 1995), Planning and the Historic Environment (PPG15 1994) and Planning and Noise (PPG24 1994)

The policy contained in guidance notes constitutes a material consideration which local planning authorities, and indeed the Secretary of State himself, must take into account in the determination of planning applications.

9.4.3 Development plans

Development plans play a vital part in the system for the control of development. They constitute the main framework against which applications for planning permission are determined and decisions are made about whether or not to issue enforcement notices against unauthorised development. The development plan system helps ensure that there is both a rational and consistent basis for making these decisions. They also influence the scale, location and timing of development or redevelopment of land, having regard to the extent and availability of the necessary infrastructure.

Until 1991, there had been a presumption in favour of granting planning permission. The Planning and Compensation Act 1991 changed that by stating that planning decisions must be made in accordance with the development plan unless important considerations indicate otherwise (section 26). Major legislative changes to the development plan system were introduced in the Planning and Compensation Act 1991 which amended the legislative basis for new style development plans in Part II of the 1990 Act.

Now, county councils are required to prepare a single structure plan to cover the whole of their area. Previously, under the old provisions of the 1990 Act, local district authorities were able to prepare a structure plan for part of their area. Also, the local authority must now prepare a single local plan covering the whole of their administrative area. Previously, this requirement was discretionary and involved three types of plan: district plans, action area plans and subject plans.

However, the basic relationship between a structure plan and a local plan remains as before. In essence, a structure plan is a set of written policies relating to land use considerations taking into account social, economic and environmental issues. Any illustrative matter in a structure plan is quantitative or diagrammatic due to its broad based nature. The local plan is prepared on a district wide basis by the local planning authority and contains detailed local policies and proposals for the district. It cannot be adopted unless certified as being in accordance with the provisions of the structure plan for the area. The land use proposals are shown on an Ordnance Survey base map.

Outside the shire counties the system is different. Since 1986, the metropolitan districts and London boroughs have had the responsibility to prepare Unitary Development Plans (UDPs) for their areas. UDPs consist of two parts. Part one contains general policies and proposals for the whole metropolitan district and is similar in concept to a structure plan. Part two contains proposals of a detailed local nature and is similar in concept to a local plan.

The preparation and updating of all plans must follow procedures laid down in the Town and Country Planning (Development Plans) Regulations 1991. They contain regulations relating to, among other things, surveys, consultations, publicity and public participation and adoption of plans. The partial reorganisation of local government in England and Wales has led to the creation of additional unitary authorities and the planning system in these areas will move from a two tier to a unitary system.

9.4.4 Development control

With few exceptions the development of land in the UK may only be undertaken with permission of the local planning authority. 'Development' is defined by section 55 of the Town and Country Planning Act 1990 as the carrying out of building, engineering, mining and other operations in, on, over or under land or the making of any material change in the use of any buildings or other land.

Where a person intends to carry out an act of development they must, therefore, obtain planning permission. If they carry out development without planning permission, they are liable to the process of enforcement. However, certain operations which fall under the definition of 'development' are allowed by legislation. The Town and Country Planning (General Permitted Development) Order 1995 (GPDO) sets out in schedule 2, in 33 separate parts, a list of types of development that are granted automatic planning permission by the state. These sorts of development are known as 'permitted development' or 'PD rights'. Examples are:

- Certain enlargements to dwellings, e.g. garages and extensions
- The erection of walls and fences
- Building operations on agricultural land
- Temporary buildings and uses
- Certain industrial development
- Some local authority operations
- Some developments carried out by statutory undertakers
- Certain types of demolition

Almost all permitted developments are subject to qualifications and restrictions, e.g. the amount a dwelling can be extended before planning permission will be required, whether the site is in a conservation area or whether the property is a listed building, etc. Permitted development rights can be removed by conditions put on a planning permission by the authority or by a direction under article 4 of the GPDO. Article 4 directions are commonly, although not exclusively, used in conservation areas and normally they must have the approval of the Secretary of State.

The Town and Country (Use Classes) Order 1987 sets out 16 classes of use in four parts and it provides that a change of use from a use in one use class to another use in the same use class does not involve development. Although changing from a use in one use class to a use in a different use class generally will require permission, the question must still be asked if there is a 'material' (important) change. Furthermore, the GPDO specifically grants planning permission for certain changes of use, for example, from a use in class A3 (cafe, hot food takeaway) to a use in class A1 (shop use), but not vice versa.

9.4.5   The planning application

The architect should always consult the planning authority at an early stage (see Chapter 7, section 7.1). Pre-application consultation can help to identify the major issues or problems or provide advice about the type of supporting information that may be required with a particular type of proposal. A planning application should be made on a form issued by the local planning authority and must be submitted properly completed together with relevant plans, documents and the fee. There are two main types of application: full (or detailed) application and outline application.

In certain cases of operational development, it may be prudent to first seek outline planning permission to establish that the principle or certain aspects of the development, for example access or siting, are acceptable. Any details not provided at this stage can be reserved for subsequent approval (a 'reserved matters' application). Thus, without incurring substantial cost, a developer may establish at an early stage the likelihood of a proposal being approved by the local planning authority.

A full or detailed application must provide all the details of a proposed development including design, external appearance, access, parking, landscaping as appropriate and so on. Additional information, depending on the scale and nature of the proposals, may also be required, for example, traffic impact assessment or retail impact assessment. Both types of application must include a certificate A, B, C or D as appropriate. They are used as follows:

A   Where the applicant is the owner of all the land which is the subject of the application
B   If the applicant has given an appropriate notice to everyone who was an owner of any part of the land during the period 21 days before the application date
C   If neither certificate A nor B can be issued and the applicant has given notice of the application to known owners and stating steps taken to identify unknown owners
D   If no owners are known

Publicity for planning applications is required by the 1990 Act. The type of publicity required involves combinations of:

■   Advertisements in the local papers
■   A site notice
■   Neighbour notification

The type of publicity required will depend into which category of development the application falls, for example, major, minor, those that involve a departure from the development plan, or those that require an environmental statement or affect a public right of way. Applications in conservation areas or which will affect the setting of a listed building require a notice in a local paper and a site notice.

The planning authority is under a duty to consult certain interested parties before they make a decision on certain types of application. For example, the highway authority must be consulted for developments that will affect access or highway conditions. The authority must come to a decision within 8 weeks of the application date unless agreement is reached to extend this period. If there is no such agreement and the authority fails to determine the application within 8 weeks, the applicant can appeal against 'non-determination', but once an appeal is lodged, the decision is taken out of the hands of the authority. If discussions were continuing and a decision was imminent, it might be quicker to allow the decision to be made rather than subject the application to the appeal process.

The authority may grant permission or grant it subject to conditions or refuse it giving reasons for the conditions or refusal. Outline permissions are normally valid for 3 years. Full permissions are normally valid for 5 years. Permission is usually given for the land; it is rarely personal to the applicant. Therefore, when the land is sold, the permission is transferred also. It is very common for a planning authority to impose standard conditions on every permission together with special conditions to suit particular sites.

A planning authority cannot approve an application for certain types of development which are not in accordance with the development plan without going through a special procedure as detailed in the Town and Country Planning (Development Plans and Consultation)(Departures) Directions 1999. This provides that such applications be notified to the Secretary of State who will then decide if he wishes to 'call in' the application for his decision.

An applicant can find out if planning permission is necessary by formally seeking a determination on the matter from the planning authority under section 64 of the 1990 Act.

9.4.6 Planning agreements

Section 106 of the 1990 Act (as amended by the Planning and Compensation Act 1991) provides that developers may enter into a 'planning obligation' which may restrict the use of land, require specified operations to be carried out or require sums of money to be paid to the local authority. By doing so, the local authority may be prepared to grant planning permission. In other words, authorities may try to achieve 'planning gains' for the community through the use of these agreements that they could not achieve through the use of conditions. The obligation may be done either by agreement with the authority or by the developer giving a unilateral undertaking. Common examples are the carrying out of off-site highway or drainage works to allow land to be developed or in relation to agricultural workers' dwellings which tie the existing land and property to the agricultural holding. In more recent years, the agreements have been used frequently to secure funding and provision of affordable housing and public open space, particularly in connection with larger residential developments.

9.4.7 Remedies

Completion notice

Under section 94 of the 1990 Act, a local authority may serve a completion notice on a developer where they are of the opinion that, although construction has been started, it will not be completed within a reasonable period. The notice must then specify a reasonable time, which must not be less than 12 months, to complete the development. Failure to comply will result in the planning permission being invalidated.

Enforcement

The local authority is empowered under the provisions of Part VII of the 1990 Act, as amended by Part I of the Planning and Compensation Act 1991, to take action to enforce against unauthorised development. The weapons at their disposal are:

(1) *Enforcement notice*
     The authority has power to serve an enforcement notice where there has been a breach of planning control, such as development undertaken without permission or in contravention of the condition imposed by the authority[1]. The notice must require the building owner or occupier to do whatever is necessary to remedy the breach. A reasonable time limit must be imposed. An appeal on specified grounds may be lodged with the Secretary of State within 28 days. While the Secretary of State is deciding the appeal, the notice is of no effect. It is not unknown for a building owner to appeal for that very reason. The authority has other powers, however.

(2) *Stop notice*

The authority may serve a stop notice[2] to ensure that construction ceases or to prevent a material change of use. It can only be served after an enforcement notice if it seems that the building owner is intent on pressing ahead with work during the appeal procedure. There is no appeal against a stop notice. If the appeal against the enforcement notice is successful, the stop notice is automatically void. Failure to observe a stop notice results in very heavy penalties and further daily penalties for continuing failure. In some instances, a building owner may be able to obtain compensation after a successful appeal against an enforcement notice which was followed by a stop notice. For this reason alone, planning authorities are reluctant to serve stop notices.

(3) *Planning contravention notice*

This is a procedure introduced under the Planning and Compensation Act 1991 whereby a local planning authority can obtain information about activities being carried out on a site where a breach of planning control is suspected. The owner, occupier or any other recipient is required to reply within 21 days.

(4) *Breach of conditions notice*

From 27 July 1992, the local planning authority has had power to serve a notice requiring compliance with a condition in a planning permission. There is no appeal against such a notice and failure to comply within 28 days is a summary offence.

Appeal

An applicant may appeal against refusal of planning permission, conditions attached to the permission and various other matters. Notice must be given to the Secretary of State in the appropriate form within a stipulated period from the date on which the refusal was received or, in the case of non-determination, within the period from the date on which the determination should have been made. The actual period allowed for lodging the appeal varies depending on the subject matter of the appeal. The range is from 28 days to 6 months. An appeal may be dealt with in one of three ways:

■ Written representation: if the parties waive their right to an inquiry and the Secretary of State agrees[3]. This is the most common type of appeal and it is used in about 75% of planning appeals. It has the benefit of speed and relative cheapness.

- Public local inquiry: The Secretary of State must hold an inquiry if either the appellant or the local authority so desire. These inquiries will deal with the most complex applications and they usually involve legal representation and the cross-examination of witnesses[4].
- Informal hearing: a simple procedure with some characteristics of written representations and public local inquiry. It may occur where the Secretary of State considers the case to be appropriate and where one or both parties has indicated their wish to be heard by an inspector. The purpose is to save time and money for the parties and to allow the inspector to lead a discussion about the matters at issue. It is a more relaxed and less formal atmosphere than a public inquiry.

The local planning authority will provide details of the appeals procedure and helpful guidance is provided by the Planning Inspectorate[5].

9.4.8   Other permissions

Renewal of permission

Renewal of an existing permission is not automatic because there may be a change in circumstances following the original permission. A full permission is normally valid for 5 years and renewal must be sought before the expiry of this period.

Listed building consent

The Secretary of State has power to compile lists or approve lists compiled by other bodies of buildings of special architectural or historic interest[6]. A building may be listed for its exterior, interior or any feature. The local planning authority must notify owners and occupiers of listed buildings. Religious bodies which have approved systems of control, including the Church of England, the Church in Wales and the Roman Catholic Church, benefit from exception from listed building control ('ecclesiastical exemption'). All other religious bodies not benefiting from exemption are subject to normal listed building and conservation controls.[7].

It is an offence to demolish, alter or extend a listed building unless the planning authority or the Secretary of State has granted a written listed building consent. If work is carried out without such consent, it may be possible to make out a defence on the grounds that the works were urgently necessary for safety, health or to preserve the building, but the local planning authority must be notified in writing as soon as possible. Temporary protection can be given to an unlisted building which is in danger of demolition or alteration, by the service of a building preservation notice by the authority. Its effect is immediate and it lasts for 6 months during which time the Secretary of State can decide whether or not to list it.

Conservation area consent

The planning authority has power to declare certain areas to be of special architectural or historic interest as conservation areas where it is required to preserve and enhance their character[8]. The controls in a conservation area include the need for consent for demolition of buildings and for the felling of trees. Planning applications must be advertised and consideration has to be given to preserving and enhancing the character and appearance of the conservation area. The controls on development are not as extensive as for listed buildings, but more restrictive tolerances may be applied in certain instances[9].

Trees

Each local planning authority has the duty to ensure that adequate provision is made for the preservation and planting of trees when planning permission is granted[10]. It may also make 'tree preservation orders' for trees, groups of trees and woodlands which contribute to the amenity of the area. Notice must be given to the owners and occupiers of the land and neighbouring land owners who may be affected by it, who are entitled to object.

It is an offence to cut down, lop, top or wilfully damage such trees without the consent of the local planning authority unless they are deemed to be dangerous, dying, dead or the work is executed in compliance with another Act of Parliament. Even in such cases, the prior consent of the authority should be sought. The authority are entitled to insist on the replacement of a tree by another of appropriate size and species. A provisional tree preservation order is made in the first instance which is valid for six months, to allow for the resolution of objections and any changes to be made to the order. The order becomes permanent upon confirmation by elected members.

Certificate of lawfulness of existing use or development

Section 191 of the 1990 Act allows anyone who wishes to do so, to apply to the local planning authority to determine whether the following matters are lawful and, if so, to be granted a certificate of lawfulness of existing use or development (a 'CLEUD') to that effect. The matters are:

- An existing operational development on land
- An existing use of land
- Any other matter constituting a failure to comply with any condition or limitation subject to which planning permission was granted

The burden of proof is on the applicant, but the local authority must grant a certificate if the case is proved. A CLEUD may be revoked if it was obtained on the basis of false information or if important information was withheld.

Certificate of lawfulness of proposed use or development

Section 192 of the 1990 Act provides that any person who wishes to ascertain whether any proposed use of buildings or other land or any operations proposed to be carried out on the land would be lawful, may apply to the local authority for a certificate (a 'CLO-PUD'), specifying the use and operation in question. A certificate must be issued:

- If the proposed use or operation does not constitute development; *or*
- If it constitutes development, but is permitted by the GPDO; *or*
- If carrying it out would be in accordance with an existing planning permission.

The onus of proof is on the applicant who must accurately describe the proposal in sufficient detail to enable the authority to make their decision. As regards a proposed use, if the use falls within a use class, then the certificate must specify the class. Once a CLO-PUD has been granted, the use is conclusively presumed to be lawful. These two forms of certificate replace the former 'certificate of established use'.

Advertisements

Throughout England and Wales, local planning authorities are responsible for the day to day operation of the advertisement control system and for deciding whether a particular advertisement should be permitted or not. The control relates to a wide range of advertisements and signs including posters, notices, placards, fascia and projecting signs, directional signs, flag adverts, captive balloon adverts, etc. The rules[11] which govern advertisements effectively divide them into three main groups:

- Advertisements which are deliberately excluded from the planning authority's control
- Advertisements for which the rules give a 'deemed consent' so that the planning authority's consent is not needed, provided the advertisement meets certain criteria
- Advertisements for which the planning authority's 'express consent' is always needed

Applications must be made using the appropriate forms accompanied by a fee. In deciding an application, the local authority may consider only two issues: amenity and public safety. Consent when granted is normally for 5 years (although a shorter period can be stipulated). However, unless a condition is imposed that requires removal of the advertisement after the consent expires, the sign can continue to be displayed without making further application. In the case of refusal or imposition of a condition with which the applicant is dissatisfied, there are rights of appeal to the Secretary of State.

9.5 Other approvals

A development may be subject to a great many approvals other than planning and building control (see section 9.2). The following are building types which require special approvals of various kinds:

- Licensed premises and restaurants
- Music and dance halls
- Cinemas
- Petrol stations
- Nursing homes
- Abattoirs

In addition, approval may be required from landlords or funders of development.

9.6 Property

9.6.1 Boundaries

Boundaries are the demarcation lines between separate properties. They can be the source of many problems when the properties either side of the line are in different ownerships, as is usually the case.

When investigating the feasibility of building, the architect should make it an early task to establish or verify the apparent boundaries of a site. The only safe way to do this is for the architect to request verification from the client's solicitor. Since deed plans and the deeds themselves are often unclear on the matter, the solicitor will often be loath to put forward a definitive view. On occasion, boundaries are so vague that all the adjoining owners have to agree the boundaries afresh. Certain presumptions may be made from inspection of such things as fences, ditches and hedges.

Very great care must be taken when dealing with old properties which adjoin. Ownership of a cellar may extend under the ground floor of the other property and the buildings themselves may actually interlock, i.e. first floor project over neighbouring ground floor and under second floor. Such cases, however, would more usually fall under a consideration of party walls (see section 9.6.2).

If a building is constructed so as to infringe a neighbouring boundary, the building owner will have committed trespass against the neighbour. The matter can only be rectified by the removal of the building or the purchase of the portion of neighbouring land on which it stands, probably at an inflated price. Common infringements occur in the projection of footings or eaves across the boundary. Where a neighbour permits an eaves to project onto his or her land, the building owner is said to have a 'right of eavesdrop'.

9.6.2 Party walls

There are three types of party wall. The most common type is where the wall is divided vertically and reciprocal easements are in force over the whole wall. The second type is where the wall is divided vertically into two strips, one strip belonging to each owner. The third type is where the wall belongs completely to one owner and the adjoining owner has the right to have it maintained as a dividing wall.

There are now special procedures for party walls under the Party Wall Act 1996 which came into force on 1 July 1997. It applies only to England and Wales at present. What follows in this section is not a substitute for reading the Act itself which affects all architects. If anything is to be done to a party wall as defined by the Act, notice is to be given in certain forms. A party wall is defined as a wall, standing on land of different owners not taking account of projecting foundations, which is part of a building; or that part of a wall which separates buildings belonging to different owners. A 'party structure' is a party wall, floor or other structure separating parts approached by separate entrances, while a 'party fence wall' is a wall, standing on land of different owners not taking account of projecting foundations, which is not part of a building, but separates adjoining lands.

If the two adjoining owners do not agree (and it is often unwise to agree in advance), each party must appoint a surveyor to whom certain powers are given by the Act to determine the difference and to decide, subject to the provisions of the Act, what contribution each party is to make to the cost of the works. Both building and adjoining owners have statutory rights which they can exercise under the Act and those rights can never be overlooked or set aside. Care must be taken to adhere to the periods of notice laid down. When acting for the building owner and in view of the time required for notice, counter-notice and negotiation, the architect must take early steps to set the machinery in motion.

There are three basic situations covered by the Act:

- Building a new party wall
- Work to existing party walls
- Adjacent excavations and constructions

Building a new party wall

Where adjoining land is not built on at the line of a junction or is only built on by a boundary wall (i.e. not a party fence wall or the external wall of a building) there are two situations. If the wall is intended to straddle the boundary, one month's notice of a wish to start work must be given. The notice must indicate desire to build and describe the intended wall. If notice of consent is received, the wall must be built half and half or as agreed, the cost borne by each in proportion to use. If the wall is wholly on the applicant's own land, one month's notice of a wish to start work must be given. The notice must indicate a desire to build and describe the intended wall as before, but the building owner has the right to project foundations, if necessary, under adjacent land any time within 12 months from expiry of the notice, but the work must be at the building owner's own expense and the adjoining owner or occupier must be compensated for damage caused by building the wall or the foundations. This also applies where the adjoining owner refuses consent to a party or party fence wall.

Work to existing walls

A building owner has certain rights in respect of existing walls. The scope is very broad and the following is a brief summary. The building owner has the right:

■ To underpin, thicken or raise, but if not due to defect or lack of repair, must make good all damage to adjoining premises, internal furnishings and decorations and if a party structure or external wall, must carry up any adjoining owner's flues and chimneys which rest on or form part of the party structure or external wall as may be agreed or settled by the disputes process.
■ To repair or demolish and rebuild a party structure or party fence wall if the work is necessary because of defects or lack of repair.
■ To demolish a partition which does not conform with statutory requirements and build a party wall which does conform.
■ To demolish structures over public ways or passages belonging to other persons and rebuild so as to make them conform to statutory requirements.
■ To demolish a party structure and rebuild so as to make it of sufficient strength or height for any intended building of the

building owner or to rebuild to lesser thickness or height provided it is still sufficient for any adjoining owner, but must make good all damage to adjoining premises, internal furnishings and decorations and if a party structure or external wall, must carry up any adjoining owner's flues and chimneys which rest on or form part of the party structure as may be agreed or settled by the disputes process.

- To cut into a party structure or away from a party, party fence, external or boundary wall any foundation, chimney breast or other projection over the building owner's land or take away or demolish overhanging parts of wall or building of adjoining owner to the extent necessary to enable a vertical wall to be erected or raised against the wall or building of an adjoining owner, but all damage to adjoining premises, internal furnishings and decorations must be made good.
- To cut into an adjoining owner's wall to carry out weatherproofing of new wall erected against it, but must make good all damage to the wall.
- To carry out other necessary works incidental to the connection of a party structure with the premises adjoining.
- To raise a party fence wall or to raise it for use as a party wall or to demolish it and rebuild it as a party fence or party wall.
- To reduce or to demolish and rebuild a party or party fence wall either to not less than 2 metres if not used by an adjoining owner other than as a boundary wall or to a height currently enclosed by the building of an adjoining owner, but must reconstruct or replace any existing parapet or construct one if needed.
- To expose a party wall or structure, but adequate weathering must be provided.

A building owner may exercise these rights with the written consent of the adjoining owner. If adjoining land is built on at the line of a junction as a party or party fence wall or the external wall of a building, before exercising any right under the Act the building owner must give a two months 'party structure notice' of the date when work will start. The notice must state the name and address of the building owner, particulars of the proposed work, whether special foundations are intended and plans, sections and details including the loads to be carried. The notice ceases to have effect if the work is not begun within 12 months of the date the notice is served or if it is not continued with due diligence. There is provision for the adjoining owner to serve a counter notice. If no consent is received within 14 days of the date of service of party structure or counter notices, dissent is deemed and a dispute is deemed to have arisen.

Adjacent excavations and constructions

There are two situations:

- Where a building owner proposes to excavate and erect a structure any part of which is within 3 metres horizontally from any part of a structure of an adjoining owner and which extends to a lower level than the level of the bottom of the foundations of the adjoining structure.
- Where a building owner proposes to excavate and erect a structure any part of which is within 6 metres horizontally from any part of the structure belonging to an adjoining owner and which extends to a lower level than a point measured at 45° from the point of intersection of the external face of the adjoining structure and the bottom of the foundation.

The owners of such structures are deemed to be adjoining owners for the purposes of this section even though the property is not touching the boundary.

The building owner must give one month's notice of the date when work will start. The notice must set out the proposals and whether underpinning or other strengthening or protection is proposed. Plans and section must show the site and the depth of any excavation proposed and if the erection of a building is proposed, its site. The notice ceases to have effect if work is not begun within 12 months of the date on which the notice is served or if the work is not continued with due diligence. The building owner may at their own expense strengthen the foundations of the adjoining structure or may be required to do so by the adjoining owner. If there is no consent within 14 days of the date of service of notice, dissent is deemed and a dispute is deemed to have arisen.

There are various other provisions in relation to matters such as disputes and access which should be carefully studied.

9.6.3 Neighbouring land

A difficult problem can arise when it is necessary to enter upon a neighbour's land in order to carry out work. Neighbours could be held to ransom where the work was essential to deal with weather ingress or structural problems. The Access to Neighbouring Land Act 1992 was intended to deal with such matters. Like the Party Walls Act, it only extends to England and Wales. The Act deals with 'basic preservation works'. The term is broad and it includes, but is not necessarily restricted to, such things as maintenance or repair of a building, clearance or repair of a drain or cable, treatment or cutting back of any growing thing and the filling in or clearance of a ditch.

An application must be made to the court which must be satisfied that the work is reasonably necessary for preservation and it cannot be carried out without substantial difficulty without entry on the adjoining land. The court cannot make an order if the adjoining owner would suffer interference with use or enjoyment of the land or would suffer hardship. Of course, the court may include whatever terms and conditions it deems appropriate to protect the adjoining owner's property or privacy. These terms may include the payment of money to the adjoining owner by the person desiring to carry out the work.

9.6.4 Trespass

This is a category of the law of tort. Trespass to land is of most concern to the architect. The general rule is that if a person enters upon, remains upon or allows anything to come into contact with another's land, that person is committing trespass. Trespass can occur under land, on the surface or to a reasonable height over the land. Contrary to popular misconception, there is no necessity to prove damage in order to sue for trespass. There is a requirement for damage before action in the case of nuisance, however, with which trespass is often confused. If a person demolishes a wall by pushing it onto adjoining property, that is trespass; if the wall simply collapses with old age and falls onto adjoining property, that is nuisance. Building a foundation across a boundary is trespass; allowing tree roots to grow across is nuisance. Trespass is a direct invasion of another's land.

The usual legal remedies for trespass are to take action for damages, if any, and/or an injunction to prevent further or continuing trespass. A form of self help is for the person in possession of the land to forcibly evict the trespasser who refuses to leave, but this option should be a last resort and exercised with great care.

A builder carrying out work on a site is said to have a licence to be on the site for the purpose of carrying out the building. There may be an express licence, but it is more usual that the licence will be implied. A builder who stays on the land after the work is complete or after determination of employment will be a trespasser. Trespassers, particularly children, can be a real problem on building sites and those in possession of the site have an especially strict duty to ensure that children do not suffer injury[12].

An occupier owes a duty to trespassers by virtue of statute[13] if:

'he is aware of the danger or has reasonable grounds to believe that it exists; . . . he knows or has reasonable grounds to believe that the other is in (or may come into) the vicinity of danger; . . . the risk is one against which in all the circumstances of the case, he may reasonably be expected to offer the other protection.'

The duty is to take such care as is reasonable in all the circumstances of the case to see that the entrant to the property does not suffer injury on the premises by reason of the danger concerned. This duty may be discharged by giving warning of the danger on an appropriately worded notice.

9.6.5 Nuisance

Nuisance has been mentioned briefly under trespass. It is another category of the law of tort. There are three types of nuisance:

■ Public nuisance
■ Private nuisance
■ Statutory nuisance

Public nuisance

Public nuisance is an act or omission without lawful justification which causes damage, injury or inconvenience to the public at large. It is a crime as well as a tort. It must affect a reasonably sized category of people or the nuisance cannot be categorised as public. An example is the obstruction of a highway. A private person has no remedy for public nuisance unless that person suffers from that nuisance over and above the damage suffered by the public at large.

Private nuisance

Private nuisance is an unlawful interference with the use or enjoyment of land. The usual examples are smell, smoke, noise and tree roots. If a person wishes to sue for nuisance, damage must be proved. Remedies available are damages or an injunction. The suffering party may take action to abate the nuisance in wholly exceptional circumstances only. In some instances, building work can be held to be nuisance[14]. It is now rare for actions to be brought in this respect, however, because building operations are generally of quite short duration. It is usually reasonable use of property to permit or cause building works to be carried out from time to time and there are statutory powers for the local authority to regulate building works to prevent excessive noise, dust, etc.[15]. Nuisance is a complex subject and should any problem arise, the architect should advise the client to seek legal advice.

Statutory nuisance

Statutory nuisance is anything which is declared by statute to be a nuisance[16]. The local authority may serve an abatement notice to require the perpetrator to bring the nuisance to an end.

9.6.6   Rights of light

Rights of light is sometimes called 'ancient lights'. It is a negative easement (see section 9.6.7) which entitles an owner to prevent his neighbour building so as to obstruct the flow of light through particular windows. The right is not acquired in respect of the whole building, unless it is entirely glazed, but only in respect of the window openings. For this reason, when considering the redevelopment of a property which has rights of light to certain windows, it is essential that a careful measured survey is carried out so that any new windows will be replaced exactly in the same positions as the original windows. The right is usually acquired under the Prescription Act 1832 which requires the right to be enjoyed for 20 years without interruption and without written consent.

The existence of a building with rights of light on adjoining land can put severe constraints on the development potential of a site. In order for an act to be considered as an interruption, it must continue for at least a year. At one time, it was necessary to erect a screen to block the light to prevent the right being acquired. Since the Rights of Light Act 1959, the owner of land over which a right of light might be acquired may register as a land charge a notice identifying the properties and specifying the size and position of a notional screen. Parties likely to be affected must be given prior notice and the notice itself is in force for a year during which time an affected party may seek to have it varied or cancelled. In order to prevent the right being acquired, it is necessary to re-register at least every 19 years.

If a party considers that another is infringing his or her right of light, the injured party must show that the light which remains is not sufficient for the comfortable use and enjoyment according to the ordinary notions of mankind[17]. Any action would be brought in nuisance (see section 9.6.5) and a practical test which is often adopted is whether the light can flow into the window without interruption at an angle of 45° from the horizontal measured at the cill. The nature and use of the building will determine the amount of light entitlement. Thus a greenhouse will need more light than a private house[18].

9.6.7 Easements

Easements are rights held by one party to use the land belonging to another or to restrict the use of such land by another. Common examples are: rights of way and rights of drainage or for services. They are known as positive easements as compared to easements such as rights of light or right of support which are negative easements. An easement relates to land, not people. The land which enjoys the right is called the dominant tenement; the land on or against which the easement is exercised is called the servient tenement. It is essential that the two pieces of land have different owners.

There is often confusion with regard to right of support although the position is very clear. All land enjoys right of support from adjoining land. In the present state of the law, no successful action would be possible against a person excavating near a neighbour's boundary unless the excavation caused actual physical damage to the adjacent land. A neighbour could not successfully bring an action for the cost of building a retaining wall to prevent possible future slippage. That is simply economic loss and it is not recoverable in tort. There is no natural right of support for buildings (however, see section 9.6.2 relating to the Party Wall Act).

If, however, the removal of support from land causes the collapse of that land and the building standing on it, the building owner would have the right to bring an action. The right of support when applied to a building is usually acquired by prescription, but it can also be acquired expressly. A fairly common situation is where a property has been in existence for some years when the adjoining owner builds next to, taking support from, the original property. There may be an express agreement entered into before building or to regularise the position, or the owner of the original property may take no action for 20 years.

A *profit a prendre* is a right to remove something from another's land, for example turf. Easements and profits may be created by Act of Parliament: express grant, usually by deed; express reservation, when land is sold; prescription (see section 9.6.6).

9.7   Contract selection and implications

If the architect is carrying out his or her normal duties in contract administration, it is the architect's duty to advise the client about the most suitable form of contract to use for the particular project. This is recognised by the Standard Form of Agreement for the Appointment of an Architect (SFA/99) (see Chapter 6, section 6.4.3). No two projects are exactly the same and, therefore, very careful thought must be given to the appropriate form. Architects do not have a good reputation in this field. In the rush of practice, it is all too easy to advise the client to use a contract form with which the architect is familiar. There are a considerable number of standard forms to suit varying situations and procurement routes.

The forms commonly used for building works are summarised in Fig. 9.1 together with available supplements. Ideally, the architect should have a thorough knowledge of each contract so as to be able to properly advise the client. It has been suggested that an architect who advises the use of the wrong form of contract which results in the client suffering loss would be negligent[19]. We can see no good reason in principle to doubt that view although assembling the necessary proof might be a different matter. In any event, it is certain that an inappropriate choice of contract will make it very much more likely that problems will occur and that when they do, the contractor will have a justifiable claim for additional money. There are various publications which can assist the architect[20].

Sometimes, a client will insist that the company solicitor draws

---

Joint Contracts Tribunal (JCT) series

Standard Form of Building Contract 1998 (JCT 98)
 Private With Quantities
 Private With Approximate Quantities
 Private Without Quantities
 Local Authorities With Quantities
 Local Authorities With Approximate Quantities
 Local Authorities Without Quantities

Intermediate Form of Building Contract (IFC 98)

Agreement for Minor Building Works (MW 98)

Standard Form of Building Contract With Contractor's Design (WCD 98)

Standard Form of Prime Cost Contract (PCC 98)

Management Contract (MC 98)

Measured Term Contract (MTC 98)

Principal supplements:
 Sectional Completion for JCT 98, IFC 98, WCD 98
 Phased Completion for MC 98
 Contractor's Designed Portion for JCT 98
 Fluctuation clauses for JCT 98, IFC 98

There are amendment sheets available for use with JCT 98, IFC 98, MW 98 and WCD 98 in Northern Ireland
Scottish contracts are available to amend the JCT 98, MW 98 and WCD 98

Association of Consultant Architects

Form of Building Agreement 1982 (ACA2) 1998 revision

BPF Form of Building Agreement 1984 (BPF/ACA) 1998 revision

Institute of Civil Engineers

Standard Form of Engineering Contract (ICE 6)

Engineering and Construction Contract 1995 (NEC)

Fig. 9.1   Standard forms of building contract.

---

up a suitable contract. The task of drawing up a suitable form of contract would be daunting to say the least even if the solicitor is well experienced in construction matters. In most cases, the result will be disastrous. It is always worth while the architect explaining to the client the basic advantages of using a standard form. They are:

- It is comprehensive, covering most common construction situations.
- It is drawn up and updated at regular intervals to take account of the most recent legal decisions.

- It is known to the contractor and widely accepted in the industry. The contractor will be aware of the advantages and shortcomings and thus there will be no necessity for the employment of specialist professionals to advise on the pitfalls. Thus there will be no inflation of the tender figure from this cause.
- Many of the standard forms have a range of related documents.
- Some of the standard forms and all the ones current in the JCT range are negotiated documents and will not normally be caught by the *contra proferentem* rule: the rule of interpretation of a contract which states that where there is an ambiguity in a document which other means of interpretation have failed to resolve, the court may choose the meaning least favourable to the party seeking to rely on it.

The choice of contract should be the end of a sequence of activity on the part of the architect and the client. The contract should fit the procurement system (see Chapter 7, section 7.4)[21].

Once a decision has been made in regard to the procurement system, the number of possible standard forms will be reduced. There will be some procurement systems which have no standard form. A current example is construction management which is commonly dealt with by the use of purpose written forms or the use of unsuitable standard forms with amendments. Figure 9.2 shows a flowchart method of getting a rough idea of the appropriate form of contract.

It is not unusual to find that after a contract has been chosen as being most suitable, it still leaves a great deal to be desired in detail. It is possible to amend the standard forms, but five points should be noted:

- Any amendments must be kept to a minimum, because amendments often cause problems during the course or at the end of a contract period.
- Amendments invariably lead to concomitant amendments being required elsewhere in the contract and it is easy to overlook them. (For instance, deletion of delay on the part of nominated subcontractors as a ground for extension of time under the Standard Form of Contract JCT 98 requires no less than 16 other amendments to be made.) Failure in this respect can have dire results.
- Amendments should be drafted by someone with specialist building contract expertise.

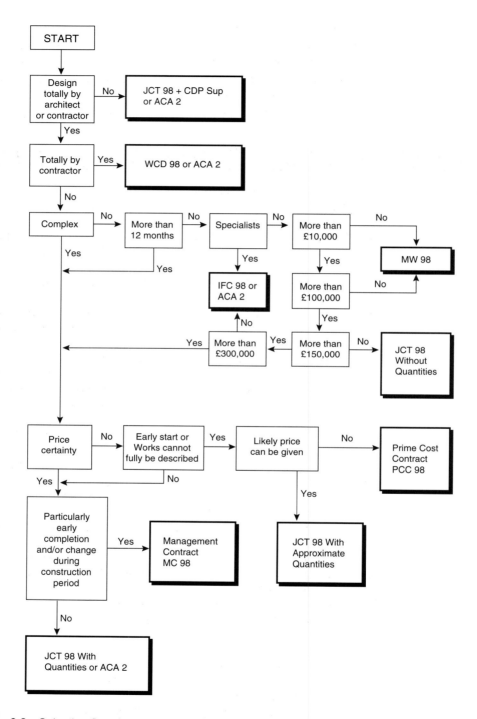

Fig. 9.2   Selection flowchart.

- Since many standard forms contain a clause giving the printed form priority over other documents, amendments should be made on the printed form itself or the clause should be struck out. If the amendment is simply made in the specification or the bills of quantities, it will be ineffective[22].
- The *contra proferentem* rule may apply to amendments.

References

(1)   The Town and Country Planning Act 1990, Part VII, sections 172–182, as amended by the Planning and Compensation Act 1991, sections 1–11.

(2)   The Town and Country Planning Act 1990, Part VII, sections 183–187, as amended by the Planning and Compensation Act 1991, sections 1–11.

(3)   DOE Circular 15/96, Annex 1, sets out the form which the statements should take.

(4)   Town and Country Planning (Inquiry Procedure) Rules 1992 and Town and Country Planning Appeals (Determination by Inspectors) (Inquiry Procedure) Rules 1992.

(5)   The Planning Inspectorate, *Making Your Planning Appeal* (Feb 1999).

(6)   Planning (Listed Buildings and Conservation Areas) Act 1990. This Act consolidates all listed building and conservation area legislation and covers such things as listing, getting listed building consent, appeals and enforcement.

(7)   Ecclesiastical Exemption (Listed Buildings and Conservation Areas) Order 1994.

(8)   Planning (Listed Buildings and Conservation Areas) Act 1990, section 69.

(9)   The Town and Country Planning (General Permitted Development Order) 1995, schedule 1 (termed article 1(5) land).

(10)   The Town and Country Planning Act 1990, sections 197–214, covers the requirement for local authorities to consider the protection and planting of trees and the making of tree preservation orders.

(11)   The Town and Country Planning (Control of Advertisements) Regulations 1992.

(12)   *Pannett v. McGuiness & Co* (1972) 2 QB 599.

(13)   Occupiers' Liability Act 1984, section 1(3).

(14)   *Andreae v. Selfridge & Co Ltd* (1938) Ch 1.

(15)   Control of Pollution Act 1974.

(16)   Public Health Act, sections 91 and 92.

(17)   *Colls v. Home & Colonial Stores* (1904) AC 185.

(18)   *Allen v. Greenwood* [1979] 1 All ER 819.

(19)   Jackson & Powell, *Professional Negligence*, 4th edn (1997) and second supplement (1999), Sweet & Maxwell.

(20)   JCT Practice Note 20, *Deciding on the appropriate form of JCT Main Contract*, revised August 1993 (deals only with JCT forms).

(21)   These factors, together with systems of contract choice, are explained in Chappell D. (1991) *Which Form of Building Contract*, Longmans.

(22)   *M. J. Gleeson (Contractors) Ltd* v. *London Borough of Hillingdon* (1970) EGD 495.

10 Stages E and F: Final Proposals and Production Information

10.1 Final design proposals

This stage of the architect's work is essentially a completion of the design stage. The architect must collaborate and co-ordinate the work of the design team. This is easy to say and less easy to do.

During this period, the architect must ensure, so far as possible, that all conflicts between consultants' work are ironed out. If any specialist subcontractor design work is involved in the project, this must also be coordinated, together with final details from statutory and other authorities. As a general rule, the use of subcontractors in a design capacity is not to be advised, because it can cause complications. In any event, the client must authorise such design delegation (Chapter 6, section 6.4.3). However, it has to be acknowledged that there are some instances where the use of specialist subcontractors in a design capacity cannot be avoided due to the nature of the specialism. In such instances, the use of a form of collateral warranty is required to protect the client.

The contractor is entitled to receive correct information. It is not the contractor's responsibility to look for errors and inconsistencies[1]. Careful cost checks will be made by the quantity surveyor if the project is large enough to support one, otherwise the architect must carry out this exercise.

If the project is sufficiently large to support a design team, they will be carrying out specific functions during the period, culminating in a meeting of the full team under the chairmanship of the team leader. This may be a project manager especially appointed by the client, but this will usually be as the employer's technical representative (Chapter 7, section 7.3). The separate functions of members of the design team will depend on the type of project, but as a general guide, they may be expected to be carrying out the following tasks:

Quantity surveyor/cost manager

- Reviewing the cost plan in the light of the client's comments and decisions on the scheme design. The review highlights

potential additional cost and risk areas and indicates scope for maximising value.
■ Carrying out cost studies and cost checks as the design team finally shape their details. There must be a constant flow of information between the architect and the consultants, the architect and the quantity surveyor and the quantity surveyor and the architect (Fig. 10.1 shows the principle).

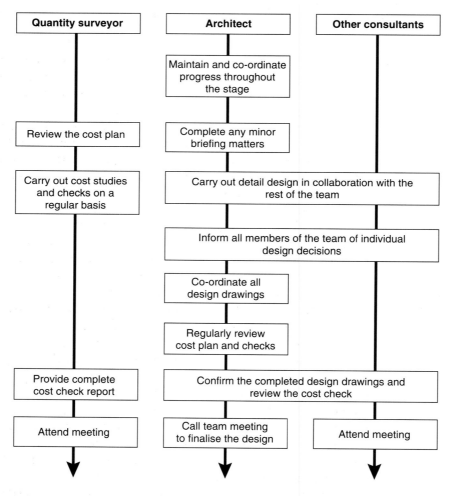

Fig. 10.1   Stage E: flow of information.

Civil and structural engineers

- Collaborating in the cost plan review and cost checking procedures
- Finalising all details in respect of dimensions, levels, loadings, concrete mixes, etc.
- Developing the specifications in detail

Mechanical and electrical engineers

- Refining the design of all services to be incorporated in the building
- Developing the specifications in detail

Strenuous efforts must be made to obtain the client's decision on any outstanding items. If the client makes any change in the size, location, shape or cost of the scheme after this stage, there will be a cost penalty to pay for the redoing of work already carried out. Ideally, there should be no changes at all in the design after this point, but in practice, it is impossible to eliminate all changes. Particularly in the case of some projects such as hospitals, the brief will be constantly evolving and the client just has to accept that there is a price to pay for changes. The difficulties may sometimes be eased by the choice of a particular procurement path and/or contract form, but it can never be removed entirely.

Stage E (final proposals) of the RIBA Plan of Work usually merges imperceptibly into Stage F (production information) and both stages amount to what would once have been termed 'working drawings'. To be precise, final proposals are probably composed in roughly equal parts of completion of design and commencement of working drawings. It does not matter. Indeed, it is perfectly proper that the process of design should not be divorced from the crucially important construction process.

The architect will continue the important two-fold function of designer and manager throughout this and the next stage. It is likely that, insofar as the architect can ever be said to have reached a finite end to this stage, he or she will have a large collection of design studies in a very final condition and covering every part of the project. This is the raw material from which the production information will take shape. There are several systems of setting out production information (section 10.3), but in every case, the architect cannot simply start by drawing a foundation and work up, or start with the roof and work down.

It is essential that the architect knows the form of each part of the building and it is during this stage, more than any other, that the building takes shape as a whole. It cannot be overstressed that all parts must progress together so that the architect is aware, when considering the ducting details, what effect they have on the foundation designs, lift wells, room plans and so on. This is in fact the most important stage in the architect's work on a project.

10.2   Building Regulations 1991

10.2.1   General

The Building Regulations in England and Wales are made by the Secretary of State under the Building Act 1984. Their purpose is to secure the health, safety, welfare and convenience of people in or about buildings and of others who may be affected by buildings or matters connected with buildings, to further the conservation of fuel and power and to prevent waste, undue consumption, misuse or contamination of water. This Act does not extend to Scotland or Northern Ireland.

Most cases of building or alteration to buildings must be notified to the local Building Control authority except where the services of an approved inspector are employed. The following building types, at present subject to certain conditions, are exempted from the Regulations but are controlled under other legislation:

- Prison buildings and buildings for the detention of criminals: Prisons Act 1952.
- Buildings required for the purposes of any educational establishment erected to plans which are approved by the Secretary of State, The Department for Education and Employment (other than houses).
- Buildings of Statutory Undertakers held and used for the purpose of their undertaking (other than offices, showrooms and sales areas).
- Buildings subject to the Explosives Acts 1875 and 1923 and to the Health and Safety at Work Act 1974.
- Buildings (other than dwellings, offices and canteens) on a site with a licence under the Nuclear Installations Act 1965.
- Buildings subject to the Ancient Monuments and Archeological Areas Acts 1979.

- Buildings (other than dwellings, offices and showrooms) which are used in connection with any mine or quarry.
- Buildings into which people cannot or do not normally go, subject to siting.
- Detached buildings containing fixed plant or machinery to which people only go intermittently to inspect or maintain the plant or machinery.
- Greenhouse (unless used for retailing, packing or exhibiting).
- Any building used for agriculture, including fish farming, sited one and a half times its height from any point of a building containing sleeping accommodation and having no point more than 30 metres from an exit which may be used in the case of fire (unless the main purpose of the building is retailing, packing or exhibiting).
- Building intended to remain where erected for less than 28 days.
- Mobile homes subject to the Mobile Homes Act 1983.
- Any building on a site used in connection with the sale of buildings or building plots, provided there is no sleeping accommodation.
- Any building used by people in connection with the erection, extension, alteration or repair of buildings and containing no sleeping accommodation.
- Small detached single storey buildings not exceeding 30 square metres floor area containing no sleeping accommodation and either sited more than one metre from the boundary of its curtilage or constructed substantially of non-combustible material.
- Nuclear, chemical or conventional weapon shelters not exceeding 30 square metres and which do not affect the foundations of adjoining or adjacent buildings subject to depth of excavation plus one metre.
- Any conservatory, porch, covered way or carport at least open on two sides. The extension which has a floor area not exceeding 30 square metres subject to glazing requirements of Approved Document N.
- Certain temporary exhibition stands.
- Tent or marquee.
- Moveable dwelling under section 269 of the Public Health Act 1936.
- 'Static' mobile accommodation (e.g. caravan).
- Certain engineering structures (e.g. dock, tunnel).
- Tower or mast not attached to building (not chimney).

- Plant or machinery.
- Storage racking (unless supporting a floor).
- Amusement or fairground equipment.
- Scaffolding or falsework.
- Street furniture.
- Fences, wall or gates.
- External storage tank.

The Regulations are much shorter than previous editions, being expressed fairly simply in functional terms, but there is a set of Approved Documents which indicate ways in which compliance with the Building Regulations may be achieved. However, it is possible to show compliance with the Regulations by reference to other standards or by calculation. Important new features have been introduced allowing building control by local authorities and by private certification. The latter system operates under The Building (Approved Inspectors, etc.) Regulations 1985. Control is operated through three procedures.

10.2.2   Notification

It is an offence to commence building operations without first depositing plans or a building notice giving at least two clear days' notice to the local authority. Note, however, that it is not necessary to await approval before commencing work. The notice procedures are:

Deposit of full plans

Deposit of full plans is the traditional system. A full set of plans must be deposited with the local authority in duplicate together with completed forms which may vary in layout from authority to authority, but which all contain requests for the same basic information. Where Part B Fire Safety imposes a requirement, two further copies must be deposited demonstrating compliance except in regard to dwelling houses. It is now possible to request, at the time the plans are deposited, that the local authority issue a completion certificate in accordance with the regulations. The Building (Local Authority Charges) Regulations 1998, in force on 1 April 1999, give the local authority power to determine the scale of plan or inspection charges as may be necessary to discharge its duties under the appropriate regulations. Charges can relate to the passing and rejection of plans, site inspections, building notices, reversion, regularisation and determinations. Charges are now payable when appeals are made to the Secretary of State. Current charges are available from any building control department of the local authority.

The drawings, each of which must be signed by the applicant or appointed agent, are generally expected to consist of the following:

- A block plan, not less than 1/1250 scale, showing the size and position of the building in relation to adjoining buildings, boundaries, position of all buildings within the curtilage, width of adjoining streets, lines of drainage, size, depth and gradient of drains and means of access, position and level of drain outfall and sewer connection.
- Sufficient plans and sections to suitable scales (usually not less than 1/100) showing full details of the intended construction of the project including site and floor levels, number of storeys, foundations, construction of floors, walls and roof, windows, doors, barriers to moisture, fire safety, means of escape, insulation, ventilation and access for the disabled.

The local authority must give written notice of approval or rejection of the application within 5 weeks of the date of deposit of plans provided the requisite fee has been paid and a reasonable estimate of the cost of the work has been submitted. The period may be extended in writing to a total of not more than 2 months by agreement of both parties. If the authority fails to give written notice, it is in breach of its duty and the plan charge must be refunded. There is no deemed approval and indeed, even if there were such deemed approval it would be of little value if there was any disconformity, in the face of the applicant's obligation to construct in accordance with the Building Regulations. If the application is rejected, the applicant may appeal to the Secretary of State.

Building notice

There is no approval of plans by the authority where the building notice is adopted and work can be commenced subject to the submission of notices (see above). A building notice is now valid for 3 years if work is not started and it cannot be given for a building which requires a means of escape and which is designated under the Fire Precautions Act 1971 or if so altered. The building, new or existing, including alterations or extensions would become subject to the Fire Precautions (Workplace) Regulations 1997 and would require full plans application to comply with the Act. There is no prescribed form for the notice, but it must contain certain basic information: the name and address of the person intending to carry out the work, notice that it is given under Regulation 11(1)(a) of the Building Regulations and a description including the use of the building to which the application relates. In addition, appropriate drawings and the prescribed charge must be deposited.

The drawing, to a scale of not less than 1/1250, will usually show the size and position of the building, its relationship to adjoining buildings, boundaries, position of all building within the curtilage, width of adjoining streets, numbers of storeys, building use, means of drainage and building over sewers. Details of insulation and hot water storage systems must be given in a detailed statement.

The authority may request the submission of whatever additional drawings or information they require to enable them to carry out their duties. It is now possible, where unauthorised work has been undertaken on or after 11 November 1985, for the owner to apply to the local authority for a Regularisation Certificate which is subject to a non-refundable charge at the time of submission[2].

Initial notice

The initial notice is used if private certification is to be employed, using an approved inspector (see section 10.2.1). The notice must be in the prescribed form and must contain a description of the work, whether it is 'minor work' under the Building (Approved Inspectors, etc.) Regulations 1985, an undertaking to consult the fire authority, a statement of awareness of statutory obligations and a declaration that an approved insurance scheme is in operation. (Fig. 10.2 is an example of such a notice). The notice must be signed by the inspector and by the applicant. It must be accompanied by an appropriate drawing. The drawing must be a site plan to not less than 1/1250 scale showing location of the site, boundaries, connections to sewers and any proposed work over a sewer.

The local authority has 5 working days from the date of receipt of the notice to accept or reject it. If the notice is not rejected within this period, the authority is presumed to have accepted without conditions. The authority may impose various conditions when accepting the notice.

The Building Act 1984, section 47, and the Building (Approved Inspectors, etc.) Regulations 1985

INITIAL NOTICE

To: The Brudax Metropolitan District Council, Department of Planning (Building Control Section), Old Town Hall, Bruddax, BX1 2FT

1. This notice relates to the erection of a home for frail elderly persons, corner of Low Road and High Street, Bruddax, BX2 4EV

2. The approved inspector for the work is:
   Seymore Thanniew RIBA
   Canny Buildings
   Bruddax, BX5 6PC
   Tel: Bruddax 0111 234567

3. The person intending to carry out the work is:
   Hope Furthurbest
   Penury House
   Neely Spent
   Bruddax, BX2 7EV
   Tel: Bruddax 0111 345678

4. The following documents relating to the work are enclosed with this notice:
   A copy of the approved inspector's notice of approval.
   A scheme of insurance approved by the Secretary of State, issued on behalf of Yorisk Insurers plc relative to the work described.
   A plan to 1:1250 scale indicating site location, boundaries, drainage, connection and location of existing sewers.

5. The work is not minor.

6. I, Seymore Thanniew, declare:

   a) that I have no professional or financial interest in the work; and
   b) that I will consult the fire authority before giving a plans certificate in accordance with section 50 of the Act or a final certificate in accordance with section 51 of the Act in respect of any of the work; and
   c) that I am aware of the obligations laid upon me by Part II of the Act and by regulation 10 of the 1985 Regulations.

Signed   Signed

Approved Inspector   Person intending to
                                                    carry out the work
2 May 2000   2 May 2000

Fig. 10.2   Example of an initial notice.

A local authority may reject an initial notice on the following grounds only:

- The notice is not in the prescribed form
- The work is not within the area of the authority on which the notice has been served
- The person signing as approved inspector is not an approved inspector
- Insufficient information about description, use of building, location or drainage
- An initial notice is not accompanied by notice of the inspector's approval
- There is no evidence of insurance cover
- There is no undertaking to consult the fire authority (if applicable)
- The inspector has a professional or financial interest in the work (unless 'minor work' involved)
- The drainage proposals are unsatisfactory
- The authority is not satisfied that it may consent to building over a public sewer (if applicable)
- Local legislation will not be complied with
- There is an overlap with a still effective initial notice

Upon acceptance, supervision of the work becomes the responsibility of the inspector and the authority's powers to enforce the Building Regulations are suspended until either the initial notice is cancelled by the inspector or it ceases to have effect on the lapse of certain defined periods.

10.2.3 Commencement, completion, etc.

Where full plans have been deposited in the traditional way, building works must be commenced within 3 years of the date of deposit of plans with the local authority. Once work has started, neither the Regulations nor the Act itself stipulate the speed at which the work must progress, probably because it would not be feasible to so specify. It is possible for the work to be carried out over a very protracted period without the applicant incurring any penalty.

If the local authority is to supervise the work by means of its own inspectors, the Regulations require the applicant or the builder to give the following notices in writing. The authority may, and often does, inspect on the basis of a telephone call, where it is permitted by the Regulations, but it is preferable from every point of view if the proper written notices are served and that:

- At least 2 days have elapsed before commencement of work on site
- At least 1 day has elapsed before any excavation is covered
- At least 1 day has elapsed before any foundation is covered
- At least 1 day has elapsed before any damp-proof course is covered
- At least 1 day has elapsed before any site concrete is covered
- At least 1 day has elapsed before any drainage or sewer is covered
- Not more than 5 days have elapsed after the covering of any drain or sewer
- Not more than 5 days have elapsed after completion
- At least 5 days have elapsed before occupation (if the building is occupied before completion)

('Day' excludes any Saturday, Sunday, Christmas Day, Good Friday, bank or public holiday.)

Local authorities must now issue completion certificates in the following cases:

- When requested at the time of full plans submission
- Where due notification has been received that the building will be put to a designated use (Fire Precautions Act 1971 and the Fire Precautions (Workplace) Regulations 1997)
- When notices have been received for completion or part occupation before completion

Where an approved inspector is involved, the inspector must issue a final certificate when work is complete (not the same as the final certificate under the provisions of JCT contracts). The local authority is deemed to have accepted the certificate if it does not reject it within 10 days of receipt.

10.2.4 Dispensations and relaxations

The local authority has the power to dispense with or relax a regulation. This is a power delegated from the Secretary of State. The authority must be satisfied that the requirement would be unreasonable in a particular instance. Unless it concerns internal work only, a relaxation application normally must be advertised in a local newspaper by the authority at least 21 days before a decision is to be made. If the authority refuses the relaxation or because of failure to respond within two months it is deemed refused, the applicant has the right to appeal to the Secretary of State. The applicant must appeal within one month of refusal setting out the grounds for appeal and all relevant information.

The Secretary of State may also grant what is known as a 'type relaxation' with or without any representations being made. Conditions may be attached to such relaxations or they may be made for a limited period only.

10.2.5   Contraventions

The local authority may require the removal or amendment of work which is carried out in contravention of the Regulations. This is normally done by service of a notice on the building owner. Failure to comply with such notice within 28 days entitles the authority to take action itself to correct the contravention and charge such costs to the owners. Such notice may not be served after the expiry of 12 months from the date of completion of the work. Appeal from such notice is to a magistrates court. An alternative is for the building owner to obtain a written report from a suitably qualified person in regard to the subject of the notice. The time for compliance with the notice is then extended to 70 days. On receipt of the report, the authority may withdraw the notice and may pay the building owner appropriate expenses.

10.2.6   Fire precautions

Fire has proved to be a major hazard in buildings for centuries. The Building Regulations 1991, Schedule 1, Part B, Fire Safety, now contains five requirements:

B1   Means of escape from all buildings, including dwelling houses
B2   Internal fire spread (linings)
B3   Internal fire spread (structure)
B4   External fire spread
B5   Access and facilities for the fire service

In large and complex schemes, the only viable and acceptable standard would be achieved by the fire engineering approach coupled with consultations with the Building Control Authority and the fire authority at every stage in any project.

The Fire Precautions Act 1971 is designed to ensure adequate means of escape and related fire precautions in premises the use of which, broadly speaking, involves members of the public being present in any number. Its object is to protect life in the event of fire and it cannot be applied directly to the protection of buildings and their contents.

The Act is enforced by the fire authorities and it provides that a fire certificate shall be required for all premises put to designated uses. The fire certificate will be issued only after the fire authority for the area is satisfied that the means of escape and other fire precautions for the particular premises are such as may be reasonably required.

The classes of use which may be designated under the Act are:

- Use as sleeping accommodation
- Use as an institution providing treatment or care
- Use for entertainment, recreation or instruction, or for purposes of any club, society or association
- Use for any teaching, training or research
- Use for any purpose involving access to the premises by the public whether by payment or otherwise
- Use as place of work (also covered by other legislation)

Application for a fire certificate must be made to the fire authority in the prescribed form and the applicant must be ready to supply such further information as the fire authority may require and within any time specified. The fire authority must have an inspection of the premises made. If the authority is not satisfied, it must serve a notice specifying what needs to be done within a specified time. The fire certificate when issued must specify:

- The use of the premises
- Means of escape in case of fire
- Means with which the building is provided (other than fire fighting equipment) for securing that the means of escape is capable of being safely and effectively used at all material times
- Type, number and location of all fire fighting equipment
- Type, number and location of means of giving warning in case of fire

The certificate may impose such other requirements as the authority consider to be appropriate in the circumstances.

A person who is aggrieved by the contents of the certificate or by the authority's refusal to grant such certificate and other connected matters may appeal to the magistrates court within 21 days.

This is an important piece of legislation which is closely linked to the Building Act 1984. Architects should be familiar with its provisions so as to be able to advise clients broadly concerning its application in particular instances.

The construction of buildings and their subsequent alteration or adaptation for other use is becoming more complex and may be subject to other Acts and regulations which may be outside the remit of the Building Regulations. The following list is an aide memoire of other legislation connected with buildings and structures, but it is not intended to be fully comprehensive. Scotland and Northern Ireland are not always included. Most local authority staff are happy to confirm whether a particular Act or regulation is applicable to a scheme:

- *Health & Safety at Work Act 1974*

- *Building Regulations and Amendment of Building (Scotland) Act 1959*

- *Offices, Shops and Railways Premises Act 1963*
  Health, safety and welfare of employees, fire precautions, means of escape and certain contiguous fuel storage premises.

- *Fire Precautions Act 1971*
  Further provision for the protection of persons from fire risk, certified premises, material and/or structural alterations.

- *Highways Act 1980*
  Means of access to premises from highways, bridges in England and Wales, certain footpaths in buildings by agreement, footbridges over highways linking buildings, doors not to open onto highway, power to prescribe building lines, control of builders' skips, dangerous land adjoining highway.

- *Mines and Quarries (Tips) Act 1969*
  Provision in relation to tips associated with mines and quarries, to prevent disused tips constituting a danger to members of the public, etc.

- *Factories Act 1961*
  Health (general provisions), safety (general provisions), means of escape in case of fire, welfare – drinking water/washing facilities.

- *Public Health Act 1961*
  Certain sections repealed by the Building Act 1984 (in schedule 7), provision of foul and surface water sewers in new streets.

- *Mobile Homes Act 1983*
  To station a mobile home on land forming part of a protected site and occupy the home as the only or main residence.

- *Safety of Sports Grounds Act 1975*
  Not applicable to Northern Ireland. An Act to make provision for safety at designated sports stadia and other sports grounds where accommodation is in excess of 10,000 spectators.

- *Disabled Persons Act 1981*
  An Act providing that provisions must be made for access to buildings, premises and signs.

- *Fire Safety and Safety of Places of Sport Act 1987*
  Provisions in respect of stands at sports grounds, indoor sports premises, amending statutory provisions, regulating entertainment licences, charges for fire certificates. The Act does not extend to Northern Ireland and there are certain sections which apply to England and Wales only and to Scotland only.

- *Local Government (Miscellaneous Provisions) Acts 1976 and 1982*
  Sanitary appliances at places of entertainment, dangerous trees, certain dangerous excavating.

- *Building Act 1984, Schedule 3, Part I*
  Certain sections of this Act do not apply to inner London; see Schedule 3, Part I for application. See also The Building (Inner London) Regulations 1985 and 1987.

- *The Disability Discrimination Act 1995*
  Buildings should be designed for access and use by everyone and designed to create a barrier-free environment. From October 1999, Part M of the Building Regulations will apply to new dwellings (separate regulations are in force in Northern Ireland and Scotland).

- *The Party Wall Act 1996*
  See the fuller description in Chapter 9, section 9.6.2.

- *The Fire Precautions (Workplace) Regulations 1997*
  These arise from two separate European Commission Directives and affect employers and workplaces. They do not at present apply to Northern Ireland, but the situation is under review. They are very extensive and they apply to all, other than specified 'excepted workplaces', to assess risk in relation to workplace or process. Assessment must be in writing where more than five people are employed. The local authority is

responsible for enforcement. Prohibition notices can be served depending on premises considered dangerous.

■ *Smoke Detectors Act 1991*
No commencement order has been made to bring this Act into force.

■ *Licensing Act 1964*
Consent required for certain alterations to licensee premises, power to require structural alterations on renewal of licence, time limit on orders, appeals, club premises, fire risks, restaurants, etc. providing entertainment, distribution of licensed premises in new towns.

■ *Cinemas Act 1985*
Licence required, giving of notice to the local authority and chief of police, powers of entry.

■ *The Workplace (Health, Safety and Welfare) Regulations 1992*
Implement provisions of the EU Workplace Directive, general duty imposed on employers to comply with the regulations, ventilation, lighting, adequacy of room dimensions, washing facilities, etc.

10.3   Production information

10.3.1   General

This is Stage F of the RIBA Plan of Work. It has already been remarked that this stage merges imperceptibly with Stage E. However, this stage does mark the firming of all construction decisions and the completion of all information in readiness for the quantity surveyor to produce bills of quantities if that is part of the chosen procurement route.

During this period, the architect prepares drawings, specifications and schedules. These are the instructions to the contractor to tell him what is to be built and the quality required. Although some architects leave the detailed specification to the quantity surveyors, this is thoroughly bad practice because the architect is ultimately responsible for the specification and from every point of view it is best if the architect prepares it.

It is also the time for agreeing details of the contract with the client and for obtaining quotations from those who are to be nominated, named or listed subcontractors. The architect must be in a position to inform the quantity surveyor of the nature and amounts of all prime cost and provisional sums which are to go into the bills of quantities. Stage F is now divided into F1 and F2. Broadly, F1 is the preparation of sufficient information for tenders to be invited whereas F2 is the further information which will be required to amplify the contract drawings and to enable the contractor to carry out and complete the Works by the date for completion in the contract. If the architect provides an information release schedule, it is the information on that schedule which is produced in stage F2.

10.3.2   Drawings

There are several different ways of producing the kind of drawings which make up the bulk of the production information. The design presentation drawings usually form the starting point for the preparation of working drawings. It has already been observed that by this stage the design drawings will be very detailed. Computers are now rapidly becoming standard practice for the production of drawings (Chapter 15, section 15.9). Although at one time a slow and laborious task, with the right equipment and architects who are practised in its operation, drawings can be produced quite quickly. A substantial number of practices, however, still use traditional methods.

Under most standard forms of building contract, the responsibility for supplying the contractor with correct information lies with the architect[3]. Mistakes will always occur, but in view of the cost of rectifying a mistake on a drawing which no one has spotted until too late, it is of the utmost importance that the drawing system should be simple and capable of highlighting errors. Of course, there is no such foolproof system, but some methods are probably better than others.

Traditionally, architects worked on all aspects of the building at once, having half finished drawings showing plans at each level, elevations, sections and rough sketch drawings of all the major details to a large scale. These 'typical details' were often drawn on the same sheet as a plan or section which included the detail to a much smaller scale. The drawings were all brought to completion together and generally formed a well integrated set. Such sets of drawings were characterised by very many more lines than strictly necessary to tell the story and an apparent desire on the part of the architect to leave no square millimetre of paper unused. Notes littered the drawing and they were often repetitive in nature.

This kind of drawing system is quite satisfactory, although expensive, if the building is relatively small and uncomplicated by special services. It is likely to be accurate because it is produced as a set and it has the advantage of having all the large scale details on the same sheet as the small scale information to which it relates. Moreover, the bricklayer can see what the carpenter has to do and the steel erector can readily appreciate the reason for any fine tolerances which have been specified. In fact, each part of the building can be understood in relation to every other part.

The problems with this kind of drawing system stem from the advantages. Although the system is fine for small buildings, it is very difficult to build a medium to large building from such drawings. One problem is the change in number of drawings from perhaps an optimum of two or three to perhaps fifty or more for a building only marginally larger and more complex than a large detached family house. The other problem is the unstructured way in which the information is presented. If details are drawn on the same sheet as small scale drawings, finding such a detail will be difficult if there is more than one drawing showing the small scale item, but the large detail is only on one. There is a rule, whose name escapes the authors at present, which states that whichever drawing the site agent picks up, the detail will be on another. The sheer complexity of such drawings, when multiplied for a large building, makes errors almost certain (see Chapter 11, section 11.1).

A drawing system which attempted to overcome the defects of what can be termed the traditional method was the elemental drawing. The idea of this was that each element of the building was given a special drawing or set of drawings. Each item of information was given just once, in the appropriate place and to an appropriate scale. Among other things, the alteration of a drawing was made easier than where a traditional drawing was involved. Thus there was a complete set of reinforced concrete drawings showing every detail of the concrete including dimensions, but nothing else. Similar sets were provided for brickwork and blockwork, plastering, joinery, plumbing, etc. Further drawings in outline were provided to show the way in which the elements fit together.

This system was developed into a four stage and more practical drawing method:

- Location drawings
- Assembly drawings

- Component drawings
- Details/schedules

Location drawings

Location drawings are produced to a small scale, typically 1:100, but sometimes, for very large buildings, 1:200 is used. The purpose of the drawings is reflected in the content. They are intended to show the location of the building and other elements on the site, so as to enable the site agent to set them out properly, and to show the position of all the other major elements in the building itself. Thus there is a site plan, plans at each level, elevations and sections through every difficult portion of the building. Such plans and sections are not intended to show how the building should fit together, they are principally to serve as an index or menu from which the site agent can get a reference number for the required drawing. Some additional information may be included, such as finished floor and foundation levels and setting out and other dimensions, but the golden rule is that every line must be on the paper for a definite purpose. Very often, these drawings are produced on a standard grid basis to simplify location of walls, doors and windows.

Assembly drawings

Assembly drawings show how the components of the building fit together. They are the successors to the traditional 'half inch sections' although they may not be sections and the scales can be any standard scale from 1:50 to 1:10. These drawings tend to contain the information which is not to be found elsewhere.

Component drawings

Component drawings show how the parts of the building are to be manufactured. Such items as fitted joinery, windows, doors, stairs, screens, concrete products and standard panels would be shown on these drawings. Generally, there is a separate drawing for each component. Components are often drawn full size or to some other appropriate large scale.

Details/schedules

The final category of drawings includes large scale details of specific items of construction not shown sufficiently clearly elsewhere. Special details of damp-proof courses, weatherings, eaves, junctions and external hard landscaping may be included. This category also includes schedules. Schedules are a very good way of presenting information for categories of building element. They also impose a good discipline on architects who learn a lot about their buildings in particular and construction in general by producing schedules. The architect who schedules everything possible will make a friend of the quantity surveyor. Common schedules include the following:

- Ironmongery
- Sanitary fittings
- Precast concrete
- Doors
- Windows
- Floor, wall and ceiling finishes
- Lighting
- Glazing
- Tiling
- Colour
- Inspection chambers and manholes
- Lintels

Some less obvious subjects for schedules, but which are well worth doing include:

- Architraves
- Skirtings
- Casings
- Pipe runs
- Gulleys
- External paving

References

(1)   *London Borough of Merton* v. *Stanley Hugh Leach Ltd* (1985) 32 BLR 51.
(2)   A number of excellent books have been published to guide and assist the architect or building designer to meet the ever-increasing legal responsibility applied to buildings. *Knights Building Regulations (With Approved Documents)*, Supplement 31, (1999) Charles Knight Pub-

lishing, is perhaps the most extensive and detailed general guide, but it is not a substitute for legal advice or for the wording of the various Acts and Regulations. Billington M.J. *The Manual to the Building Regulations*, (1999) Stationery Office, is also a detailed source of information regarding procedure.

(3) *London Borough of Merton* v. *Stanley Hugh Leach Ltd* (1985) 32 BLR 51.

Stages G and H: Tender Documentation and Tender Action

11.1 Co-ordinated project information

One of the prime causes of disruption of building operations on site has been highlighted as being shortcomings in drawn information together with a lack of compatibility in project information generally, i.e. the drawings, specifications and bills of quantities all say something different.

In order to improve the situation, the Co-ordinating Committee for Project Information (CCPI) was set up by the major bodies in the construction industry and after consultation with all interested parties produced a Common Arrangement of Work Sections for Building Works (CAWS). They also produced Codes of Project Specification Writing and Production Drawings and also worked with the producers of the Standard Method of Measurement for Building Works (SMM7).

The purpose of CAWS, as set out in its introduction, is to define an efficient and generally acceptable identical arrangement for specification and bills of quantities. The main advantages are:

■ Easier distribution of information, particularly in the dissemination of information to subcontractors. One of the prime objects in structuring the sections was to ensure that the requirements of the subcontractors should not only be recognised but be kept together in relatively small tight packages.
■ More effective reading together of documents. Use of CAWS coding allows the specification to be directly linked to the bill of quantities descriptions, cutting down the descriptions in the latter whilst still giving all the information contained within the former.
■ Greater consistency achieved by implementation of the above advantages. The site agent and clerk of works should be confident that when they compare the drawings with the bill of quantities they will no longer ask the question 'Which is right?'.

CAWS is a system based on the concept of work sections. To avoid boundary problems between similar or related work sections, CAWS gives, for each section, a list of what is included and what is excluded, stating the appropriate sections where the excluded item can be found.

CAWS has an hierarchical arrangement in three levels, for instance:

- Level 1   R   Disposal systems
- Level 2   R1   Drainage
- Level 3   R10   Rainwater pipes/gutters

CAWS includes some 300 work sections encountered in the construction industry. They vary widely in their scope and nature reflecting the extensive range of products and materials that now exist for use by contractors, subcontractors and specialists. Although very much dependent on size and complexity, no single project will need more than a fraction of this number: perhaps as a very general average 25-30%. Only level 1 and level 3 are normally used in specifications and bills of quantities. Level 2 indicates the structure, and helps with the management of the notation. New work sections can be inserted quite simply without the need for extensive renumbering.

11.2   Bills of quantities

11.2.1   General

The work of quantity surveyors/cost managers is described in Chapter 1 and was traditionally described as being to measure and value, but as will have been seen today covers a much wider range of activities. The comments in this chapter are restricted to the preparation of bills of quantities, a key part of the measuring and valuation function.

11.2.2   Time for preparation of quantities

The quantity surveyors' work is the last stage before receipt of tenders, except estimating by the contractors. Consequently, there is a tendency for the cumulative result of delays during the earlier stages of a scheme to have its effect on the time allocated for preparation of quantities. With drawings completed and everything apparently cut and dried, it is sometimes difficult for clients to understand further delay, and the surveyor is accordingly pressed.

Surveyors can and will work at high pressure when necessary, but they cannot do so for everybody and all the time. They are, after all, preparing a contract document, which will define the contract work precisely, and accuracy in the bill depends on a systematic checking of each stage, and a very careful reading through of the final draft. Excessive pressure can only result in work being done hurriedly or in part omitted, with dangerous results. Therefore no attempt should be made to reduce the period for taking off the quantities to compensate for earlier delays.

It is a great help in shortening the time required for preparation of a bill if the quantity surveyor is fully involved throughout the design stages and is able to plan ahead and ensure the necessary resources are available. They should be kept informed of the programme and advised of any slippages as they arise. When drawings are approaching the final stages they should be given a definite date, which, when once given, will be adhered to. They will then be able to plan their work so that the job can be done in the minimum of time. Moreover, if surveyors are expecting drawings they can do the work in, say, six weeks; the same period may not be sufficient if the drawings turn up a fortnight late, or if they come slowly in batches.

The period is fixed having regard to the work expected to be in hand at the time, and assuming that all particulars will be available together, unless otherwise arranged. The architect may be confident that surveyors, for their part, will do the work as quickly as possible, as it is in their interest to do so.

11.2.3   Procedure in the quantity surveyor's work

In order that the architect may appreciate the requirements of quantity surveyors in the way of drawings and particulars, it is necessary to give some idea of how they set about their work.

The building is divided into sections structurally, and each section is individually measured one section at a time. A list of sections in a typical building might be:

(a) Substructure   (1) Substructures
(b) Superstructure   (2) Frame
                         (3) Upper floors
                         (4) Roof
                         (5) Stairs
                         (6) External walls

		(7)	Windows and external doors
		(8)	Internal walls and partitions
		(9)	Internal doors
(c)	Finishes	(10)	Wall finishes
		(11)	Floor finishes
		(12)	Ceiling finishes
(d)	Services	(13)	Sanitary appliances
		(14)	Disposal installations
		(15)	Water installations
		(16)	Heating installations
		(17)	Electrical installations
		(18)	Gas installations
		(19)	Lift installations
		(20)	Communications installations
		(21)	Builder's work in connection with services
(e)	External works	(22)	Site works
		(23)	Drainage

This list is obviously elastic, and a particular building might introduce additional sections, e.g. kitchen equipment or laboratory installations. The list is in a logical order, more or less following the construction of the building. The surveyors going through these sections see the erection of the building carried through in their mind's eye and must see every detail (even the fullest of drawings cannot show everything); they must decide for themselves what that detail is, for they cannot measure without something definite in mind.

Obviously it will be of great assistance to the surveyors if all the drawings are made available at one time but if certain drawings are delayed the surveyors will not necessarily be held up. It must be the right drawings which are kept back. Surveyors may be able to do without joinery fittings or drains and not upset their organisation; but if they are sent foundation drawings and are told by the architect 'You will have to wait for the depths', it is worse than useless.

Even if they are told 'It's all there except the bar reinforcement, I'm waiting for the engineer', surveyors are bound to lose time. They would normally measure reinforcement whilst the foundations are fresh in their mind. If they have to go over the whole again, there is much wasted effort. When complete drawings are not going to be available the surveyors should be consulted as to priorities.

11.2.4   Standard methods of measurement

Standard methods of measurement have been introduced over the years to ensure that all bills of quantities are prepared on the basis of a set of rules accepted and agreed by the industry.

The most common in use is the Standard Method of Measurement of Building Works agreed between the RICS and the Construction Confederation (formally BEC). This is currently in its seventh edition (SMM7), revised in 1998 and is a set of rules structured in CAWS which provides a uniform basis of measuring. Under the JCT forms of contract, bills of quantities are deemed to have been measured using SMM7 unless specifically stated to the contrary. SMM7 is accompanied by a Code of Measurement Practice for use as a non-mandatory explanatory document.

For engineering works the ICE publish a Civil Engineering Standard Method of Measurement which like its counterpart in the building field provides a uniform basis for measuring. This method of measurement does not have the same contractual significance as SMM7 in that it is not mandatory under the ICE form of contract.

Other standard methods of measurement available include a Method of Measurement intended for Work Overseas, published by the RICS.

Deviation from a standard method of measurement is to be avoided unless there are very good reasons for doing so. If deviations are chosen it is essential that they are made clear to tendering contractors otherwise disputes are certain to arise.

11.2.5   PC and provisional sums

For various reasons it is not always possible to define finally, at design stage, everything necessary for the completion of the building. For instance it may be necessary for the architect to select certain articles such as sanitary appliances, ironmongery and the like in consultation with the client, and the details of these may very well not have been considered at the early stage when tenders are being sought. It is therefore not unusual to include *prime cost* (PC) sums for these items which the estimator will include in the tender for goods to be obtained from a supplier, but which are subject to adjustment against the actual costs of the articles selected. These suppliers are known as *nominated suppliers.* The contractor has to be given the opportunity in the tender to add profit for each of these items.

Further, it may be desirable to select specific specialist firms to carry out certain works and not leave the choice to the main contractor: for instance, curtain walling, mechanical and electrical services and lift installations. If possible, estimates for these works will be obtained from specialist firms and PC sums will be included in the tender for work to be carried out by a *nominated subcontractor* (see Chapter 1). Alternatively the chosen firm will be 'named' and the tendering contractor left to obtain a price to include in the tender. In the case of nominated subcontractors under JCT 98 a combined system of tender, offer and nomination leading to a formal subcontract is available. A similar system is available for named subcontractors under IFC 98.

Provisional sums are included for work for which there is insufficient information available for proper measurement and/or pricing. They may also be included to cover possible expenditure on items which may be required but for which there is no information available at tender stage. Provisional sums may either be for 'undefined' or 'defined' work: i.e. work which can be described fairly fully but not measured, perhaps because the extent is not known or some other finite detail inhibits full description. In respect of the latter the contractors are expected to have taken into account all their own costs and when the actual sum expended is ascertained for the final account no other adjustment to prices or time is made. On the other hand if the works are 'undefined' then other prices, such as items of plant, may have to be adjusted when the work is valued for the final account and the contractor may be entitled to an extension of time and loss and/or expense.

In most if not all construction projects there are bound to be unknown matters arising such as changing ground conditions, new by-law requirements or problems emerging when an old building is opened up. In order to ensure that money is available to pay for these unexpected extras it is usual to include in the bill of quantities a sum of money known as a *contingency sum* to be used if required or if not omitted in whole or part as the case may be. It should be emphasised that a contingency sum, which of course is an undefined provisional sum, is there for the very purpose described and is not there to be spent because the architect has had a change of mind or has forgotten to include part of the client's brief.

11.2.6 Figured dimensions

Figured dimensions on drawings may be divided into three categories:

(1) Overall dimensions of the building
(2) Subdivision of the last for setting out, showing spacing of structural openings for frames, windows and doors
(3) Internal dimensions of rooms

Quantity surveyors will require (1) and (3). They use (1) to calculate the girths of the walls, and a whole series of items are dependent on these girths: trench excavation, concrete foundations, brickwork, damp-proof courses, facings, copings etc. They must have (3) to record the measurements of ceiling and floor finishes and to establish the girths of the rooms for wall plaster, skirtings etc.

Architects should ensure, therefore, that they give overall dimensions of all sides of the building and that the exact dimensions of every room in either direction can be seen at a glance. Where there is a range of rooms of similar dimensions, obviously the figuring need not be repeated for each, but otherwise the two dimensions should be clearly given on the plan. The dimensions of piers, recesses, cupboards, etc. should be clearly marked. The figuring of heights on sections must not be forgotten, with no doubt as to whether they are floor-to-floor or floor-to-ceiling heights.

Category (2) of the figured dimensions is not of interest to quantity surveyors but, of course, is absolutely necessary on drawings from which the building is to be constructed.

Contractors also require the overall dimensions (except where setting-out is for a steel frame) as they will be setting out the corners of the building before they have to think about the position of the window or door openings, etc. In the same way, the inside sizes of rooms will assist them in setting out the internal walls and partitions.

All figured dimensions on plans will normally be of the shell of the building, i.e. between wall faces before plastering. It should be made quite clear whether heights are to finished level or surface of the structure; the allowance to be made for thickness of finishes should be definitely given so that the agent has figures to follow. Architects must, however, remember that where there is any requirement of minimum height for rooms, such minimum will be between finished surfaces, and they must make allowance accordingly.

It may be found convenient to mark floor levels on each floor in relation to some datum, particularly where they vary on a floor. It should be made clear by a note on the drawing whether these are finished or slab levels (usually the former).

11.2.7   Specification notes

Drawings need to be supplemented by descriptive information. This may be either a full specification such as would be used if there were no quantities, or in the form of notes expressing the architect's requirements (see also section 11.3). Where the Government Form of Contract (GC/Works/1) is used the specification is a contract document, and is usually supplied to the quantity surveyor in full. In the JCT Standard Forms with Quantities the specification is not a contract document and so need not be in so full a form.

Following the introduction of co-ordinated project information (CPI) referred to above, the specification now plays a key role in tender documentation and whilst not itself a contract document, the relevant parts need to be incorporated in some way. The fuller the information given to quantity surveyors, the more will the bill represent the architect's requirements and the less trouble there will be in answering questions raised by the quantity surveyors. The surveyors, as already explained, have to pass the whole building before their mind's eye; they must decide every detail that is not shown on the drawings or included in the information. These must be ascertained by enquiry to the architect.

Specification notes are sometimes found written all over the drawings. If they are at all full, they hinder easy reading of the drawings, particularly if the same note is repeated in several places. For instance, a note '255 mm cavity wall' is sufficient, if the bricks are known to be 102.5 mm thick. Detail as to bond, ties, etc. is not necessary for the drawing but is, of course, essential for the specification.

11.2.8   Corrections to drawings

The very detailed analysis made by surveyors can be of great assistance to architects in that it will bring to their notice any errors or inconsistencies in the drawings or specification. Even if not definite errors, points raised by the surveyors may sometimes involve alteration. After the bills of quantities have been completed it will be found beneficial to ask the surveyor to lend a copy of the drawings marked with any amendments which have been discussed and agreed, so that the necessary corrections can be made to the architect's drawings before they are issued to the contractor.

The contract drawings must correspond with the bill of quantities and they must also be identical to the tender drawings, so if, as sometimes happens, alterations are discovered to be necessary after the bills have been prepared, and the surveyor is told to leave the alteration to be adjusted as a variation, it is most important that the drawings to be signed with the contract should not show the alteration. When it comes to signing the contract, if prints of the original drawing cannot be made, or if the architect, not realising the discrepancy which arises, supplies the revised prints, inconsistency is caused between drawings and the contract bills of quantities and the employer may be put to some expense.

If, during the preparation of the bill of quantities, the architects propose to alter the drawings, they should give immediate warning to the quantity surveyor. Even a line altered or erased may involve substantial alterations to the dimensions. Such changes as reducing the length of a building by 250 mm or the pitch of a roof by 5° involve complications not apparent at first sight.

Alterations made during the progress of the measuring are not only a waste of valuable time, but mean that, when it comes to adjusting variations, it is necessary for the quantity surveyor to hunt in two or three places to find what is in the contract. The adjustment is therefore complicated. If revised prints are to be sent to the quantity surveyors to correct drawings which they have, it is most useful if the architect circles the revision using a coloured pen, otherwise much time is spent searching for the alteration and there is no guarantee that minor alterations will not escape notice.

11.3   Specifications

11.3.1   General

In the context of tender and contract documentation the specification has always played a key role. With the introduction of CPI, as described above, the specification has become more important than ever. CCPI in their publications make it clear that the specification is the key document from which all other information, either for drawings or bills of quantities, will flow.

The writing and use of specifications is a subject in its own right and as such warrants separate study[1]. Suffice it therefore in this book to restrict comment to what a specification is for and the changes that have come about in recent years in the way that specifications are drafted.

11.3.2   What is a specification for?

The specification has three main purposes, in each case in conjunction with the drawings:

■ To be read by the contractor's estimator as the only information available on which to prepare a competitive tender
■ To be read by the quantity surveyor to enable a bill of quantities to be prepared as a basis for such competitive tenders
■ To be read by the contractor's agent and the clerk of works during the progress of the contract as the architect's instructions for carrying out the work

11.3.3   The specification as a basis for tenders

In small contracts, usually those under about £100,000 in value, contractors prepare their tenders from drawings and specifications only. Estimators take their own measurements of the work from the drawings and build up their estimates, relying on the specification for a full description of quality, materials and workmanship. Besides this, drawings and specifications, when read together, must indicate everything required to be included in the estimate. If anything is omitted, something that is required or very obviously necessary or implied, is not mentioned or shown, such work will not be part of the contract. If its carrying out is insisted on, the contractor will be entitled to extra payment.

The writer of a specification for this purpose will, therefore, realise the importance of the work necessary. Instructions must be crystal clear and complete in detail. The specification will be one of the contract documents and it is not to be hurriedly thrown together. It must have all the preciseness of an agreement (in fact it will be part of such an agreement) conveying exactly to the contractor what is wanted and protecting the building owner from claims for extra payment which would arise from vagueness and uncertainty.

11.3.4   The specification for the quantity surveyor

For contracts where it has been agreed that bills of quantities are to be supplied to the contractor on behalf of the client in order to obtain competitive tenders, the measuring work, which in the previous case would be done by all the tenderers, is in these circumstances done for them by the quantity surveyor who puts the facts before them, but each tenderer is left with the estimating, this being largely a matter of individual judgement.

In order that the quantity surveyor may prepare the bill, instructions must be given by the architect. While such instructions need not be as complete as those required by the contractors when taking their own measurements, they must be sufficient to ensure that all cost significant matters are fully described. In this case the architect's full specification is not usually a contract document, although bearing in mind the dictum of CPI it may very well form an adjunct to the bill for cross-referencing purposes. It can however be less formal and convey the information in the form of notes either separately or on the drawings. For certain standard clauses reference may, with care, be made to similar clauses in other contracts.

While such a specification should be as complete as possible, omissions are not as vital as in the first case. The quantity surveyor will find the gaps, since in taking off the quantities every stage in the erection of the building has to be visualised and questions will arise whenever further information is required.

The specification preambles will be in CAWS order to facilitate easy reading with the measured items, which themselves will also be in CAWS order. These specification preambles must convey the specific information so that when read in conjunction with the measured items (the bills) they 'fully describe and accurately represent the quantity and quality of the work' as required by the SMM.

11.3.5   The specification for site agent and clerk of works

When erection of the building starts the work will be supervised on behalf of the contractor by the agent. On large projects a clerk of works will be employed as an inspector on behalf of the building owner, since constant inspection will be necessary and the architect is not expected to be continuously on the site. Both site agent and clerk of works require instructions and they take these, subject to any variations ordered by the architect, from the contract documents, i.e. drawings and specifications or drawings and bill of quantities. Where quantities have been prepared, the quantity surveyor will have incorporated the specification in the descriptions or in the bill preambles.

There is, however, certain information required by the site agent and clerk of works, which will have been excluded from the bill. The locations of items, for instance, will not usually be mentioned in the bill because they do not normally affect price; however, the site agent must have this information when it comes to erecting the building. Spacing of joists, colour schedules and fittings location are other matters which, while not included in a bill of quantities, need to be available to the site staff.

11.3.6   Drafting specifications

For many years it was common practice for specifications to be hand-written, albeit often using previous documentation suitably amended. Over the intervening years the practice of writing specifications fell into decline. Regrettably on many occasions specifications became a matter of a few sheets of hastily drafted notes; more often it was a case of 'It's all on the drawings'.

Today, owing to the advances in computer technology, slowly at first but with gathering momentum, standard specifications have become the order of the day. Now architects and surveyors can enjoy the benefits of having the facility to call up mark-up copies of a standard specification to be adapted for each specific project.

11.3.7   National Building Specification

The National Building Specification (NBS) is not a standard specification, rather it is a large library of specification clauses all of which are optional; many are direct alternatives and often require the insertion of additional information. NBS thus facilitates the production of specification text specific to each project, including all relevant matters and excluding text that does not apply.

NBS is available only as a subscription service, and in this way it is kept up to date by issue of new material several times a year via disk and hard-copy for insertion into loose-leaf ring-binders. NBS is prepared in CAWS (section 11.1), matching SMM, and complies fully with the recommendations of the CPI Code of Procedure for Project Specifications (section 11.3.1). There are three versions of NBS, the Standard Version, an abridged Intermediate Version and a Minor Works Version.

11.4   Schedules of work

A schedule of work is a list of items of work required to be done and should not be confused with a specification. It is mainly used in works of alteration to spell out the items that are only covered in the specification in general terms. Recently schedules of work have started to appear as an adjunct to the specification but they have to be used with care.

A specification, like a bill of quantities, incorporates contract particulars, employer's requirements, contractor's liabilities as well as a full specification of the materials and workmanship. A specification, however, should never contain quantities; these are matters for the quantity surveyor where there are bills and the contractor when there are no bills.

To quote quantities in a specification is inviting trouble: the contractors will say 'We've priced the quantities we were given' whereas they should have priced everything that they considered necessary from their own measurements to arrive at a lump sum price. Where the specification option is used in some standard forms of contract, the inclusion of quantities can lead to those items gaining priority over the drawings.

In the same way problems can arise when the description of the work is set out in schedule form following the materials and workmanship clauses. Old-fashioned specifications used to end up with words such as 'Carry out all the work shown on the drawings'. Today there is a tendency on the part of the employers to require the lump sum to be broken down into component parts, and schedules of work are appearing indicating specific packages – alterations, substructure, brickwork, roofing etc. – and a £ sign is appearing against each of these packages.

While this can be of some assistance in checking interim valuation applications, in giving the client a breakdown of the price and in some ways costing variations, the same problem exists: 'We only priced what was written down', whereas the intention was that they should have priced everything necessary. Because of these problems the same care must be taken in drafting these schedules of work as is taken in drafting the specification itself. It must be very clear to the estimator exactly what is wanted and nothing must be missed.

11.5   Activity schedules

A recent development has been to obtain tenders based on priced activity schedules (e.g. the Engineering and Construction Contract, JCT 98 and IFC 98). Such a schedule is either prepared by each tenderer or alternatively is provided as part of the tender documentation in order to aid ready comparison of tenders submitted. An activity schedule is a list of activities, normally relating to programmed activities, that the contractor needs to carry out in order to complete the works. Activity schedules are considered by some to be more suited to method driven projects, e.g. those of a civil engineering nature; however they are becoming more widely used on building projects.

11.6   Tendering

11.6.1   Procedure in preparing a tender

The preparation of a contractor's estimate may be divided into two parts: the ascertaining of facts and the application of judgement. The facts are the nature and quality of the materials and the workmanship required, which must be set out in a form suitable for pricing. A bill of quantities provides this. Where no bill of quantities is supplied the tenderers must, with the guidance of the specification, prepare their own quantities from the drawings.

The deciding factor in the preparation of a tender when quantities are supplied is the tenderers' judgement on prices. They should not follow rule-of-thumb or price books (although some inexperienced firms have been known to do so) because every contractor's office has to take different circumstances into account.

Tenderers will in all probability have from their own records the actual cost on different projects of the main components of a building, and these costs will help them as a basis for pricing new work. They may have particularly good workmen in some trade, or may have special opportunities of buying some materials advantageously. They must consider the particular location of the project in question, its distance from the office, its accessibility etc., and adjust their costs accordingly. An isolated site involving transport and travelling time for workmen can make a big difference to the real cost of an hour's work. There will be many items for which tenderers must obtain quotations in order to build up suitable rates.

They may well adjust their tender according to their need for new work. If they are short of work they may be satisfied with a low level of profit and sometimes with no profit at all, although this can cause problems on all sides as the work progresses and the contractor is faced with unexpected costs. If they are busy they may not want the work unless they can get it at an advantageous price.

It is important to remember that in submitting competitive tenders a mistake may involve serious financial loss. Contractors do not enjoy the facility of correcting their mistakes as do architects, engineers and quantity surveyors. It is therefore most important that contractors should have all possible information available and every facility to acquire as full a knowledge as possible of the circumstances of the proposed work.

11.6.2 Documents for tendering

Where a bill of quantities is supplied, it will be accompanied by a copy of the general 1:100 or 1:50 scale drawings together with any component details required. The supply of this type of drawn information gives tenderers a better idea of the nature of the project and their probable commitments than does a hurried look in the architect's office. Where no quantities are supplied, each tenderer must, of course, be given a complete set of all the drawings from which to prepare their estimate.

In the case of works of alteration, a set of drawings issued to each tenderer is almost indispensable. If, however, for some special reason each is not issued with a set, one should be made available on the premises to be altered; the difficulties of an estimator going round a building pricing spot items without a drawing must be appreciated. Where there are substantial alterations to be priced a set of drawings to be inspected at the architect's office is of no use.

In works of alteration, where rooms are divided or two or more are to be made into one, rooms should be given serial numbers on the drawings according to the existing plan. The specification and the bill of quantities should be similarly referenced. The numbers then have a clear meaning to the estimator walking around the building before any alterations have been made. If identification of new rooms is required in a similar way, a series of letters can be used (or vice versa).

Where there are no quantities, a full specification will be supplied to each firm tendering, but not when quantities are provided: everything affecting a price should be in the bill of quantities.

11.6.3   Selection of contractors

The selection of contractors to tender for each project should be made having full regard to its size and nature. It should be the aim to have contractors of similar standing tendering in order to make tenders properly comparable. A small house will warrant a different list from that for a civic centre and contractors who may be suitable for a civic centre contract may not necessarily be suitable for a steel-framed factory. Whereas many contractors could tackle a dozen houses in a housing scheme, the number in the locality who could undertake a contract for 200 houses is certainly more limited.

The nature of the work and the financial capacity of the prospective contractor must always be taken into consideration. Reference should be made to the Code of Procedure for Single Stage Selective Tendering (1996) and the similar Code of Procedure for Two Stage Tendering (1996) both published by the National Joint Consultative Committee for Building (NJCC).

In many lists of tenderers there are some who are ineffective. A firm will perhaps agree to tender because they think (often quite wrongly) that they might offend the architects or prejudice future enquiries if they do not do so. They might feel that the work is not 'in their line', or though quite suitable, they may be so pressed with other work that they cannot undertake the project. The result is the practice of 'taking a price' from another tenderer: someone who has prepared a genuine tender gives a price somewhat higher than their own (known as a *cover price*) which, therefore, is certain to be rejected. The tender form is filled in accordingly and, if the priced bill of quantities is to be delivered sealed with the tender, it will often be found, if opened, to be blank.

Certain public authorities, by their standing orders, are required to advertise their contracts publicly. This can result in a mixed list, and many of the better firms, as long as they have plenty to do, will refrain from tendering in such circumstances. They have to compete with inexperienced firms, who may cut the price merely to get a start in the contracting business. As they are often unknown, tendering in this manner is the only way in which to make a start. The lowest price in those circumstances is not necessarily the best, or even the most economical in the end. If the authority could be persuaded to advertise that it will select a list from the applicants, there would probably be an actual saving in public money instead of an apparent saving which turns out to be illusory.

Where open invitations are issued it is not uncommon for the employer to require the successful contractor to provide a guarantee bond, and this may be obligatory to comply with the standing orders of some public authorities. The guarantor undertakes to meet any deficiency due to the failure of the contractor to carry out the contract, up to an agreed specified limit, commonly between 10% and 20% of the contract sum. The details of the bond are a matter for the employer's solicitor and are usually outside the province of the architect.

Public sector construction contracts within the European Union over approximately £4 million (5.15 million ECUs) must be invited and awarded in accordance with the procedures laid down in EC Directives. The Directives provide for 'restricted tendering procedure', which permits the selection of technically and financially competent contractors following advertisement in the official journal of the European Communities circulating throughout member states.

11.6.4   Time for tendering

With the object of ensuring that contractors have every opportunity of preparing a proper tender which they can safely stand by, the time allowed for tendering should be as long as possible. An excessively short period results in rushed work and inability to get estimates in proper time, and in consequence increases the risk of errors.

When a bill arrives in a contractor's office for pricing, the usual procedure is for the estimator to go through it and mark up those parts for which quotations are required, either for the supply of materials or the subletting of work. The marked portions will then be copied with any adaptions necessary and these portions will be used for competitive enquiries. The bill will then be put aside because it cannot be priced until all replies have been received, as to do so piecemeal is a waste of time. When the replies are received they are sorted and examined and the most suitable used, with the necessary additions for profit and fixing if appropriate.

While it is always advisable to ask contractors in good time if they would like to tender, where time is short for some reason they should be given warning as to when documents will be sent out and the date for delivery of the tenders. The Codes of Procedure for Tendering already referred to make provision for such a preliminary invitation. Any firm that cannot tackle the project in the time will then be able to say so and last-minute requests for extensions of time will be avoided. Four weeks should be regarded as the minimum time for tender.

It is obvious that when contractors are tendering on a specification and drawings only they will need longer to tender than when a bill of quantities is supplied for a similar building, as they will have to prepare their own quantities.

11.6.5   Sending out documents

The architect or the quantity surveyor will send to each firm tendering a copy of the specification and tender form and a complete set of drawings or, if a bill of quantities is used, that too with a selection of drawings under a covering letter which should state:

- Invitation to tender, if not already sent
- List of enclosures
- Date and place for delivery of tenders
- Whether the site is open for inspection and if so what arrangements should be made to visit it
- Request for acknowledgement

Figure 11.1 illustrates a typical letter.

Tenders will usually be delivered to the architect or the quantity surveyor, unless the employer particularly wants them to be delivered to them. In the case of public authorities both the sending out of documents and receipt of tenders will be handled by the clerk to the authority. A recommended form of tender is illustrated in Fig. 11.2. The documents should be accompanied by a suitable envelope for delivery of the tender ready addressed and marked 'TENDER FOR. . .' on the face. These envelopes will on receipt be recognised as containing tenders and will be left unopened until the time stated for delivery has passed and a check has been made that all have been delivered. If this procedure is not scrupulously observed the employer may be liable for a tenderer's abortive expenditure[2].

Where there is a bill of quantities much the same procedure is followed, though the documents are usually (but not in the case of

Dear Sir

[insert heading]

I refer to your letter of the [insert date] in which you expressed willingness to submit a tender for the above project. I now have pleasure in enclosing the following:

1. Two copies of the bills of quantities.
2. Two copies of each of drawings numbers [insert numbers] giving a general indication of the scope and character of the works. These will become the contract drawings.
3. Two copies of the form of tender.
4. An addressed envelope for the return of the tender and instructions relating thereto.

Please note the following:

(a) Drawings may be inspected at [insert place].
(b) The site may be inspected by arrangement with [insert person and telephone number].
(c) Tendering will be in accordance with the Code of Procedure for Single Stage Selective Tendering 1996.
(d) Examination and adjustment of priced bills: alternative 1 / 2 [delete as appropriate] of section 6 of the Code will apply.

The completed form of tender is to be sealed in the endorsed envelope provided and must arrive at [insert place] not later than [insert time] on [insert date].

Please acknowledge safe receipt of this letter together with the enclosures noted and confirm that you will submit a tender in accordance with these instructions.

Yours faithfully

Fig. 11.1 Letter to contractor: invitation to tender (assumes bills of quantities used).

a public authority) sent out by the quantity surveyor on completion of the printed bills, so saving a little time. There will be a selection of small-scale drawings with perhaps typical details and special drawings required by the SMM to accompany tenders, indicating broadly the scope and quality of the work, and the covering letter will state where the remaining drawings can be inspected if required (usually the office of the architect or surveyor).

If the bill is to be delivered with the tenders, as is often the case, the documents must include a separate envelope of suitable size and strength to hold the bill, addressed in the same way as the envelope for the tender. The tenderers should be notified in the covering letter to put their name on the outside of the bill envelope so that only the bill accompanying the lowest tender is opened. The remaining bills should be returned unopened.

Tender for [describe works]
at [insert location]

To [insert name and address of employer]

I/We, having read the conditions of contract, articles of agreement, appendix and specification/ schedules of work/ bills of quantities [delete as appropriate] delivered to me/ us and having examined the drawings referred to therein, do hereby offer to execute and complete the Works described in accordance with the terms therein for the sum of _____

_____ (words) £ _____

In consideration of the sum of £1.00 receipt of which I/We hereby acknowledge I/ We undertake to keep this offer open for a period of [insert period] days from the date of this tender.

I/We agree that

(a)   The employer is not bound to accept the lowest or any tender.

(b)   Persons tendering do so at their own cost.

(c)   If errors in pricing or errors in arithmetic are discovered in the priced specification/ schedules of work/ bills of quantities [delete as appropriate] before acceptance of this offer, such errors will be dealt with in accordance with alternative 1 / 2 [delete as appropriate] of section 6 of the Code of Procedure for Single Stage Selective Tendering published in 1996.

(d)   Unless and until a formal agreement is prepared and executed, this tender together with your written acceptance thereof shall constitute a binding contract between us.

Dated this . . . . Day of . . . . .20 . . . .

Signed . . . .

in the capacity of . . . .

duly authorised to sign tenders for and on behalf of:

Name . . . .

Address . . . .

Fig. 11.2   Form of tender.

11.6.6   Opening of tenders

Before opening the tenders it is important to see that they have all been delivered, and care is necessary if any tender is delivered late. Most contractors will find out quite easily the identities of the other tenderers. After the time fixed for delivery there may be enquiries from one contractor to another on the telephone as to figures and one must accordingly be sure that no late tenderer has taken advantage of this.

If tenders are delivered to the architect's office they will be opened and a list prepared, arranged in order of price, for submission to the client. Any special conditions attached to the tender should be noted and entered against the tenderer's name in the list. If tenderers are required to state a contract period as well as a price, as is often the case, this too will be entered against each name. If the tenders are being opened by the clerk to a public authority (often in the presence of an elected member), the same procedure will be followed for submission of the result to the council or committee concerned.

11.6.7   Reporting of tenders

In considering tenders other factors than the price may be important. The time required to carry out the work, if stated on the form of tender, may be compared, as time may be very important financially to the client. The time stated by a reputable contractor may be taken as a reasonable estimate, having regard to the circumstances as known.

The architect, having considered these matters in consultation with the quantity surveyor, or the clerk to a public authority, will report the tenders to the client or committee concerned. If there is any doubt, the arguments in favour of acceptance of one tender or another need to be clearly set out for consideration. Other matters that may be considered are the proposed teams, quality and safety.

When tenders are invited from a selected list of contractors, the lowest, or potentially lowest, should be accepted. All go to a good deal of trouble and expense in preparing a tender, and the object of such tendering is to decide which among a number, all acceptable to the building owner, will do the work at the lowest price. Whether expressly disclaimed in the invitation or not, there is no legal obligation to accept the lowest or any tender.

However, when tenders are advertised and any contractor who can raise the required deposit and surety may submit a tender, the circumstances are different. One can justly say 'I didn't ask you and I don't want you', though even then, when the expenditure of public money is involved, there may be repercussions.

As soon as the lowest or any tender is accepted, all the tendering contractors should be notified (see section 11.6.10).

11.6.8   Examination of a priced bill

If the employer decides to proceed with the work, the tenderer whose offer is under consideration will be asked to supply a copy of the priced bill (if it has not already been submitted with the tender), either a blank copy being sent for the purpose or the contractor making a photocopy. This will be examined by the quantity surveyor who will make a mathematical check and will also look generally through the rates for any possible serious errors or omissions in the pricing. If there are no serious errors, and provided there are no other inhibiting circumstances, then the tender can be safely recommended for acceptance.

However, if mistakes are found the contractor must be notified. Then one of two things will happen according to the principles previously decided on and notified to tendering contractors: the contractor will be invited either to stand by the tender price or withdraw, in which case a commercial decision will need to be taken. The mistake may be of such magnitude that withdrawal of the tender is the only option, in which case the next lowest bid is considered in the same way. However, the contractor may be prepared to stand by his tender and the contract sum will remain as the tender. It is not usually good policy to press a contractor who has made such an error to stand by the tender. The inevitable effort to recover the position is fairly certain to give trouble.

While the contract sum will remain as the tender sum, correction of any material errors should be made in the body of the text solely for the purpose of providing a fair schedule of rates for the adjustment of variations. The principle to be followed is that the total of the bill must be unchanged and must agree with the contract sum: the adjustment due to correction of errors will be treated as a rebate or as a plusage on the whole of the prices (except prime cost and provisional sums) and will appear immediately before the final total on the summary by way of a percentage.

However, if it was made clear at the time of tendering that genuine errors would be corrected, then the corrections are made and a revised tender sum is established. If the resultant figure shows that the revised tender is now in excess of the next lowest tender, it is the next lowest tender which comes into contention and is subject to a similar examination. The way in which corrections of errors found in tenders are to be treated is set out in the NJCC Code of Procedure for Single Stage Selective Tendering previously referred to.

11.6.9   Reductions

Unfortunately, it is not uncommon for tenders to be higher than expected, sometimes due to too optimistic an attitude of architect and quantity surveyor at the approximate estimate stage or, more probably, because a full cost-planning exercise has not been carried out. If employers are not prepared to meet the higher cost, ways and means have to be found to get down to their figure, and at the same time meet their requirements as to accommodation etc.

The architect will have to re-examine the drawings and specification with this in view. Here the help of the quantity surveyors can be useful as they may be able to suggest from the analysis which the priced bill has provided, where the architect's requirements are costly; less costly alternatives could be considered. A list of possible reductions will be prepared and valued in consultation with the quantity surveyors. They will prepare a bill of omissions and any counterbalancing additions, from which the tender sum can be adjusted.

For what sounds quite a simple reduction, adjustment on a bill of quantities may be lengthy. To take 150 mm off the length of a building (which may only mean a few broken lines and figured dimensions on the architect's drawings) affects a large number of items through many sections in the bill of quantities, from stripping surface soil to the paint on the walls and ceilings.

There is one cause of excessive tenders and consequent reductions which should be avoided: the inclusion of something which the architect wants, in the hope that the clients can be persuaded to want it when they discover that it is included in the tender. The architect may feel that it is easier to cut out such an item when tenders come in than to add it afterwards. Such conduct on the part of an architect may amount to professional negligence. Unless there is a reasonable hope of keeping within the client's price, it should be cut out in the first instance. Reductions in a tender only make additional work for architects and quantity surveyors in altering drawings and specifications and preparing reduction bills and, moreover, involve the client in additional fees and expenses.

11.6.10   Informing tenderers

Preparation of competitive tenders is today a very expensive activity. Much time and effort and consequently money are expended and it is only reasonable that tendering contractors should be made aware of the result. The winner will want to know 'how much they left on the table', i.e. what margin there was between their bid and the next lowest. The losers in their turn will need to know, for future pricing and policy purposes, just where they stood.

Much is made of the need for confidentiality in competitive tendering and it is sometimes argued that publication of tender results breaches that confidentiality. Actual confidentiality is perhaps questionable; there are too many common contact points by way of suppliers, ready-mix concrete firms etc. whereby it is not unknown for a tender list to become public knowledge. Once tenders are submitted it is quite common practice for tender amounts to be exchanged by the competing contractors.

However, none of this alters the duty to publish the list and, with the confidentiality referred to above in mind, this can best be done by publishing a list of amounts without the firms' names being given. Each tendering firm will recognise their price and where they came. If in addition they are able to put names to sums that is their business. An alternative is to publish the list of contractors in alphabetical order and the tenders received in order of value.

11.6.11 Negotiated tenders

All that has gone before in this chapter assumes that competitive tendering procedures are being adopted. However, perhaps the contractors are known to both employer and architect for whom they have performed well in the past; or it is a further stage of a contract upon which the contractor has already worked or is still working; or perhaps an advantage of gaining time is being sought. For any of these or similar reasons a decision may be taken to negotiate a tender.

The procedures that are to be gone through are similar to those required for competitive tendering except that before the final tender is submitted it will have been examined by the quantity surveyors, who may have been involved in the pricing themselves, and the tender prices will have, if necessary, been negotiated. Such negotiations can lead to several advantages referred to above, and although the price can be shown to be the right price it can never be proved to be the cheapest. If the cheapest price is the criterion for letting the contract then negotiation has no place.

11.7 Preparing the contract documents

The duty of preparing the contract by completing the various blanks in the articles of agreement usually falls on the architect although the quantity surveyor is commonly asked to do it. It may be necessary to add special clauses to the conditions of contract and to amend other clauses; if so, they must be written in, and the insertion or alteration must be initialled by both parties at the time of signature. Any portions to be deleted must be ruled through and similarly initialled. All other documents contained in the contract (each drawing and the bill of quantities) should be marked for identification and signed by the parties, e.g.:

> This is one of the drawings
> *or*   This is the bill of quantities
> referred to in the contract
> signed by us this   day of   20

In the case of the bill of quantities this identification should be on the front cover or on the last page and the number of pages can be stated. If the standard form is used (with quantities) the specification as such is not part of the contract, and will not be signed by the parties. Where there are no quantities the full specification is a contract document and must be signed accordingly. All the signed documents must be construed together as the contract for the project.

Contracts are either signed under hand, when the limitation period is six years, or, when 12 years is required, they are completed as a deed (formerly under seal). In the latter case it is important to ensure that this is duly recognised, as failure to do so could have serious implications[3].

Case law exists that illustrates the importance of ensuring that all the contract documents are in agreement with each other. There was a discrepancy between completion dates set out in the contract bills and the completion date in the appendix to the JCT form of contract. Delays had occurred, and the question was which date was to be taken in calculating liquidated damages. The court held[4] that under the relevant clause of the standard form in use at that time (JCT 63 clause 12(1)) the date in the appendix prevailed, but the litigation would not have occurred if all the contract documents had been checked for inconsistencies. The equivalent clause in JCT 98 is 2.2.1.

References

(1) Willis C.J. and Willis J.A. (1997) *Specification Writing for Architects and Surveyors*, Blackwell Science.

(2) *Blackpool & Fylde Aero Club* v. *Blackpool Borough Council* (1990) CILL 587.

(3) The Companies Act 1989 and the Law of Property (Miscellaneous Provisions) Act 1989 state the requirements for companies and individuals respectively (see Chapter 6, section 6.4).

(4) *M.J. Gleeson (Contractors) Ltd* v. *London Borough of Hillingdon* (1970) EGD 495.

Stages J and K: Mobilisation and Construction to Practical Completion

12.1 Contractor's programme

The value of a programme is that it will enable the contractor to plan ahead, give early and precise notice to subcontractors, avoid the risk of overlooking the ordering of materials or fittings in good time, and enable adequate steps to be taken to reinforce or reduce the labour force as the occasion demands. Finally, it constantly signals to contractor, agent, clerk of works, architect and client whether or not the work is proceeding at a satisfactory rate.

On large contracts it is customary for the contractor to include in the programme the dates by which full details are required of the various parts of the Works from the architect or other consultants, together with instructions regarding the expenditure of prime cost and provisional sums. Many JCT contracts now make provision for the architect to provide the contractor with an information release schedule which, if used, should render the practice obsolete. As the contract proceeds it may be necessary to expand the progress schedule to show in more detail the co-ordinated installation and commissioning of complex engineering services.

The question whether, in the absence of an information release schedule, an architect is obliged to provide information to suit the contractor's programme is often asked. The programme may well show a completion date earlier than that fixed in the contract. There is legal authority that, although the contractor is entitled to finish early, the architect is not obliged to provide information to suit the shortened programme. The architect's duty is simply to provide information at such times as will enable the contractor to carry out and complete the Works by the contract date for completion[1]. JCT 98 and IFC 98 now enshrine that principle in clauses 5.4.2 and 1.7.2 respectively.

Clause 5.3.1.2 of JCT 98 contains an optional requirement for a master programme. This is not a contract document, but the clause gives the architect the right to have a copy of the contractor's programme. The clause also requires the contractor to update the programme whenever the contract period is extended. That is quite unsatisfactory in practice, because the contractor may be in culpable delay and the architect may wish to see a revised programme. Unless an extension of time is given, the architect has no right to require the updated programme. The clause would benefit by amendment which requires the contractor to provide the update upon the architect's reasonable demand.

The master programme should be drawn up by the contractor before starting work and it should be monitored on a regular basis by both architect and contractor. It should be prepared so that all the information can be clearly tabulated and it should be placed in a prominent position in the site office. It must not be too complicated, but it should at the same time give a precise indication of the progress planned by each trade each week, together with the actual progress achieved.

The most common programme is the *Gantt* or *bar chart* on which proposed and actual progress can be indicated. A line is plotted in black (or any other chosen colour) against each trade or operation commencing at the week in which the particular work is due to start and continuing through the number of weeks that it is expected to proceed. This may not, of course, be a continuous line, as it may be necessary to suspend the particular work while some other operations proceed and then return for a second spell. The actual progress should be recorded by a line or lines in a different colour.

Other forms of programmes include network analysis, precedence diagrams and PERT (Performance Evaluation and Review Technique) charts. These show the planning of the work as a set of activities related to each other. The facility becomes available to plan alternatives and variants to the critical, or chosen, path when for some reason or other there has to be a change to the planned path. The architect is able to monitor the effects of delays to the work especially where one of the many computer software programmes is used. Such matters as estimating extensions of time are much simpler and indeed the courts appear to advocate extensions of time calculated by this means[2]. A programme in this form (showing resources) should always be requested in addition to the more common bar chart.

As an architect is not empowered under the terms of any JCT contract to give instructions to the contractor about the programme, the requirement to provide a programme in the form noted above should be made in the bill of quantities or in the specification if there is no bill of quantities. This will not create a conflict between the bills of quantities and the printed form, because there is no attempt to override or modify what is in the form, but merely to require something which is not already in the contract or, if there is a provision for a master programme, the item in the bills merely seeks to amplify the requirement.

12.2   Meetings

Every architect will be involved in meetings. There really is no escaping meetings although most people affect to consider them a waste of time. A meeting will be a waste of time unless there is a clear purpose and unless the participants are carefully selected and relevant to the purpose. It is useful to work on the basis that if the most effective meeting consists of two people, every extra person reduces the effectiveness in inverse ratio to the numbers attending. The meetings in which architects may be involved can be roughly divided as follows:

- Staff meetings
- Client meetings
- Design team meetings
- Site meetings
- Meetings for special purposes

12.2.1   Staff meetings

This is the kind of meeting which all members of staff attend, to talk about office reorganisations, expansion, contraction, etc. Many offices make a practice of having a regular staff meeting every month or two months to discuss points of interest to the whole office. It is a good way to air problems. How successful such meetings are depends on the maturity of the participants. In some offices, staff meetings may be called rarely to deal with major concerns, and contributions 'from the floor' may be discouraged. How staff meetings are used, indeed whether they are used effectively at all, depends on the management styles of the partners or directors responsible.

12.2.2   Client meetings

The best meetings are one to one. A client meeting may involve one person other than the architect, or the client may be a board of directors or local government committee. Meetings between the architect and a board of directors should be few. It is only really necessary when the commission is being set up and possibly when the architect is demonstrating the initial design proposals. At other times, the board should nominate someone with authority to deal with the architect on the board's behalf, otherwise progress will be slow. Generally, the architect will initiate client meetings to make decisions, receive reports, view proposals and so on. Occasionally, there may be other professionals present. These may be the client's legal and financial advisers or the other members of the design team.

12.2.3 Design team meetings

In planning this kind of meeting, the architect should be guided by, but should not slavishly follow, the RIBA Plan of Work. Depending on the size of the project, the personalities of the participants and the stage of the work, the client may be present at these meetings. In any event, all the consultants should be present. This meeting is necessary in order to co-ordinate the effort of the team and to create the right sort of enthusiasm which is essential for the success of any major project. Normally, these meetings are called at key points in the scheme rather than, say, 'every month just to make sure that everything is proceeding smoothly'. Such meetings are usually counter-productive.

The general rule about numbers is equally valid with reference to team meetings and the architect will often find it easier to work on a one to one basis with consultants as well as the key point meetings mentioned above. In practice, it is common to find that the necessity for full design team meetings ends at tender stage. After that, one to one meetings are the norm.

12.2.4 Site meetings

Architects commonly have regular fortnightly or monthly site meetings, although one school of thought considers that there is little to commend them. The purpose of site meetings is presumably:

- To measure actual against predicted progress
- To answer queries
- To provide information

Progress is in the hands of the contractor, whose best interests will be served by a quick and workmanlike conclusion to the contract. The architect's principal role in assisting progress is to ensure that all necessary production information is provided at the proper time. The clerk of works, if appointed, can be asked to submit a weekly progress report in any format and incorporating whatever information the architect may desire. The contractor can be asked to submit a separate weekly report. Any problems with the progress of the project can be taken up directly between the architect and the contractor, in person, by telephone or, best of all, by correspondence.

The site meeting is not the correct forum for answering queries. Most queries arise between meetings and they should be answered immediately. In any event, it is best to answer queries and provide information in writing so that there is a proper record. Site meeting minutes are notorious as vehicles for what the architect wished had been said! Site meetings are always preceded by a site inspection, but an inspection can be carried out without a site meeting.

A final point against regular site meetings is the number of expensive man-hours which are swallowed up. At every meeting there are many people in attendance who have an interest in only a small part of the proceedings. Indeed, in some cases, a professional may be there just in case, rather than for a specific purpose.

Obviously, there must be a meeting for all interested parties before the project commences on site. This is usually erroneously called the 'pre-contract' meeting rather than the more accurate 'pre-start' meeting. After the first meeting to sort out procedures and deal with the many preliminary matters which must be resolved before work can actually start, site meetings should be reserved for specific purposes. Then, the meeting becomes an important occasion, not to be taken lightly. Before arranging a site meeting (or any meeting for that matter) it is useful to ask what the meeting can achieve which cannot be achieved in some other way, more effectively and at less cost.

12.2.5 Meetings for special purposes

There will always be the kind of meeting which cannot be properly categorised except under this heading. Meetings with local government officers, members of an amenity society or ministry officials fall into this group.

It should go without saying that every meeting must have a

purpose and a clear idea of what it intends to achieve. So also, a good meeting will be the result, among other things, of careful preparation. It is usual to prepare an agenda and to circulate it to participants together with any papers which should be read before the meeting. Provided that the date of the meeting has been agreed in advance, it is best to circulate the agenda and supporting papers no more than a week before. This gives people the time to read the information, but does not really allow time for it to be put on one side. The generally accepted format for any kind of meeting is:

- Record of those present including status
- Apologies for absence
- Agreement to minutes of the last meeting
- Any matters arising from the minutes of the last meeting
- Items for discussion
- Any other business
- Date and time of next meeting

An example of an agenda for a pre-start meeting is shown in Fig. 12.1. That is only the merest outline of course. Architects should not assume that the pre-start meeting is an opportunity to put restrictions on the contractor. By this time, the contractor should be in contract with the employer on clear terms. The architect has no power to vary those terms and if variations of work or materials are instructed during the meeting, there will be a price to be paid. The meeting is to give everyone the opportunity to meet and hopefully form the beginnings of a team and to remind everyone of the important points about the project. There will also be a certain amount of business to be carried on regarding insurance policies, bonds and the like unless these have been dealt with already.

It is usual, and desirable, for architects to chair their own meetings. This is a difficult task to do properly. The chairman must lead the discussion and be prepared to silence the talkative. Minutes should be brief, recording decisions, not the perhaps endless discussion leading to the decision. Minutes should be circulated within 24 hours to everyone attending the meeting or who has an interest in the results of the meeting. Anyone receiving the minutes of a meeting should read them immediately and carefully in order to check for mistakes, omissions and sometimes insertions which should be reported in writing to the author of the minutes without delay. Such a letter should also be sent to all those people noted on the circulation list. It is fatal to wait until the next meeting to attempt to rectify a mistake; memories will have faded by then.

Shops, Offices and Garage Development, High Street, Bruddersfax, South Yorkshire

Agenda for pre-start meeting

To be held on 3 September 2000 at 11 AM in the site office.

1. Personnel
2. Production information
    a) Prepared
    b) To be prepared
3. Contractor's copy of contract documents
4. Insurances
    a) By employer
    b) By contractor
5. Bond
6. Subcontractors
7. Employer's licensees
8. Architect's instructions
9. Clerk of Works directions
10. Oral instructions
11. Queries and information requests
12. Further meetings and participants
13. Contractor's programme, form and updating
14. Progress reporting
15. Role of the clerk of works
16. Samples
17. Covering up work
18. Setting out
19. Services
20. Signboard
21. Consultants and their roles
22. Procedural matters not otherwise covered
23. Any other business
24. Date, time and place of next meeting if appropriate

Fig. 12.1   Example of a pre-start meeting agenda.

12.3   Site inspections

'Inspection' and 'supervision' are often confused. Architects are commonly referred to as being responsible for 'design and supervision'. That, of course, is quite wrong. Inspection involves looking and noting, possibly even carrying out tests. Supervision, however, not only covers inspection, but also the issuing of detailed directions regarding the execution of the works. Supervision can only be carried out by someone with the requisite authority to ensure that the work is carried out in a particular way. That is the prerogative of the contractor.

Inspection is not something to be carried out lightly. Many architects simply wander onto the site with no very clear idea of what they expect to find or indeed what they should be looking for. Before commencing an inspection of the Works, the architect must have a plan of campaign as follows:

■ Inspections should have a definite purpose. They should coincide with particular stages in the Works. It is sensible for the architect to sit down beforehand and draw up a list of parts of the construction which must be inspected on that particular visit together with items of secondary importance to be inspected if possible[3]. The composition of the list and the frequency of inspections will depend on factors such as the employment of a clerk of works and the size and the complexity of the project. Comments can be made against the checklist as the inspection progresses. The list and the comments are for the architect's own files, not for distribution. Although an architect's inspection duties are quite onerous, he or she will be better able to defend themselves in court against an allegation of negligent inspection if they can show, by reference to contemporary notes, that inspections were carried out in an organised manner[4].

■ Times of inspections should be varied so that a devious contractor cannot rely on getting poor work covered up between inspections.

■ The architect should always finish an inspection by spending a few minutes inspecting at random.

■ Action should be taken immediately the architect returns to the office, whether or not any defects have already been pointed out to the site manager. It is wise to put in writing all comments regarding defective work.

■ During site inspections, the architect is bound to be asked to answer queries. It is prudent to give answers on return to the office when it is possible to sit down calmly and assess the situation. Many decisions made on site are either amended or regretted later.

12.4 Safety

The health and safety of those employed on a building site is governed by Act of Parliament and subsidiary regulations. The principal Acts are:

- The Health and Safety at Work Act 1974
- The Factories Act 1961
- The Offices, Shops and Railway Premises Act 1963

The Construction (Design and Management) Regulations 1994, commonly known as the CDM Regulations, resulted from EC Directive 92/57. They apply to all construction operations except some minor works. The emphasis is on safety right through the construction process and including design. An entirely new discipline, that of planning supervisor, has been spawned by the Regulations. The preparation of a health and safety plan at the beginning and a health and safety file at the end of the process are important stages. All participants, including clients, have a responsibility under the Regulations. Standard form contracts have been amended to make failure to comply with important aspects of the Regulations a breach of contract. Many architects also practise as planning supervisors, but in any event, all construction professionals should be well briefed on the Regulations[5].

Some of the regulations under the Factories Act are:

- The Construction (General Provisions) Regulations 1961
- The Construction (Lifting Operations) Regulations 1961
- The Construction (Health and Welfare) Regulations 1966
- The Construction (Working Places) Regulations 1966
- The Notification of Accidents and Dangerous Occurrences Regulations 1980

The architect should have a reasonable knowledge of safety regulations and be on the lookout for any infringement on site. The architect should take basic precautions such as reporting to the site manager immediately on arrival, wearing a hard hat and other protective clothing as appropriate and conforming with all reasonable safety rules set up by the site management. Every office should have its own safety policy which should be clearly set out to all members of staff besides, of course, conforming to statutory safety regulations.

12.5 Architect's instructions and variations

Building contracts generally give architects wide powers to issue instructions and they must adopt a systematic method for documenting all variations to the contract. In the past many architects have used standard forms for this purpose which were called 'variation orders' (usually abbreviated to VOs). The term 'variation order' itself does not appear in the JCT form of contract and its use is to be discouraged. The RIBA standard form is entitled 'Architect's Instruction' (Fig. 12.2).

JCT forms of contract require that all variations must be the subject of architect's instructions which are contractually defined. A letter or memorandum signed by the architect is actually sufficient authority for an instruction, but a form has the advantage of keeping the information complete and orderly for every instruction throughout the project. It will appear distinct from other correspondence and forms, especially if a coloured paper is used and all copies are filed separately. The following information should be on every architect's instruction:

■ Name of project
■ Name of contractor
■ Date of instruction
■ Serial number, each project starting with the figure 1
■ Subject matter of the instruction or instructions
■ Architect's signature

The last requirement is very important. Each instruction must be signed by the architect. It is also useful to indicate the distribution of all copies on the instruction. On the architect's and quantity surveyor's copies the approximate cost of the variation may be put and, if desired, a summary of the balance remaining from the contingency sum. It is not advisable to put any value on the contractor's copy, as such value for an extra will tend to be treated by the contractor as a minimum. However, if the quantity surveyor has been prudent, it will be a maximum and complications could arise when it comes to agreeing the final account.

Issued by:	Smith and Jones Architects		**Architect's**
address:	Address		**Instruction**

Employer:	Willow Developments Ltd	Job reference:	456
address:	Address		
		Instruction no:	10
Contractor:	ABC Construct Ltd	Issue date:	DATE
address:	Address		
		Sheet: 1 of 1	
Works:	Shops and Offices		
situated at:	Willow Centre		

Contract dated: Date

Under the terms of the above-mentioned Contract, I/we issue the following instructions:

	Office use: Approximate costs	
	£ omit	£ add
Construct inspection chamber and install drainage pipework in accordance with drawings 456/12B, /13C and /14D	ON ARCHITECT AND QS COPIES ONLY	

To be signed by or for the issuer named above

Signed _J. Smith_

Amount of Contract Sum	£	
± Approximate value of previous Instructions	£	
Sub-total	£	
± Approximate value of this Instruction	£	
Approximate adjusted total	£	

Distribution						
	☐ Contractor	☐ Quantity Surveyor	☐ Clerk of Works	☐	
	☐ Employer	☐ Structural Engineer	☐ Planning Supervisor	☐	
	☐ Nominated Sub-Contractors	☐ M&E Consultant	☐	☐ File	

F809 for JCT 98 / IFC 98 / MW 98   © RIBA Publications 1999

Fig. 12.2 RIBA Architect's Instruction (courtesy RIBA Publications).

Where an instruction involves something quite different from the original requirements a definite estimate may, of course, be obtained from the contractor and accepted by the architect on behalf of the employer as a firm price. In such cases it is, however, advisable to consult the quantity surveyor who, before acceptance, will examine the detailed build-up of the estimate and ensure that proper credit has been given for balancing any omissions that there may be.

When instructing variations it is wise to mark each clearly with whether they are omissions or additions to the contract and to give each item a subsidiary number within the overall instruction. A variation can be described in one of two forms, for example:

(1)   For softwood door to entrance hall substitute oak to detail; *or*
(2)   OMIT   Softwood door to entrance hall
      ADD   Oak door to detail.

It is not advisable to quote item reference numbers from the bill of quantities to define a variation or to mention prices except when a definite quotation is being accepted. The architect will not be fully aware of what bill items other than those noted might be affected. It is better to specify the variation in normal terms and leave it to the quantity surveyor to look up the dimensions and see which items need to be adjusted.

Architects cannot generally delegate their powers or duties under the contract other than the customary delegation within a practice, and not even that without the client's permission if the architect has been appointed on a personal basis. Accordingly, an instruction signed by a clerk of works cannot constitute a variation within the meaning of JCT 98. As mentioned earlier, duties of a clerk of works are solely that of an inspector. While certain inspection duties may be delegated, instructions to vary the contract must be given by the architect.

Some contractors keep a 'variation order' book on the site, into which the agent enters all instructions purported to have been given and the architect may be asked to sign them when visiting the site, afterwards receiving a copy. Remember that if a contractor confirms a verbal instruction to the architect in writing, perhaps on a form titled 'Confirmation of Architect's Instruction', then this constitutes a formal notification under clause 4.3.2 of JCT 98 and, unless dissented from in writing by the architect within 7 days of receipt, it will take effect as an architect's instruction.

With the subcontract procedures set out in JCT 98, notification of a nomination must be made by way of the issue of NSC/N which confirms all the negotiations completed under the tender documentation NSC/T and gives to the contractor all the information necessary for the completion of the subcontract NSC/A. In these circumstances the issue of written covering instructions as well, while not out of order, could lead to confusion.

One copy of all architect's instructions and revised or supplementary drawings should be sent to the quantity surveyor if one is employed.

12.6　Variations and their valuation

12.6.1　General

Most building contracts include provision for changes in both design and construction if these are found to be required either for reasons of a change of mind by the architect or employer or because of the exigencies arising from construction. These changes are better known as 'variations'. Variations in their nature can be very expensive matters and architects need to think very carefully before authorising them. They must in particular adhere strictly to the terms of the contract and ensure that they do not act outside their powers.

The variation procedures under the JCT forms of contract are covered in the main by clause 13 of JCT 98 and clauses 3.6 and 3.7 of IFC 98. The procedures under the government form, GC/Works/1(1998) are somewhat different in that facility is provided for the pre-costing of variations and there is a much closer relationship with loss and expense, as is the case with the more recently published NEC Engineering and Construction Contract which provides for the submission and agreement of quotations for compensation events as the contract proceeds.

The JCT contracts draw a clear distinction between valuing variations (usually tied to rates in the contract bills or in the schedule of rates) and ascertaining loss and expense which may arise over and above the value of the actual variation. As mentioned above, this is not the case with the government form whereby loss and expense for prolongation and disturbance are required to be included in the costing of variations; only such loss or expense which arises from events other than variations is treated separately.

The line between the two is not always easy to draw in practice and, even if it were, there is the problem of reconciling costs which differ considerably from the rates in the contract. Clearly the latter apply to variations but the question arises should the employer have to pay costs which may greatly exceed rates simply because they rank as a loss and expense rather than an item to be valued. This dilemma can be partly resolved by listing the reasons that can give rise to such differences:

- Underestimate in the rate
- Remedial work
- Inefficiency and default
- Inflation
- Non-reimbursable costs (e.g. those caused by nominated and domestic subcontractors)
- Disruption caused by act, omission or default of the employer or his agent

12.6.2 Definition of a variation

A variation is defined as the alteration or modification of the design, quantity or quality of the works as shown on the contract drawings and described by or referred to in the contract bills (or specification if there are no quantities). The addition, alteration or omission of certain of the obligations or restrictions imposed by the employer also fall within the definition of a variation. In the case of the standard forms this includes:

- The addition, omission or substitution of any work
- Alteration of the kind or standard of any of the materials or goods to be used in the works
- Removal from the site of work or materials
- Changes to access to the site or part thereof
- Limitations in working space or hours
- Changes to the order of the works

It excludes nomination of a subcontractor.

12.6.3 Valuing variations

Items to be dealt with by valuing under JCT 98 clause 13 and IFC 98 clause 3.7 are:

- Variations
- Provisional sums both defined and undefined
- The effect of variations on the remainder of the work

Items to be excluded from valuation under JCT 98 clause 13 are:

- Variations the price of which is agreed between the employer and the contractor
- Disruption to regular progress and any items to which clause 26 (JCT 98) and clause 4.11 (IFC 98), the loss and expense clauses, apply

Factors relating to work which can properly be valued by measurement and which is varied by addition or substitution can be summarised as follows:

Character	Conditions	Quantity	Basis of valuation
(1) Similar	Similar	No significant change	The rates and prices in the contract bills
(2) Similar	Similar	Significant change	As last but make due allowance for the change
(3) Similar	Not similar	No significant change	As last
(4) Not similar	—	—	Fair rates and prices

Other matters that need to be considered in the valuing of variations include the following:

- Work that cannot properly be valued by measurement is valued by reference to daywork. Daywork sheets must be delivered for verification within detailed timetables (JCT 98 clause 13.5.4; GC/Works/1 Condition 42 (12).
- Omitted work is valued at rates in the contract bills.
- Work that is not varied *per se* but is affected by a variation (including an omission) is valued as if it were the subject of a variation.

■ Where work is valued by reference to bill rates, allowance must
   be made for:
   (a) measuring to the same rules (SMM) as applied to the
        contract bills
   (b) any percentage or lump sum in the contract bills
   (c) adjustment of preliminaries

As bill rates form the key to the valuation of variations it is
important that any errors and/or inconsistencies are removed
before the contract is signed. Alternative rules for achieving this
are laid down in the NJCC Code of Procedure for Single Stage
Selective Tendering (Chapter 11, section 11.6.3).

The above procedure for pricing variations could be described as
the traditional route and applies to the valuation of variations
under the government form when it applies to other variations or
variation instructions where a lump sum quotation has not been
called for. Under condition 42 the project manager, as stated above,
has the right if so wished to call for a lump sum quotation. These
quotations must include the cost of the work and the cost of prolongation and disturbance (if any), each to be separately identified.
A strict timetable is laid down for submission of the quotation and,
if called for, supporting documentation and for the subsequent
acceptance or non-acceptance of the quotation. In the event of non-
acceptance, the traditional route is reverted to.

A similar procedure is set out in JCT 98 in clause 13A, which
allows the architect to require a quotation. Both JCT 98 and IFC 98
now include reference to the contractor's 'priced statement'. The
effect is to allow the contractor to submit a quotation (including
loss and/or expense and extension of time if he so wishes), whether requested or not. In each case, failure to agree or accept the
quotation results in a reversion to the traditional valuation route.

The question often arises as to how work should be priced where
there is an obvious inconsistency or downright mistake in the
original pricing. Practice suggests that the fair solution is to hold
the contractor to the wrong rate for the original quantity but to
apply a corrected rate for any additional quantity. There is however case law[6] which lays down that a contractor can be held to
the original rate irrespective of quantity. Although this was
something of a special judgment, more recent case law tends to
support it[7].

Although the contract does not require the parties to 'agree' the
final account, it is obviously sensible to do so if possible. It is often
the case that the quantity surveyor, on behalf of the architect,

agrees a final account with the contractor and thereafter has to resist attempts by the employer and/or the auditors, be they local or central government finance officers or (in the case of private clients) their professional accountants, to amend or challenge this. These attempts have to be resisted as these matters are decisions of the architect whose powers are expressly laid down in the contract. The remedy for an aggrieved employer lies elsewhere in arbitration or through the courts.

12.7   Controlling costs

Possibly the most common criticism that is made by clients of their architects (and quite often quantity surveyors as well) is that they never keep them informed of how their money is being spent. They have in most cases signed what has been described to them as a 'lump sum firm price' contract and they have the greatest difficulty in understanding why they are now being asked to pay a lot more money.

For this reason architects have a particular duty to watch the expenditure of their clients' money. When clients want changes made, not only must they be advised whether or not such changes are feasible but also what the cost is likely to be both in terms of time and money. Equally, they must be kept so informed when unavoidable changes have to be made for matters such as changed ground conditions or unexpected problems arising when an existing building is opened up. Finally of course, architects must resist the temptation to change their designs to suit their revised thoughts. If such architects' changes are envisaged then the clients must be consulted and again advised of any financial effect on the total budget. If the financial effects are of any magnitude the chances of the client concurring in the changes being made are slim.

A running record of cost can be kept by having a valuation of each variation recorded and totals of omissions and additions to the contract sum made from time to time. Prime cost sums must be adjusted against specialists' estimates as these are accepted, if formal written architect's instructions are not issued to cover them. Such a record depends very much for its accuracy on the prompt issue of written instructions. Obviously if they are neglected, figures will be of little value. Price adjustment increases and payments made for loss and expense must also be taken into account.

Ideally a statement of the financial position should accompany each interim certificate so that clients when paying the contractors have in front of them a financial picture of the project. The statement needs to be tailored to meet specific client requirements. Certain clients will only require a summary statement of the current financial position (see example in Fig. 12.3); others will require a detailed report identifying the cost implication of each instruction, whether issued or anticipated. It is very important that the figures contained in such statements should be, if not accurate,

---

SHOPS AND OFFICES, WILLOW CENTRE, ANYTOWN
FOR
WILLOW DEVELOPMENTS LTD

FINANCIAL REPORT 6

Smith & Jones	Date	8.9.99
Chartered Architects	Contract week	27
	Date for possession	6.3.99
	Date for completion	1.3.01

	£	£
Approved contract sum		4,268,750
Less Contingencies/daywork		85,000
		£4,183,750
Estimates for instructions issued	£	
Architect's instructions 1 – 16 as report 5	28,640	
AI. 17 Revolving doors	285	
18 Redesign of balustrades	(2,500)	
19 Additional fire officer's requirement	1,170	
		27,595
Estimates for instructions to be issued	£	
Lift	2,500	
Atrium paving	6,000	
		8,500
Ascertained claims		—
Estimated final total (excluding contingencies)		£4,219,845
Current approved sum		4,268,250
Balance of contingences		£ 48,405

NOTES
3 weeks extension of time granted. Contract completion date now 22.3.01. Anticipated actual completion date 14.4,01, i.e. contractor estimated to be in 3 weeks culpable delay.
Loss and expense claim received in the amount of £26,500. Sum not ascertained or certified – not included above.
All figures exclusive of VAT and professional fees.

Fig. 12.3 Example financial report.

then on the pessimistic side. There is nothing worse for clients than to be lulled into a sense of false security only to receive a bombshell at the end of the contract.

12.8   Workmanship and materials

Workmanship and materials are the very essence of a building and they should be specified by the architect in accordance with the design. Materials are inextricably bound up with the appearance and use of the building and specification of the wrong materials can ruin the concept and possibly leave the architect open to an action from the client for failing to take proper care. Examples would be if the architect specified an unsuitable roof covering which subsequently let in water, or a floor finish which was inappropriate to the expected traffic and became badly marked or worn.

The specification of workmanship is less obvious and less clearly defined, yet poor specification in this area can be just as detrimental to the building as a whole. If poor workmanship is applied to the task of erecting the finest materials, the result will be worse than if less expensive materials had been erected with first class workmanship. Good workmanship is difficult to define, but easy to recognise. The specification of workmanship is more difficult that the specification of materials. Certain aspects of good workmanship can be described, such as the way in which bricks are to be laid, but generally good workmanship is described by the result expected. Thus, materials are the basic building elements; workmanship is the process which puts the elements together.

It is one of the architect's functions, and of the clerk of works if appointed, to check that the correct materials have been used by the building contractor and that the workmanship of the building is in accordance with the specification. Depending on the size of the project, a clerk of works may spend a great deal of time checking materials and, for example, taking samples of concrete for testing in the laboratory. Under most standard forms of contract, the architect has wide powers to reject materials or work not in accordance with the contract. Under JCT 98, for example, the contractor must provide materials in accordance with the contract so far as they are procurable. That is a valuable protection for the contractor whose obligation seems to come to an end if the materials are truly not procurable. Of course, not procurable at a price or at a date the contractor considers reasonable does not fall within the meaning of this provision. Workmanship is to be to the standards described in the bills of quantity or specification if there are no bills. If no standards are described, the workmanship is to be to a standard 'appropriate to the works'. That is fairly broad, but probably as good a standard as any in the absence of precise specification.

It is always open, and provided for in the contract, for the architect to specify materials or workmanship to be to his or her satisfaction, in which case, the contract stipulates that they are to be to the architect's reasonable satisfaction. This is obviously intended to prevent the architect from insisting on an inappropriately high standard. Whether the standard is inappropriate or not is something which, in the last resort, must be settled by adjudication or arbitration if the parties cannot agree. Architects must be sure that they inspect such work carefully, because the issue of the final certificate will be conclusive evidence of satisfaction in such instances (see Chapter 13, section 13.5). Clause 8.2.2 requires the architect to express dissatisfaction within a reasonable time of the execution of work which is to be to the architect's satisfaction. No doubt, some architects may be tempted to advise their clients to delete this particular clause as being a potential cause of trouble.

JCT 98 has elaborate provisions, in clause 8.4, to allow the architect to order the removal from site of work or materials which are not in accordance with the contract. The architect may also or alternatively allow the work to remain and make an appropriate deduction from the contract sum; or issue reasonably necessary instructions requiring a variation at no additional cost, no extension of time and no loss and/or expense; or require the contractor to open up or test the work to establish whether there is the likelihood of similar failure at no additional cost, but with an extension of time if the work examined is found to be in accordance with the contract. There are certain conditions which have to be satisfied and the architect should become familiar with them.

The Intermediate Form IFC 98 has provisions which are less far-reaching, but to similar overall effect. Both JCT 98 and IFC 98, in clauses 8.3 and 3.12 respectively, give the architect power to order opening up and/or testing of work or materials. If the work or material is found to be in accordance with the contract, the contractor is entitled to an extension of time, if appropriate, and whatever direct loss and/or expense can be shown to have been suffered.

12.9   Certificates and payments

12.9.1   Responsibility for certificates

It usually falls on the architect under a building contract to certify from time to time the amount of instalments on account to be paid to the contractor and to certify the total of the final account. It is generally provided that certificates shall include the value of work properly executed and unfixed materials on site, less a specified percentage to be retained which is known as the retention sum or reserve.

While the quantity surveyor will usually make valuations and recommend to the architect the amount to be certified, the architect is nevertheless responsible for the issue of the certificate[8], the surveyor's recommendation being possibly affected by deductions for unsatisfactory work, delays in payment to subcontractors etc. A standard valuation form is published by the RICS (Fig. 12.4) for completion by the quantity surveyor. Public authorities often have their own form for this purpose.

On smaller contracts architects should quite easily be able to make their own assessment. Where there are no bills of quantities the contract schedule of works (if priced) can be used, or the contractor may ask for the original estimate to be used as a guide to the subdivision of the contract sum. Provision can be made in the contract for the contractor to provide a detailed statement with each application, which can then be checked.

12.9.2   Method of valuation

How architects make their valuations will depend on the size and complexity of the project. In the case of repetitive housing it may be possible to fix values per house at each of half a dozen stages, say:

- Damp-proof course level
- First floor joists fixed
- Roof plate level
- Roof completed
- Plastering completed
- Second fixing and decoration completed

To this would have to be added the proportion of drainage and external works completed plus an allowance for the preliminary

Valuation

Chartered Quantity Surveyor
Brown & Partners
Address

Valuation No: 6
Date of Issue: **Date**
QS Reference: 123

To Architect/Contract Administrator

Smith & Jones Architects
Address

Employer
Willow Developments Ltd
Address

Contractor
ABC Construct Ltd
Address

Contract sum   £ 4,268,750.84

Works
Shops and Offices
Willow Centre

I/We have made, under the terms of the Contract, an Interim Valuation

as at   **Date**   * and I/we report as follows:

Gross Valuation
(excluding any work or material notified to me/us by the Architect/The Contract Administrator in writing, as not being in accordance with the Contract).

£ 411,280.00

Less total amount of Retention, as attached Statement.

£ 11,878.00

£ 399,402.00

Less total amount stated as due in Interim Certificates previously issued by the Architect/The Contract Administrator up to and including Interim Certificate No. 5

£ 280,000.00

£ 119,402.00

Balance (in words)

ONE HUNDRED AND NINETEEN THOUSAND
FOUR HUNDRED AND TWO POUNDS

Signature: W. Brown

Chartered Quantity Surveyor FRICS/ARICS
(delete as applicable)

Notes:
(i)   All the above amounts are exclusive of V.A.T.
(ii) The balance stated is subject to any statutory deductions which the Employer may be obliged to make under the provisions of the Finance (No. 2) Act 1975 where the Employer is classed as a 'Contractor' for the purposes of the Act.
(iii) It is assumed that the Architect/The Contract Administrator will:—
      (a) satisfy himself that there is no further work or material which is not in accordance with the Contract.
      (b) notify Nominated Sub-Contractors of payments directed for them and of Retention held therein by the Employer.
      (c) satisfy himself that the previous payments directed for Nominated Sub-Contractors have been discharged.
* (iv) The Architect's/The Contract Administrator's Interim Certificate should be issued within seven days of the date indicated thus
(v)   Action by the Contractor should be taken on the basis of figures in, or attached to, the Architect's/The Contract Administrator's Interim Certificate.

© 1980 RICS

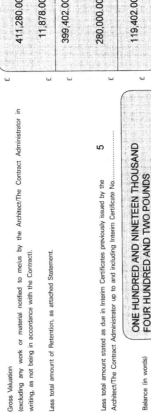

Fig. 12.4   Standard valuation form (courtesy The Royal Institution of Chartered Surveyors).

costs. As a valuation this would only be approximate but would be sufficient for the purpose.

In contracts for larger buildings the architect, if without the help of the quantity surveyor, will have to go through the bill of quantities and, taking one work section at a time, pick out in a general way (without bothering too much about minor items) the work which has been done and its value. A total will thus be built up. Again a suitable proportion of the preliminary bill would be included together with any percentage addition made pro rata and any sums for insurances etc. shown in the summary.

Another variant is payment in accordance with a predetermined stage payment chart or table, either provided as a tender document or submitted by the contractor at the time of tender. Payments will then be made at regular intervals based on the stated percentage. Allowances can be made to amend these percentages either up or down according to whether the contractor is ahead or behind the programme.

Where the contract is based on a priced activity schedule, the assessment of the amount due in each interim certificate is the value of each completed activity adjusted to reflect the impact of any relevant variations. The valuation process tends to be easier than with contracts based on bills of quantities as there are usually substantially fewer items to consider and they are programme related.

Architects should beware that if they carry out work normally undertaken by quantity surveyors they could find themselves without appropriate insurance cover (see Chapter 17, section 17.5).

12.9.3 Unfixed materials

Most forms of contract provide for interim payments to include the value of unfixed materials properly brought onto the site. The contractor should be asked to prepare a priced list of these at the date of the valuation, which can be checked by the clerk of works (if any) or by the architect. If verification of cost of any of the items is required this can be asked for and at the same time assurances sought regarding retention of title to ensure that they are the property of the contractor and can safely be passed to the employer.

When these materials are paid for they become the property of the employer. Being the property of the employer, they must not, of course, be removed without permission, and in the event of the contractor's bankruptcy they would not be an asset vesting in the trustee, but could be removed or, as is more likely, used by the employer.

A matter that needs careful consideration is the inclusion in a valuation of the costs of unfixed materials that are not on the site and so outside the physical control of the employer and agents (JCT 98 clause 30.3). If the employer is prepared to agree to payment for materials off-site, a list must be prepared at tender stage and, in due course, fixed to the contract documents. If materials or goods are not included in the list, they will not be included in certificates. The list is divided into uniquely identified materials (such items as boilers, baths etc.) and non-uniquely identified materials (such items as bricks, sand etc.) and a bond is usually required.

If payment is to be made for materials off-site the contract requires that:

- Reasonable proof of ownership and adequate insurance shall be provided
- The materials shall be complete in all respects ready for inclusion in the works
- The materials shall be set apart and clearly marked as to ownership and ultimate destination

12.9.4 Nominated subcontractors

Architects when issuing certificates must notify the contractor of the amounts included for nominated subcontractors. A form is published by the RICS which sets out these details, for use by the quantity surveyor (Fig. 12.5) and provision is made in the RIBA certificate form for the information to be included (Fig. 12.6). The RIBA also publishes a form for individual notification to each subcontractor (Notification to Nominated Sub-contractors). It is only by notifying these amounts and asking for the contractor to produce proof of payment that the architect can enforce the authority given under clause 35.13 of JCT 98 to certify payments of the accounts of nominated subcontractors direct by the employer.

12.9.5 Price adjustment

Where provision is made for price adjustment on account of fluctuations in cost of labour and materials, this must be taken into account in the valuation under the relevant contract clause.

Statement of Retention and of Nominated Sub-Contractors' Values

Chartered Quantity Surveyor
Brown & Partners
Address

Works
Shops and Offices
Willow Centre

This Statement relates to:
Valuation No : 6
Date of issue : Date
QS Reference: 123

| | Gross Valuation | Amount subject to: | | | Amount of Retention | Net Valuation | Amount Previously Certified | Balance |
		Full Retention of 3 %	Half Retention of %	No Retention				
	£	£	£	£	£	£	£	£
Main Contractor	346,280	330,930	-	15,350	9,928	336,352	280,000	56,352
Nominated Sub-Contractors:-								
G&H Engineering	40,000	40,000	-	-	1,200	38,800	-	38,800
I & J Electrical	15,000	15,000	-	-	450	14,550	-	14,550
K & L Windows	10,000	10,000	-	-	300	9,700	-	9,700
TOTAL	411,280	395,930	-	15,350	11,878	399,402	280,000	119,402

No account has been taken of any discounts for cash to which the Contractor may be entitled if discharging the balance within 17 days of the issue of the Architect's/Contract Administrator's Interim Certificate. The sums stated are exclusive of V.A.T.

Fig. 12.5 Statement of retention and of nominated subcontractors' values (courtesy The Royal Institution of Chartered Surveyors).

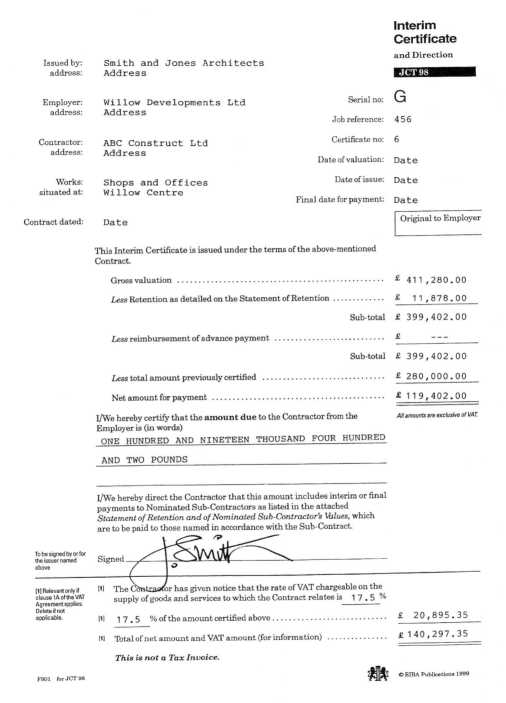

Fig. 12.6 Interim certificate (courtesy RIBA Publications).

Before any increased cost is included under the price adjustment clauses, the contractor should submit a statement showing the price adjustment formula computations for checking. If the adjustment is to be by way of wages and materials increases, the necessary information (backed up by time sheets, invoices, vouchers etc.) must be produced. Increased costs (or in rare cases decreased costs) cannot be taken into account in interim certificates until they have been incurred and no profit is added (or deducted).

12.9.6 Nominated suppliers

Nominated suppliers fall into the same category as ordinary merchants supplying materials to the industry; the only difference is that they are nominated by the architect. The protection given to nominated subcontractors under clause 35 of JCT 98 is not available to nominated suppliers under clause 36. Furthermore there is no obligation for the architect to notify the amounts due to each or the power to certify direct payments.

12.9.7 Retention sum

In preparing certificates, architects have to take into account the sum to be retained under the contract. If the quantity surveyors have submitted a statement, the amount retained will be shown. The retention sums outstanding on various contracts constitute a substantial part of a contractor's capital. While they are part of the financing which is expected of contractors they should not be expected to do more than the contract requires of them. The architects should therefore see that, so far as they are concerned, there is no delay in releasing balances at 'practical completion' and at the end of the defects liability period. To this end they should be prompt in making their final inspection and in giving notice to the contractor of defects to be remedied.

The retention provisions of JCT 98 are set out in clauses 30.4 and 30.5 and the appendix makes provision for stating the percentage of the value of the work done and materials supplied that is to be retained. The footnote suggests figures which are commonly adopted. In calculating the amount of retention to be held at any one time the total value of the contractor's work and of the nominated subcontractor's work, together with the value of materials on site (and sometimes off site: see section 12.9.3), must be taken into account when applying the percentage. Amounts notified are gross and the contractor will deduct the relevant retention monies together with discount before paying the subcontractor.

Clause 30.2 of JCT 98 indicates which work is subject to retention and which is not. The first category includes the value of work done, the materials on and off site and fluctuations computed under the price adjustment formula; the second category includes loss and expense claims and fluctuations adjusted on the rise and fall of labour rates and material prices. The requirements of the government form in this respect are slightly different.

The employer's interest in the retention sum is fiduciary as trustee for the contractor; under the private edition of JCT 98 the employer is required, if asked, to set the money aside in a separate account in the joint names of the employer and the contractor. This means that in the event of default or bankruptcy of the employer the money is available to pay off the contractor and it is not lost in the general funds which may or may not remain. When the employer is a local authority the same circumstances apply but there is no requirement for a separate bank account although it seems that a contractor could insist[9]. A trustee always has the obligation to keep trust funds separate[10].

12.9.8 Final check

When the certificate has been completed a careful check should be made to ensure that the figure shown as already certified is correct, as a slip here can cause a serious error in the valuation.

12.9.9 Release of part of retention

It is usually provided that half, or some other part, of the retention shall be released when the work is complete, the balance being retained until the end of the defects liability period. Clause 30.4.1 of JCT 98 provides for this release on 'practical completion' of the Works, the architect being required to issue a certificate of practical completion under clause 17.1. It is not, therefore, necessary for the contractor to have completed his contract (see Chapter 13, section 13.2).

Under JCT 98 nominated subcontracts are now treated as contracts in their own right and the rules for ascertaining and releasing retention are the same as for the main contract. When the valuation has been prepared by the quantity surveyor and the standard form of valuation has been used (Figs 12.4 and 12.5) the second sheet is of particular importance. An examination will show that the recommendation is in three parts:

- Works still going on: subject to full retention
- Work which has reached practical completion but for which defects have not been cleared: subject to half retention
- Work completed and cleared of defects: no retention

These categories are shown for both main and subcontractors and this sheet will be particularly important as it shows at a glance what the financial position of the job is at each interim valuation.

12.9.10   Release of final balance

Under clauses 17.4 and 30.6 of JCT 98 the whole of the balance of the retention sum is to be released forthwith on the issue of the certificate that making good of defects has been completed. Provision is made for adjustment later of any balance (either way) when the total of the final account is known. Release of the final balance may be delayed because the accounts are not complete. If variations are reasonable, the final figure should be available by the end of the defects liability period.

12.9.11   Form of certificate

Certificates are usually issued in a standard form such as that published and sold in pads by the RIBA (Fig. 12.6). Each certificate form in such pads is in quadruplicate, the distribution being employer, contractor, quantity surveyor and file. Certificates need not be in any prescribed form, but they should use the words 'I (or we) certify', stating the name of the contract, names of contractor and employer, the amount certified as due and the date, and they must bear the signature of the architect. It is an obvious advantage if they are given a serial number. As referred to above, provision is available for the amounts due to nominated subcontractors to be identified[11].

Under the JCT forms (of all kinds) as indicated above, the certificate is issued to the employer with a copy to the contractor. It is now no longer necessary for the contractor to present the certificate to the employer in order to receive payment.

12.9.12 Need for promptness

Finance is an important factor in the running of any business and contractors are no exception; like all business men they naturally want to reduce to the minimum the amount of capital they have tied up. The intervals at which interim certificates will be issued is usually dictated by the contract, and architects should see that they give prompt attention to the matter at the specified intervals. If the architect is slow, delays visits for valuations and does not deal with the matter promptly on return to the office, particulars given by the contractor quickly become obsolete and the time-lag between valuation and payment increases.

While it may seem that a delay of a week or two in payments of what may be relatively small sums of money may not be very important, the aggregate of such outstanding amounts can be substantial. Where the contractor has no very great margin, delays in payment may cause financial difficulties from which the employer may ultimately suffer. Quite apart from anything else, the architect would be in breach of contract for which the employer would be liable[12].

12.10 Delays and extensions of time

Contracts entered into between employers and contractors usually take the form of an agreement that the Works will be constructed for a certain sum of money, or at least specify the way in which that sum will be computed. In addition all contracts include an agreement as to the length of time that the Works will take to complete. Accordingly either starting and completing dates are stated or a set period is given. In either case an end or *contract completion date* is established.

In many cases, for various reasons, a project overruns and finishes on a date later than that originally set. This later date is the *actual contract completion* date. The fact that contractors have to spend longer on site than they contracted for means that unless the contract completion date is amended they become liable to pay liquidated and ascertained damages for late completion. It is important to ensure that the level of liquidated and ascertained damages inserted in the contract is a genuine pre-estimate of loss, which can be deducted without proof of actual loss.

Most contracts provide for architects to have the power to extend the original contract completion date if they are satisfied that the reasons for the overrun were those set out in the contract.

Certain contracts, the standard forms in particular, set out very clearly the duties of contractors and architects in this respect. The contractor has to give notice as soon as it becomes apparent that delay has or is likely to arise, to state the reasons and give an estimate of the length of delay. Architects in their turn have, within prescribed periods, to decide first whether or not in their opinion delay actually is going to occur and second what the true reasons are for the delay. To assist in the second of these requirements what are known as *relevant events* are set out in the contract. In the case of JCT 98 the relevant events contained within clause 25 are as follows:

- *Force majeure*
- Exceptionally adverse weather conditions
- Loss or damage from a specified peril or perils
- Civil commotion, strikes etc.
- Architect's instructions
- Late instructions
- Delay by nominated subcontractors
- Work by employer's own employees
- Act or statutory power by government
- Inability to obtain labour and/or materials
- Delay by local authority/statutory undertaking
- Failure by employer to give ingress to site etc.
- Deferment of possession
- Approximate quantities not an accurate forecast
- Change in statutory requirements affecting performance specified work
- Use or threat of terrorism
- Compliance or not with CDM Regulations
- Suspension of contractor's obligations

It will be seen that these 'relevant events' fall into two categories: those which are neutral, i.e. neither the fault of the employer nor of the contractor; and those for which the employer or his or her agent is responsible.

Once architects are satisfied that the delay is due to one or more of these relevant events then they are empowered to fix a new contract completion date and the threat to the contractor of the implementation of damages is lifted for that period. While an architect has to state the events taken into account there is no requirement to give separate time allocation for each event. In the event of the full overrun not being awarded as an extension of time then the contractor is in what is known as a *period of culpable delay* and remains liable for the specified damages.

Other JCT contracts have similar clauses but contain significant variations. For instance, the JCT Intermediate Form, because it does not recognise nominated subcontractors as such, does not include delay by such firms as a ground for an extension of time. Equally the effect of an Act or statutory power of the government is also excluded. Under CG/Works/1 the project manager has the power to grant extensions of time for any matter which is considered applicable, with the notable exception of weather conditions, which are specifically excluded.

When questions of extensions of time arise architects must study carefully the particular contract clause and act accordingly. Certain basic facts have to be borne in mind, as follows.

Unless the contract includes an acceleration clause the original contract completion date cannot be improved on: i.e. there is no facility to shorten a contract.

A contractor has a duty to make every endeavour to prevent delay arising short of expenditure of large sums of money. The obligation is to continue to work regularly and diligently. However, once delay has arisen there is no requirement that time lost must be recovered.

Extensions of time provisions are to put the contractor back into contract and provide relief from the damages provisions. They can also be, as pointed out below, of benefit to the employer.

No question of additional costs being paid arises at all[13]. These are matters dealt with elsewhere in the contract (see section 12.11).

Extension-of-time provisions are inserted in building contracts for the benefit of the employer as much as for the contractor. As far as employers are concerned they protect their right to receive liquidated damages. If such provisions were not included and contractors were caused delay by the employer or any of their agents then the right to recover damages would be forfeited and the contract would become (as the lawyers say) *at large*: i.e. the only obligation on the part of the contractor would be to complete within a reasonable time.

12.11   Financial claims

The word 'claim' as such is not used in the JCT forms of contract at all. What have come to be known under the generic head of claims are in fact an entitlement to reimbursement of direct loss and/or expense, to use the exact terminology of the contracts. Before considering claims at all it is necessary to define the differences between the two types of claim that the law recognises: common law claims and contractual claims.

Common law claims are claims for breach of contract when the claimant must prove a breach of contract and is then entitled to recover damages calculated on common law principles. These claims have to be pursued by way of litigation or arbitration and the architect has no authority to deal with them unless expressly authorised to do so by the employer. Any resulting payment must be made outside the terms of the contract.

Contractual claims arise because some provision in the contract entitles the contractor to payment for 'loss' or 'expense', made and settled under machinery provided by the contract itself. In some cases events which give rise to such a claim will also be breaches of contract and as such will give rise to a common law claim. In other cases they will not; for example, the issue of a variation order may give rise to a loss and expense claim even though it is authorised by the contract itself. In both cases the burden of proof lies with the claimant.

Before considering claims at all it is also necessary to define what the phrase 'direct loss and/or expense' means. Perhaps it is easier to say what it does not mean. It is not the difference between what the contractor thought the costs would be and what they actually were. This is a commonly held fallacy believed by some contractors; it overlooks the possibility that the initial estimate might have been optimistic. It is what it says it is: direct loss and expense. The word 'direct' in this context means 'close to' or 'appertaining to the event causing the disruption'. 'Expense' means 'actual disbursements'. 'Ascertainment' means 'find out', not, as many claimants appear to think, 'work out'. In several cases, when considering JCT contracts, the courts have held that loss and/or expense is subject to the same principles as are applied to common-law damages.

Claims, to use the generic term, in the construction industry fall into two categories: extensions of time, and loss and/or expense for disruption to the regular progress of the Works. Claims for extensions of time have been covered in section 12.10. Claims for loss and expense can be subdivided into prolongation and disruption elements, and while the JCT forms of contract do not recognise any distinction (each being treated as part of the whole), it is necessary to consider the difference when it comes to the computation of a claim.

A *prolongation claim* arises from delay in completion of the contract works beyond the date when they would otherwise have been completed. Such a claim is sometimes erroneously called an extension of time claim.

A *disruption claim* is one that arises from the effect of an event on the contract works which does not in itself necessarily involve a delay in the completion of the works. A popular misconception is that there cannot be disruption without prolongation. This supposition is quite false and it is no defence for an architect to say that no extension of time has been granted and therefore there can be no claim for loss and/or expense; there certainly can be.

The subject of financial claims and their ascertainment warrants textbooks on its own, and indeed a variety of such books exist for further reading[14]. Suffice it to say that architects will from time to time have to make judgements by way of ascertainment and will occasionally have to be judge and jury on their own mis-demeanours.

In making these decisions architects must bear in mind two main principles:

■ Can any wording of the contract, though not specifically mentioning it, be reasonably applied to the point?
■ The value of the claim should not affect a decision on the principle. If the claim is very small, however, whichever party is concerned might be persuaded to waive it, or it may be eliminated by a bit of 'give and take'.

Some claims may be due simply to misfortune which neither party could have foreseen, and it may be reasonable for the employer to meet the claim *ex gratia* to a greater or lesser extent.

References

(1) *Glenlion Construction* v. *The Guinness Trust* (1987) 39 BLR 89.
(2) *John Barker Construction Ltd* v. *London Portman Hotels Ltd* (1996) 12 Const LJ 277.
(3) A useful check-list is included in: Aqua Group (1996) *Contract Administration for the Building Team*, 8th edn, Blackwell Science.

(4)   *East Ham Corporation* v. *Bernard Sunley & Sons Ltd* [1965] 3 All ER 619; *Sutcliffe* v. *Chippendale and Edmondson* (1971) 18 BLR 149; *Brown & Brown* v. *Gilbert Scott & Payne* (1993) 3 Con LR 120; *Alexander Corfield* v. *David Grant* (1992) 59 BLR 102; *Bowmer & Kirkland* v. *Wilson Bowden* (1996) 80 BLR 131.

(5)   Summerhayes, S. (1999) *CDM Regulations Procedures Manual,* Blackwell Science; *Managing Construction for Health and Safety: Approved Code of Practice* (1994) Stationery Office.

(6)   *Dudley Corporation* v. *Parsons & Morrin* (1967) unreported.

(7)   *Henry Boot* v. *Alstom Combined Cycles* (1999) 90 BLR 123.

(8)   *R.M. Burden Ltd* v. *Swansea Corporation* (1957) 3 All ER 243; *Sutcliffe* v. *Thackrah* (1974) 1 All ER 889.

(9)   *Rayack Construction Ltd* v. *Lampeter Meat Co Ltd* (1979) 12 BLR 30.

(10) *Wates Construction* v. *Franthom Property Ltd* (1991) 53 BLR 23.

(11) Three helpful guides to completion of all kinds of contract administration forms and other useful hints are published by RIBA Publications in respect of JCT 98, IFC 98 and MW 98. They are each entitled *Contract Administration Guide.* Anticipated publication date is 2000.

(12) *Croudace Construction Ltd* v. *London Borough of Lambeth* (1984) 1 Con LR 12.

(13) *H. Fairweather Ltd* v. *London Borough of Wandsworth* (1987) 39 BLR 106.

(14) Chappell, D. *Powell-Smith & Sims Building Contract Claims* (1998) 3rd edn, Blackwell Science. Trickey, G.E. & Hackett, M. (2000) *The Presentation and Settlement of Contractors' Claims,* 2nd edn, E. & F.N. Spon.

13 Stage L: After Practical Completion

13.1 Determination

Most forms of building contract provide that either party can bring the contractor's employment to an end on the occurrence of certain events. The contract itself is not ended, because it is important that the contract continues in existence to govern the situation after determination. It should be noted that there are some forms of contract which make no provision for contractors to determine their own employment, e.g. GC/Works/1. The act of bringing the contractor's employment to an end must never be taken lightly by either employer or contractor. The provisions are intended to be used as a last resort, which indeed they are so far as those contractual parties are concerned.

If there were no determination provisions in building contracts, determination could only be achieved under the general law. In that case, the contract itself would come to an end. There are four ways in which a contract can be ended:

- By performance
- By agreement
- By frustration
- By breach

13.1.1 Performance

Most contracts end by performance, when both parties have carried out their obligations properly. The contract then ceases to have a purpose and comes to an end.

13.1.2 Agreement

It is open to the parties to a contract to agree at any time that the contract should be ended. In theory, all that is necessary is for both parties to agree to walk away. In practice, because human nature is sometimes frail, it is wise to record the agreement in writing. For the agreement to have binding effect, it must either contain consideration from both parties (i.e. both must gain and/or lose something) or it must be completed as a deed (see Chapter 6, section 6.4.1).

13.1.3 Frustration

Frustration is a term with a specific legal meaning in relation to contracts. When an event completely outside the control of the parties results in the contract becoming fundamentally different from that contemplated by the parties at the time the contract was made, the contract is said to have been frustrated. It is not sufficient simply that the contract has become more expensive to carry out than the contractor intended[1]. A good example of frustration would be if a contractor was unable to carry out a refurbishment contract because the building burned down before the date for possession. There are less extreme examples such as a government order which restricts the work.

13.1.4 Breach

Breach is an unjustified failure to carry out contractual obligations. If it is a serious breach, it may entitle the other party to treat the contract as ended. The breach itself does not discharge the contract, it has to be accepted by the other party. The terms of a contract are either conditions or warranties. A breach of a warranty entitles the innocent party to sue for damages. A condition is an important term, breach of which entitles the innocent party either to treat the contract as ended and sue for damages or to treat the contract as continuing and to sue for damages. Such a breach is known as 'repudiatory', because it is a repudiation of the contract.

The difficulty is knowing whether a term is a condition or a warranty. If a party wrongly accepted a breach as repudiatory and refused to continue with the contract, that party would then be the one in breach. As a general guide, a breach will be repudiatory if it is clear that, by the breach, a party demonstrates an intention not to be bound by the terms of the contract. Great care must be taken, however, because it has been held that where a contractor in breach of contract suspended work, that was not a repudiatory breach. Far from indicating an intention not to continue with the contract, the word 'suspension' indicated only a temporary cessation of activities[2].

13.1.5 Determination under the contract

The conditions which have to be satisfied before the contractor's employment can be brought to an end under the contractual machinery can be far less onerous than those required under the general law. Typical grounds for determination by the employer are:

- If the contractor completely or substantially abandons the Works.
- If the contractor fails to proceed regularly and diligently. This concept has caused some trouble in the past. It really has to be clear and unambiguous[3].
- If the contractor refuses or neglects to rectify defective work and the Works are seriously affected as a result. There are usually other more suitable contractual remedies.
- If the contractor does not observe the provisions of the assignment and subletting clauses.
- If the contractor does not comply with the CDM Regulations 1994.
- The contractor's insolvency.

Since determination is such a draconian step, the courts are likely to look very closely at the procedure. The party wishing to determine must comply strictly with the contractual terms governing determination. If the contract stipulates that notice must be given by special or recorded delivery or delivery by hand, other forms of communication such as e-mail or facsimile will not suffice. In JCT 98, for example, although the architect is to give the prior notice of default, the actual notice of determination (if given) must be issued by the employer. There is no substitute for carefully reading the particular contract being used.

Where the contract requires that a certain number of days' notice must be given before determination, the determination will not be valid if attempted even one day early. In such a case, the contractor may be able to sue for damages for repudiation although much depends on the extent to which the employer has relied on the contract provision, even if mistakenly[4]. As the person charged with administering the contract, the architect has important duties to administer the provisions carefully after determination. The best drafted contracts expressly provide that the contractor must give up possession of the site after determination. Although it may seem obvious that the contractor must leave the site, there have been problems where the contractor has disputed the determination[5].

Most standard form contracts provide that the employer has the right to make use of the contractor's plant and engage others to finish the Works, taking over contracts for the supply of work and/ or materials. Generally, the employer will not be obliged to make any further payment until the Works are complete. It will then fall to the architect and the quantity surveyor to take all the expenditure into account including additional professional fees (some contracts include provision for the employer to include his loss and damage in the calculation) and certify a final payment of the balance either to employer or to contractor.

If the contractor determines, the situation will be very serious, not to say catastrophic, for the employer. The architect should make every effort to prevent such an occurrence. Many contracts provide that a contractor who determines may claim the loss of the profit which would have been made had the contract continued[6]. Quite apart from that, the employer will have to shoulder the burden of completing the Works using another contractor at increased cost of building and fees and to an extended time scale. There are four danger areas which cause problems:

- The employer's failure to pay certified sums within the period stated in the contract
- Interference by the employer in the issue of any certificate
- Actions, inactions or defaults by the employer or the architect causing suspension of the Works for a protracted period
- The employer's insolvency

Most contracts provide for determination by either party for such things as prolonged suspension of the Works due to causes outside the control of either party. Normally, the consequences are simply that the contractor is paid up to date and the parties have no further liabilities to each other. Of course, the employer still has the problem of paying extra and waiting longer to complete the Works.

A contractor has nothing to gain and everything to lose by determining employment as a result of suspension. Having said that, the contractor cannot wait forever and the architect should attempt to obtain some agreement if it seems that suspension will last long enough to allow determination to take place. A most important provision is that the determination notice must not be given unreasonably or vexatiously. That provision must be interpreted in the ordinary commonsense way.

13.2   Practical completion

Practical completion is a term used in the JCT series of contracts. The ACA Form of Building Contract (ACA 2) uses the phrase 'fit and ready for taking over'. The Engineering and Construction Contract refers to the project manager certifying 'completion'. This almost certainly means the same as 'practical completion'[7]. There are conflicting views regarding the meaning of practical completion, but it is certainly not when the building is totally complete:

> 'I take these words to mean completion for all practical purposes, that is to say for the purpose of allowing the employer to take possession of the works and use them as intended. If completion in [the possession and completion clause] meant completion down to the last detail, however trivial and unimportant, then [the liquidated damages clause] would be a penalty clause and as such unenforceable.'[8]

There is much sound commonsense in that view.

It has also been said that the architect may certify practical completion when the architect is satisfied that the Works are reasonably in accord with the contract with no obvious defects, even though there are some minor things left to be done[9]. The is probably the best view and receives support from an earlier decision of the House of Lords[10]. A vexed question concerns the extent to which an architect is justified in certifying practical completion, because the employer has retaken possession of the Works. The brief extract quoted above does not support that approach. Indeed, often an employer will re-take possession long before the building is complete for that purpose. The golden rule must be that architects must not certify practical completion before they are of the opinion that practical completion has taken place. The certificate is a formal demonstration of the architect's opinion and, therefore, not something to be taken lightly. Certainly, practical completion is not achieved simply because the employer has occupied the Works[11]. The architect is not entitled to certify practical completion merely because the employer or the employer's solicitor has instructed the architect to do so.

Although practical completion is something which the contract generally leaves to the opinion of the architect, it can be seen that in reality the architect has very little discretion. Practical completion is very largely a question of fact in each case. Following the introduction of the CDM Regulations 1994, JCT contracts set two criteria before practical completion may be certified:

■ Practical completion of the works must have taken place in a physical sense as usual; *and*
■ The contractor must have complied with the obligation to provide the health and safety file to the planning supervisor.

The, perhaps unexpected, result is that the certificate may be withheld for weeks, because the health and safety file is not complete. The contract provisions allow the employer to deduct liquidated damages until the date of practical completion in such circumstances. The only glimmer of light is that the contractor must have 'sufficiently' complied with his obligations. This no doubt allows the certificate to be issued when there are some outstanding pages missing from the file. However, the question whether liquidated damages would become a penalty has yet to be resolved. At the first site meetings, architects should stress to contractors the importance of completing the file before practical completion can be certified.

The contractor will be anxious to see the certificate because it marks a very significant date. In most contracts it marks the date at which:

■ The contractor's liability for damage to the Works and goods intended for the Works ends
■ The contractor's insurance liability ends
■ Liability for liquidated damages ends
■ Half the retention must be released
■ Liability for subsequent frost damage ends

Most contractors will notify the architect when practical completion is about to be achieved although it is rare for a contract to have a provision to that effect. A contractor will often serve notice prematurely. Architects must be on guard against this tactic which is possibly designed to suggest that the architect is being very unreasonable. The contractor may well write to the effect that it is two months since practical completion was achieved and still the architect refuses to issue a certificate. Such manoeuvres are highly reprehensible of course, but it must be said that some architects can be slow to certify.

The architect should inspect the building and, if it is not complete, write a very firm letter to the contractor pointing out that, at present rate of progress, it seems to be ....weeks from practical completion and that practical completion had not been achieved on the date suggested by the contractor. Fig. 13.1 shows an example of a form of certificate of practical completion.

There is nothing wrong and much to be said for architects who point out defects to the contractor. They should not be persuaded to carry out detailed inspections of every part of the building and prepare long lists for the contractor – so-called 'snagging lists' beloved of clerks of works. A danger with such lists is that the contractor will rely on the architect and clerk of works to do what the contractor's site supervisory staff should be doing. Another danger is that the contractor will frequently consider that when the listed defects are rectified, practical completion will be certified. In fact, the architect may well carry out another inspection two days later and add further items to the list. The architect is perfectly entitled to do so, but it does not make for good relations with the contractor. Far better to get the facts straight at the beginning, i.e. it is the contractor's obligation under the terms of the contract to construct the building strictly in accordance with the contract; the architect has no duty to point out defects.

It has already been noted that the employer may try to persuade the architect to certify practical completion before it has really been achieved so that the employer can move into the building. Of course, as one of the parties to the building contract, it is open to the employer to agree with the contractor to take over the building at any time. However, it has been seen that the architect has no power and, therefore, it would be very unwise, to issue the certificate before practical completion has actually been achieved. If the employer takes the building before practical completion, the architect's duty depends on the form of contract. Under the provisions of JCT 98 or IFC 98, if the employer takes possession of any part or parts of the Works with the contractor's consent, the architect must issue a written statement identifying the part taken into possession and the date.

Many contracts have provision for such partial possession. The idea is that where there is just one date for completion in the contract, but during the progress of the Works, the employer wishes to take possession of some part of it before practical completion of the whole, this can be achieved provided that the contractor agrees. It is important to remember that the provision does not enable sectional completion to be achieved. Where it is known at time of tender that sectional or phased completion is desired, care should be taken that the appropriate form of contract

Certificate of

**Practical
Completion**

Issued by: address:	Smith and Jones Architects Address
Employer: address:	Willow Developments Ltd Address
Contractor: address:	ABC Construct Ltd Address
Works: situated at:	Shops and Offices Willow Centre

Job reference: 456

Certificate no: 1

Issue date: Date

Contract dated: Date

Under the terms of the above-mentioned Contract,

I/we hereby certify that Practical Completion of

*Delete as
appropriate

*1. the Works

~~XX XSemxxxxNxx~~ XXXXXXXXXXX ~~xX theWorks~~ XXX
_____

was achieved on

_____ Date _____   19 _____

To be signed by or for
the issuer named
above

Signed _J Smith_____

Distribution	Original to:	Duplicate to:	Copies to:	
	☐ Employer	☐ Contractor	☐ Quantity Surveyor	☐ Clerk of Works
			☐ Consultants	☐ File

F853   for JCT 80/IFC 84/MW 80   © RIBA Publications Ltd 1991

Fig. 13.1   RIBA Certificate of Practical Completion (courtesy RIBA Publications).

is used. Some contract forms have sectional completion supplements.

It is not usually sufficient to put a list of handover dates in the specification or bills of quantities if there is only one completion date in the contract form. In such circumstances, the architect will be unable to insist on sectional completion due to the priority clause in the contract[12]. He will be unable to give extensions of time to individual sections of the work and the liquidated damages clause might well become a penalty and thereby unenforceable.

13.3 Defects liability period

Most forms of building contract provide for a period of time after the practical completion of the Works during which the contractor will be liable to make good defects which appear during that period. The usual period is 6 months, but 12 months is commonly specified in respect of mechanical services to allow the system to be exposed to the full yearly cycle. This is incorrect, because the contract does not allow differing defects liability periods to be specified. The solution is to specify 12 months for the defects liability period for the building as a whole.

The reason for the period is often misunderstood. It must be remembered that, during the contract period, the contractor is said to have a licence to be on the site (the employer's property) for the purpose of carrying out of the Works. It is generally accepted that the licence allows the contractor to remain on the site until the Works are completed. If the contractor were to stay on site or allow equipment to remain on site beyond that point, it would amount to trespass for which the employer could mount an action for whatever damages could be proven. The defects liability period allows defects to appear and provides for the architect to give a schedule to the contractor with a requirement to rectify them. The contract gives the contractor a licence to enter upon the site again to make good the notified defects. The contractor, therefore, has a right under the contract to rectify those defects[13].

Were it not for this clause, the employer would be entitled to engage another contractor to carry out the work and charge the cost to the original contractor (after due notice and time to inspect of course). This is a very valuable right to the contractor because the cost to the contractor for doing the remedial work will be very much less than the cost to the employer of getting in another contractor to do the same work. Some contracts allow the employer to decide not to allow the contractor to make good the defects and to make 'an appropriate deduction' from the contract sum. This sum is not the cost of engaging another contractor, but what it would have cost the original contractor to do the work[14].

Another misconception is that at the end of the defects liability period, the contractor has no further liability for defects. If only life were as simple as that. The contractor is liable for all defects (i.e. work not in accordance with the contract) until the expiry of the limitation period (see Chapter 6, section 6.4.1). Thus if it was discovered 3 years after the end of the defects liability period that a contractor had omitted a number of wall ties specified to be used in the cavity walls, a legal action could be successfully brought against the contractor for the cost of making the defect good, not just what it would have cost the contractor, but all the costs involved in getting another contractor to do the work[15]. A contractor is liable beyond that period, but the Limitation Act operates to allow a contractor faced with an action in respect of breach of contract to escape the consequences after a period of 6 years from the date of the breach (or 12 years if the contract is a deed). It is a basic principle, of course, that if the employer wants to recover the cost of making good defects from the contractor it is essential that the contractor is first given notice of the defects and afforded the opportunity to inspect.

Most forms of contract provide for the architect to issue a certificate to the contractor when all the listed defects have been made good and, in some standard forms, there is then provision for the second half of the retention to be released. The retention acts as a safeguard to the employer if the contractor fails to make good the defects. The contractor should make good the defects within a reasonable time after notification by the architect. What is a reasonable time will depend on many factors. It is not possible to fix a period which applies to all circumstances. The criteria to be taken into account include the complexity of the work, the size of the project, the number and type of defects and the difficulty of making good.

If the architect is of the opinion that the contractor is not attending to the contractual obligations with reasonable expedition and does not respond to pressure, the architect should seriously consider giving notice on behalf of the employer that if the making good is not commenced/completed within 7 days, the employer will engage others to do the work and will charge the full cost to the contractor. That would normally amount to making a deduction from the retention fund.

Some contractors and even some forms of contract refer to the 'maintenance period'. The term is quite misleading and it should never be used because it suggests an obligation to keep the works in pristine condition rather than an obligation to correct defects. The only kind of defects which most forms of contract require the contractor to make good are those which are due to the work not being in accordance with the contract or to frost occurring before practical completion. Clearly, ordinary wear and tear is excluded as are the consequences of inadequate specification.

13.4 Adjustment of contract sum

It seems to be the fashion for architects to leave the calculation of the final account entirely in the hands of the quantity surveyor. In most instances, the result will be no less than satisfactory. Architects should remember, however, that they are the contract administrators and that when the final certificate is issued it will be conclusive (under most JCT contracts) that all the clauses which provide for adjustment of the contract sum have been correctly operated. The consequences of a failure in this regard could be quite serious. The only safe process is to check through the contract and make sure. To take the JCT Standard Form of Building Contract 1998 as an example, it contains no fewer than 26 different clauses which permit or require adjustment of the contract sum. They are indicated in Fig. 13.2. Each clause should be carefully considered and a positive decision should be made that the matters referred to in the clause have been dealt with.

Architects should not leave everything to the quantity surveyor; they should check through the material provided by the contractor. Although it is probably inappropriate for architects to attempt the kind of financial reconciliations which are in the province of the quantity surveyor, architects can usefully see what sort of information has been sent by the contractor and the work categories concerned. Architects who do this may spot errors which the quantity surveyor has missed because the quantity surveyor was not so closely involved with the carrying out of the work. Needless to say, the quantity surveyor must have a full set of all the instructions issued by the architect during the course of the project. Included should be not only the standard Architect's Instruction forms, but also any instruction given by the architect in any other way.

If the contract is small and no quantity surveyor has been

Clause	Adjustments
2.2.2.2	Errors in the contract bills
2.3	Discrepancy in contract documents
3	Contract sum adjustments
6.1.3	Divergence between contract documents and statutory requirements
6.1.4.3	Emergency in complying with statutory requirements
6.2	Fees legally demandable under Act of Parliament
7	Levels and setting out
8.3	Opening up the works and testing
9.2	Royalties and patent rights
13	Variations
17.2, 17.3	Defects, shrinkages and other faults
21.2.3	Insurance payments by the contractor under clause 21.2
22B.2	Contractor insuring if employer defaults
22C.3	Contractor insuring if employer defaults
26.5	Loss and/or expense
28.2.2.2	Work begun but not completed at date of determination
30.6	Final adjustment of contract sum
32.3	Works required after outbreak of hostilities
33.1.4	Removal of debris and protective work after war damage
34.3.3	Loss and/or expense due to antiquities
35.24.7	Re-nomination of subcontractor
36.3.2	Expense in obtaining goods from a nominated supplier
38, 39, 40	Fluctuations

Fig. 13.2   Adjustment of the contract sum under JCT Standard Form of Building Contract 1998.

engaged, the architect will be responsible for checking the account in detail. All invoices of subcontractors and suppliers should be requested and they should be checked against entries in the account and the amounts allowed in the contract. All extra items should be authorised by architect's instructions and where there is no contractually precise method of valuation set down, care should be taken that prices are in accordance with any agreed pricing document or that they are reasonable. The mathematics of the account must be finally checked.

When the final account has been sent to the contractor and hopefully agreed, it should be sent to the employer. It is usually best to do this in a simplified version. The employer, of course, has the right to see the full final account and any other papers, but unless the employer has some professional expertise, a simple version will be appreciated. It is appropriate for the architect to prepare the simple version. It should not miss out anything important nor attempt to whitewash over difficulties. An example is shown in Fig. 13.3. Where architects are dealing with local authorities or companies who have their own technical staff, they will almost certainly require the full accounts to be submitted and they will equally certainly have a great many queries which must be answered.

	£
Contract sum	
Deduct contingencies	
Add sundry additional works (brief details)	
Deduct [or *Add*] adjustment of PC and provisional sums	
Deduct [or *Add*] adjustment of measured work	
Add fluctuations	
Add amount ascertained for loss and expense	
Final amount	

Fig. 13.3   Statement of final account to client.

The architect should have kept the employer up to date throughout the contract with the assistance of the quantity surveyor. It should have been made clear that changes from the agreed scheme will inevitably result in extra cost. Any instructions from the employer to the architect should be confirmed in writing by the architect so that at final account stage there is no doubt about which costs have been incurred by the employer. Architects should never give instructions to the contractor which involve variations and extra cost unless so instructed by the employer. It sometimes happens that, towards the end of the contract, the architect may make savings which could usefully be spent on improving some aspect of the building. In such instances, the architect may never instruct the contractor without first seeking appropriate authorisation from the employer.

Architects should always keep in mind that no matter how experienced the employer or how firm his or her views, it is for the architect alone, assisted by the quantity surveyor, to carry out the function of settling the final account. It is helpful if the contractor agrees the figure, but if not and if the architect and quantity surveyor are of one mind on the matter, they should simply inform the employer that there has been no agreement with the contractor. It is always open to the employer to come to some special agreement with the contractor as the two parties to the contract. This has nothing to do with the architect and the quantity surveyor.

13.5   Final certificate

There is a great deal of mythology about the final certificate. The significance of the final certificate has swung violently one way and then the other since the last edition of this book was written. Architects may still be dealing with some contracts entered into under older forms of contract. For that reason and because it is a very common subject for questions, the situation is set out as it has developed since the last edition.

At one time, when the architect issued the final certificate it was a statement that the whole of the Works were complete in all respects in accordance with the contract. That was certainly the position under some early editions of the JCT 1963 form of contract. In later editions of JCT 63 and under JCT 80 and IFC 84 the position was substantially modified.

Some forms of contract made the issue of the final certificate conclusive about certain things. Other forms did not state that it was conclusive about anything, not even the amount finally due. The final certificate under the JCT Agreement for Minor Building Works (MW 98) was, and is, an example of the latter category and, therefore, these comments relate to the conclusivity of the final certificate and do not apply to MW 98. At the other extreme, JCT 80 made the final certificate conclusive in four instances. CD 81 (With Contractor's Design), JCT 87 (Management Contract) and IFC 84 (Intermediate Form) had similar wordings.

When a final certificate is said to be 'conclusive', what is meant is that if neither party has entered into adjudication, litigation or arbitration before the issue of the certificate and does not do so within a stipulated period (usually 28 days) after its issue, the certificate is conclusive (i.e. unchallengeable) evidence in any such proceedings in regard to the stipulated matters. Thus, if a final certificate is said to be conclusive in regard to the amount of the final sum certified, it will not prevent an aggrieved party from seeking satisfaction by way of arbitration if the sum is considered to be wrong[16]. However, the other party has simply to produce the final certificate for the matter to be at an end. Certificates under JCT 80, CD 81, JCT 87 and IFC 84 were conclusive in respect of the following:

■ *That where the quality of materials and standards of workmanship are to be to the reasonable satisfaction of the architect, the architect is so satisfied.* This referred back to an early clause (2.1 in JCT 80) stating the contractor's obligations and it was a failure to realise what this meant which gave rise to many misconceptions. Part of the contractor's obligations was to ensure that if the architect had stated that certain things were to be to the architect's satisfaction, such things were to his or her satisfaction. Note that the architect *must first have stated* (presumably in the specification or in the bills of quantity) that certain things were to be to the architect's satisfaction. This may have been done by stating that specified items must be 'approved' or 'to the architect's satisfaction' or some other form of words to the same effect. When the final certificate was issued, it was conclusive evidence that the architect was satisfied with any matters which were so specified whether or not the architect had in fact specifically expressed approval or even looked at the item in question. It will readily be appreciated that to insert some such phrase as 'All workmanship and material unless otherwise stated, must be to the architect's satisfaction' was opening the door to the blanket conclusivity of the final certificate again. It was the business of the architect's satisfaction which gave rise to all the problems and it will be considered in detail below.

■ *All the provisions of the contract requiring adjustment of the contract sum have been complied with.* The mechanics of this were covered in section 13.4, but the final certificate was conclusive evidence that all necessary adjustments had been properly carried out. Claims by the contractor after the appropriate period had elapsed from issue of the certificate, that the figures were wrong would be fruitless. The only exceptions were if there had been accidental inclusion or omission of work or materials, fraud or if there was an obvious arithmetical error. This sub-clause still applies unchanged.

■ *All due extensions of time have been given.* This was to prevent the contractor raising the question after the final certificate when the employer may have deducted liquidated damages and all financial matters appear to have been settled. This subclause still applies unchanged.

■ *That reimbursement of loss and/or expense is in final settlement of all contractor's claims in respect of clause 26 matters whether the claims are for breach of contract, duty of care, statutory duty or otherwise.* This is a very widely drawn clause intended principally, like the previous clause, to ensure that the final certificate really does spell the end of the financial road. It should be noted, however, that the conclusivity is effective only in respect of the clause 26 matters. It will not operate to prevent the contractor from making claims in regard to breaches of contract outside this parameter. This subclause still applies unchanged.

The effect of the issue of the final certificate, especially in regard to the architect's satisfaction with workmanship and materials, was considered by the Court of Appeal[17]. Much to the concern of architects, the court decided that the final certificate under JCT 80 was conclusive that the architect was satisfied with the quality and standards of *all* materials, goods and workmanship. The consequence was that the employer found it very difficult to take subsequent action against the contractor for latent defects.

The RIBA responded to the situation by issuing guidance notes. They proceeded on the basis that the interpretation put on the final certificate by the Court of Appeal was not what the parties to the contract understood and intended when they entered into contract. Therefore, the notes suggested that the architect should invite both employer and contractor to sign a 'declaration' to that effect before the issue of the final certificate. When subsequently issuing the final certificate, the architect was advised to put sticker B on it which recorded the basis of the declaration. Another set of stickers (stickers A) were provided for putting on certificates of all kinds (practical completion, making good of defects, interim, etc.) stating that the certificate was not intended to indicate that workmanship or materials conformed to description or were in accordance with the contract.

When the Court of Appeal considered the effect of the final certificate and came to its decision, it was not making new law. What it was doing was telling everyone what the terms of the contract meant even though until that moment perhaps no one (including the Court of Appeal) had realised it. What the parties intend to do when they enter into a contract is, of course, important, but only in so far as they give effect to their intentions by the written terms they agree in the contract. In turn, the court can only interpret their intentions by looking at the contract terms. Evidence as to their intentions outside a written contract is normally inadmissible. The court's interpretation of the contract term was very much in the contractor's favour, but that is what the parties agreed in law when they signed the contract.

Anecdotal evidence suggests that most contractors refused to sign the declaration when approached by the architect. That was not surprising, because the contractor was being asked to agree to give up a valuable right. Even if the contractor and employer signed the declaration, it is not certain what effect it would have had. Clearly, it would not vary the original terms – it would require a separate contract to do that. It is possible that it would have some other standing, such as a waiver by the contractor of specific rights, a clarification or in some circumstances an estoppel.

The status of the final certificate if the declaration was signed and both stickers were affixed is uncertain. If the declaration was not sufficient to vary the original terms, it seems that the final certificate may still have been conclusive to the extent decided by the court. Affixing the stickers in those circumstances could have had one of two effects: either they would have made the final certificate void or voidable; or they would have been ineffective, because they were affixed to a certificate which the contract said was conclusive when issued.

If the declaration had been reworded so as to provide for some payment by the employer in return for the contractor giving up his right to a conclusive final certificate, or if the declaration had been completed as a deed by both parties, the contract would indeed have been varied and the problem would have been over. It seems unlikely, however, that a contractor who was hesitant about signing the declaration at all could have been induced to complete it as a binding contract. As far as the contractor is concerned, nothing had changed. The terms of the contract required the architect to issue a final certificate within a specific timescale. If the architect did not so issue he, and through him the employer, was in breach. The architect's position was straightforward if he or she had been engaged on the usual (SFA 92) terms of engagement or similar. During the progress of the Works the architect must carry out inspections with reasonable skill and care. There is a duty to issue the final certificate in accordance with the building contract. If subsequently, a latent defect was discovered, the employer may have been unable to recover the cost of remedial work from the contractor. The employer might then have turned attention to the architect. If the employer was to have been successful in recovering the loss from the architect in negligence, it would have to be shown that the architect failed to carry out administrative duties, including inspection, with reasonable skill and care. That would not have been very easy, but perhaps easier than most architects would have wished.

It was common, in former times, for architects to be so concerned about the conclusiveness of the final certificate that they often neglected to issue a final certificate at all, leaving a minute sum of money outstanding in the knowledge that the contractor would not seek arbitration in respect of such a small amount. By this method it was hoped that the matters otherwise made conclusive by the final certificate would be left open and the employer would not be precluded from obtaining redress from the contractor if any latent defects appeared. Of course, it had also to be borne in mind that, if successful, such a ploy would effectively deprive the employer of the conclusive benefit of the other three matters. The courts have put an end to any likelihood that an employer could proceed against the contractor if the final certificate was not issued at the proper time. The court's view was that if the failure to issue was a breach of contract, the employer cannot take advantage of that breach[18].

Following the *Crown Estates* case[17], the JCT issued amendments to each of the affected forms of contract which were intended to remove the effect of the Court of Appeal decision by rewording the subclauses relating to the conclusivity of the architect's satisfaction. Essentially, therefore, the position was restored that the final certificate was conclusive about the architect's satisfaction only if the architect had specifically stated in the bills of quantities or specification that some item of goods, materials or workmanship was to be to his or her satisfaction or approval. The RIBA issued further stickers (sticker C) and a revised declaration to refer to the amendments. These stickers, like the first set, may be best forgotten. The latest reprinted forms (JCT 98, IFC 98, MC 98, WCD 98 and PCC 98) incorporate the amendment. MW 98 is still unaffected, because the final certificate is still not conclusive.

The only thing which can be said of the final certificate under all building contracts is that after the architect has issued the final certificate, he or she is said to be *functus officio,* having no further powers under the contract. The architect, for example, cannot then issue further extensions of time. An example of a final certificate is shown in Fig. 13.4.

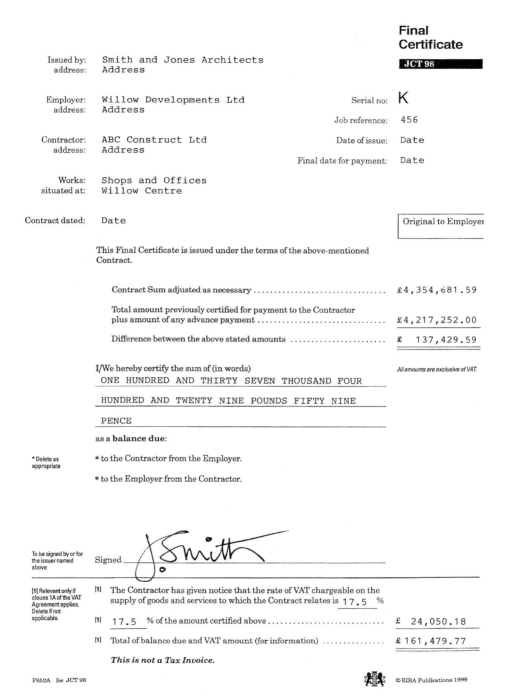

**Final
Certificate**

Issued by: Smith and Jones Architects
address: Address

`JCT 98`

Employer: Willow Developments Ltd   Serial no: K
address: Address
                                             Job reference: 456

Contractor: ABC Construct Ltd   Date of issue: Date
address: Address
                                             Final date for payment: Date

Works: Shops and Offices
situated at: Willow Centre

Contract dated: Date   Original to Employer

This Final Certificate is issued under the terms of the above-mentioned
Contract.

Contract Sum adjusted as necessary £4,354,681.59

Total amount previously certified for payment to the Contractor
plus amount of any advance payment £4,217,252.00

Difference between the above stated amounts ....   £   137,429.59

I/We hereby certify the sum of (in words)   *All amounts are exclusive of VAT.*
ONE HUNDRED AND THIRTY SEVEN THOUSAND FOUR

HUNDRED AND TWENTY NINE POUNDS FIFTY NINE

PENCE

as a **balance due**:

* Delete as   * to the Contractor from the Employer.
appropriate
                  * to the Employer from the Contractor.

To be signed by or for   Signed _____
the issuer named
above

[1] Relevant only if   [1]   The Contractor has given notice that the rate of VAT chargeable on the
clause 1A of the VAT   supply of goods and services to which the Contract relates is 17.5   %
Agreement applies.
Delete if not
applicable.   [1]   17.5   % of the amount certified above ....   £   24,050.18

                        [1]   Total of balance due and VAT amount (for information) ....   £ 161,479.77

                        This is not a Tax Invoice.

F852A for JCT 98   © RIBA Publications 1999

Fig. 13.4 RIBA Final Certificate (courtesy RIBA Publications).

13.6   Feedback

This is a most important stage of the building process. One of the most valuable references is an architect's own experience. Memory grows dim, however, and often it confuses facts. Records of projects become increasingly valuable as the numbers of projects completed increase.

At the end of each project a routine should be established to extract the maximum amount of useful information. Ideally, records should be building up during the running of the project. In practice, everyone connected with the project will be so busy during the construction process that they will put off doing anything which does not seem to be urgent. An architect does not simply come to a conclusion on one scheme and then the following day start work on another. The reality is that work on one project overlaps work on another. Depending on size, an architect may well be working on several different schemes at once. Finding time to carry out a feedback and appraisal exercise is not usually a priority. It has to be done, however, if the architectural practice is to develop.

If all parties can be gathered around the table for an appraisal session at the end so much the better. Theoretically, all parties are terribly frank with each other and the contractor takes part. There is no doubt that such a session would be very useful, but the chances of achieving it are remote. By the end of the project, all parties probably know what they think of each other. They may not be on speaking terms at that stage and quite possibly, though regrettably, arbitration or litigation may be in the air and adjudication may have taken place.

Architects can produce quite a lot of useful feedback information simply by consulting the files and by spending an afternoon going through a prepared agenda and discussing among the design team within the architect's office just what was done and whether it could have been done in a more effective way. It is important that the discussion is carefully structured or it will achieve nothing. The first thing in preparation is to record the key dates and other information. Some suggested, but by no means an exhaustive list of, items may be:

- Dates of commencement of each Plan of Work stage, i.e. when was the first contact with the client
- Projected and actual dates for commencement and completion of the contract on site

- The cost history: estimates of cost from inception until tender stage, then accepted tender price, contract sum and final certificate figure
- Project type, construction system, services
- Procurement method and form of contract, amendments

This is a useful starting point for discussion which should attempt to answer the question 'why?' in relation to each item. Other matters which should be examined are:

- Drawings preparation and issue
- Architect's instructions, content, pricing, reasons for issue
- Site meetings and minutes
- Cost control
- Claims
- Communications within the design team, with the client and the contractor
- Client's brief compared to finished building, compared to building in use
- Appropriateness of materials including reviews at set time periods
- Appropriateness of details including reviews at set time periods
- Areas where improvements can be made

Some architects consider that the client should be involved in the process and a questionnaire can be sent inviting comment on specific issues. Others think that to do so would be inviting trouble, rather like asking the client to consider whether it is appropriate to serve a writ. That is perhaps to take a rather gloomy view. The client should appreciate that the architect is simply concerned to give a good service and always anxious to improve. Whether the client is involved or not, it is certain that architects will get much out of a thorough feedback exercise. Among other things, it promotes the questioning of long established but possibly ineffectual practices. Many architects would be astounded to realise just how many times they have issued revised versions of certain drawings, just how long it took them to provide the answer to certain queries from the contractor, and just how many people-hours were spent on site meetings.

One final point: the feedback exercise is intended to help all concerned. It is not intended to be a witchhunt to discover the culprit behind failed details or exceeded cost targets. If it is used as a method of apportioning blame by an office, there will only ever be the one exercise.

References

(1) *Davis Contractors Ltd* v. *Fareham UDC* [1956] 2 All ER 145.

(2) *F. Treliving & Co Ltd.* v. *Simplex Time Recorder Co (UK) Ltd* (1981) unreported.

(3) See the courts' views in *Greater London Council* v. *Cleveland Bridge & Engineering Co Ltd* (1986) 8 Con LR 30 and particularly *West Faulkner Associates* v. *London Borough of Newham* (1995) 11 Const LJ 157.

(4) *Woodar Investment Development Ltd* v. *Wimpey Construction UK Ltd* [1980] 1 All ER 571.

(5) *London Borough of Hounslow* v. *Twickenham Garden Developments Ltd* (1970) 7 BLR 81.

(6) *Wraight Ltd* v. *P.H. & T. (Holdings) Ltd* (1968) 8 BLR 22.

(7) *Emson Eastern Ltd (in receivership)* v. *EME Developments Ltd* (1991) 55 BLR 114.

(8) Salmon LJ, *Westminster City Council* v. *J. Jarvis & Sons Ltd* [1969] 1 All ER 1025, CA.

(9) *H.W. Neville (Sunblest) Ltd* v. *Wm Press & Son Ltd* (1981) 20 BLR 78.

(10) *Westminster City Council* v. *J. Jarvis & Sons Ltd* (1970) 7 BLR 64 HL.

(11) *BFI Group of Companies Ltd* v. *DCB Integration Systems Ltd* (1987) CILL 348.

(12) *M.J. Gleeson (Contractors) Ltd* v. *London Borough of Hillingdon* (1970) 215 EGD 165.

(13) *City Axis Ltd* v. *Daniel P. Jackson* (1998) CILL 1382.

(14) *William Tomkinson and Sons Ltd* v. *The Parochial Church Council of St Michael's and Others* (1990) 6 Const LJ 319.

(15) *Pearce and High* v. *Baxter* (1999) 90 BLR 101.

(16) *P. & M. Kay Ltd* v. *Hosier & Dickinson* (1972) 10 BLR 126.

(17) *Crown Estates Commissioners* v. *John Mowlem & Co* (1994) 70 BLR 1.

(18) *Matthew Ortech Ltd* v. *Tarmac Roadstone Ltd* (1998) 87 BLR 96.

Part 3
General Office Matters

14 Management Principles

14.1 Objectives

There are broadly two kinds of objectives: the objectives of the firm and the objectives of the individual. As a rough guide, the most successful firms are those in which the objectives of the firm and its employees most nearly correspond, because they can all go forward together without jostling for advantage.

The objectives of an architectural practice might well be to enjoy and to produce fine architecture, contribute to the environment, and make a reasonable profit. The architects in the practice will have joined because they have similar objectives and they are also perhaps, looking for career advancement. A good manager will ensure that these personal goals are capable of satisfaction within the overall framework of the practice objectives.

Many large organisations have problems because the members of staff have rather different objectives from those of the organisation. It is not uncommon to encounter the kind of individual who considers that his or her objective is achieved if the pile of papers in the 'IN' tray can be transferred to the 'OUT' tray by the end of the day. In the context of that company, the objective may be valid, but everyone should ask the question, 'Is what I am doing assisting in achieving the objectives of the organisation?' Sometimes, it is difficult to see how particular tasks are helping to achieve objectives. In such cases, the employee should ask the manager for an explanation (see section 14.5).

Objectives, of course, both for individuals and organisations are long and short term. A short term objective for a practice might be to complete a particular project. In the shorter term, completing a stage, such as the client's acceptance of outline proposals, may be crucial. Longer term objectives are probably associated with expansion, specialisation, movement to better premises, etc. It is clear that the longer term objectives can only be achieved if the shorter term objectives are secured first. Personal objectives have similar structures.

Achieving objectives can involve admitting mistakes, indeed must do so. Whoever first decided that it was a weakness to admit mistakes was very misguided. Everyone makes mistakes and it is only by acknowledging a mistake that progress can be made. For example, it is essential to know how to put a cost on a project so that appropriate fees can be charged. In order to achieve this objective, careful historical records must be kept to indicate just how well the practice's own cost and time targets are achieved. An essential part of these records are staff time sheets. It is not unknown, however, for some architects to put down a proportion of their time to other work when they begin to see that they are in danger of exceeding the budgeted figures. The only clear result is that the practice builds up a set of unreliable records and it will continue to underestimate time periods, project after project, until the laying-off of time against other projects ceases (see Chapter 16, section 16.15).

Every practice should have a policy of admitting mistakes, including those of the partners, so that something can be done about them. Once a mistake is admitted, there should be commiserations all round then the mistake should be forgotten and the concentration should be on objectives. Every architect should learn to take decisions on the basis of the practice objectives; if a mistake is made, an admission will save much time and files of internal memos. Architectural practices who try this approach experience team work, often for the first time. There really is no place for a practice with an infallible sole principal and six frightened assistants. Common objectives eliminate this problem.

If the objectives are clear, the best route towards them may be difficult to find. If the objectives are not defined, everyone will be setting off in different directions.

14.2   Leadership

Architects are called upon to practise leadership in different ways. In a small way, it is required in chairing a meeting. A principal, partner or director has to exercise leadership. If the office is large enough, a group leader is aptly named.

In the long run, the best leaders are low profile. There is much inconsequential verbiage written about leadership. A good leader really has only two functions:

- To decide objectives for those being led
- To set the pace

The importance of objectives has already been discussed. Deciding objectives is a clear function, if difficult to carry out. Setting the pace is more complex. How a leader sets the pace depends on many factors including the objective to be achieved, the circumstances, the personalities of others and, not least, the personality of the leader. This is what is sometimes referred to as leadership style. Some architects, with large outgoing personalities, like to lead from the front, building up an office image which is essentially their own image. This is not necessarily or even usually, effective. It results in a practice which is essentially one person plus helpers.

The real art of leadership is to appear to be following, hence the phrase 'leading from behind'. A good partner will ensure that everything is in place to make it as easy as possible for project architects to carry out their tasks. A good leader must also be a good facilitator, prepared to do the things which would distract the architects from their essential tasks. Good leaders put forward their ideas in such a way that the project architects think they are their own ideas. The true measure of successful leadership is the performance of the leader's staff.

14.3 Communications

Communication is the most vital aspect of management. Ineffective communication will render the most splendid ideas useless. Communication is a two-way process. Many of the problems associated with building contracts result from failure on both sides. The general principle is that if a message is misunderstood, it is the fault of the originator. It is in the nature of the profession that architects can only get their concepts realised if they communicate them effectively. So architects must be excellent communicators. Good communication involves:

- Clarity
- Certainty
- Brevity
- Comprehensiveness

14.3.1 Clarity

Architects should look at their drawings, specifications, reports and letters as though they were the recipients. Many architectural drawings need second sight to decipher. Preparing production information (see Chapter 10, section 10.3) requires the application of a mind which having analysed the problem can synthesise the solution to produce easily digestible information. It is not easy. Eccentric and flamboyant drawing styles do not help matters.

14.3.2   Certainty

Certainty goes arm in arm with clarity although there is a distinction. When the architect communicates with the contractor there should be only one interpretation possible. Very often, a message which may be a model of clarity in itself may be capable of two meanings when read in context with other messages or with the project as a whole. The architect should take care, therefore, that any communication, drawn, written or spoken, is incapable of misinterpretation. The message may be uncertain in itself, of course, as in such phrases as 'as soon as possible' or 'when convenient' or 'quality'. It has becomes fashionable to talk about 'quality products' or a pub serving 'quality food'. Such phrases are meaningless. 'Quality' is a characteristic or an attribute. Unless it is qualified, it means nothing. But '*good* quality food' or '*poor* quality products' get the message across. Even if a time period is specified, uncertainty may still exist as in, 'You have only 7 days to respond.' Does that mean 7 days from the date, or from the receipt of the letter, or 7 days from some other date which may be implied when the phrase is read in context with the rest of the letter?

14.3.3   Brevity

It is difficult to be brief. Extra words are added to a sentence or clause and extra lines are added to a drawing to make the meaning clearer. Often, they make the meaning more obscure. This is in part, because it is more difficult to read. To be brief in a written document involves writing out the message as clearly and briefly as possible, then carefully editing out the superfluous, doing some rearranging, then writing it out again. It will take the architect longer to prepare the document, but it should save time in the long term, because the contractor should be able to act on the document without any, or too many, questions.

14.3.4 Comprehensiveness

It is very common to assume that a recipient knows more than actually is the case. The golden rule is to assume that the recipient knows very little and proceed accordingly. This will involve more time in preparation, but again it should save questioning time and it is also useful when drawings or other documents have to be consulted long after they were produced. Brief messages in the style of 'Got your message, and agree your suggestion' are unfortunately quite common. The only thing one can say is that they encapsulate in one an ignorance of three of these principles, thus making the fourth, brevity, another fault. Messages of this kind are not the hallmark of the busy executive architect, but careless almost to the point of negligence. These principles hold good not only between architect and contractor, but between architect and fellow consultants and between the project architect and the other architects in a particular group. Regrettably, architects' drawings are not always good examples of communication documents. The eminent architect, Sir Edwin Lutyens, once said that a drawing should be like a letter to the builder telling him exactly what is required, not a pretty picture to impress an idiotic client. Not very complimentary to his clients, but very true for all that.

14.4 Delegation

It is common to hear architects say that the architect above them in seniority does not know how to delegate. Grumbles of this sort usually indicate that the architect in question insists on keeping an eye very firmly on everything that is going on. That architect, however, will probably say that since he or she takes the responsibility in the end, such close supervision is justified. That kind of response puts the cart before the horse. Delegation is a key function of management and the art of delegation is to know what to delegate, when and to whom. Of course the senior takes overall responsibility; that is one of the reasons for the larger salary cheque.

The rule is to delegate work to the least qualified/paid person who is capable of doing the work. It is important to understand the principle properly. It does not mean that work should always be delegated to the least paid or least qualified. The important criterion is that the person should be capable of doing the work. Therefore, if the quality required is of a very high order it might well be that the person capable is actually the best qualified and highest paid. If there are three people who can do the work, the least qualified and least paid should be chosen. To do otherwise is to squander talent and money.

Delegation encourages people to take responsibility. Architects in control of staff may be reluctant to delegate because they think that the task will not be carried out properly. What they really mean is that it will not be carried out precisely in the way they would have tackled it. In fact it could be carried out with greater efficiency.

An example will make it clear: There may be a meeting scheduled at which an important client will meet the contractor to settle some crucial matters relating to a large contract. The senior architect may well feel an obligation to attend even though there is a very competent project architect dealing with that contract. The truth is that if the senior architect delegates the attendance at that meeting, the preparation for it and report after the meeting will receive the kind of attention the senior architect is unlikely to be able to give it. The senior architect should delegate attendance to the project architect (with reasonable notice) with the message that whatever he or she agrees will be backed. The project architect will appreciate the confidence and will spend long hours, not all of them office hours, in preparation to make sure of achieving the best possible outcome. The senior architect will be freed to do non-delegable work.

An important rule is not to delegate work and interfere. A manager who does that has lost his nerve. Architects in a position to delegate work should pick the right person and then demonstrate total confidence in the delegation. They will rarely be disappointed. If they are, it will usually reflect their bad judgement.

14.5 Motivation

Motivation is in two parts: motivation of self and motivation of others. Self motivation is very complex. It may depend on the solving of a problem or the desire to improve an already satisfactory situation. The desire for status, money, power, social position, security, happiness, acknowledgment, service, etc. fall in either or both of those categories. Without a strong motive, little is achieved. A common term for a person with a strong motivation is 'self starter'. It describes the situation very well. Most professional activity is motivating for the participant, possibly none more so than architecture. It offers challenge and the opportunity to rise to the occasion.

An unmotivated architect will probably stay in the same office for the whole of a working life, maybe doing unrewarding work and progressing slowly, if at all, at the whim of others. If such a person changes offices or progresses more quickly, it will be as a reaction to some external pressure. To that kind of person, the professional challenges which motivate others may simply be depressing, particularly if they are beyond that architect's capabilities.

A self starter will determine his or her goals in life, long and short term, and create the appropriate internal pressure required to attain the goals. In fact, the unmotivated architect noted above is not really unmotivated. It is just that the motive is not the accepted kind. It may be to drift along to retirement with the minimum of fuss because the architect in question has some extra-office activity to which work is just a necessary interruption. Self motivation in this context, however, is generally taken to mean the ability of an individual to drive him or herself without the necessity for any external pressure.

The motivation of others is very difficult. The secret is to discover what the individual goals of team members are. Motivators are generally seen as achievement, recognition and advancement. Whether an individual acts in particular circumstances depends largely on whether the action is seen as resulting in the desired outcome. The art of motivation, therefore, is to let the individuals see that their actions are achieving the desired end. The carrot is more effective than the stick. The golden rule for motivating others can be summarised as follows:

- Find out what they want
- Show them how to get it by doing what you want
- Ensure they are not disappointed due to your fault

15 General Office Practice

15.1 Introduction

There are certain basic skills which every architect should have in addition to specific professional skills. This chapter addresses the basic office skills which are essential to everyone who works in the office environment. Architects are usually left to acquire these skills as part of the practice experience. That is not the best way of learning. All architects should have a thorough understanding of good office practice before they enter the office in which they are to work and in which very bad office practice may be the order of the day. What follows is simply an outline of the key areas in which the architect should be proficient in the office. Some are relevant only to architects, some are of wider application.

15.2 Telephone, facsimile (fax) and e-mail

A telephone is essential. There is sophisticated equipment available today which will allow virtually any installation appropriate to the office organisation. Installations may range from a single line to any number of separate lines incorporating facilities for inter-office communication, conference facilities, answerphones and speakerphones. Where offices are spread over several buildings, it is possible to have the telephone system set up so that callers to the central switchboard are rerouted to the appropriate building.

Telephone calls should be made and answered promptly and they should be kept as brief as consistent with the object of the call. This is always important, because telephone calls can be costly, but it is particularly important if there are few lines and there may be a risk that outside callers cannot communicate with the office. A competent telephone operator with a good voice and manner is a boon to any office. Such a person is the firm so far as telephone callers are concerned. If the first impression is not good, they will not call again.

There are some basic rules for good telephone management. They include never keeping anyone waiting and keeping a record

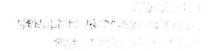

of incoming calls and messages if the recipient of the call is unavailable. Architects should always keep a written record of telephone calls. The degree of detail in the record will depend on the importance of the call, but the minimum must be the name of the caller and the time of the call. Most telephone calls will warrant more detail than that.

A particularly annoying habit, so far as the recipient is concerned, is to have a secretary or the switchboard make a call. At the very least, it sends a clear message that the caller is much busier than the called and his or her time is much more valuable. An excuse often given for the practice is that telephoning and getting a busy number or discovering that the particular person is out is time consuming and much better carried out by someone who is costing the firm less than the architect. At first sight there seems to be some merit in that argument, but it is axiomatic that when the switchboard have eventually made contact with the required person and got that person waiting on the telephone, the original caller has vanished from the desk and cannot be traced for several minutes if at all. Before indulging in such annoying one-upmanship, the architect should judge the likely reaction of the person receiving the call.

Except when returning a call, the person telephoning is doing so with an aim in mind, a particular reason for calling. Courtesy requires that such a person must do the waiting, not the person called.

Although mobile telephones are a real boon to the single-handed practitioner, they must be used with consideration for others. Under the right conditions, listening to one side of another's animated mobile phone conversation may be a source of amusement to while away a tedious train journey, but usually such things are merely irritants. Save for the most pressing of reasons, there can be no excuse for leaving a mobile phone switched on during a meeting. Even then, the permission of the chairperson must be obtained and not assumed. To leave the phone on in normal situations shows the most flagrant disregard for the time of others. It sends everyone a message that the offender believes that he or she is the busiest and most important person present. Some companies arrange important meetings away from the office precisely because they do not want the participants interrupted by telephone calls or urgent consultations. To take a mobile telephone into that environment defeats the object.

Although the telephone has provided a means of transmitting the spoken word for many years, other means are available which enable the user to send letters, pictures and drawings almost instantly from one side of the world to the other. The facsimile (fax) machine has revolutionised the way business is conducted. Sketches can be faxed directly to site and there is no longer any excuse for a delay before the architect confirms oral instructions. The fax is best employed when it is reserved for matters which are urgent enough to warrant a message being transmitted the same day. Unfortunately, it has become the practice to fax all letters and follow up with a hard copy of the letter in the post. Although a hard copy is essential, the automatic sending of all documents by both means simply doubles the paperwork. In many cases, nothing is achieved by same day delivery.

More recently, e-mail has replaced faxing in large measure for those unwise enough to reveal their e-mail addresses to the world at large. The authors saw a recent news item to the effect that office workers receive an average of about 170 e-mails daily. This seems excessive and difficult to believe, because we have yet to meet anyone who admits to half that number. The principle, however, is clear. The ease with which an e-mail can be sent encourages the sending of messages about the most trivial matters. E-mail is really valuable for the transmission of large quantities of text from one place to another. The system is especially useful, because the recipient of the text can make alterations. Large quantities of text can be transmitted by fax, but it cannot be amended without retyping or, if the text is very distinct, by scanning.

15.3   Information technology

Many architectural activities that were formerly paper-based are now replicated or replaced by computer applications. Although it is beyond the scope of this book to describe them, or indeed information technology generally, in any detail, the architect should be familiar with them and they warrant a brief mention.

E-mail and computer aided design (CAD) are described elsewhere in this chapter, but there are other common applications. Word processing software is used by most practices these days. The key advantages are that everyday typing is more efficient, corrections and edits are readily made and standard documents of all kinds can be electronically stored for amending and issue. Word processing packages today are becoming more and more sophisticated with the facility to manipulate text in a variety of ways, to check spelling and grammar and to reference text. Crucially, it is possible to search thousands of files within seconds to find a particular word or phrase.

Spreadsheet programmes allow arithmetic and logic operations on numeric data to be performed and they are now available for a wide variety of tasks. Databases are effectively computerised filing systems, which enable data to be manipulated and produced in many different ways to suit different purposes. Therefore, records can be stored for retrieval against different designated criteria. Project planning software is a boon for architects who have to decide the appropriate amounts of extension of time. It allows logic links to be inserted with lead and lag times and the appropriate resources for each activity. This method of working out the amount of extension of time due to the contractor has received judicial approval[1] and every architect's office should have the software. It is also useful for monitoring progress as the work progresses.

The quality of printers available now allows inexpensive documents of textbook quality to be produced. For improved presentations there are easy-to-use desktop publishing-programmes available.

15.4   Letter writing

The object of writing a letter is essentially to convey what is in the mind of one person to the mind of another, albeit the writer may not always wish to be entirely frank and open in the communication, and at the same time to make a permanent record of the communication. The other person is obviously not present to be addressed orally, therefore the writer must convey what would be clear from facial expression or tone of voice by the skill of combining words. Without embarking on a full exposition of the subject a few suggestions may be made:

■ Be sure that the points made are clear.
■ Be as brief and simple as possible. Do not use two words if one will do. Avoid long words and convoluted phraseology.
■ Start a new paragraph whenever a new point is to be made even if the paragraph is only two lines long. Do not split a point into more than one paragraph.
■ If the letter becomes very long, consider whether it might be better to put the contents in the form of a report or schedule with a short covering letter.
■ Be sure to write with the reader in mind. Technical terms may

provide a useful short cut when writing to like disciplines, but they should be strictly excluded when writing to non technical persons. Despite what some architects may think, trying to impress a lay client with difficult words and concepts does not succeed.

- Avoid commercial and business cliches, journalese, Americanisms, slang and jargon.
- Avoid spelling mistakes and grammar. They give a poor impression to the reader.
- Avoid the impersonal. 'It is regretted' means nothing. Regret is a personal sentiment; if regret is felt, say 'I regret' or 'We regret'. It may or may not be prudent to say 'the Board' or 'the directors' regret.
- Be definite. Do not say 'this appears to be correct'. If satisfied that it is correct, say so.
- Standard reference books are available which can prove useful in ensuring that well-written letters are sent out[2].

Some care should be taken over forms of address. Traditionally, men have been addressed as Esquire and women as Mrs or Miss. Today the mode of address is more likely to be Mr, Mrs, Miss or Ms. Whatever form is adopted, qualifications and honours should not be forgotten. When opening a letter, the usual form is 'Dear Sir' or 'Madam' and the ending 'Yours faithfully'. Depending how well the parties know each other these forms may become less formal, but in a business letter it is unwise to go beyond Mr, Mrs, Miss or Ms. Remember that letters sometimes end up in court and too much familiarity may come to be regretted.

The fashion for first names to be used when the writer does not even know the recipient is unfortunate. It is a rather hypocritical trend, because traditionally first names are only used between friends and close colleagues. Architects must certainly move with the times, but they should take care while doing so.

15.5 Reports

The architect may be specifically asked to write a report, or may decide to do so when a letter looks like becoming long-winded. The art of report writing is a considerable subject on its own, but a few words of guidance are offered by way of assistance:

- Remember who is going to read the report. If it is to be a technical person then technical phraseology is quite acceptable, probably inevitable; the reader will understand what is being said. If the reader is to be a non technical person or a lay committee, they will be completely at sea unless the report is written in language they can understand.

■ Plan the structure of the report. There is nothing worse than a report which is clearly the thoughts of the author just as they have arisen, put down on paper without any thought as to logical order.

■ A report should start with an introduction setting out the subject matter and, if appropriate, who the writer is and his or her qualifications. Then follows the body of the report: it is most logical and effective to note the facts first before going on to matters of opinion. The report should end with a conclusion and usually a request for instructions. It should be signed and dated.

■ Adopt a simple and consistent system of numbering. For example:

1.00 *Introduction*
1.01 My name is ... etc, etc.
1.02 I am asked to report on ... etc, etc.
2.00 *Extensions of time*
2.01 Extensions have been granted as follows:

■ Take care with the English, the punctuation and the spelling. A good report reads well; bad English, poor punctuation and a plethora of wrongly spelled words give the worst possible impression.

■ Report on that which has been asked for. Cut out all unnecessary verbiage; it may add to the bulk of the report, but it adds little or nothing to the content. Better a short, pithy report than a long rambling version, which runs the risk of boring the reader and never being read.

■ Read over the final version very carefully; much may hinge on your efforts.

There are several useful books available on the subject of report writing[3].

15.6   Filing

15.6.1 Correspondence and reports

Once the letters and reports have been written, the office copies together with letters, reports, facsimiles, etc received have to be filed.

The secret of good filing is to ensure that any document can be found quickly. Much time and cost, to say nothing of frustration and temper, can be expended in trying to trace a wrongly filed document.

The complexity of the filing will depend largely on the complexity of the project. A simple project will probably warrant a single file. More complicated ones may require a series of files for, say, architect, client, contractor, quantity surveyor, engineer, etc. Other files will be required for special matters such as partner's personal file, insurances and professional bodies.

As well as letters, the files should contain such things as reports, telephone messages and internal memos. These will help to complete the history of the project and they may prove to be invaluable later, particularly in legal matters where the side with the best records is going to be at a great advantage.

Typical files for a medium-to-large project might be:

- Correspondence: client, funder, etc.
- Correspondence: statutory undertakings, planning, building control
- Correspondence: consultant quantity surveyor
- Correspondence: contractor
- Correspondence: prospective nominated subcontractors
- Mechanical and electrical services
- Structural
- Landscaping
- Clerk of works' reports
- Site meetings
- Architect's instructions
- Certificates, valuations, nominated subcontractor directions
- Financial reports

Another system which should not be overlooked is electronic data storage. There are many advantages to storing all data this way. Only one of these is space. Obviously, enormous quantities of information can be stored on hard disk, on floppy disk, on Zip disks and on CD-rom. Technology has advanced to the stage that documents of all kinds can be scanned onto disk very rapidly. The document can be retrieved and read on a monitor in an instant. Moreover, the system can be arranged to search for and display all documents of a particular kind or documents which deal with a particular topic. In short, it is easier to find a piece of correspondence after it has been stored electronically than before. The material can be guarded so that 'read only' access is available, or it can be manipulated in any convenient way.

There are some warnings. Electronic data is much more ephemeral than something on paper. It is essential to keep back copies of the data because disks, even hard disks, can corrupt without warning and it is also possible to corrupt a disk physically or, for example, by trying to remove it while the computer is trying to read from, or write to, it. Even though documents may be scanned and consigned to disk in some form, the original documents should not be destroyed straight away. There are some documents which must never be destroyed, for example, contracts and various statutory permissions. It could be argued that ordinary documents, such as correspondence associated with administering a building contract, should never be destroyed. There is always a risk that a document will be needed many years after the building is completed. Most architects, however, would probably feel comfortable destroying original correspondence 6 years after the issue of the final certificate if the contract was executed under hand and 12 years after if the contract was executed as a deed. The fact that copies are still held electronically should suffice to deal with any queries after that date. Nowadays, there is no excuse for destroying all trace of any document.

15.6.2   Drawings

Drawings in current use should be filed flat in plan-chests or vertically in cabinets. They should not be folded or rolled. Negatives, office prints and specialists' drawings, if possible, should be kept separate. Rough sketches which are probably prepared on pieces of paper of various sizes can be folded and kept in large paper envelopes or box files.

When a drawing has been revised, the out of date print should be clearly marked 'superseded' and filed separately. Large paper envelopes can be procured for filing such drawings which, of course, can be folded if necessary. All drawing cabinets, box files or envelopes which are used for storing drawings should be marked with the appropriate number or reference.

Drawings which are removed from the plan chest should be returned as soon as possible, and in a large office it will be necessary to devise a form of register in which a record can be kept of any drawings which have been taken out, with the names of the borrowers. In some large local authority and government offices the filing and registration of drawings are undertaken by a clerk who is solely responsible for ordering prints, loaning drawings and keeping them in safe custody.

For convenience, except in a very large office, the drawing cabinets will be kept in the drawing offices, so that quick reference can be made to drawings of current jobs. It should be part of the daily routine to put all drawings away at night; they should not be used as dust sheets or for rough sketches.

When a job is finished, the drawings should be brought up to date, removed from the drawing office and suitably filed. That is a counsel of perfection, but it will pay dividends later if it is observed. Unless a large amount of storage accommodation is available, only the negatives need to be retained, as it will be more convenient to order new prints if they are subsequently required. Old prints can probably serve a more useful purpose as scrap paper!

Traditionally, old negatives were filed in metal tubes which were stacked in racks. A tube 150 mm in diameter will store about 200 drawings. An alternative method of storage was in large paper envelopes which had the advantage of storing the drawings flat. These envelopes could be stacked vertically or clamped with wooden strips on one edge and slung from a bar rather like a coat hanger on a rail. An index should, of course, be kept of all old drawings in store.

However, even the smallest businesses can microfilm important information. Saving as it does tremendous space and being easily catalogued and retrieved, microfilm and microfiche is probably the best method of storage for architectural drawing records. Drawings produced by CAD will obviously be stored electronically on disk or tape.

15.7   Office based meetings

See Chapter 12, section 12.2.

15.8 Drawing office practice

Although the use of computers to produce drawings is widespread (see section 15.9), many practices still rely on hand drawing. Every architect should study the relevant British Standard on drawing practice[4]. Where, as in the construction industry, clear communication is all important, there is no room for an architect who employs exceptionally personalised drawing techniques. Many of the mistakes which occur on a construction site undoubtedly stem from a misreading of drawings and any attempt to co-ordinate symbols, hatching and representational methods of all kinds is to be welcomed. In some cases, an exception may be made for drawings which are purely for the purpose of explaining the proposals to a client. It is not proposed to dwell especially on this type of drawing, because this is one thing which architects quickly learn to do very well[5].

Certain basic information must be included on every drawing:

- Firm's name
- Address and telephone number
- Project title
- Drawing title
- Drawing number with revision number and description if appropriate
- Scale
- Date drawn and dates of revisions if appropriate
- Name or initials of draftsman
- North point on plans

It is common for a practice to have a set of standard-sized drawing sheets pre-printed with the basic information and firm's logo if applicable. Where grid lines are used to position structural elements or for modular purposes, they should be carefully referenced. It is usual to use numbers along one axis and letters along the other. Vertical positioning is best done by levels referenced to a datum. Such horizontal and vertical references must be used consistently, not only by architects but also by other consultants.

If all parties creating or using the drawings stick to this system of referencing, the chance of errors due to ambiguous descriptions will be minimised and time saved. Thus the vague: 'wall next to splayed abutment opposite general office on second floor' becomes more simply and accurately: 'wall between refs R4 and 5 on floor level 10.600'. The 'general office' will be unidentifiable during building operations (and perhaps after practical completion) and what constitutes a 'splayed abutment' is anyone's guess.

Time and clarity are served if symbols are used to show such items as WCs, washbasins, kitchen units, etc. rather than having them drawn out in meticulous detail.

Some offices adopt the practice of using standard details. This can be very useful for items which recur, such as access panels, cills, lintels, eaves, door frames and casings, windows, skirtings, etc. Although the same standard details will not be suitable for every project, architects should resist the temptation to design a totally fresh detail for everything on every project, bearing in mind that standard details should evolve over the years to represent the very best detail for a particular situation which that office can produce.

15.8.1   Dimensions

Dimensions form one of the most important items of instruction to the quantity surveyor and later to the contractor. Incorrect dimensions are a constant source of problems on site.

A block plan must give overall dimensions of the building, setting out dimensions for all foundations and walls, together with their thicknesses. In practice, many architects do not understand what information a contractor needs in order to be able to set out properly on the site, yet most standard form contracts make the architect responsible for producing that information and probably such responsibility would be implied if not expressed. The contractor needs to be able to locate at least one, and preferably two, base lines on site. To do that each point at the end of the base line must be securely fixed, by triangulation, from an already established known point (see Fig. 15.1).

If a building has a steel or reinforced concrete frame, the setting out of the centre lines of stanchions should be shown on the foundation plan. The contours of the site should be shown and the levels of foundation bottoms, with positions of steps indicated. Levels should be referenced to an established datum. A key on the drawing should make clear the difference between existing and proposed levels. A simple system is to put each existing level in a small box.

Floor plans should show levels, detailed dimensions of rooms, corridors, thicknesses of walls and partitions, widths of openings,

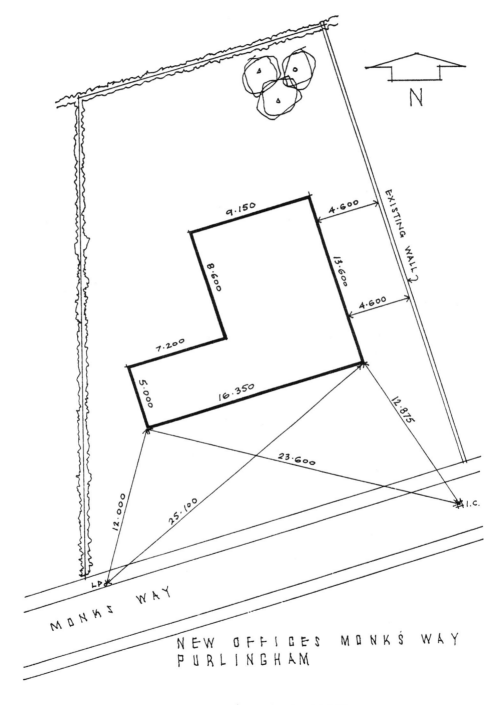

Fig. 15.1   Setting-out plan. Orignal was drawn to scale of 1:200.

etc. Care must be taken that dimension lines are not capable of confusion with lines representing part of the building. It is usual to show the extremities of each dimension by a clear arrowhead, cross, dot or other symbol. Figures must be clearly written, particularly the stop separating the metres from decimal parts.

In a new building, the quantity surveyor and the contractor should have no doubt about the exact heights and dimensions between walls in both directions of all rooms, including all recesses, cupboards formed by partitions, passages, etc. Where working between existing walls, it may be necessary to leave one of a series of dimensions to be verified on site, but all others should be given.

The finished floor and roof levels should be shown on the plans as well as on the sections, and it should be clear what allowance the builder is to make for the difference between structural and finished surfaces. All doors and windows must be referenced so that they can be easily found in appropriate schedules.

Sections should be drawn through portions of the building where floor or roof levels vary, at the intersection of parts of the building, through staircases and any other places which are not shown elsewhere. To explain really difficult parts of the construction, isometric and planometric should be used. The position at which sections are taken should be clearly marked on all floor plans. Floor levels and heights of rooms should be shown and on 1:20 scale sections it is a good idea to incorporate a brick/block scale, so that the levels of lintel, cill, wallplate, floor bearings, etc. can be properly related to courses. It is also helpful if the materials in the larger sections are indicated by appropriate cross hatching.

The elevations, besides indicating the external appearance of the building, the different materials used and the finished ground levels against the building, should also show the floor and basement levels dotted on and dimensioned, the levels of damp-proof courses, the opening portions of windows, external flashings and weatherings, vent pipes, rainwater pipes and the stepping to foundations. Windows and doors can be numbered on elevations as well. The common practice of never showing anything on an elevation that can be found elsewhere may save a little time, but it sacrifices the very useful extra check provided by the inclusion of such details.

It is sensible to include a note on each drawing that figured dimensions are to be followed in preference to scaled measurements. The need for figured dimensions can be reduced considerably if grids are used to represent, not only locations, but also standard dimensions; 300 mm is a common grid measurement.

15.8.2 Lettering

Neatness and clarity in lettering are essential and to achieve the best results, the letters should not be too large and should be evenly spaced. The lettering should be kept as simple as possible and individual styling should be eschewed. Italic script, for example, can be very attractive in a letter and when carefully executed, but in the hands of many hard-pressed architects it can become neat, but unreadable. Stencils can be used, but they are never as quick as good hand lettering. Another option is the typed adhesive strip (the typescript must be dense) or the rub-off transfers which can be used for other parts of the drawings as well as lettering.

15.8.3 Negatives

Drawings may be prepared on translucent material, so that several copies can be obtained for distribution, but it is now common for drawings to be printed onto plastic sheet rather than being drawn directly on it.

There are various grades of tracing paper, generally being used for sketching and scribbling. It is well worth using a good, stout quality of paper, as not only will it stand up to frequent handling much better, but it will allow quite a lot of ink erasing without falling to pieces. Many architects still prefer detail paper for sketching. Different types of plastic sheet are available, and growing in use, which have a very good ink surface, and are more transparent than stout tracing paper and better able to stand handling and erasing.

Negative prints can easily be obtained. This process enables architects to have basic information reproduced on a number of additional negatives to enable working up into various forms. For example, the basic floor plans may be copied before notes and additional information are added so that separate drawings can be provided for heating and electrical layouts, floor and ceiling designs, duct layouts, etc.

A frequent problem is that when the contract documents are to be prepared, the architect finds that the drawings on which the contractors tendered and which must, therefore, or with agreed amendments, become the contract drawings, have been altered and updated. Problems of this kind can be avoided if a set of negatives is taken at tender stage especially for the purpose of preparing the contract documents in due course.

15.9   Computer aided design

The number of offices using computers to assist design is increasing, but there are few offices in which computers are the only design tool. The reason is probably because all computer aided design (CAD) takes time and application to master. Even when mastered, and some systems are easier than others, it can be a relatively slow process.

The only way to learn to use CAD and to understand the possibilities is to sit at the computer and experiment after the initial period of instruction in the particular system. At the current state of the art, computers are not capable of thinking for themselves. The old adage 'rubbish in, rubbish out' is still true. The computer will only do what the operator instructs. It is unlikely that computers will replace the pencil and paper approach of the designing architect for some time to come. But computers are very useful for testing a design once produced. They can reveal the design in three-dimensions from any chosen viewpoint, and they can be programmed to produce a virtual reality impression of a walk through the building if sufficient data are input into the system.

If basic design information is put into the computer at an early stage, it can eventually form the basis of computer drafted production information. Computer images can be combined with programmes which allow investigation of acoustics, heating, day lighting levels and so on. There is also the benefit of being able to plot all services and reproduce perspective views to identify possible conflict areas.

CAD is moving forward very quickly and highly sophisticated software enables full interrogation of designs at an early stage. No architect can afford to ignore these developments.

15.10   Presentation

The way in which architects choose to present proposals to clients is largely a matter of personal choice. The truth is that whatever works is right. A client's capability to understand a scheme should never be overestimated. Many otherwise highly intelligent people find difficulty in understanding plans, sections and elevations, which is why models and perspectives are so popular. It is useful for architects to get into the habit of producing working models. Models which clearly explain the scheme at the stage it has reached are worth any number of drawings to a client.

When making a presentation to a client, a model should be the basis so that the client can quickly get an idea of the scheme. Then plans can be used to elaborate, and freely drawn perspectives used to show what it will actually look like. Sections and elevations are of little use to a client. A building never looks like its elevations, and sections are too complex for the average client to understand. It is easier to make a quick sectional model to explain any complex parts of the building and it is many times more effective. The virtual reality walk through, mentioned above, can also be invaluable to a client who may have difficulty visualising the building by means of drawings and models alone.

Plans should be clearly drawn with the room name printed in each room. The use of a key at the side of the drawing together with a number in each room can be irritating. It is helpful to include a drawn scale on the drawing and also one or two dimensions. Any part of the building which is especially important or which needs particular consideration should be drawn out to a larger scale and a separate model prepared if possible.

Some architects produce highly intricate drawings and involved renderings to impress the client. The client may well be impressed and also confused. If the client fails to understand the drawing, approval may be given for something which may be a source of disappointment and aggravation when built.

15.11   Reproduction

Drawings are still commonly reproduced by prints. Light sensitive paper is used and the image turns black. Many practices have their own print machines which require relatively little skill to produce acceptable prints. In large urban areas, specialist printers will provide a service. Small drawings, up to A3, are often printed by photocopier which tends to give a clearer, crisper image than normal printing.

15.12   Work programming

Programming of any kind is a difficult business. Programming a project in an office is complex because there so many imponderables. Yet there is a need to programme such work, otherwise when the client asks, 'Will it be ready to go out to tender in two months?' the architect has no way of answering.

The basis for planning any project should be the RIBA Plan of Work. The stages usefully split up the work to be done. The next stage is probably to decide whether the project deserves one, two or more people working on it for any or all of the stages, for example, it is quite possible that a project may need only one person in the early stages and expand to require more people at stage E. The question, of course, is how many people and for how long.

The only safe way of getting to this answer is to consult historical records and look at the fees. In most cases, the fee will depend on how long the architect estimates involvement. Every office should have time sheets for this purpose. Only by looking at the time needed to carry out a comparable project can an estimate of future time requirements be formulated after adjustment to take account of any differences. Work programming is a serious matter where failure can result in disaster for the practice. All members of staff, including partners, must realise that the accurate completion of current time sheets is essential (see Chapter 16, section 16.15).

References

(1) In *John Barker Construction Ltd* v. *London Portman Hotels Ltd* (1996) 12 Const LJ 277.

(2) *Concise Oxford Dictionary* (1999) 10th edn, Oxford University Press; Gowers, E. (1987) *The Complete Plain Words*, 3rd edn, Stationery Office; Fowler, H.W. (1994) *Dictionary of Modern English Usage*, 4th edn, Oxford University Press; Palmer, R. (1992) *Write in Style*, E & F Spon; Chappell, D. (1996) *Contractual Correspondence for Architects and Project Managers*, 3rd edn, Blackwell Science.

(3) Chappell, D. (1996) *Report Writing for Architects and Project Managers*, 3rd edn, Blackwell Science.

(4) BS 1192 *Construction drawing practice*.

(5) Hill, M. (1999) *Drawn Information*, RIBA Publications.

Chapter 16 Finance and Accounts

16.1 Introduction

The subject of finance and accountancy is now part of most undergraduate courses. It is a practical form of economics and as such is important to the architect in general. It is also useful to have an elementary understanding of the subject. Larger practices and companies will have finance and accounts departments with specialist accountancy staff, whereas within smaller organisations all financial matters are dealt with by senior management.

16.2 The accounts

The primary purpose of keeping accounts is to provide a record of all the financial transactions of the business, and to establish whether or not the business is making a profit. The accounts will also be used:

- In determining the distributions to be made to equity shareholders
- In determining the partners' or company's tax liabilities
- To support an application to a bank for funding
- To determine the value of the business in the event of a sale
- As a proof of financial standing to clients and suppliers

All limited companies are required under the Companies Acts to produce accounts and to file them annually with the Registrar of Companies in order that they are available for inspection by any interested party.

The principal accounting statements are the profit and loss account and the balance sheet.

16.3 Profit and loss account

The profit and loss account records the results of the business's trading income and expenditure over a period of time. For an architectural practice, income will represent fees receivable for the supply of architectural services; expenditure is likely to include such items as salaries, rent and insurance. After adjustments have been made for accruals (revenue earned or expenses incurred that have not been paid or received) and pre-payments (advance payments for goods or services not yet provided), an excess of income over expenditure indicates that a profit has been made. The reverse would indicate a loss.

The preparation of the profit and loss account will enable the business to:

■ Compare actual performance against budget
■ Analyse the performance of different sections within the business
■ Assist in forecasting future performance
■ Compare performance against other businesses
■ Calculate the amount of tax due

An example of a simple profit and loss account is shown in Fig. 16.1.

Profit and loss account for the two months to 28 February 1999		
	£	£
Income		
Fees received		300,000
Expenditure		
Salaries	150,000	
Rent	50,000	
Others	30,000	
Depreciation	20,000	
		250,000
Profit for the period		50,000

Fig. 16.1 Example profit and loss account.

16.4 Balance sheet

The balance sheet (Fig. 16.2) gives a statement of a business' assets and liabilities as at a particular date. The balance sheet will include all or most of the following:

■ *fixed assets:* those assets held for long-term use by the business, including intangible assets

```
Balance sheet as at 28 February 1999

                                              £              £
Fixed assets
    Fixtures and fittings                                200,000
    Less: Depreciation                                    20,000
                                                         180,000

Current assets
    Fees receivable                        60,000
    Cash at bank                           60,000
                                          120,000

Current liabilities                        50,000

Net current assets (working capital)                      70,000

Net assets                                               250,000

Capital                                                  200,000
Retained profits                                          50,000
                                                         250,000
```

Fig. 16.2   Example balance sheet.

- *current assets:* those assets held as part of the business' working capital
- *liabilities:* amounts owed by the business to suppliers and banks
- *owner's capital:* shareholders' funds (issued share capital plus reserves) in a limited company, or the partners' capital accounts in a partnership

The various types of asset and liability accounts are considered in more detail below.

16.5   Assets

The term 'assets' covers the following:

- *intangible assets*, which include goodwill, trademarks and licensing agreements, usually at original cost less any subsequent write-offs
- *fixed assets*, which include land and buildings, fixtures and fittings, equipment and motor vehicles, shown at cost or valuation less accumulated depreciation
- *current assets*, which are held at the lower cost or net realisable value. Current assets include cash, stock, work in progress, debtors and accruals in respect of payments made in advance

Depreciation, referred to above, records the loss of value in an asset resulting from usage or age. Depreciation is charged as an expense to the profit and loss account, but is disallowed and therefore added back, for tax purposes. Depreciation is recorded as a credit in the balance sheet, reducing the carrying value of the firm or company's fixed assets.

16.6   Liabilities

Liabilities include amounts owing for goods and services supplied to the business and amounts due in respect of loans received. Strictly it also includes amounts owed to the business' owners – the business' partners or shareholders. Note that contingent liabilities do not form part of the total liabilities, but will appear in the form of a note on the balance sheet as supplementary information.

16.7   Capital

Sources of capital may include proprietors' or partners' capital or, for a limited company, proceeds from shares issued. Capital is required to fund the start-up and subsequent operation of the business for the period prior to that period in which sufficient funds are received as payment for work undertaken by the business.

The example in Fig. 16.2 identifies an initial capital investment of £200,000; however, this investment is soon represented not by the cash invested but by various other assets and liabilities, as shown.

To illustrate the movement of cash in terms of receipts and payments a simple example of a summarised bank account statement is given in Fig. 16.3. This statement is produced periodically, usually monthly, and is the source of the cash postings to the other books of account.

16.8   Finance

There are several ways in which a business can supplement its finances. The most common way is by borrowing from a bank on an overdraft facility. The lender will be interested in securing both the repayment of the capital lent and the interest accruing on the loan. The lender will therefore require copies of the business' profit

Receipts	£	Payments	£
Capital introduced	200,000	Salaries	150,000
Fees received	240,000	Rent	50,000
		Other expenses	30,000
		Fixtures and fittings	150,000
		Balance carried forward	60,000
	440,000		440,000

Fig. 16.3   Bank account summary statement.

and loss account and its balance sheet and details of its projected cash flow.

16.9   Cash forecasting and budgeting

It is necessary for a business to predict how well it is likely to perform in financial terms in the future. Budgets are therefore prepared, usually on an annual basis, based on projected income and expenditure. Once a business is established, future projections can be based to a certain extent on the previous year's results.

As mentioned above, in the event that it is the intention to borrow money from a bank then the bank is likely to request a cash-flow forecast for the next six or twelve months. The preparation of a cash-flow forecast is a relatively easy process and in practice a computerised spreadsheet package or accounting software will be used to project the likely phasing of receipts and payments.

The example cash-flow forecast in Fig. 16.4 illustrates the starting-up of a professional business. It identifies the initial introduction of capital, the borrowing facility requested and the projected effect of expenditure and receipts over the period. It can be seen from the forecast that an additional £10,000 of funding will be required in April and a further (£25,000 − £10,000) = £15,000 in May.

This cash flow is typical of a business start-up, when substantial sums are spent in advance of income being received. Provided the business is run profitably the outflow should be reversed before too long.

	January	February	March	April	May	June
Capital introduced	200,000	—	—	—	—	—
Fees received	60,000	180,000	50,000	110,000	100,000	200,000
Asset sales	—	—	—	—	—	—
Receipts	260,000	180,000	50,000	110,000	100,000	200,000
Salaries	75,000	75,000	75,000	75,000	75,000	75,000
Rent	25,000	25,000	25,000	25,000	25,000	25,000
Equipment	100,000	50,000	20,000	30,000	—	—
Others	15,000	15,000	15,000	15,000	15,000	15,000
Payments	215,000	165,000	135,000	145,000	115,000	115,000
Movement in cash	45,000	15,000	(85,000)	(35,000)	(15,000)	85,000
Balance brought forward	—	45,000	60,000	(25,000)	(60,000)	(75,000)
Balance carried forward	45,000	60,000	(25,000)	(60,000)	(75,000)	10,000
Borrowing facility	50,000	50,000	50,000	50,000	50,000	50,000
Additional requirement	—	—	—	10,000	25,000	—

Fig. 16.4   Example cash-flow forecast.

16.10   Books of account

The underlying books of account are likely to comprise the general ledger (which will include all general items such as salaries and rents) and totals from the subsidiary ledgers such as the sales ledger (fees or other income receivable), the bought ledger (accounts payable), the cash book (a record of the bank transactions) and the petty cash account. Other books, such as fee and expenses books, may also be kept.

In addition to the books of account, businesses must retain vouchers such as receipts, invoices, fee accounts and bank statements to support the accounting records. These are required by businesses' auditors and for VAT purposes.

16.11   Fee invoicing

Fees are the lifeblood of all professional organisations and their payment at the earliest opportunity aids cash-flow and limits the need for borrowings. It is prudent therefore to make provision for the payment of fees by instalments at regular intervals or, as is becoming more common, relative to achieved milestones.

Fees can either be in the form of lump sum(s), a percentage of the construction work, reimbursement of time expended at agreed rates or a combination of these, all depending on the basis of the agreement entered into (see Chapter 6, section 6.3).

Fee accounts can be raised either as VAT invoices or as applications for payment, which have different implications with regard to VAT as described in the next section.

A schedule of all raised fee accounts should be kept in order to monitor payments, pursue outstanding debts and for accounting purposes.

16.12 VAT

VAT is a UK tax collected on business transactions in the form of output and input taxes. Output tax is the VAT due on taxable supplies, which in relation to professional consultants is charged on the fees for the provision of services to clients. Input tax is the VAT charged on most business purchases and expenses.

The time of supply of the services is defined as the 'taxpoint'. In respect of the provision of professional services this is generally the date of issue of a VAT invoice. Such invoices must include specific information including the VAT registration number and must separately identify the fees invoiced exclusive of VAT, the rate of VAT and the value of VAT charged.

An alternative within the construction industry to issuing VAT invoices is the use of 'authenticated receipts', which can be used for the supply of goods and services made under contracts which provide for periodic payments to be made. They must include all the relevant detail as on a VAT invoice, but their use has the effect of delaying the taxpoint to the time when payment is received and the authenticated receipt is issued.

Up to date VAT records must be kept for completion of VAT returns and to enable Customs and Excise to readily check the figures. Tax returns are sent to Customs and Excise together with any tax due, i.e. excess of output tax over input tax during the tax period concerned.

16.13 Computerisation

Accounting functions have become less time-consuming through the use of computers for the regular and routine entries and calculations that are necessary. Entries can be allocated to different accounts, and up-to-date information can be retrieved quickly and efficiently in a variety of formats to meet particular needs. This greatly assists in the financial management of a business.

16.14 Annual accounts/auditing

At the end of a business' financial year a set of 'end of year' accounts are prepared bringing together all the previous year's financial information in the form of a profit and loss account and balance sheet as described earlier.

In most circumstances, accounts will be audited by an independent accountant; indeed this is a requirement for all larger limited companies under the Companies Acts. Audited accounts will carry more authority with the Inspector of Taxes and are also useful to prove to third parties, including prospective clients, that the financial status of the business has been independently scrutinised.

16.15 Staff time records

It is necessary for detailed records to be kept of the time worked by each member of staff, for two purposes:

- As a basis on which to build up an account for fees for services that will be charged for on a time basis.
- To establish the cost for each particular project. Such costs will be used primarily to establish whether a particular project is making a profit or a loss, but may also be used to estimate a fee to be quoted for similar future work.

Clause 5.9 of the RIBA Standard Form of Agreement for the Appointment of an Architect commits the architect to maintaining records of time spent on services performed on a time basis. These records must be produced to the client on request. Even without this stipulation, it is difficult to see how a time charge could be made without timesheets.

Unless the means is available for an office to monitor its progress in a methodical way and assess performance at the end of a project, project planning remains pure guesswork. Although practice varies, the filling in of timesheets is usually restricted to technical staff, with secretarial and administration costs being treated as overheads as it is difficult to allocate such time to projects. For the same reason, principals and partners rarely complete timesheets for the whole of their time. Of course partners must keep a record of their time if it is intended to charge a client on this basis and indeed it is good practice for partners to keep proper timesheets in order to check how time is allocated against each project.

Most offices have their own ideas about recording time and costing. However, a typical procedure is as follows. Timesheets are completed at the end of each week and collected. All hours worked are then input into the accounts system, and when costed out it is possible to determine whether the project is financially on target, from a practice point of view. Graphs can also be plotted to show the relationship between forecast and actual expenditure. Time charges to the client become simply a matter of extracting the hours for each member of staff and multiplying it by the appropriate rate.

It should never be thought that it does not matter whether the timesheet is filled in accurately or not. It is common for architects to be lax in filling in timesheets, often leaving them until the end of the week when it is possible that inaccurate records are set down.

It is important to log every time a different project is worked on and therefore the time-sheet should be kept to hand at all times (or as more likely nowadays be readily accessible on the PC) and be filled in throughout the day. Most solicitors work in this way and there could be a lesson in that! It is equally important not to become overly scrupulous about timesheets, but to use commonsense.

Prompt and accurate feedback to the architects responsible for each project is an indispensable part of the system. If it can be seen, at an early stage, that the allocated time will overrun, steps can be taken to deal with it. If a particular project is taking up too much time, all attempts should be made to recover the situation, but this should not include allocating time to other projects. This undermines the whole purpose of keeping accurate time records. Furthermore, the reason that a particular project is overrunning may be as a result of the original estimate of time being low or because the client changed his mind at an important stage and should be charged extra fees. If the timesheets are fabricated a nonsense is made of the office records on which future estimates will be made.

An example of a timesheet is shown in Fig. 16.5.

Weekly Timesheet	Name									Grade				Wk Ending				
	Mon		Tues		Wed		Thurs		Fri		Sat		Sun				
Project description	Basic	O/T	Basic	O/T	Basic	O/T	Basic	O/T	Basic	O/T	Basic	O/T	Basic	O/T	Code	Project no.	Rate
Office administration																	
Training/study leave																	
Public holidays																	
Annual holidays																	
Sick																	
Other																	
TOTAL																	

Fig. 16.5 Sample timesheet.

Chapter 17 Insurance

17.1 Introduction

The topic of insurance is included here because it is important for every architect. Insurance is a contract between the insurer and the insured. Some kinds of insurance, however, are more important for some architects than others. For example, the insurance of premises and public liability rests firmly with the partners or directors, but professional indemnity insurance affects every architect. What follows is of necessity a brief summary of the main kinds of insurance which an architect meets during a professional career.

Insurance is very complex and an experienced broker should always be consulted. There are, however, two important principles which should be understood by anyone taking out insurance:

- *Uberrimae fidei*: of the utmost good faith
- Subrogation: standing in the place of another

Uberrimae fidei

The basic principle is that the party seeking insurance must disclose all material facts whether the insurer specifically asks for them or not. Failure to make such disclosure can render the contract voidable. Thus an architect must reveal all circumstances in the past which might lead to a future claim, etc. when seeking professional indemnity insurance.

Subrogation

If an insurer pays out to a third party in respect of a claim against the insured, the insurer has the right to stand in the place of the insured for the purposes of recovering against any other person who may be liable in respect of the claim. A simple example will make this clear. Where a firm has professional indemnity insurance (see section 17.5), an employee may perform a negligent action which leads to the firm being sued for negligence by its client. If the insurer pays out in respect of the claim, it is entitled to stand in the place of the firm and take action against the employee to recover the full amount paid out. To avoid this distressing situation, most professional indemnity policies contain a waiver of subrogation in favour of the firm's employees. In other words, the insurer agrees not to exercise rights of subrogation against any employee whose negligent action lay at the root of the claim against the firm.

17.2 Premises and contents

Loss or damage of the office and contents is potentially disastrous for a practice. The first thing to decide is the beneficiaries under the policy. In the case of a partnership, all the partners may own the property jointly or one may own and lease to the rest. Alternatively, the premises may be leased from a landlord and the practice may be only one of a number of tenants in the same building.

It is essential that the policy should provide protection for the partners or directors and the possibility of the insurance company exercising rights of subrogation should not be ignored. Thus, in the case of a tenant responsible for fire damage to the landlord's property, the landlord will be able to claim from the insurers, but they may subsequently take action to recover from the negligent tenant.

The basis of insurance will usually be 'full reinstatement', i.e. the insurers make no deductions for dilapidations. Care must be taken that sufficient cover is purchased and that the appropriate perils are included. If the premises are underinsured, the result will be that in the case of loss, the insurers will only pay out a proportion of the amount claimed.

The contents of an architectural practice are particularly vulnerable to damage, consisting as they do largely of paper representing many hours of work. It is essential that a practice takes a proper inventory of the contents of the office and updates it regularly. So far as drawings are concerned, their value for insurance purposes must include the estimated cost of redrawing them after total destruction. Expensive pieces of equipment such as computers must receive special consideration and if equipment is to be used outside the office, the insurance must cover such use.

17.3   Public liability

Public liability insurance must be taken out and maintained to cover the liability of the practice to third parties for injury or death or damage to property as a result of the negligence of the partners or one of its employees. The insurance does not cover professional negligence (see section 17.5). A large indemnity limit should be specified (£2,000,000 plus) and it should be upgraded at regular intervals, because if a court gives an award in excess of the insurance cover, the additional amount must be borne by the practice. Where the practice becomes involved in other activities, such as social events or car parking facilities etc., the insurance cover should be appropriately extended.

17.4   Employer's liability

A practice is required by law to take out insurance to provide an indemnity against its liabilities to its employees[1]. The indemnity should be unlimited. The policy is to cover death or injury and it includes sickness provided that:

- It arises in the course of employment; *and*
- The employer has legal liability.

Examples of such liability could be employer's breaches of the Factories Acts or Employer's Liability (Defective Equipment) Act 1969, unsafe systems of work or the negligent acts of other employees or an employee being attacked while going to the bank.

17.5   Professional indemnity

Professional indemnity is probably the most important area of insurance for all architects. Every practice should have an adequate level of insurance to cover the possible negligence of its staff. This is a requirement of the ARB Code of Professional Conduct and Practice (Standard 8). Although no architect likes to contemplate the possibility of facing a claim for professional negligence, few practices escape such a claim or the threat of such a claim at some period. The insurance is for the benefit of both practice and clients. It ensures that there is a fund to compensate a client if the architect is found to have been professionally negligent and it also protects the partners of a practice against the chance that they are held liable in respect of a large sum which they would otherwise have to find from their own resources. Although one might hope that a client would not press a claim to the extent of making all the partners bankrupt, it does happen and the good nature of a client facing a huge bill to correct the consequences of an architect's negligent design could be over-stretched. The subject is complex and a specialist text on the subject should be studied[2].

There are certain important points to bear in mind regarding professional indemnity insurance:

- Premiums are high.
- It is difficult to decide on the amount of cover required, because the value of commissions actually being carried out is no indication of the likely maximum amount of any claim.
- Insurers prepared to provide the necessary cover are relatively few.
- The cover is only effective on a yearly basis, for example in respect of matters notified during that year. Thus if cover is not maintained, perhaps because a practice has fallen on hard times, a claim made during that period cannot be referred to the insurance company even though cover may have been in place for ten years before.
- The policy normally covers the amount of any damages awarded against the insured together with the amount of legal costs up to the limit of indemnity noted in the policy. It should be noted, however, that all policies carry excesses which may be substantial.
- Insurers usually claim the right to defend any claim. Alternatively they may decide to settle. Whichever course they take, it will be on the basis of sound business principles. This may not suit the architect. Policies should contain a clause which allows the insured to demand opinion from leading counsel and the insurers are obliged to proceed accordingly.
- Once cover is in place, the insured must immediately notify the insurers of any circumstance which may give rise to a claim. Failure may lead to the insurers repudiating liability.

It is possible to extend the cover to deal with certain other matters such as pursuing a claim for infringement of copyright, to provide indemnity in an action alleging libel or slander, etc.

17.6   BUILD insurance

BUILD stands for 'building users insurance against latent defects'. It was the subject of a NEDO report in 1988 which recommended that this type of insurance should be available for buildings. At first, the insurance was not available in the UK although it was common in many European countries. More insurers are interested in offering this type of insurance in this country. Some of its characteristics are:

- It is non-cancellable for a period of 10 years from practical completion.
- Cover is generally limited to structure, weathershield envelope and optional loss of rent.
- Risk assessment is carried out on behalf of the insurer by independent consultants. This may necessitate amendments to proposals in certain instances.
- Policy is taken out during the early design stages and a single premium paid.
- Benefit to the employer.
- Waiver of subrogation against architect, contractor, etc. can be purchased for an additional premium.

If this kind of insurance becomes general or even mandatory by law, the burden of liability on the architect and other professionals could be eased. However, there is little benefit unless subrogation is waived and that is usually quite costly. It is also unlikely that an employer would be prepared to pay an extra premium for this purpose. Even where subrogation is waived, it should be noted that the cover provided is fairly limited.

17.7   Other insurances

Some other common forms of insurance which a practice may take out are:

- Partnership – to cover the situation which may arise if a partner retires or dies and the practice loses a large slice of capital in consequence. A partnership will usually also insure the lives of all partners in favour of the others.
- Pensions – for the benefit of the partners and staff.
- Medical insurance – a popular 'perk'.
- Insurance of company cars.
- Personal accident insurance.

References

(1) Employers' Liability (Compulsory Insurance) Regulations 1998.
(2) Ray Cecil (1991) *Professional Liability*, 3rd edn, Legal Studies & Services (Publishing) Ltd.

Chapter 18 The Architect as Employee

18.1 Finding employment

18.1.1 Self assessment

Whether the architect is newly qualified looking for a first appointment or an experienced architect seeking a change, obtaining employment is not easy. It is relatively easy to get a job (depending on the current economic climate), but it is not easy to get just the job required. To a large extent, the principles of getting a job are the same whether the person concerned is an architect, solicitor or a financial director. The field is known as professional and executive. But the aspirations of an architect are unique and demand a rather different approach to job hunting. For the most part, the principles are widely known and widely neglected. In the last analysis the successful outcome depends on the person and their particular talents, experience and personality; neglect of the principles will put the job seeker at a severe disadvantage. Most architects have experienced the interview at which the 'whizz-kid' gets the coveted job. Often, they fail to fulfil expectations and quickly whizz off to another, better, position somewhere else. The common denominator is that this type of person knows how to set about finding a post, applying for it and making a good impression at interview. The art of finding employment is very much the art of self presentation.

Just as a salesperson cannot market a product effectively unless they know all about it, architects cannot market themselves unless they know their strengths and weaknesses. Architects should be adept at the art of selling; after all they are regularly called upon to make presentations of schemes to clients. The first step is to sit down and carry out a self appraisal (Fig. 18.1) so that the prospective job seeker thoroughly knows the 'goods'. It is a good idea to do it in note form following the headings below.

```
■  Formal qualifications
■  Experience
   Most recent appointments
   Duties in each post
   Achievements
■  Talents
■  Personality
■  Career objectives
   Job satisfaction
   Pay
   Advancement
   Responsibility
   Ancillary
      Location
      Security
      Working hours
      Opportunity for initiative
      Personality of partners
      Type of work
      Design philosophy
```

Fig. 18.1   Self appraisal.

Formal qualifications

This should be easy: degrees, diplomas, certificates and memberships of professional bodies. Listing of minor institutes, which may
give the right to certain affixes on payment of an annual subscription, should be avoided, because they tend to dilute an
architect's principal qualification by giving the impression that the
architect is scratching around to find something to put down.

Experience

It does not pay to be vague. If qualification is recent, experience
will be slim, but the most should be made of it. It is useful to put
down experience as follows:

■ Most recent appointments (say during the last five years).
■ Duties in each post. This is not nearly so important as:
■ Achievements. This heading repays careful thought. It is an
   important selling point. Architects should consider whether
   they have played a major part in a really good building or
   brought a contract back from the brink of disaster or introduced
   a system which made the office more cost effective. In other

words, whether they have ever done anything which makes them outstanding in a particular field. It is not uncommon to become quite depressed about this section of the self-appraisal. Architects may feel that they have achieved very little. What they are probably feeling is that they have not achieved as much as they would have liked – not the same thing at all. Architects who take it slowly, going through all the work they have done, are often surprised at the extent of their achievements.

Talents

The things that the individual architect does best. To identify talents it is necessary to look at what one most and least likes doing.

Personality

Relationships with colleagues, persons in authority and team members are important as is the way in which an architect deals with contractors, manufacturer's representatives and officials of public bodies. An architect should consider his or her most vulnerable points. It might be age or youth and inexperience or difficulty in mastering some new technique or aspect of architectural practice. Some architects, for example, feel very exposed when they have to carry out a site inspection. It is important to acknowledge such things at this stage so that the architect can be prepared if they arise during interview.

Career objectives

The next step is for the architect to decide what is really required from a career. Presumably, an architect qualified in the first place because of a desire to participate in the creation and maintenance of a delightful, satisfying and durable environment for the benefit of everyone who will inhabit or pass through it. Ultimately, that should be the aim. All actions should be carried out with that end in mind. Efficient management and competent design work are not ends in themselves. Few people actually sit down and plan their careers, but it pays to do so even if things do not work out according to the plan. It is not unknown for architects to drift into satisfying, well-paid appointments, but it is not the norm. The following are a few headings to guide the thoughts:

- *Job satisfaction*. Most architects want this, but it means different things to different architects. What kind of architectural work is wanted? Very large or very small projects, mainly designing, contract administration, technology, new work or rehab? It is important to try to define one's ideal post.
- *Pay*. Thought should be given to how much money will be needed to justify a move. Sometimes an architect will be prepared to accept the same salary, or less, in order to secure just the right job. It is important to decide how much money is actually needed and what difference it would make if the job was 300 miles away. The two vital ingredients of a good job are job satisfaction and pay.
- *Advancement*. An architect must consider whether it really matters. Most people have a desire to progress, but not all. Usually, something must be relinquished to secure promotion. Although the absence of good prospects may suggest that a job is not worth having, it is generally true that a good architect will create prospects.
- *Responsibility*. An architect who wishes to be completely responsible is aiming for the top of the tree. Such an architect must decide whether status matters more than the opportunity to practise particular skills.
- *Ancillary*. There may be many other things which an architect would include on the list of ideal job attributes. They may be important, but the question must be asked whether they are as important as job satisfaction and pay. If requirements are kept simple, securing a job will be easier. Among other things which might influence the job seeker are:
  Location
  Security
  Working hours
  Opportunity for initiative
  Office environment
  Personality of partners

Completing this checklist should clarify the thoughts and, incidentally, reveal certain facets of the architect's character which were unacknowledged before. The complete self-appraisal is the unrefined raw material which must be used to find employment.

18.1.2 Opportunities

By this time, architects should have a clear idea of their own capabilities and the kind of post being sought. The next stage is to consider how to set about locating the sort of job vacancies required. It is always possible, of course, that someone will telephone unexpectedly and offer just the job being sought. Although this happens more regularly than might be thought, the main ways of locating vacancies are:

■ Reading advertisements in the professional, technical or local press
■ Making speculative approaches to potential employers
■ By word of mouth, through contacts in other offices and recruitment consultants

It is possible to persuade an employer that there is a need for just the kind of architectural expertise being offered. A number of architects have found their niches in this way. There are techniques to help job seekers achieve success.

18.1.3 Answering advertisements

Answering advertisements is probably the way in which most architects find employment. Besides looking at the obvious professional press, the less obvious construction journals should not be neglected. They occasionally have advertisements for architects and they may also advertise posts which are not aimed specifically at architects (see Chapter 3). National and regional newspapers are a fruitful source of jobs. Some small practices rarely advertise beyond regional level. Some large organisations have their own magazine or journal in which they advertise vacancies before they appear nationally. Local authorities, in particular, sometimes have a policy about advertising 'in-house' as a first step. Of course, it is impossible to keep abreast of all such advertisements, but an architect with a clear idea of the post being sought will be rewarded by scanning as many relevant publications as possible. It should be remembered that advertisements on a national scale will almost certainly attract more applicants than regional advertisements.

The kind of advertisement encountered will vary widely. Some give masses of information, others hardly anything at all beyond the job title. A salary may or may not be quoted. Large organisations commonly ask the reader to write for further details and an application form while private practices usually ask for a CV. The techniques for preparing these are discussed in section 18.1.6.

The first rule of answering advertisements is to do exactly as they say. It is pointless sending a CV if they want an application form completed. It simply creates a bad impression. A firm which has its own application form usually does so because it always wants to see the information presented in the same order. Some firms still ask applicants to fill in forms or write to them in handwriting. It may seem a trifle weird in the age of computers, but the instruction must be followed. Generally, employers are just trying to find out if the handwriting is decipherable, but it is possible that they have retained a graphologist to comment on your personality. There are some employers who believe that character can be read in handwriting: a clear neat hand indicates a logical neat person, etc. Without passing judgement on such theories, all that can be said is that one's usual hand should be employed and care should be taken that it is legible. Otherwise, it is better to have the application typewritten.

If a CV is required, it should be sent with a covering letter. If there is an application form, it should be requested with a simple letter and returned when completed with a covering letter which should take the opportunity to briefly emphasise a couple of key points. If selection is to be by means of a completed application form, it makes little difference whether the form is returned immediately or just before the closing date, because usually all applications are considered together after the last date. Private practices asking for a CV will seldom state a closing date. It often pays to submit promptly.

Some forms invite the applicant to telephone for an informal chat. If the architect is confident of a good telephone manner and is quick thinking, it makes sense to telephone. Some posts are virtually secured on that basis, making the interview a formality. The architect telephoning a prospective employer should have some notes prepared as if for an interview, with questions ready. To approach the informal telephone chat casually can be fatal. It should be remembered that the telephone can magnify vocal mannerisms and the listener concentrates on the voice, because there is nothing else. There may be a bad line, the person on the other end of the telephone may seem abrupt and a thousand and one things can conspire to upset the friendly chat. In a face to face meeting, the participants can relate much better.

18.1.4 The speculative approach

It may be thought that writing to a firm of architects to offer one's services is a waste of time. Whether or not that is true will depend on the firm and its circumstances when they receive the letter. There are four possible scenarios:

- The approach may be rejected out of hand.
- The firm may be about to advertise a vacancy and they may decide to interview the writer before incurring the expense of inserting the advertisement in the press.
- The firm may be sufficiently impressed to create a post especially to suit the writer's expertise. (This does happen quite frequently.)
- The firm may be sufficiently impressed to interview the writer, which may lead to a post in the future when they have the right opening. Firms do not enjoy the hassle of large scale interview sessions. They do not like to waste the time and the money. If they have a post and they know of someone who can fill it, they will often contact that person.

The reason for making a speculative approach may well be that the architect knows the firm by reputation, admires their work and, therefore, wants to join them, even though they are not advertising any vacancies. There is nothing demeaning about a speculative approach. The recipient should be flattered. Some firms never have any need to advertise, because architects are anxious to join them.

Anything which looks like a mass-produced application should be avoided at all costs in these circumstances. Each application should be given an individual bias. At the very least, the letter should be addressed to the person in the firm who deals with staffing. This is easy to discover by means of a telephone call to the firm's receptionist. Even in this age of apparent informality, it is still prudent to address the letter 'Dear Mr/Mrs/Ms...' and finish it 'Yours sincerely'. It should be brief and to the point. There are no hard and fast rules about whether a CV should be included. Generally, it is probably better not to send a CV. The letter should give just enough information to convince the recipient that it is worth while meeting the writer. The sole purpose of the letter is to secure an interview. It is the purpose of the interview to secure the post. Therefore, the first few lines of the letter deserve a great deal of thought if quick despatch into the waste basket is to be avoided.

Starting a letter, 'I am writing to enquire whether you have any vacancies for an architect' invites rejection in all but the most patient of recipients.

Speculative approaches should not be attempted by telephone. In communications, a telephone conversation is halfway between a letter and a face to face meeting. In a letter it is possible to say as much or as little as one wishes. It is impossible to be drawn into a hurried response. During a meeting what is said can be moderated or emphasised by gesture or facial expression and silent signals can be received from the interviewer. In comparison, the telephone can be a very coarse instrument of communication. Its danger lies in the fact that it seems to convey a better picture of both parties whereas in fact it gives only a partial picture, and that perhaps the worst part.

Speculative approaches should never be sent by facsimile or by e-mail, because both are too often employed to send informal notes and memos.

18.1.5   Contacts

Everyone has contacts. Every architect has contacts in the architectural world and many elsewhere. If it becomes known that a talented architect is seeking another appointment, the results can be surprising. There may be an approach from a firm who had not thought of approaching previously, because the architect may have seemed settled for life. More often, a contact can sometimes tell of opportunities which have not yet been advertised, thus enabling a speculative approach to be made.

There are a number of other avenues for job seekers, for example, the University Appointments Board, RIBA at national and regional level and recruitment consultants. The latter can be very effective, but it is important to keep up the pressure and to remember that their objectives are not quite the same as the architect's objectives. Some consultants are commissioned to search for and find suitable applicants. They may carry out the initial weeding out of unsuitable applicants. They collect their fees from the employers. They are always on the lookout for architects seeking new posts and they welcome approaches. The more people they can successfully place and the higher the salaries, the more money they make. There are many recruitment consultants who carry out their jobs with the utmost professionalism. Unfortunately, there are others who will try to place the architect in any kind of job. Other than recommendation, it is probably safest to try those consultants who specialise in the architectural and construction markets.

18.1.6   Career history and CV

CV stands for 'curriculum vitae' – the story of a life. What most firms actually mean when they ask for a CV is a career history. They do not want to know about early childhood or anything which is not absolutely relevant to the application. Even though a career history may be submitted, it is diplomatic to head it 'Curriculum Vitae' if that is what is requested.

Ideally, the CV should occupy no more than one sheet of A4 paper. Most CVs take up more than one page, but six page long CVs become very tedious to read, particularly if the recipient is faced with reading several of them. The CV should be written to suit the post for which application is being made. The layout should be clear, it should be typed and the following should be borne in mind:

■ If age may be a problem, the date of birth should be omitted. Employers often have a preconceived notion about a 50-year-old as opposed to a 30-year-old applicant. At 50, a person is less likely to move again, but experience and skill is evident and enthusiasm can be just as marked as in a much younger person. The only disadvantage with older persons is that they may be slower than their younger colleagues but that is by no means always the case.

■ Degrees and professional qualifications should be included, but not usually school examination results. The exception is if the school examination results show an aptitude for something which is not strictly architectural, but which could prove useful to a potential employer. An obvious example is an examination result which indicates proficiency in a foreign language.

■ The current appointment should be described first, followed by the next most recent and so on. Ten years ago is ancient history; any posts held earlier than ten years ago should simply be listed.

■ Achievements must be emphasised rather than duties, and brevity is the watchword.

■ Titles of some posts may be obscure and there is nothing wrong with amending them to make them more comprehensible to the reader. For example, 'Deputy to the Chief Architect', if true, is easier to understand and creates a better impression than 'Architect Grade ABC'.

■ If the architect is currently self-employed, the prospective employer may wonder why the decision to change to employment has been made. The thought may arise that the architect is a business failure. A convincing reason for giving up self-employment should be stated.

■ Generally, however, it is best not to include reasons for wishing to leave the current or last post. If appropriate, reasons can be discussed at interview.

■ It is a mistake to include details of present salary. Architects are worth an objective amount, not merely £1,000 more than the last salary. They may have been underpaid.

■ 'Additional information' should only include items which are strictly relevant. The fact that an architect is a keen fisherman is not relevant; it may suggest a loner. Involvement in local societies, however, indicates public spiritedness and possibly contacts which may be useful in the future.

That is only a guide and there may be good reasons to ignore some of the advice. The individual use of judgement is all important. Applying for a new post should be approached with the same skill and care which is applied to any important task. There are few things more important than a career in view of the length of time spent working in it, but it is surprising how many applicants dash off an application in a few minutes. The recipient will probably give it the same sort of cursory treatment.

18.1.7 The application form

Many application forms are exceedingly badly arranged. The form should be used for the applicant's own advantage. It may sound trite, but it is important to read every bit of information about the post before completing the form. All questions should be answered in the spirit of the information given, using the same words if possible. For example, if the information calls for an architect with a 'flair for design', the same phrase should be included in the application form. The form should be completed neatly, but it is important to fill the available space adequately. Additional sheets should be attached to detail experience if the space is too small (it usually is). Most application forms are straightforward, but some forms have one or more questions which are difficult to answer. A selection of such questions and outlines of possible answers are given below. The details, of course, will depend on the individual.

What do you consider are your greatest strengths and weaknesses?
This offers both a chance and a trap. There is no place for modesty. Strengths should be clearly stated, whether they are the much sought after 'flair for design' or project management or the restoration of old buildings. If there is space, examples should be given. This is an opportunity for the architect to emphasise achievements. For example, 'I directed the design team on XYZ Building'. That can be very effective if XYZ is a well-known project. The second part of the question is a trap. It is an invitation for the applicant to give the firm a reason for exclusion from interview. On no account must such things as 'I tend to get bored with office work' or 'I find it difficult to get up in the morning' be put down. They may be true, but they will not help secure an interview. It is possible to turn such a question to advantage by stating as faults what others will probably see as good points. For example, 'I tend to concentrate on detail, but I am capable of seeing the broad picture' or 'I become frustrated if all members of the team are not pulling their weight. I tend to deal by face to face discussion with the person involved.' It is not suggested that these 'weaknesses' be invented; merely that the architect should take something about which he or she is a shade too fanatical, state it as a weakness (which it is) then say how it is overcome.

What has been your greatest disappointment?
Once again, this is a potential trap. It will be fatal to say, 'I have not got as far as I would have wished in my career', or 'I failed to solve the cladding problem on XYZ Buildings and there has always been a rain problem'. The same technique should be used as for 'weaknesses' above. The perfectionist is always bitterly disappointed that a near perfect conception is not actually perfect. The architect's greatest disappointment might be that an award-winning design had a minor flaw or there was an absence of technology to achieve the whole concept.

Why are you applying for this post?
Another opportunity to relate achievements and show how they apply to the particular post. The aspects of the firm or organisation which are most appealing should be stressed, for example, reputation for good design, efficiency, new technology, etc. These points will impress the prospective employer who will be equally

unimpressed if the reasons include nearness of office to home or the need for extra money.

What are the major ways in which you consider that you can contribute to the work of this organisation?
As above.

Reasons for leaving your present post?
Being fired, made redundant or major policy disagreements with the boss are *bad* reasons. Anxiety to further a blossoming career in the firm to which application is being made is a *good* reason.

Which of your duties gave you the most satisfaction?
Another opportunity to state achievements. Care must be taken to avoid the danger of appearing too much of a specialist, unless that is what the advertiser requires.

If you are offered the post, where do you see yourself in 10 years' time?
This is always a difficult one. It really is a silly question if taken at face value. But the totally honest answer that the applicant has absolutely no idea is probably a mistake. The safest way is to stick to generalities, stressing progress so far and concentrating on personal development as contracts administrator, designer, technologist, etc. which is seen as continuing in logical progression depending on the opportunities offered.

Describe, in detail, how your experience relates to this post?
This question often appears in a very much longer form. It is not an invitation to submit a life story. It is important to be clear and to the point. Those achievements which relate most closely to the new post should be set out. Many architects ramble in trying to answer this question. 'In detail' simply means that the prospective employer wants actual examples to be quoted.

Other points

There are a few further points to remember about application forms:

- *Health:* Unless the applicant is disabled, health should be excellent. Past operations and treatments, if successful, should be ignored.

- *Leisure activities:* The employer is looking to see that the architect is a well balanced personality with the ability to mix easily. A brief statement regarding any involvement with a couple of sports and pastimes is better than a complete list of all activities.
- *Interests:* This is the architect's opportunity to show involvement with local branches of the RIBA, RSUA or RIAS and memberships of other societies. Private firms encourage members of their staffs to develop a wide circle of acquaintances; it promotes work. All honorary posts or public duties should be included, such as Justice of the Peace.
- *Documents:* Drawings, photographs and diplomas should not be included with the application even if (rarely) they are requested. If appropriate, it should be made clear that these documents will be brought to an interview.
- *Projects:* The types and values of projects should be stated.
- *Expertise:* Areas of expertise which are useful adjuncts of architectural practice should be stated, e.g. CAD, models, perspectives, arbitrations.
- *Referees:* Referees should be as senior as possible. It is a mistake to choose people merely because they are friends. The opinion of the person on the next drawing board is of little value. The most senior architect in the applicant's current employment, if well briefed, will be best placed to give a good reference. It is the kiss of death to include the name of a referee without permission, besides being grossly discourteous. Architects are sometimes afraid that they will get a poor reference, because of some incident in the past. The law provides some reassurance. The employer, in writing a reference, assumes responsibility and the employee relies on the employer's skill and care in its preparation. It is not sufficient that the employer believes what is said to be true. The employer must have exercised reasonable skill and care in checking the truth of any allegations[1].

18.1.8 Before the interview

The whole purpose of filling in application forms, producing curricula vitae and sending letters to prospective employers is to obtain an interview where applicants can demonstrate to the employer that they are the persons most suited to the posts advertised. It is a matter of matching skills and experience to the employer's requirements. To be effective, applicants must be fully prepared.

The first thing to remember is that the employer must have been sufficiently impressed by the application to consider offering the post subject to interview. Finding the right post is a two-way process. Both parties should be finding out as much as possible about each other, because:

■ Something discovered may influence the applicant's decision to join the firm
■ The applicant needs information on which to base questions
■ An employer will usually be impressed that an applicant has taken trouble to do research

Among the points an applicant will want to know is the firm's policy on hiring and firing, how long the firm has been established, the ages and experience of the partners, and the buildings they design. Apart from many standard reference books, the applicant should not neglect to enquire of past clients and employees, and local chambers of commerce and the RIBA at local and national level. It is important to visit the buildings produced by the firm to get to know something about them.

A list of points needing clarification at the interview should be prepared. The chances are that most of the points will be covered by the employer, but experience shows that without a list of questions, the applicant often forgets to ask something important. A checklist of such points is shown in Fig. 18.2. It should be used as a guide only.

Very little can be done about the timing of the interview. If one appointment only is to be made, there could be up to seven interviewees. It is common to take candidates in alphabetical order. A candidate whose name begins with either ABC or XYZ will probably be seen either first or last respectively, which are supposed to be the best positions. Sometimes other considerations affect the order, such as distance of travel. The middle of the list is supposed to be the worst place, because a candidate in this position becomes confused with other candidates in the mind of the interviewer. Someone in that position has to impress a bit more if they are to secure the post. Most architectural posts call for the architect to take along visual material. There are exceptions, of course, if the post is purely administrative or concerned with contracts. Some architects refuse to take drawings to an interview as a matter of principle, presumably with the view that, being architects, they have no need to show their quality – it is taken for granted. That is a very mistaken view. Whether or not requested, the architect should always take along visual material to show not only competence but

- Hours of work
- Holidays
- Salary and bonus
- Fringe benefits, car, telephone, mobile telephone, health scheme, insurance, pension, sabbatical
- Prospects for advancement
- Office organisation and range of disciplines
- Clarification of job description
- Particular office expertise
- Current workload
- Possibilities of working in other branches
- Initial programme of work for the successful applicant
- The design philosophy of the office. Do they believe in a house style?
- Use of computers
- Any particular method of working?
- Company policy about staff doing spare time work
- Is it a new appointment? If not, what happened to the previous holder?
- Any particular problems associated with the post?

Fig. 18.2 Checklist of points to clarify at interview (Note that it is not possible to be specific because of the wide range of posts for which an architect might apply).

also that the approach to problem solving is what the firm requires. Some or all of the following may be taken:

- *Drawings*. They should be flat not rolled and prints not negatives. Drawings should be chosen to suit the post. For example, if the firm does a lot of housing, the drawings should be domestic in character; if the post is for an architect to design warehouses and factories, industrial work should be taken. Unless the work is very specialised, it is always a good idea to take along a brief selection of other work to show the breadth of expertise. The newly qualified will have to take one or two projects produced during training, but they must be prepared to face keener criticism of such work and they should have answers ready to the inevitable question, 'Why did you do that?' Unless the post particularly indicates otherwise, only one or two production drawings should be taken, but they should be good. There is nothing wrong with taking drawings produced by others provided the architect makes that fact clear. The drawings may show the extent of a building on which the architect had an important role as supervisor or co-ordinator of the design team. An architect in that situation must be prepared for keen questioning.
- *Photographs*. They must be first class large prints, but the

architect will have to work hard to demonstrate a key role in the building if there are no supporting drawings.

■ *Glossy brochure about the architect's work.* In theory, this is very good, but it does give the impression that the architect makes a career of attending interviews.

■ *Complete file of correspondence concerning the post.* This must be taken. A copy of the career history or the application form must be included together with a list of points to raise and questions. Some architects think that it is bad form to take notes to an interview; they are mistaken. The interviewer will certainly use notes. An applicant who also uses notes will appear well organised and confident.

The above is merely a guide. There is no point in taking a portfolio of drawings if the last post was administrative and the application is for a similar post. One last thing which can be done in preparation for interview is to take along a 150 mm scale rule and a soft pencil.

18.1.9   The interview

The applicant should arrive about a quarter of an hour early. Later, and there is little time to compose oneself. It is useful to arrive with a quarter of an hour in hand, if only to absorb the atmosphere. There are often examples of the firm's work on display in the reception area. If it is one of those interviews where it is necessary to wait with the other interviewees, it is always better to listen rather than talk so as to assess the strength of the competition.

Local authorities and large firms will have a special form for claiming expenses. Smaller firms are unlikely to have a form, but they will normally pay basic expenses, in which case it is usual to list expenses and leave them with the secretary. It is not something to bring up at interview.

There are two basic types of interview:

■ One-to-one
■ Committee or panel

The one-to-one interview offers the best chance to establish a relationship with the interviewer and, therefore, the best chance of obtaining the post. A committee interview can be very difficult. There is usually a chairman, and each member asks questions in turn. When answering questions, it is important to reply directly to the person asking the question. Although difficult, the applicant should try to remember the names of the committee as they are introduced and to use them during the interview. It is difficult to be sure of the relationships between members of a committee. They may be more interested in impressing one another than in the candidate. The interviewer will almost certainly be an architect if a post as an architect is the subject of the application, but not invariably so. Other panel members may be personnel or managerial, related construction disciplines or, in the case of a local authority, councillors.

The *RIBA Handbook of Practice Management* sets out some useful guidelines for interviewing from the point of view of the employer. It also forms a useful guide for applicants, because they know the kind of things the employer is looking for.

Interviews may be structured or unstructured. The first follows a pattern set by the interviewer, the second rambles and gives the applicant the opportunity to set the pattern. The latter form of interview is very common, because interviewing is a skill which few employers bother to learn properly. A typical interview often runs as follows:

- The interviewer chats for a few moments to help the applicant relax
- A description of the firm is given
- A description of the post is given
- The interviewer asks questions relating to answers on the application form
- The applicant is asked half a dozen 'technical' questions
- The applicant's portfolio is examined, with more questions
- The applicant is given time to ask questions

Arrangements vary greatly. The interview may take place across a desk or around a conference table or sitting in easy chairs with coffee. Quite a lot depends on the type of job for which the applicant is applying. An interview for a first post might well take place formally across a desk. Progression to more senior posts is marked by a steady decrease in formality, because the interviewer wants to get to know the applicant thoroughly. That is particularly true in the case of posts which may lead to partnerships. The applicant must:

- Speak slowly and clearly
- Look at the interviewer, not look down

- Be enthusiastic
- Think before answering

Applicants should be wary of making a gift of their expertise. If asked to solve problems, they should try to show that they know how to set about solving it without actually doing so. Applicants should always open portfolios even if not asked to do so. A useful opportunity comes at the end of the interview when the interviewer asks for further points. It strikes a strong note to preface answers by 'yes' or 'no'. Answers should be elaborated, but not too much. No opportunity to display experience, achievements and skill should be missed. Although it is helpful to ask questions which show that the applicant has studied the firm's work, it does not pay to be too critical, unless the decision has already been made that the post is not wanted.

Interviews really are two-way affairs. They may not seem that way in practice, but they are. Applicants must decide whether they want the posts. If they are good at what they do, employers will be anxious to impress them. An applicant's approach should be positive, stressing achievements and interest in the post applied for.

Every interview contains awkward questions. The ability to deal with them depends on experience and confidence. The interviewer should always be humoured. It is never appropriate to say that a question is silly. If really at a loss for an answer, the interviewer should be complimented on devising such a difficult question and the admission should be made that the applicant is beaten. The device is particularly effective in a panel interview. Although awkward questions can never be entirely foreseen (one reason why they are awkward), the following is a selection of such questions which regularly make their appearance at interviews.

Why do you want to leave your present post?
Furtherance of career and joining the firm to which one is applying are acceptable answers; being fired, made redundant or seeking more money are not.

Do you think that you are too old/too young/too inexperienced for this post?
The answer to this is simply to stress interest in the post together with achievements and skills.

Given the opportunity, how would you reorganise this firm to make it more efficient?
This is a really silly question. The only reason for asking it is to see if the applicant is silly enough to attempt an answer. The only

sensible response is to express delight in the question and ask for sufficient time to study the firm in order to give a worthwhile answer. This sort of question does give applicants an opportunity to explain how they reorganised some aspect of their present firm.

Who is your favourite architect?
It is important to be ready for this question and to say who and why. Jargon should be avoided. The why is more important than the who. It should not matter that the architect is not a favourite of the interviewer. Effective things to admire are attention to detail and planning.

Why did you stay so long at your last firm?
It is important to emphasise the additional responsibility taken on over the years and progress within the firm. It is unwise for the applicant to say that he or she was on the point of leaving many times, but stayed after being offered more money. Among other things, the current application could be seen as just a ploy to increase the salary yet again. This question inevitably leads to the one about reasons for leaving at this stage. The reasons can only be that it seems to be the right career moment. Be warned, however, that employers will want to know why such a long serving member of staff does not warrant a partnership in the current practice. Only the applicant knows why, but it is unwise to directly criticise the current firm.

It seems to us that a person with your particular skills/experience/ qualifications should be ... (doing something else)
This is tricky. It may also be true. On the basis that an applicant for a job wants the job, the only answer is to say why the job is wanted and to emphasise interest in it.

Why do you think you are the person for this post?
Another opportunity to stress achievements in the previous post and to relate them to the requirements of the new post.

How would you motivate others?
Books have been written about this. It is useful to read one of them. Put very simply, motivating someone else involves getting them to want to do what the motivator wants by letting them see it is in their own best interests.

What salary are you looking for?
This is a question to be avoided if possible. It is up to the employer

to make an offer, but in any case salary discussions should not take place until the end of the interview. As a general guide, it does not usually pay to accept less than desired for the promise of something indefinite such as promotion in 2 or 3 years' time. Bonuses too, have a habit of disappearing unless the percentage is written in as a definite part of the remuneration package. If there is no alternative but to state a salary, it is useful to state a range. If the applicant is confident of commanding a particular salary, it should be stated, but not tentatively.

The list of awkward questions is endless. In addition, applicants may be asked to sit what amounts to a short examination, spot mistakes in a drawing or undergo a psychological test. It is important to co-operate fully with the employer's whims unless the applicant has already decided that the job is unsuitable. Remember, what may seem a silly waste of time may be something in which the employer puts the utmost faith. That in itself may say something about the likely relationship with the future employer.

As in any other meeting, misunderstandings can arise during the course of an interview, which can be the reason why the post is not offered. To overcome the possibility, it is sensible to ask a question at the end of the interview which exposes any reservations on the part of the interviewer. It can be phrased in different ways, but it should be something like, 'Did any points arise during the course of the interview which lead you to believe that I am not suitable for the post?' If the answer is 'No', the post should be secured. If the answer is 'Yes', the applicant has the opportunity to correct the misunderstandings. The employer cannot really refuse to give an answer.

18.1.10 After the interview

If all the candidates are being interviewed on the same day, it is common practice to announce the result shortly after the last interview is completed. In other cases, the result will be made known by post. No applicant should have to wait longer than about a week. If there is no word after two weeks it may be that:

■ The post has been offered to another candidate and the employer is waiting for an acceptance before notifying the others; *or*

■ The employer is unsure whether any applicant is suitable; *or*

■ Points raised during the interview have caused the employer to rethink some basic office policy.

It is not good policy to telephone to find out the situation. The employer may be embarrassed and forced into making a quick decision which is unlikely to be favourable. A carefully worded letter, on the other hand, which emphasises interest in the post and in the firm may just tilt the balance. Even if the post has been offered to someone else, it may be turned down and the letter pushes that applicant's name to the front of the list of alternatives.

18.2 Acceptable job titles

The use of the title 'architect', when applied to a person carrying on a business, is governed by the Architects Act 1997 (see also Chapter 2, section 2.4). Such a person must be registered and, therefore nowadays, qualified. The RIBA have issued a Practice Note 2 setting out job titles and descriptions which are acceptable and unacceptable. They are:

Acceptable titles
Chief architect
District architect
Principal architect
Project architect

Acceptable descriptions
Chartered architect
Experienced architect
Architect at B/C/D level of responsibility

Each of these titles or descriptions adds something to the basic 'architect' so as to indicate the status or job. The professional status, however, is not in doubt.

Unacceptable titles
Assistant architect
Senior assistant architect
Chief assistant architect

Unacceptable descriptions
Registered architect
Qualified architect
Fully qualified architect

Each of these titles or descriptions detracts from the status of the architect. The descriptions suggest that it is possible to be termed 'architect' while at the same time being unregistered, partly or wholly unqualified. To qualify 'architect' by 'assistant' indicates that the unfortunate title holder is somehow less than an architect. Some titles are of course unlawful, such as where a job advertisement calls for the post of architect but the requirements are clearly for a person who need not be registered. Such phrases as 'architect at or about qualification standard' fall into this category. So do 'student architect' and 'trainee architect' as a matter of law.

18.3 Employment

18.3.1 Employed or self-employed?

The Inland Revenue have introduced strict rules to outlaw the use of self-employment as a device when the situation is really one of employment.

The first thing an architect should be sure about is whether he or she is an employee. It is possible to work on an employed or self-employed basis. An employee enters into a *contract of service*, someone who is self-employed enters into a *contract for services*. The difference is very important:

- Employment law applies only to employees
- Statutory rights apply only to employees
- Duties at common law will be implied only in an employment situation

It may seem obvious into which category a person falls, but that is not always the case. Often the situation is straightforward. An architect working for a client in return for a fee is self-employed, whereas most architects working in practices for a salary are employed. A self-employed person is sometimes referred to as an independent contractor. If the matter comes before the courts, they will look at the actual situation rather than the title[2]. Thus a person referred to as a 'consultant architect' may be held to be employed while a 'project architect' may in reality be self-employed. In order to resolve the issue in situations where there may be some doubt, the courts have devised some tests which can be applied. Briefly, they are as follows.

Control

If the employer has control over the architect's method of working, the architect is an employee. The greater the degree of control, the greater the likelihood that the architect is an employee. Although this is quite a good test where the work is of a manual nature, whether skilled or unskilled, it is less satisfactory in the professional context where even an employee must have quite a lot of freedom to exercise his or her profession. The test is relative, therefore, and the amount of control exercised over a particular architect must be compared with the usual degree of control exercised in architectural practice.

Integration

Architects who are integral parts of a business are likely to be employees. This test is probably more telling than the last so far as professional people are concerned. Thus it is easy to see the difference between an architect who freelances, self-employed, but working perhaps for a day or two a week for several practices, increasing or decreasing involvement to suit varying office workloads, and the permanent staff member. It used to be common for some self-employed architects to work permanently for one office.

Multiple test

This is probably the best test. If the other tests are inconclusive, the questions to ask are: Does the architect work for an agreed salary? Is the degree of control such that there is a master and servant situation? Are the other provisions of the contract consistent with employment? For example, who is responsible for paying the architect's tax? Is there a company pension scheme to which the architect belongs? Who owns the drawing equipment which the architect uses?

Before the introduction of the stricter Inland Revenue rules referred to above, there was a growing tendency for architects to be employed on a self-employed basis. This was possibly because of the uncertain economic climate. The position used to be that an employer took less risk by using self-employed persons, because they were not protected by statute like an employee.

There are advantages to being self-employed. Architects in this situation pay tax on a different system, usually in arrears, and there is greater scope for claiming expenses against tax. In addition, many architects like the freedom which self-employment brings. Of course, if an architect was self-employed but nevertheless engaged permanently for one practice, the situation was mainly for the benefit of the office, with no commitment on either side. It should also be noted that the self-employed can be caught if they are negligent and the practice has to make a claim against the insurance policy. In such cases, the insurer does not waive rights of subrogation, as is usual in the case of employees, and the self-employed may face the prospect of a personal writ from the insurer.

18.3.2   Employment contract

A contract of employment may be written or oral. The only problem with an oral contract is the problem with all oral contracts; the parties may have conflicting recollections of the terms. The contract can also be implied as the result of the conduct of the parties. Some firms, so it is said, still engage staff with a shake of the hand. There is nothing illegal in this and if the firm is equally relaxed about all aspects of its relations with employees, it may be the ideal environment for some. In general, however, a written contract of employment is an advantage, because both sides then know for certain the basis of the relationship, at least in respect of the main issues. In the absence of express terms between employer and employee, the general law will imply that the employer has a duty to:

■ Pay the employee
■ Provide work, if without work the employee would be unable to earn money
■ Reimburse the employee for reasonably incurred expenses in carrying out duties
■ Take care for the employee's safety

and that the employee must:

■ Provide personal (i.e. not delegated) service
■ Obey the employer's lawful instructions
■ Take reasonable care when about the employer's business
■ Show good faith in revealing to the employer that which should be revealed and in safeguarding confidential information

In addition there is much statutory law which governs the employer/employee relationship and which has now almost supplanted the common law for most purposes.

18.3.3 Written statement

The employer must give the employee a 'written statement' of the principal contract terms not later than 13 weeks after commencement of employment. The statement, however, is not the contract and, if appropriate, the employee can contend that the statement attempts to modify the terms of employment. The fact that the employee may be asked to sign a written statement is not thought to indicate anything other than acknowledgement of receipt of the statement. Many employers are slow to issue the statement because there is no effective sanction. An industrial tribunal may make a decision on the points in dispute, but that is all. The statement must be given to the employee personally, but it need not be issued at all if all the points have been covered already in a written contract of employment. It is not sufficient, however, for the employer to pin the statement to a notice board or to refer to standard conditions.

The statement must contain the following:

- The identities of the employer and employee.
- The job title.
- The date of commencement of employment and whether a previous period of employment counts as part of the period of continuous employment for statutory purposes.
- Rate of pay and interval between payment.
- Hours of work.
- Holiday entitlement, including public holidays and the method of calculating holiday pay (see section 18.11).
- Rules regarding absence from work due to sickness or injury and any sick pay provision. There is no right to sick pay under the general law, but most employers make some provision. An employer is obliged to pay statutory sick pay for 28 weeks in any year, after which responsibility for payment of statutory sick pay lies with the Department of Social Security.
- Details of the pension scheme. The employee may be referred to another document.
- The period of notice required to bring the contract to an end. The statement may stipulate any period, but if it is less than the

statutory minimum, the statutory minimum will apply. If no period is stipulated, the statutory minimum does not apply and reasonable notice must be given (unless a fixed term contract is in force).
■ Disciplinary rules and the grievance procedure. The procedures are not regulated by statute, but codes of practice have been produced by ACAS which, if adopted, tend to demonstrate to an industrial tribunal that the procedure was reasonable.

If the contract is silent about any of these points, a note to that effect must be put in the written statement. If there is any change, a further written statement must be furnished by the employer within one month of the change.

18.4   Job description

Job descriptions are often included in job advertisements. They may be brief in the extreme, of the 'project architect with flair for design' variety, or they may be extremely detailed. Although in general it might be assumed that architects know what they do, there is a tremendous range of functions in practice, depending on the kind of practice, the kind of work and the position of the architect in relation to other members of the office. It is comparatively rare for a detailed job description to be included in a contract of employment for an architect.

The general rule is that the more senior the post, the less need there is for a job description. So the lowest paid member of staff doing relatively unskilled work might have a very long job description setting out the varied tasks which might be requested of that person. The highest paid member or senior partner will have no job description because, at that level of responsibility, the person writes his or her own description day by day. The job, for such people, is whatever they make it.

The employment contract should contain some description of the general nature of the work. Professionals cannot expect their contracts to spell out every detail of their duties[3]. Those duties, however, will not be held to extend beyond the duties normally associated with the proper performance of the functions indicated. Thus an architect cannot refuse to do something on the basis that it is not in his or her contract of employment if it is consistent with an architect's normal duties. From the employer's point of view, it is useful to include a general phrase requiring the employee to carry out other activities which are reasonably incidental to his or her principal job. Part of the job description in the employment contract may be that an architect is required to work at another branch office at the discretion of any partner. Without such a clause, the architect cannot be compelled to move.

A simple form of job description was pioneered in the 1961 survey *The Architect and His Office*[4] (Fig. 18.3). It graded all architectural staff in four grades: A, B, C, D. Each grade carried a brief description of the qualities required and the person's responsibility. Thus an architect seeing that a firm was advertising for a post grade C would have a good idea of the kind of person being sought. It also formed the basis of the salary structure. Some kind of job description is essential if the office carries out job evaluation (see section 18.7).

18.5 Hours of work

The hours which an architect is expected to work should be detailed in the contract of employment, although this is seldom the case. They must, however, be specified in the written statement (see section 18.3.3), but there are no statutory provisions about the actual hours. There really is no such thing as 'normal' office hours. In London, the usual start is 9.30 AM; elsewhere 9 AM is common, the normal week being 35 and $37\frac{1}{2}$ hours respectively. On 1 October 1998, the working time regulations came into force[5]. Essentially, they provide that a worker must not work more than 48 hours including overtime in a 7 day period. In order to arrive at the figure an average is taken over 17 weeks. An employee can agree to work more than 48 hours, but the agreement must be in writing and the employee can terminate it on written notice.

It is very uncommon for any professional to keep strictly to the specified hours of work and architects are no exception. Whatever the appointed hours of work, architects will tend to work longer. (More about this in section 18.6.) In many places, some form of flexible working hours is operated. There was resistance in some quarters, but it is the norm in many local authorities and it is becoming acceptable elsewhere. In principle, an employee is required to work during a 'core' period from perhaps 10 AM to 3 PM each day, together with other hours to choice or as agreed with the employer. The overriding rule is that the employee must put in an agreed minimum number of hours every week or month. There are

Type of work which can be handled	Knowledge and initiative	Influence on others	Responsibility
'A' level Perform simple jobs offering little or no alternative methods. Simple analysis of problems for which logical answers are readily obtainable.	No initiative required.	Able to understand and execute simple instructions. A minimum influence on the work of others.	Responsible for making minor decisions. All work closely supervised.
'B' level Perform work offering a limited number of alternative methods. Solve problems for which logical answers are not readily apparent and which will have some effect on the other aspects of the job.	Limited initiative required. Limited research into common technical literature required. Knowledge of the more common types of materials.	Able to understand and execute instructions covering a limited field. Able to give simple clear instructions.	Responsible for making decisions affecting his work only, which must be reported to his senior. Parts of his work closely supervised.
'C' level Perform work offering a variety of alternative methods. Solve problems for which answers are not apparent and which will have considerable effect on other aspects of the job.	Initiative is required. Considerable research into all technical literature required. General knowledge of all types of materials.	Able to understand and execute instructions, covering a wide field. Able to give instructions to allocate work among and to control the work of, up to 5 or 6 others working as a team and to co-ordinate their activities.	Responsible for making decisions for all the work of his team within the framework laid down. Receives general supervision.
'D' level Perform work offering an infinite variety of alternative methods. Solve problems for which considerable thought is required to produce logical answers, the solution to which will have a profound effect on the whole design.	Considerable initiative is required. Considerable basic research is required into fields not normally covered by normal technical literature. Wide detailed knowledge of all types of materials.	Able to initiate a plan of working and check progress, able to convert plan into a practical method of working and give the necessary instructions. Able to control and co-ordinate the work of a number of teams working independently.	Responsible for submitting and agreeing design policy with the principal within the framework laid down by the office. Receives administrative supervision only.

Fig. 18.3 Grading table for architectural staff (from *The Architect and his Office*: courtesy RIBA Publications Ltd).

obvious advantages for the employee and the practice may become more widespread eventually. The contract should state the office policy regarding the accumulation of hours into additional days' leave.

18.6 Overtime

Attitudes to working overtime vary tremendously. Most architects will be expected to work overtime at some times when there is a heavy workload or when there is a temporary crisis which demands attention. The way in which overtime is handled will depend on the particular office. Although, particularly in difficult times, it is better to be somewhat understaffed, it is not a good idea for anyone to work regular overtime. Everyone needs time to relax and recharge batteries, otherwise tiredness becomes normal and mistakes occur.

Some offices repay overtime by offering time off in lieu. This can be useful to the employee, but if all members of staff exercise the option, there may be times when the office is seriously under-staffed. In addition, those architects who work most overtime usually find difficulty in finding a space in their workload to enable them to take normal holidays, let alone time off in lieu. No architect should allow this kind of situation to develop. Overtime should always be paid with time off in lieu as an alternative.

Some offices do not pay for overtime and still the staff work extra hours. This reflects well on the commitment of the staff and badly on the partners. Overtime payment should be on a higher scale than normal, to reflect the unsocial hours and the fact that it is over and above what an architect can reasonably be expected to work. Fair rates are usually taken to be from one and a third times the normal hourly rate to twice the normal hourly rate if the hours are especially late or during the weekend. It is not unknown for an office to pay only normal rates, however much overtime is worked. It has also been known for an office to stipulate that no overtime will be paid until the employee has worked in excess of a stated number of hours overtime on any one day.

Some architects will work overtime without requesting payment in order to gain advancement in the firm. Whether that is a good idea will depend on circumstances.

18.7   Salary

Starting salaries should be settled at the time of interview. What should also be settled, and this is sometimes overlooked, is the frequency and timing of salary reviews. Every employer is obliged by law[6] to issue full-time employees with an itemised statement of pay setting out the gross salary, details of all deductions and the net amount payable. Remuneration is the 'consideration' which the employer gives for the employee's service.

In addition to the basic salary, many firms operate a bonus or profit-sharing scheme. If the term 'bonus' is used, it is possible that the employer thinks of it as an occasional, rather than a regular thing, something with which he can reward exceptional endeavour. In law, a contractual promise to pay a bonus as part payment for work done will be enforceable although the amount of the bonus will depend on the terms laid down. A profit-sharing scheme is probably the most satisfactory arrangement. What constitutes 'profit' should be clearly stated and the sharing may take place on the basis of a points system – a greater number of points represents a greater share. Points may be allocated for length of service, salary or status or in any other way deemed fair or set in the contract of employment.

Job evaluation is a technique which is sometimes used to relate each post and its pay to every other post. There are two stages:

- Every post must be given a rank
- Appropriate salaries must be attached to each post

The system is said to have many advantages. It should produce a pay structure within the practice and an overall level of pay which is clearly recognised as being reasonable in itself and in comparison to external pay levels. In addition, the employees should feel secure from arbitrary changes in the pay structure and the practice has a method of fixing rates of pay for new posts.

It is quite difficult to grade the work of professionals. Job evaluation is usually based on a points system which is most appropriate to manual work. Although there is no reason why such a system should not work when applied to professionals, a considerable amount of sublety is required. It is the post and not the individual which is being graded. Points are normally given for effort, skill, experience, qualifications, working conditions, etc. It is open to a practice to establish its own criteria so long as they can be seen to be fair and reasonable when applied to all members of staff. A basic job description is described in section 18.4.

18.8 Perks

Perks are an important part of the remuneration package. Indeed, in some instances they may be a significant factor in determining whether an architect takes one post in preference to another. The most highly prized perk is still a company car, particularly the more expensive kinds which architects may covet but be unable to buy themselves, even though the tax penalties are increasing, particularly for larger cars. Firms have varying policies. In many practices it is still quite rare for an architect below the status of associate to be given a company car. An alternative is the 'pool' car where architects may have the use of a car, but they must take whichever car is available on that particular day.

As an alternative, a firm may require employees to provide their own cars for use on firm's business and give an annual or monthly running and depreciation allowance together with a realistic mileage payment. In such cases, the employer should also provide a generous interest-free loan facility. Problems can arise with this kind of provision. Employees who have major repairs to finance can find themselves in breach of contract if they are unable to afford the repair. If car use is essential, the car should be provided by the firm, either personally to the employee (as is common in other parts of the construction industry) or in a pool.

Second only to a car is a telephone. In the case of minor appointments, it is common for the employer to at least pay all rental charges and the cost of business calls. It is also becoming common for mobile telephones to be provided, and laptop computers. Whether this last really is a perk is open to question.

Some firms automatically enrol all employees in a medical insurance scheme. This can have obvious benefits for the employees and the great advantage for the employer is that hospital procedures can be carried out quickly and, in the case of non life-threatening conditions, to suit the employee's office commitments. Points to note are that it is usual for these schemes to exclude cover for any illness even remotely connected with a previous illness in the same employee. For example, an employee who has had investigations for a stomach ulcer prior to enrolling on the scheme might well find that cover is excluded for any abdominal ailment. The actual extent of expense which will be reimbursed should be carefully checked. Such insurance counts as a benefit for tax purposes. (see Chapter 17, section 17.7).

Parking is often a problem in centrally situated offices and a parking space is a valuable provision, although it may be going too far to call it a perk. An alternative is for the office to provide season tickets to local car parks. Many architectural practices have located in semi-rural areas to take advantage, among other things, of the easier parking situation.

18.9   Professional activities

All employees should be encouraged to take part in professional activities, but many firms are mean about such things and what should be regarded as commonplace has almost come to be regarded as an extra perk. The degree of encouragement often depends on the principal, and his or her mood on a particular day. The particular economic climate is also of prime importance. The following may be said to fall into the category of professional activities of varying degrees of importance.

Continuing professional development

Every employee should be allowed some time each year to go on courses either in or out of the office. Employers vary considerably regarding whether they are prepared to continue paying salary during days off for this purpose. The imposition of compulsory CPD by the RIBA on its members is particularly significant in this regard (see Chapter 2, section 2.2).

Examinations

Students require time off to sit their Part III examinations. They also need time for study and attendance at short courses during the period immediately before examinations. Employers must allow attendance at examinations; they should allow attendance at appropriate short courses, but pure study time is probably best left to the student to organise.

Sabbaticals and study trips

Sabbatical leave is recognised as an important constituent of some posts, particularly in education. It refreshes the mind and generates ideas. Above all, it plays an important part in the development of the employee. Study trips also assist the employee to develop a particular interest. It is rare for offices to allow such trips, except of course during the employee's own holiday period. Where an office does allow or even encourage such trips, the effect on salary payments should be clarified in advance.

Professional subscriptions

It is relatively unusual for an employer to reimburse an employee's subscription to a professional body. This kind of provision is generally regarded as a perk for architects of high status such as associates.

Journal subscriptions

It is even rarer for an employer to reimburse professional journal subscriptions, but virtually all offices subscribe to a range of journals for the benefit of staff as a whole.

Attendance at branch meetings

Architects should be as active in the local professional branch as their other commitments allow. It is a way of keeping up to date, not only in regard to technical matters, but also as far as professional matters are concerned. Most branches have a series of sub-committees and they are usually desperate for members. It is a useful way of getting to know other architects in the area and of finding out what is happening in other offices. Most of these meetings take place in the evenings and, therefore, time off is not required. Where an employee is particularly active in the local branch, it makes sense for the office to allow time off to attend any special meetings during the day. Apart from other considerations, it is a useful piece of exposure for the practice and a means of keeping the practice tuned into what is happening elsewhere.

18.10 Expenses

Expenses are often linked to remuneration. That is wrong. Employees are not expected to make a profit out of expenses, but neither are they expected to make a loss. The intention should be that they are reimbursed, no more, no less.

The general law implies a term in every contract of employment that the employer will indemnify the employee against any expense reasonably incurred in the performance of their duties. Within that statement, however, there is considerable scope for differences in application. Thus, although there is not strictly any necessity for details of expenses to be set out in the contract of employment, it is worth doing, so that both parties are perfectly clear at the outset. The key word is 'reasonable'. An expense will be reasonably incurred if authorised or, if prior authority is not possible, if it is justified by the circumstances. This later category causes most trouble and there is much to be said for giving guidelines, if not in the contract itself, as soon as possible thereafter.

The most common expense is travelling. The preferred mode of transport should be stipulated by the office: car, train, bus or taxi. Most probably, the type of transport authorised will depend on the length of journey and whether or not a client is in the party. Where cars are involved, the mileage rate should be stated as should the class where rail travel is involved. Taxis are normally reserved for transport between station and office or hotel and for emergencies.

The employee must be reimbursed if he or she incurs expense in entertaining clients. In some offices, only partners are permitted that sort of expense account. The company policy should be made clear.

The type of practice and the location of its work will determine how often an employee may be away from his or her office base on business. The rates of subsistence payments in such cases should be sufficient to ensure a fair standard of accommodation and meals.

It is essential for employees to properly record all expenses so that the practice can recover them from the client if appropriate. However, the fact that an office cannot recover certain expenses from the client should not preclude payment to the employee. Expense repayments should be prompt. Some firms get the free use of money by making employees wait several weeks before payment. Expense repayments should ideally be *on demand* and there is no good reason why they should not be *in advance* if the anticipated expense is likely to be more than the employee wishes or is able to advance from his or her own resources.

18.11   Leave

It used to be the case that there was no automatic right to paid holidays, either in statute or at common law. An employee's holiday entitlement was, therefore, whatever was agreed with the employer. Legislation, however, now provides that all employees are now entitled to four weeks' paid leave every year. Even part-time staff now have leave entitlement, but it is proportionately lower than full-time employees.

Leave must be included in the 'written statement' (see section 18.3.3), but it is preferable to have the details recorded in the employment contract. Holiday entitlement is often in excess of the minimum and commonly includes all public or bank holidays together with 20 or 25 additional days to be taken during the holiday year. This normally runs from January to December or from April to April (the financial year). It is generally stipulated that the holiday days must be taken within the holiday year to which they relate. Some firms allow a few days to be carried over to the next 'year' or give payment in lieu.

Payment in lieu of holidays is not generally encouraged by employers, because it tends to encourage employees to forego holiday entitlement which every working person needs. It is better to allow a few days to overlap into the next period if pressure of work has prevented the taking of holidays at the appropriate time. Obviously, chaos would ensue if employees enjoyed untrammelled power to save their entitlement from one year to the next until perhaps they could take six months off to tour the world. Not that such an idea is bad in itself, but there are other ways of accomplishing that kind of ambition. The taking of holidays should be tempered by the need to keep the office running smoothly.

It is good practice for an office to have all the rules regarding holidays, as other things, clearly set out. There are few things worse than the office which is full of unwritten (and therefore, constantly changing) rules. Many offices close down completely from Christmas to New Year. Employers should make clear whether this period is included or additional to the annual leave. Additional days are often added onto the annual holiday to reward long service with a firm.

In addition to holidays, there are other kinds of leave which may affect the employee architect:

- Maternity leave
- Compassionate leave

- Leave for public duties
- Unpaid leave and sick leave

18.11.1   Maternity leave

Maternity leave is subject to statutory regulations which change from time to time. The Employment Relations Act 1999 will apply to women who expect to give birth on or after 30 April 2000. To qualify for maternity pay and the right to return to work:

- The reason for absence must be pregnancy; *and*
- The woman must be employed until the eleventh week before the expected delivery week; *and*
- She must have completed one years' continuous employment by the beginning of the eleventh week before confinement; *and*
- Not less than 21 days before absence, she must inform the employer that she will be absent due to pregnancy and state whether she wishes to return to work afterwards (she is not bound by this statement); *and*
- She must produce a medical certificate if required.

A woman is entitled to a total of 29 weeks' maternity leave. She must give 21 days' notice of intention to return to work, but she may postpone her return for a further four weeks on account of illness. The employer is entitled to request written notice of intention to return to work after 49 days from the confinement week. He may also postpone her return for 4 weeks if he cannot make appropriate arrangements in time.

18.11.2   Compassionate leave

No employee has the right to compassionate leave; it is entirely at the discretion of the employer. Many firms, however, lay down useful guidelines in their employment contracts and they will allow paid leave for such things as death, serious illness or accident to a close relative. In general, such leave is dealt with on an ad hoc basis depending on the particular circumstances. Some employers lay down a maximum compassionate leave allowance in any year. Such a provision is comparatively rare, however, because it can be considered by employees to be an entitlement which must be taken before the end of the year on sometimes flimsy grounds. Most firms are generous once they know that the need is genuine.

18.11.3 Leave for public duties

Legislation stipulates that certain persons holding official posts must be allowed time off from work to attend to their duties. A common example of this is the trades union official who is entitled to a reasonable time off with pay to attend to union affairs. In most other cases, however, time off must be granted, but it need not be with pay. Common examples are JPs, members of the local authority or other authority, members of tribunals and school governors. Although, because it is a statutory requirement, there is no necessity to include references to such leave in an employment contract, many firms include a statement on the position for the avoidance of doubt. Employers can be quite generous in continuing to pay employees, less only any attendance allowance, for carrying out official duties. This may also reflect the recognition that it does the firm no harm at all to have one or more of its employees in the public eye (see Chapter 19).

Specific trades union members are allowed to have reasonable leave for all trade union activities (except industrial action). Unlike trades union officials, however, ordinary members must take the time off without pay.

Although not public duties, there are two further situations in which an employer must allow time off with pay. The first is in the case of an employee whose post becomes redundant. Reasonable time off with pay must be allowed for the purpose of seeking alternative employment. The second situation is when an employee becomes pregnant. She is entitled to reasonable time off with pay for ante-natal care.

18.11.4 Unpaid leave

The Employment Relations Act 1999 gives employees with one year's service the right to take up to 13 weeks unpaid parental leave. This applies at present only to parents of children born on or after 15 December 1999. It also gives all employees, regardless of length of service, the right to take a 'reasonable' amount of time off work for urgent family reasons. 'Reasonable' has not yet been fully defined.

18.11.5 Sick leave

Although the general law gives no right to sick pay, legislation fills the gap and most firms have quite detailed provisions of their own. If they are not in the contract of employment, they must be included in the written statement. The employer is obliged to pay statutory sick pay for a period of 28 weeks of sickness. Certain procedures must be carried out and it is usual to make compliance with the procedures a condition of employment. This is because strict adherence to the procedure is necessary if the employer is to be able to reclaim any sick pay under the entitlement from the DSS.

An employer will often undertake to pay an additional amount to bring the statutory sick pay up to an employee's usual salary. Such payment is sometimes linked to length of service and commonly consists of one or more months at full pay and an equal number of months at half pay. The more generous schemes provide for an employee to be paid for six months at half salary if a period of illness occurs after a qualifying period of two years. Less than two years' service gives rise to a reduced entitlement. This kind of provision is more likely in larger offices where the absence of a member of staff for a prolonged period is not likely to be more than inconvenient. The chances of several architects taking several months off for sickness at the same time is so unlikely as to be suspicious.

Subject to what may be included in the employment contract, there is nothing to prevent an employer terminating employment on the grounds of prolonged absence due to sickness. Some employers set out the relevant criteria in the employment contract, but it is rare. Where criteria are set out, they often include the right of the employer to ask for an independent medical examination of the employee after absence from work for a specified period or at the employer's discretion.

18.12 Disciplinary and grievance procedure

Every office should have a disciplinary and grievance procedure. There is no particular statutory requirement, contrary to popular belief, regarding the exact form of the procedure. ACAS has produced codes of practice which firms may adopt. The general principles are:

- The procedure should be described in writing
- The person who may operate the procedure should be specified
- Possible action should be specified
- Except in the case of gross misconduct, a first offence should not incur dismissal
- The employee should be informed of the complaint and he or she is entitled to representation
- There should be a warning procedure including at least one oral and one written warning followed by a sanction less than dismissal before dismissal actually takes place
- There should be an appeal system

The grievance procedure should state who the employee should approach with a complaint and to whom appeal may be made.

The procedures may be contained in the office manual. Less commonly, they are spelled out in the employment contract. Some firms appear to be a trifle coy about this as if admitting that a procedure exists is tantamount to encouraging disputes.

18.13 Notice and dismissal

Every employee must be aware of the period of notice required to end the employment contract. If the period is less than the statutory minimum, the statutory minimum will apply. Most firms give reasonably detailed terms governing the termination of employment, but it should be noted that such terms cannot override statutory provisions. The statutory periods of notice which must be given by the employer range from one week if the employee has been continuously employed for more than one month but less than two years, and thereafter one week for every complete year worked up to a maximum of twelve weeks. The employee, on the other hand, has a statutory obligation to give one week's notice of termination. If the contract stipulates a greater period, the employee will be in breach of contract if he or she gives less.

There is confusion between unfair and wrongful dismissal. The terms are often used as if they were interchangeable. There are in fact four circumstances in which employment can be terminated:

- Wrongful dismissal
- Unfair dismissal
- Fair dismissal
- Redundancy

Wrongful dismissal is a breach of contract, for example, if insufficient notice is given. Damages are available at common law. Unfair dismissal, however, is enshrined in statute and it refers to the situation when the correct notice is given, there is no breach of contract, but the reason for the dismissal is considered by statute to be unfair. In this case, the employee's remedies are prescribed by statute also. Fair dismissal is when the correct notice is given, there is no other breach of contract and the reason for dismissal is considered to be fair. Redundancy comes into a special category which lays down the particular statutory rights of the employee in such a situation. Dismissal will not be wrongful or unfair if the employee is guilty of gross misconduct or is unable to carry out the work properly. Some contracts attempt to set out precisely what may fall into these categories in order to avoid disputes later, but those contracts are rare in architectural practice.

18.14   Spare time practice

Many architects engage in spare time practice during the period they are employees. It may be a means of obtaining extra cash or a means of starting up in practice with a client nucleus. The general law will imply that an employee may so practise unless there is a term in the contract expressly forbidding it.

The employer's attitude, however, may be less than enthusiastic, either directly forbidding spare time practice, in spite of the code, or hedging it around with so many rules that it is not a practical proposition. Reasonable conditions are:

- The employee must inform the employer in advance
- The clients must be informed that the employee is carrying out the work in a personal capacity
- The clients must not be existing clients of the firm
- Private work must not be carried out in office hours or making use of office equipment or materials unless prior permission has been obtained
- The firm's interests must not be affected in any way

Many firms encourage employees to introduce work into the firm. Again, it is preferable if the policy is clearly stated. Very small jobs may not be welcome. Employees introducing work will expect something more than the usual salary for their trouble. Some employers reward the employee by a special payment related to the final profit on that particular project. Provided that the method of calculating the payment is known to all, it is a sensible way to proceed, because it associates the employees with the firm, it links the futures of firm and employee and paves the way for closer association in due time.

There is a great advantage to an employee in bringing all work into the office rather than carrying on spare time practice. The employee will have the protection of the office professional indemnity insurance (see chapter 17, section 17.5). Private work is carried out at the employee's risk. If the employee is negligent in his or her own work, the client will look to them for damages. Such employees should carry their own insurance to cover their spare time practice. The reality is that such cover may not be easily affordable. All may be well during the time the architect is employed and is not considered worth suing by clients. The situation may be different if the employee later sets up in profitable practice and earlier negligence results in a heavy claim for damages.

There are two matters which are closely associated with spare time practice: copyright and confidential information. In general, copyright in work prepared by an employee belongs to an employer[7]. Employees should be aware that permission must be obtained from an employer to produce copies of their drawings to take to interview for the purpose of securing other employment. Employees, of course, retain copyright in work which they produce during their spare time.

Confidentiality is a difficult area. Information which an employee may gain in employment was considered in *Faccenda Chicken Ltd* v. *Fowler* [1986][8] to fall into three categories:

- Information well known to people in the industry
- Confidential information which becomes part of the employee's own skill and knowledge
- Information of such confidentiality that it cannot be used lawfully to benefit anyone other than the employer

Information in the third category can never be divulged by an employee even after leaving the employment. The second category of information cannot be protected when an employee leaves, but to reveal such information while still in the original employment would be a gross breach of trust and entitles the employer to damages. The problem lies in correctly identifying what information falls into which categories. It is probably for this reason that some firms purport to state the type of information which is considered to be highly confidential in the employment contract. An employee, of course, will be bound by such terms.

Some architects in employment, usually those with considerable responsibility and possibly access to information regarded by the practice as highly confidential, may have a restraint clause in their contracts. Such a term may try to restrict an employee setting up in practice within a certain distance of the previous employer for a period of time. Terms in contracts which attempt to restrict future employment are basically void at common law as being in restraint of trade. Such terms may be valid and enforceable if:

■ They are reasonable between the parties:
   (a)   The restriction protects the employer's legally recognised interest: protection of trade secrets and/or protection of business connections
   (b)   The restriction is no greater than necessary to so protect, in respect of the period of restriction and the geographical restriction.
■ They are reasonable in the public interest, for example, they do not deprive the public of special skills which the employee may possess.

(Where a restriction is placed on ex-partners, the same principles generally apply, but it is generally considered reasonable to enforce stricter time periods and geographical areas.)

18.15   Discrimination

It may be surprising to learn that discrimination on the grounds of age, religion, politics or membership of a trades union is not directly unlawful.

An employer may not discriminate against a person on the grounds of that person's sex or marital status[9]. The Act has particular application to the recruitment of staff and to any benefits. Indirect discrimination is also unlawful, for example, if criteria are laid down which favour one sex. An exception is made in the case of occupations where decency or physiology dictates that only a man or a woman can do the work.

Discrimination against a person on the grounds of race, colour or nationality is also outlawed[10]. Again, indirect discrimination is also forbidden and the Act applies equally to fellow employees. Exceptions to the provisions are allowed, for example, if a particular racial group would have difficulty in doing certain work or if certain work could only be performed by a certain group.

A woman may not be treated less favourably simply because of her sex[11]. Pay and conditions of service are covered. The Act of course does not apply where the reasons for differences in pay are due to such things as differing job responsibilities.

It is unlawful to discriminate against disabled people in employment situations[12]. The Act applies to both mental and physical disablement. Discrimination is lawful only in very specific circumstances, for example, to safeguard health and safety. Businesses of fewer than 20 people are excluded from the provisions.

References

(1)   *Spring* v. *Guardian Assurance plc and Others* [1994] 3 All ER 129.
(2)   *Ferguson* v. *John Dawson* [1976] 1 WLR 1213.
(3)   *Sim* v. *Rotherham MBC* [1986] IRLR 391.
(4)   *The Architect and His Office* (1962) RIBA Publications.
(5)   Based on the European Union Working Time Directive, the Young Workers' Directive and health and safety measures.
(6)   Employment Act 1982.
(7)   Copyright Designs and Patents Act 1988.
(8)   [1986] 1 All ER 617.
(9)   The Sex Discrimination Act 1975.
(10) The Race Relations Act 1976.
(11) The Equal Pay Act 1970.
(12) The Disability Discrimination Act 1995.

19 Attracting Work

19.1 Active marketing

The first thing for any architect to realise is that marketing any professional service is not like selling baked beans. An altogether different approach is necessary. Not very long ago, the only acceptable way for an architect to attract work was through existing clients. Apart from a brass plate with letters of a prescribed size, there were few ways the architect could advertise the existence of the practice. The situation now is vastly changed and a wide range of activities are allowed by the code of conduct.

Every practice must develop a unique marketing strategy for that firm. Very large practices may employ one or more full-time marketing people to keep the firm in the public eye and follow up particular opportunities. The majority of firms, however, must rely on the part-time efforts of their own staff. Some architects have the gift of attracting work. They can go to a party and come back with three new commissions. Such architects are worth their weight in gold and they need never do any architectural work themselves. Such architects, however, are quite rare. Therefore, specific marketing objectives must be set so that all the staff in a practice are pulling in the right direction.

There are some simple, straightforward actions that every practice can take:

- Clients Advisory Service
- Architects' sign boards
- Lectures and articles
- Direct approach

19.1.1 Clients Advisory Service (CAS)

A practice can register with the CAS service at the RIBA. Not only does CAS promote architects in a general way, it also responds to the many queries it receives from prospective clients seeking an architect for a particular project. Architects have an entry in the

Directory of Practices which is now available to be searched on the internet. CAS has a database of architectural practices together with projects carried out. Practices are responsible for keeping the information held by CAS up to date and when an enquiry is received, CAS furnishes a client with a list of three or four names of architects appropriate for the project outlined by the client. CAS operates through a network of regional RIBA offices where further information can be obtained. The overall number of enquiries increaed by 23% from 1997 to 1998.

19.1.2   Architects' sign boards

Most practices have standard sign boards which are erected in a prominent position on new developments. If the development is of any size, the architect's board will be just one of many professionals' boards and there will be boards giving the particulars of the main contractor and subcontractors. It must be remembered that such boards require planning permission (see Chapter 9, section 9.4) and the architect is usually responsible for approving, if not actually designing, the layout of such boards.

An architect now has the right to insist that the practice is credited with the design of a building in permanent form on the outside of the finished building[1]. Although there may be isolated instances where the architect definitely does not wish to be remembered as the designer of a particular building, in most cases it is a valuable means of additional publicity.

19.1.3   Lectures and articles

Although it may be difficult for a one-man practice to find the time to give lectures or write articles, many practices contain members who can give short talks and others who can put together an interesting article on aspects of architecture in general and the work of the practice in particular. Many organisations, such as civic and amenity societies, chambers of commerce and the like have difficulty in finding speakers for lunch or evening meetings. There is nothing to prevent a practice from writing to such organisations offering a talk on architectural matters of interest. Although speaking in public can be daunting at first, practice makes perfect and provided a speaker is prepared with notes and possibly slides, the experience can be enjoyable for all parties. This is a good way of putting the firm's name in front of a wider public. An article is a more permanent record and likely to reach a wider audience provided it appears in an appropriate magazine or local paper.

19.1.4   Direct approach

Architects may now approach a client directly before there has been any initial enquiry by the prospective client. For example, an architect may hear that a company is expanding and looking for sites for additional factory production. There is nothing to stop the architect from writing to the company offering his or her services in finding a suitable site and designing the factory. Experience suggests that many commissions are obtained in this way.

19.2   Practice brochure

It has been suggested that a client will spend only seven seconds flicking through a brochure[2]. This does not tend to promote confidence that a practice brochure will do much to assist in getting work. A practice brochure is not normally produced for wholesale distribution. Pressing a brochure on an unwilling client is counter productive. The brochure should explain who is who in the firm, how long it has been established and the kind of work carried out, preferably with illustrations. Special areas of expertise should be highlighted. Although the brochure should be well designed in layout and typeface, it should avoid being too gimicky. It should be easy for a prospective client to find the way through to the information required (remember the seven seconds – quite a long time actually). The brochure should be available in the waiting area of the practice office. It should be taken by a partner and left with a client after a presentation. In other words, it should be used selectively. A small practice cannot afford a large and expensively produced brochure, but there is no evidence that a modestly pre-pared, but informative document is any less effective. Indeed, some clients are wary of architectural firms projecting a high gloss image. The question in the client's mind is, 'Who is paying for this?'

19.3 Advertising

Advertising must be used with caution. Architects may advertise their services (since 1986), but whether it is wise to do so depends on circumstances. There is still a general feeling that advertising is not a very professional thing to do. It may be that it is worthwhile for a small practice to advertise in the local newspaper or in a magazine devoted solely to the subject of the practice's principal expertise.

Looked at in a broad sense, advertising can be fruitful – that is the publicity a practice can get through the official opening ceremony of a prestigious building, or for assisting in fund raising for a charitable building. The practice can get a high profile by offering to organise foundation laying or opening ceremonies or by becoming involved in the design of the commemorative brochure. A relatively poor client might want some assistance in putting together a fund raising leaflet and the practice could well donate the services of a member of staff to draw a suitable pen and ink perspective for the front. Advertising can also be carried out by the setting up of exhibitions at galas, meetings and locations such as libraries and museums, provided the subject matter is local and topical.

19.4 Contacts

Contacts are probably the best method of attracting work. In the most basic form, the architect looks to relatives to provide commissions and to provide introductions to other sources of work. This can be easily expanded to include friends and acquaintances. It is surprising how often one reads of old acquaintances achieving positions where they can be a useful source of work or further contacts. Those contacts are more a matter of luck than anything else, but the members of a practice can work to make contacts by joining clubs and organisations of a social, religious, sporting, civic or political nature. That is not to say that an architect should join a club for the sole purpose of getting work; such an architect will not only get no work (his or her purpose will be obvious to all), but there will be no other enjoyment either.

Civic societies and conservation panels are a useful way of getting to know the local planning officers. Some architects make a practice of frequenting a local pub where solicitors, accountants and insurance brokers gather and sometimes a new commission will be obtained in that way, not usually directly, but because when the solicitor is trying to think of an architect who can carry out a particular project on behalf of a client, the drinking companion may spring to mind.

19.5 Competitions

Competitions as a way of getting business should not be overlooked, although they are not usually the first line of attack. Very often the winning of a competition can be the start of a successful career for a young architect. Whether an office will enter for a competition depends very much on the volume of work in the office and the enthusiasm of its members. The RIBA has produced a guidance handbook to assist those intending to organise an architectural competition[3].

There are various types of competition depending on the particular requirements of the promoters. In the first place, the competition may be single or two-stage. In a single-stage competition, the competitors are required to submit fairly complete small scale drawings sufficient to describe their designs, but in a two-stage competition, they are required to submit simple line drawings only in the first stage, indicating the broad outline of the scheme. From these entries, a shortlist is drawn up and the competitors on it are invited to submit a developed entry similar to the submissions in a single-stage competition. An obvious advantage of this method is that a relatively small number of entrants are expected to devote large amounts of time and effort. A variant is where the second stage consists of the competitors selected from the first stage together with a limited number of competitors specifically invited to submit schemes at the second stage. Persons invited to submit at the second stage only must be named in the conditions so that other competitors know the calibre of persons they have to beat.

Another type of competition is the 'ideas competition' which is intended to solve particular problems. This kind of competition is sometimes set by manufacturers or the professional press as well as by clients, in order to air specific issues or to encourage rising architectural talents.

Competitions may be open or limited. Open competitions are those which may be entered by any eligible architect. Sometimes clients will promote a limited competition and invite architects of established merit, or entrants may be limited to architects from within a particular geographic area. Architects who are invited to submit designs or who are successful in proceeding to a second stage receive an honorarium. All winners should receive an appropriate premium and the author of the design placed first should be appointed to carry out the work. The premium is then subsumed into the fee for the project.

The assessors must be approved by the President of the RIBA and they are debarred from competing. Neither may an architect assessor take a commission to carry out the design in the event that no submitted entry is satisfactory.

19.6 Keeping clients

The best way of building a practice is to keep every client who is attracted enough to commission work. There is nothing so comforting as repeat business. It shows that the client is really satisfied and it provides a solid base from which the practice can grow. Although such devices as regular mailshots, parties and regular correspondence on matters of interest help to show clients that their architect is concerned for their interests, the very best way of keeping clients is for the architect to give a first class service.

References

(1) The Copyright, Designs and Patents Act 1988.
(2) *Architects' Journal*, 13 December 1989, p.69.
(3) *Architectural Competitions: RIBA Code of Practice* (1986) Royal Institute of British Architects; see also McGhie, C. and Girling, R. *Architectural Competitions: a Handbook for Promoters* (1996) Constructional Research Communications for the Department of Heritage and the Department of the Environment.

Table of Cases

Index